USING INTERNET EXPLORER TO BROWSE THE INTERNET

USING INTERNET EXPLORER TO BROWSE THE INTERNET

Dustin Sullivan

AP Professional

AP Professional is a Division of Academic Press, Inc.

Boston San Diego New York
London Sydney Tokyo Toronto

AP PROFESSIONAL

An Imprint of ACADEMIC PRESS, INC.
A Division of HARCOURT BRACE & COMPANY

ORDERS (USA and Canada): 1-800-3131-APP or APP@ACAD.COM
AP Professional Orders: 6277 Sea Harbor Dr., Orlando, FL 32821-9816

Europe/Middle East/Africa: 0-11-44 (0) 181-300-3322
Orders: AP Professional 24-28 Oval Rd., London NW1 7DX

Japan/Korea: 03-3234-3911-5
Orders: Harcourt Brace Japan, Inc., Ichibancho Central Building 22-1, Ichibancho Chiyoda-Ku, Tokyo 102

Australia: 02-517-8999
Orders: Harcourt Brace & Co. Australia, Locked Bag 16, Marrickville, NSW 2204 Australia

Other International: (407) 345-3800
AP Professional Orders: 6277 Sea Harbor Dr., Orlando FL 32821-9816

Editorial: 1300 Boylston St., Chestnut Hill, MA 02167 (617)232-0500

Web: http://www.apnet.com/approfessional

This book is printed on acid-free paper. ∞
Copyright © 1997 by Academic Press, Inc.

United Kingdom Edition published by
ACADEMIC PRESS LIMITED
24–28 Oval Road, London NW1 7DX

Sullivan, Dustin.
       Using Internet Explorer to Browse the Internet/Dustin Sullivan.
          p.   cm.
       Includes index.
       ISBN 0-12-676140-X (alk. paper)
         1. Microsoft Internet Explorer.   2. Internet (Computer network)
   3. World Wide Web (information retrieval system)   I. Title.
   TK5105.883.M53S85   1996
   025.04—dc20

                                     96—41793
                                       CIP

Printed in the United States of America
96 97 98 99 CP 9 8 7 6 5 4 3 2 1

This book is dedicated to Ariel and Zeke. Writing it would have been a lot more difficult if they weren't so cute!

Contents

Chapter 4: Wandering the Web   59

Chapter 7: Customizing Explorer 139

Appendix C: Internet Explorer 2.0 for Windows 3.1   307

Introduction

Welcome to the world of the Internet! With this book and Microsoft Internet Explorer, you will be able to journey to all parts of the Internet, including the most popular area, the World Wide Web. Never before has such a source of information been so easily accessible to so many people. It seems that the Net has reached into all areas of our lives, from socialization to education to business. Even laundry detergents have Web sites that you can visit! If that doesn't signal wide acceptance of this technology, I don't know what does!

Have you been feeling left out of the whole event? Not to worry. Sure, many people have gone on-line before you, but look at it this way: the early adopters used the old, clunky Internet programs and Web browsers. You let them do all the dirty work! Eventually, they became tired of using the difficult interfaces and the archaic command line prompts, so they changed them. Now it is many times easier to get on-line than ever before. And here you come to take advantage of all of the improvements made in the last few years. I'd say that your timing is pretty good!

INTERNET EXPLORER 3.0

A browser is a program that is used to view the sites on the World Wide Web and the Internet. Lately there has been much fanfare in the Web browser business. Microsoft doesn't like to be second best in anything, so it has completely reworked its Internet Explorer Web browser to make it the best in the business. For most people, Internet Explorer will be all they need to access the Internet. Explorer offers access to all parts of the Net including the World Wide Web, FTP, Gopher, and Telnet sites, e-mail, and Usenet newsgroups. Add to this the multimedia capabilities of the World Wide Web, and you have a dynamic browsing experience.

To raise the standards for Web browsers, Microsoft went back to the drawing board. It looked at everything that users would want for surfing the Net and included them. The need for plug-ins or helper applications has been minimized because almost everything is built-in from the start! Support for all major audio and video formats, advanced security features, personalization options, speed and performance improvements, and active content all make Explorer the most complete browser ever. It is perhaps the active content features that push Explorer to the top, however. With ActiveX, Microsoft has released a format for controlling Web pages that is sure to become an industry standard. Java has become one of the fastest-growing areas of the Web, and Explorer 3.0 offers the fastest compiler around. Support for VRML and the latest version of HTML round out the offerings of this solid product.

WHAT'S IN THIS BOOK

Now that the hype is finished, what is in this book that can really help people get the most out of Explorer? Explorer itself is easy to use, but this book offers a much more rounded approach than just basic Explorer functions. Sure, the basics are in here, but in order to get the most out of your Internet browsing experiences, you need more than just the basics. You need to have a solid background in the Internet and World Wide Web as well as knowledge of the skills required to run Explorer. The Internet can still be a confusing place that shows its rough edges from time to time. Without the correct skills, a novice can easily become discouraged and quit before discovering the good parts. This book can teach you those skills.

By the time you are finished with this book, you will have learned the following:

- Basic Explorer operation
- Tricks and tips to improve your Web surfing skills

- The ins and outs of the Internet itself and how to get the most out of it
- Technical info that might help you out of a jam
- More advanced Explorer operation to customize your experiences

WHO SHOULD READ THIS BOOK?

This book is designed to start an Internet novice on the road to guru status. It gives you the information that you need to know in the best order to learn the ropes. Even if you are already familiar with the Net and know the difference between an FTP site and a Gopher server, there are still operational tips that can help you. If you use Explorer every day and need a reference that you can count on, this is the place. If you are only a casual user, this book is designed to give you the information you need as you develop your skills.

ABOUT THIS BOOK

The chapters in this book are grouped to cover information in the order that is best suited to learn the Net as well as Explorer. It is possible to skip around from chapter to chapter, but you will find that the information is presented in an order that facilitates step-by-step learning of the skills needed to get the most out of the Internet. The order of the skills is as follows.

- Introduction to the Internet and World Wide Web
- Basic Explorer skills
- Searching for information on the Net
- More advanced Explorer skills
- Using e-mail and Usenet
- Technical features

There are several conventions used in this book to present information in a more readable format.

Tip: Tips offer advice on ways to change Explorer or even Windows 95 itself to improve your performance or make features easier to use or access.

Note: Notes are included to inform you of slight differences between configurations and how those differences could affect you. Notes are also used for general information that needs to be emphasized apart from the main text..

Warning: Used less often, cautions inform you of possible negative effects from trying certain features.

BOXES

Boxes are used as asides. They generally contain background information that is not relevant to include in the main text. You could skip all of the boxes and not miss any important operational procedures, but you might miss an explanation of something that would aid in your overall understanding of the Internet and Explorer.

When describing certain operations, I have grouped several steps together. For example, to open the Options window and see the Connection tab, you must first click View on the menu bar, then select Options, then select Connection. I have condensed this to "Select the Connection tab from the View Options menu." This is much more direct and saves unneeded steps. After all, the idea here is to make Internet use quick and effortless! This convention is used throughout the book.

Windows 95 has a file management program also called Explorer. It is called Windows 95 Explorer in this book to reduce confusion. If you read something that is just called Explorer, it refers to Internet Explorer.

One minor note: this book was being written as Explorer itself was being written. As new updates and versions were released, the book was changed to reflect the features of the new release. From time to time, you will see screen shots that look slightly different from the rest. These are screen shots from the first beta, or first test, release. We kept some of the original pictures in cases where the features or operational steps did not change between the versions.

ACKNOWLEDGMENTS

This book was a collaborative effort that included many people. If you see any of us on the street, please shake our hands! In the meantime, I would like to thank several people who have been instrumental in the development of this book. First, thanks to Mike Williams and Gael

Tannenbaum at AP Professional for giving me such great constructive criticism! Thanks to Mom and Charles for their support throughout this entire process. Thanks to Tracy, Lynn, Andy, Carrie, and J.P. for not bugging me too much while I disappeared for days at a time while writing (and thanks for still being my friends when I came up for air). Thanks to the guys at the store for putting up with my weird schedule throughout this process. Thanks to Zeke for not eating too many of my manuscripts, and to Ariel for singing to me as I wrote. Finally, a special "give that man a cigar two thumbs up round of applause two triple cheeseburgers thanks" to Jeff Pepper at AP Professional for giving me this opportunity and advising me in the process of book publishing. Without him, you wouldn't be reading this and I'd still be working weekends!

KEEP IN TOUCH

I would love to hear what you think of this book. Please send your comments to **dsullivan@iquest.net.** Positive feedback may even get a reply! Please keep in mind, however, that it's just me, my cat, and my bird. I have enough to do keeping Zeke out of the bird cage, so please don't send me your technical questions or questions regarding Explorer itself. I simply am not equipped to act as a technical support center. Do send me your thoughts on what was good, what was bad, what was left out, and what should have been left out of this book.

Chapter 1

INTRODUCTION TO THE INTERNET

Have you ever seen a coworker stumble up to the coffee pot with dark circles under bloodshot eyes and say, "Man. I was surfing on the Net until 3:00! I was having so much fun, I didn't realize how late it was." Even if you don't know any Net junkies (yet), I'll bet you have talked with a few people extolling the virtues of being on-line. Did these people make you feel that you are missing something fantastic and revolutionary?

Despite creating insomniacs all over the world, the Internet is increasingly becoming a part of everybody's life. Strictly speaking, the Internet is just a collection of computers across the world that have been linked together. If you use a computer at work that is connected to other computers at work, you are probably using a local area network. The Internet operates using the same concept, but on a much grander scale.

So much can be done on the Internet that it can be a bit intimidating. Technobabble, with its terms and acronyms, can turn away even the most experienced computer users. Where can you start? Luckily, right here is a good place. Keep reading and you will learn what makes up the Internet, how to get connected, and what some of the terms mean. To get you started, I'll show you some reasons for getting on the Net in the first place.

KEY POINTS IN THIS CHAPTER:

- What can the Internet do for me?
- Who started this monster?
- Is the World Wide Web the whole Internet?
- How can I connect to the Internet?
- What do all these numbers and letters mean?

Tip: Experienced Net surfers can skip to Chapter 2 for some World Wide Web basics or Chapter 3 to get into Internet Explorer.

WHAT CAN YOU DO ON THE NET?

A better question might be "What *can't* you do on the Net?" The Internet is growing every day, and just about each day somebody finds a new way to put it to use. As corporate America gets into the action, count on even more new uses to be devised. Here is a short list of Internet uses.

Search for Information

Have you ever wondered how much your car is worth? Or what the weather is like at your friend's house in Miami? The Internet gives you a way to find both, in the same session at your computer! Even complicated information, like the gross domestic product of Spain, can be found in a matter of minutes. Think of the Internet as a library at your fingertips. And I don't just mean a card catalog (although those, too, can be reached over the Net). You can get the actual information, not just a list of sources.

Caution: Not all of the information contained in the Internet is completely factual. The Net is not regulated by any one organization, so people are free to post whatever they want, without verifying sources (or even having sources!). I'm sure you know people who talk without really knowing what they're talking about. These people can be annoying at parties. Now imagine millions of them all across the globe with their own little spot on the information superhighway. They could be dangerous to innocent Net surfers looking for some facts to add to the presentation for the boss. Be careful, and don't believe everything you read!

Send Electronic Mail

Electronic mail (e-mail) is one of the first features that attracted people and businesses to the Internet. With an Internet account, you can send a message to a friend in Japan, who will receive it only minutes after you send it. It's easy, too—no more envelopes to buy, stamps to lick, or trips to the Post Office. Just type your message and send it. With the right software, you can even attach files to these messages. Don't just send a letter explaining the sales forecast to your boss—send the spreadsheet! Don't just tell your mom about your European vacation—send her the photos!

Shop

Connecting to an on-line mall is easier than flipping through pages and pages of direct mail catalogs. Say you're looking for a sweater: navy turtleneck, 100% cotton. You could spend quite a bit of time looking in your favorite catalogs for the one tiny picture showing that sweater. Or you can log onto an on-line store, type "turtleneck, navy, cotton," and have a photo appear with all the sizing, pricing, and ordering information. And it can be done on a secure site so your credit card information isn't floating around in cyberspace for someone else to find.

Read the News

Check out the *New York Times*, *Wall Street Journal*, or *Chicago Tribune* on-line. Many other newspapers are now on the Net, including many local and small town papers. Reading the news on the Net might not be as traditional as curling up with the Sunday paper, but at least you don't get ink stains on your fingers.

Check on Your Favorite Sports Team

How are the Bulls doing? Sure, you can get the scores from TV or the newspaper. But how many points has Jordan averaged during the playoffs this year? What's his career playoff average? When did John Salley start playing for the Bulls? Who is the franchise's leading rebounder? It's not difficult to find sports sites on the Net that focus on any or all of these topics. Many are statistical almanacs, while others focus on up-to-date team information. Some even give a day-by-day listing of team news, on and off season. Add to this pictures that you can download, sound clips from broadcasts, and even some video clips, and you have a totally interactive sports experience.

Play Games

As if you need another reason to waste time! From a simple game of checkers to fully interactive shoot 'em ups, the Net has games for you. Perhaps turn-based strategy or classic dungeon exploring is more to your taste. The Internet is not short on gaming possibilities.

Download Files and Programs

Looking for hard-to-find clip art or fonts for your neighborhood newsletter? Maybe you just want a new picture to use as background wallpaper for your Windows desktop. Have you updated your antivirus software lately? Have you bought a game that requires the latest drivers for your sound card? These are just a few odds and ends from an immense collection of programs available on the Internet. Shareware (software that is distributed freely but trusts users to register it for a small fee) is abundant, as is freeware and public domain software. Utilities and program upgrades are also easily transferred to your computer over the Internet. Many of you are probably using a copy of Internet Explorer that was downloaded from Microsoft's Internet site.

Caution: Computer viruses are programs that attach themselves to or disguise themselves as real programs. Whenever you download files from the Internet you risk infecting your PC. Internet Explorer uses sophisticated techniques to verify the authenticity of software to minimize the risk of downloading a program that has been altered, but the safest course of action is to buy and use an antivirus program and be careful when choosing what files to download.

Entertain Yourself for Hours

Just like that coworker who stayed up half the night, you will soon find out how easy it can be to spend hours moving around from site to site. You might start out with a purpose, but so much cool stuff is out there that sooner or later, you'll jump in and just play around. You can rationalize your searching, but just try to explain to your spouse why you've spent the last hour reading all about llamas when all you meant to do was check on airline ticket prices.

*Caution: Pornography on the Internet has been in the news lately, and it **is** out there waiting to be accessed. Don't be frightened that you will come across it by accident—most sites are tucked discretely away from the main-stream. However, you may find references scattered around in unrelated material. Certain areas of the Net are more traditional homes for porn (these will be noted as they are discussed in this book), so if you are worried about your kids accessing them you may want to familiarize yourself with these areas. In general, it is possible to spend much time on the Net without ever coming across any offensive material. Internet Explorer has a ratings system that can be used to screen out sites that may contain objectionable material. See Chapter 7 for details.*

A BRIEF HISTORY OF THE INTERNET

An entire book can be written on the history of the Internet, so let me put extra emphasis on the word *brief*. The modern Internet was started in the 1970s when the U.S. government decided to link the various computer networks that it operated across the country. Universities thought that was a great way to share information and resources, so they got in on the act. The idea spread, and new collections of com-puter networks were added to the system, even computers that were on different continents! The first incarnations of the Internet were not fancy. Most connections were text only, with complicated commands for navigating through the system. Many of these computers worked with different operating systems, so learning one system did not mean that you knew it all. But the foundations were being laid.

The Formative Years . . .

Throughout the 1980s the Internet remained the domain of a select group of people: scientists, researchers, government workers, hackers, and college students and faculty (students especially had the free time available to learn the systems). The rest of us were pretty much left out due to the complicated nature of the operating environments. But behind the scenes, people were working on simplifying the way the Net was accessed.

The Enlightenment . . .

Even as recently as a few years ago, the Internet was still too complicated, too piecemeal for most people to learn unless they *needed* to use it. A program called Mosaic, used on a new part of the Internet called the World Wide Web, started to change the way people used the Net. Instead of text only, Mosaic offered pictures. Now a site could be designed to look like whatever the Web author wanted. Mosaic offered sound. Now voices and music could be heard. Mosaic offered a mouse interface. Now the average user could point and click to different parts of the Internet instead of using arcane computer commands that were difficult to remember.

Note: Even though the government started it, private industry has taken over much of the Internet. Don't be surprised if the next Web page you see has a small advertisement at the top. Think of it as the price to be paid for progress (and don't write your Congressperson to complain!).

The Internet has reached millions of people who, until recently, didn't know what it could do for them. Add to the limited list of users above teachers, business people, politicians, and everyday people (and students, who still have the most time to use it). Instead of going to a dedicated machine at the university, you can access the Net from home, from school, from work, and even from coffee houses.

The Future . . .

Here we are today, using Internet Explorer, a direct descendant of Mosaic. What will we use in five years? I won't be so foolish as to guess in this industry, but I can show you some of the ideas for the near future. Very soon, dedicated "Internet boxes" will be available. Think of an Internet box like a phone or a toaster. They do what they were designed to do, nothing else. Unlike your computer, with which you can play games, surf the Net, or crunch numbers, an Internet box initially will be able only to surf the Internet—much as a phone can be used only to make calls and a toaster can only toast. Neither would be very good at calculating the advertising budget for next quarter or washing the car. An Internet box may not be able to function as a regular computer. Some are designed to be countertop devices, similar in design to a fax machine. Others are designed to hook into a television set. In fact, several major TV manufacturers have designed televisions with this capability built in.

To show that the Internet is truly reaching mainstream, manufacturers of home video game systems are developing and testing add-on modules for their game consoles. Imagine playing Ridge Racer on your Sony Playstation, then plugging in an Internet module for some on-line game tips. Or following Virtua Fighter on your Sega Saturn with a session on the Web to order flowers for Mother's Day. Or unplugging Mario on your Nintendo 64 . . . you get the idea.

I don't want to predict doom and gloom for these products before they are given a chance in the market, but the Net is changing rapidly. Dedicated devices are sure to become out of date almost as rapidly. Nothing is as flexible as the good old PC for keeping up with changes. Sure, you may have to drop a pile of money into your PC every year, but it is able to change to meet new technology, so don't throw out the PC and rush out for an Internet box just yet. They will eventually come of age, however.

MAJOR COMPONENTS OF THE INTERNET

Even with slick new interfacing, some older systems on the Internet are still around, and many can be extremely useful sources of information. Just as using Windows doesn't completely free you from learning a few DOS concepts, using the modern Internet doesn't mean you can avoid the old spots. A smart user is at least aware of, if not casually familiar with, these older systems to increase the chances for a successful information search. The following is an introduction to the major systems that make up the Internet.

Electronic Mail (E-mail)

E-mail is used by almost everybody who has Internet access. With e-mail, messages and files can be sent almost instantaneously across the globe. The e-mail system is anchored by a collection of e-mail servers (a *server* is a computer that is used to store, access, and transfer data; it is the "brains" behind a computer network). When you send an e-mail message to a friend across the country or world, your message is sent from your PC to an e-mail server run by your Internet service provider

(ISP), the company that is providing you with Internet access (more on ISPs later in this chapter). The message is then sent along a chain of other e-mail servers until it reaches the e-mail server belonging to the ISP of your friend. Think of it as sending a letter that must be sorted and placed on several different trucks and planes to reach its destination. When your friend e-mails you a reply, you may be able to see a listing of the route the message took to get to you at the bottom of the reply (some e-mail programs don't show this, however). It can be interesting to trace the path of a message—and confusing, too! It's amazing that anything can get through all that mess! Figure 1.1 shows an example of a route a message takes on its way to be delivered.

File Transfer Protocol (FTP)

FTP is a part of the Internet that is still used frequently. Mostly run on servers using UNIX or other powerful text-based operating systems, FTP provides storage for almost any type of file available. When you log into an FTP site, you are presented with a list of files and directories that can be accessed. Figure 1.2 shows a typical FTP setup. Today's software takes much of the hassle out of navigating through these electronic warehouses. Instead of using UNIX commands to move through the FTP server, the mouse can be used to point and click on files to download or directories to display.

Depending on which FTP server you are browsing, you can find many types of program files: games, applications, utilities, graphics files and fonts, and more. FTP servers even serve as archives for information.

```
 -------- Original message header follows --------
From  sullivan@  uest.net  Wed May 22 02:50:29 1996 [PIM 3.2-030.   ]
Received: from  uest.net (  uest4.  uest.net [206.   .230.100]) by pimaialw.prodigy.com (8.6.10/8.6.9)
with SMTP id CAA29032 for <      Y84A@prodigy.com>; Thu, 23 May 1996 02:49:08 -0400
Received: from button by   uest.net with smtp
        (Smail3.1.29.1 #5) id mOuMUCk-00490hC; Thu, 23 May 96 01:49 EST
Message-Id: <mOuMUCk-00490hC@  uest.net>
From: "Dustin R. Sullivan" <  sullivan@  uest.net>
To: "      Y84A@prodigy.com" <      \'84A@prodigy.com>
Subject: E-MAIL EXPLANATION
Date: Thu, 23 May 1996 01:47:54 -0400
X-MSMail-Priority: Normal
X-Priority: 3
X-Mailer: Microsoft Internet Mail
MIME-Version: 1.0
Content-Type: text/plain; charset=ISO-8859-1
Content-Transfer-Encoding: 7bit
```

Figure 1.1: The twisted path of an e-mail message across the Internet.

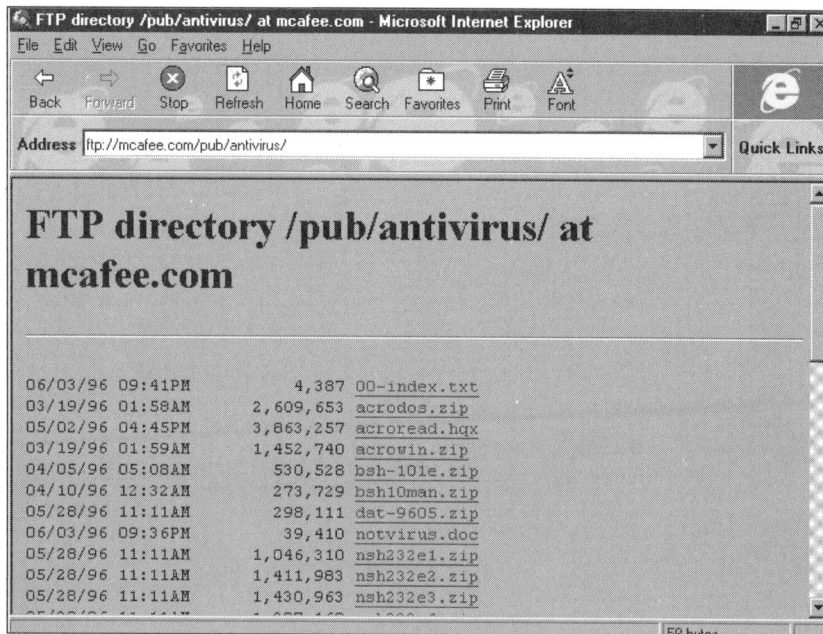

Figure 1.2: The directory tree of an FTP site.

You can pull up reports and studies that were completed years or even just days ago. FTP sites are also used to store old Usenet sessions, so if you saw an especially interesting post in a Usenet discussion last month, it may still be available on an FTP server. What is Usenet, you say?

Usenet Newsgroups

Newsgroups are one of the most popular ways of communicating on the Net. Unlike e-mail, however, newsgroups are completely public. The discussions are not like talking on the phone, though. Newsgroup messages are letters and replies to other letters that are "posted" for everyone with newsreader software to view. See Figure 1.3 for an example of a message in a newsgroup. There are literally hundreds of discussion groups, with new groups appearing all the time. Wonder what the buzz about that new movie is all about? Get on the movie review group. Want the lowdown on what' s happening in the presidential race? Get on a political group. Even if you want to argue your religious beliefs, there is a newsgroup for you.

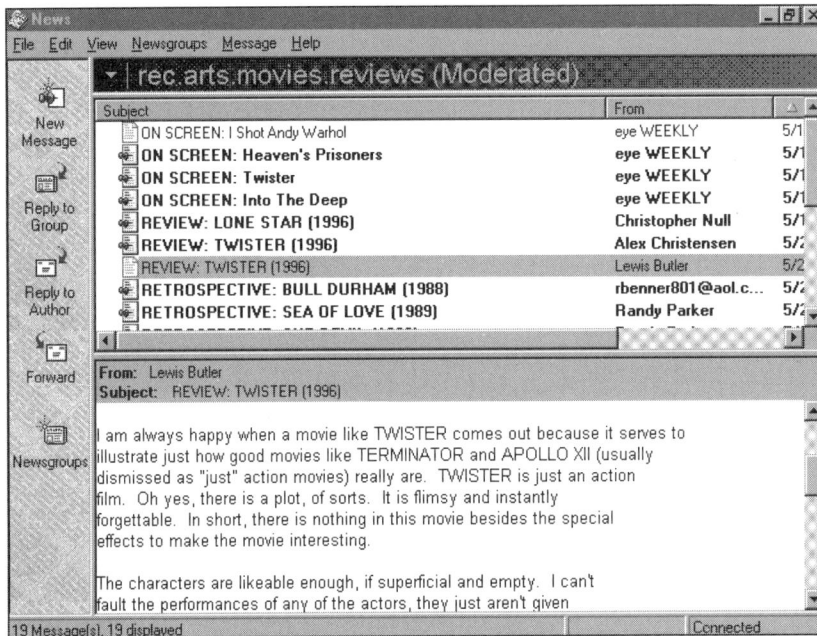

Figure 1.3: A Newsreader program displaying a list of movie reviews on the newsgroup "rec.arts.movies.reviews."

Usenet is also known for its "alternative" discussions. There are many discussion groups of an adult nature, and because the Internet is not owned or regulated by one organization, the discussions can get about as colorful as you can imagine. Pictures are also traded freely on Usenet groups. These pictures are encoded so instant viewing is not possible, but with just a few clicks you can have a full color photo on your computer screen. Pornographic pictures are not all that is available. You can find classic and original artwork, photos of cars or national parks, and stills from movies and cartoons.

Newsgroups are not for people who want to start and finish a discussion right away. While some sites have hundreds of new messages and replies each day, it often takes a few days for a topic to really be explored. For people who want more immediate satisfaction, there is Internet Relay Chat.

Internet Relay Chat (IRC)

IRC is the part of the Internet that allows real-time conversations. You don't actually speak into your computer (yet). You communicate with other users across the world by typing on your keyboard. Your message, usually just a sentence or two, instantly appears on the computer screens of other people in your group. They can then reply as they desire. Figure 1.4 shows a discussion on an IRC "channel." A *channel* is a discussion group. When you connect with an IRC server, you can display a list of channels that you can join. Once you choose a channel, you are free to speak with other people using that channel. Usually channels are divided into specific topics, but there are several "friendly" channels for people who just want to shoot the breeze. It is not uncommon for several thousand people from all parts of the world to be connected at a time.

Now, of course, I have to warn you again that there are many channels of an adult nature. Just like Usenet, these channel are completely unregulated, so the discussions may be offensive to some people. You can usually determine the nature of the discussion before you join by the channel's name. #NASCAR will probably be about racing, while #GROUPSEX, well, you get the idea. Just like the rest of the Net, IRC has something for everyone.

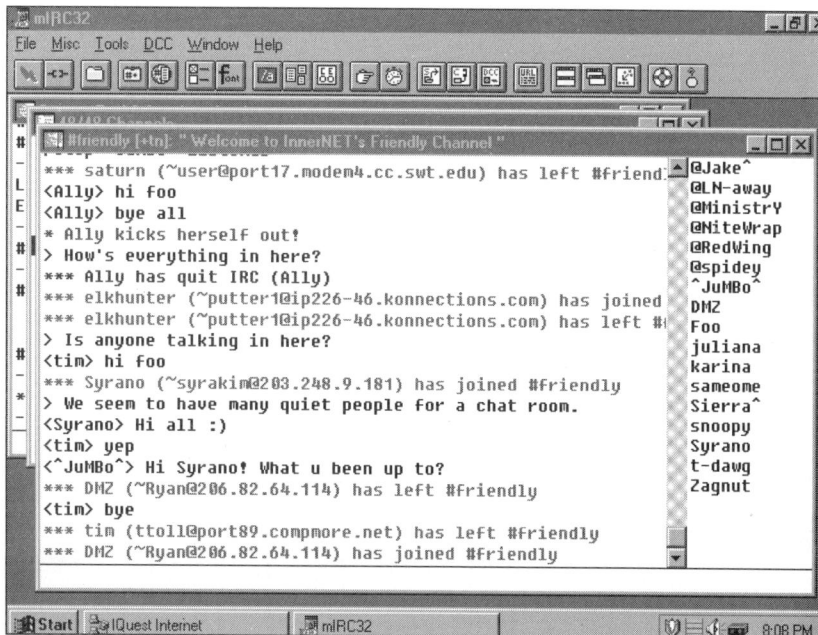

Figure 1.4: A session on the #friendly IRC channel.

Telnet

Remember the early Internet computers that were text only, each of which operated with a different system? Well, they are still around! Telnet is not the most popular place on the Net these days because of its complicated nature, but it can still be a valuable source of information in the form of databases and library card catalogs. Figure 1.5 shows a Telnet session. Telnet offers you direct control of a remotely located computer. The problem is you have to know how to use that computer, and each one can be different! Thank goodness we've progressed to the standard format of the Web.

World Wide Web (WWW)

The Web is, after all, why you are here. It is the newest, most popular, and fastest growing part of the Internet. It revolutionized access to the Internet by providing pictures, sounds, animations, and video clips

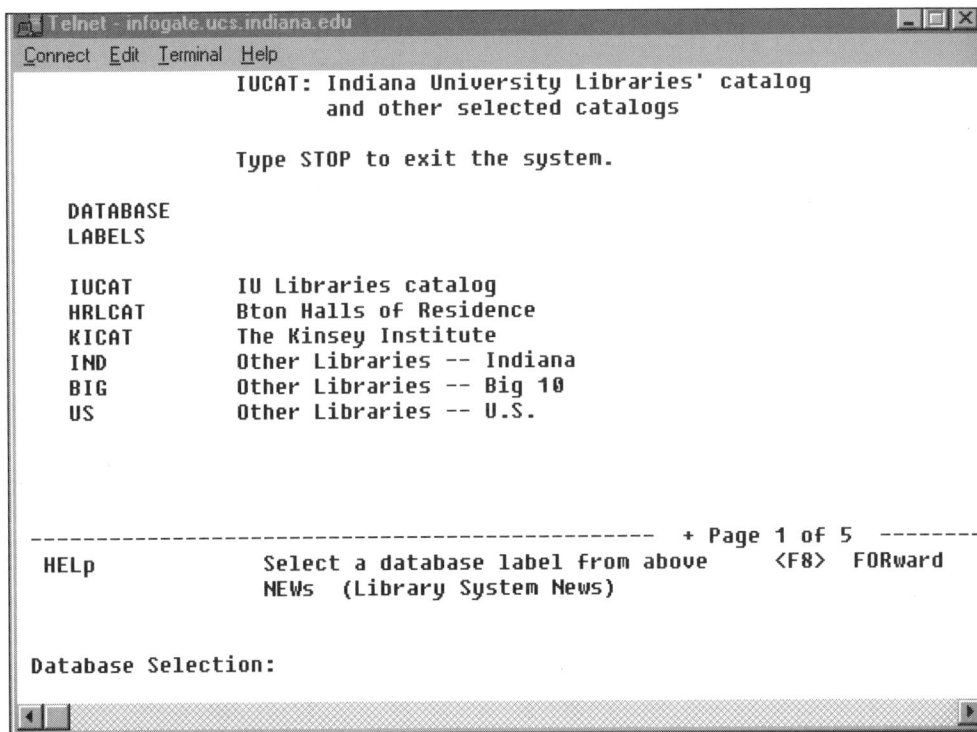

Figure 1.5: An average Telnet session's plain vanilla interface.

that are immediately accessible right on screen. It also offers a standardized point-and-click interface that allows users to move from point to point with very little knowledge of the systems with which they are working. Finally, an Internet for people who are too busy to memorize complicated commands and learn 50 different systems! Figure 1.6 shows how different the Web is from its other Internet cousins.

Today when people mention "surfing the Net" or talk about "being on-line" they are most likely referring to the World Wide Web. Even though we have just seen that the Internet is composed of several major areas, the WWW has recently become so popular that it is almost synonymous with the Internet. Many of these other areas can be reached through the Web, making it an even more powerful component of the Internet.

Figure 1.6: The graphical nature of a World Wide Web page.

CONNECTION OPTIONS

Now you are ready to become a part of the information superhighway. Where do you start? How do you get connected? You have several choices, each of which has advantages and disadvantages. In the end, however, there are really only one or two options if accessing the entire Internet is your goal. Here are your possibilities, excluding e-mail-only accounts, which don't offer any real access.

Types of Access

- Permanent connection—*very* expensive!
- Dial-up terminal—connecting to a computer that runs the access programs for you
- National on-line services—Prodigy, America Online, The Microsoft Network, etc.
- SLIP—a direct connection to the Net, with local and national providers
- PPP—a better direct connection to the Net, with local and national providers

Permanent Connection A permanent connection is so expensive that it is impractical for most people, so I won't discuss it. Essentially, it is a hard line connected to the actual "backbone" of the Internet.

Dial-up Terminal Having another computer run the access programs for you may sound like a good idea, but in reality it is much more limiting than it seems. These connections make your PC a terminal to control a computer that is actually connected to the Internet. Sound like Telnet? Well, it's close. You do get a bit more flexibility, but you are limited to a text-only environment. No fun!

National On-line Services Prodigy, AOL, and the rest have much to offer in the way of extra services, but in reality they are much more expensive and offer inferior Internet access than what you probably want. With so many free trials in the mail, you may have tried one or more of these services. At least you probably reused the disks even if you didn't try the 10 free hours of service that they offered.

SLIP and PPP SLIP (Serial Line Interface Protocol) and PPP (Point to Point Protocol) essentially are direct connections to the Internet for the time that you are on-line. They offer you complete Net access and can be very reasonably priced. Internet Explorer uses one of these two connections to link you with the Net. PPP is preferred because it is faster and more stable than SLIP accounts. If you have not yet signed up with an Internet service provider, find one that offers PPP. If you have a SLIP account, have it changed to a PPP, if possible, or change ISPs.

Note: Some national ISPs offer full PPP access. They usually have some strings attached, however. Many are more expensive than local alternatives, while others require you to use their software. Several of the major long distance phone companies now offer PPP accounts that give Internet access discounts if you use their long distance calling plans. These generally are very competitive with local providers.

INTERNET SERVICE PROVIDERS

Now that we decided that the best account is a PPP, what are your ISP options? Think of your ISP as your electric company or phone company. It offers you a service (Internet access) for a monthly fee. It won't come out to your home to install cables, though. You will connect to it using a modem and your regular phone lines.

ISP Choices

- School or work
- Community services
- Commercial services

School or Work First check to see what kind of access is offered. Many universities and offices have their own permanent connections to the Internet, and you can access them from home or office just like a PPP account. The best part about these is the cost—usually free! Some schools and companies still have older Internet connections that won't run Internet Explorer, though, so be sure to ask.

Community Services Many rural areas have received special grants that allow them to establish Internet access in towns not serviced by the major commercial services. These are often PPP and are also often free or inexpensive. Check with your city or county government or even some local nonprofit organizations. Many of these accounts are older, dial-up types that won't help you, so be sure to ask questions.

Commercial Services Commercial services are the most common way to access the Internet. Local, and some national, companies have been established across the country to provide Internet access for a fee, although it is usually fairly reasonable. Most of these should offer PPP.

MODEM TERMINOLOGY

When you call your local ISP to establish service, it will more than likely ask you a few questions about your system. It will then send you some information with some funny terms that may not be fully explained. Here are the most common terms that will come up in that process.

14.4 and 28.8 bps

These are modem speeds that refer to the amount of information that can be transferred through the phone lines. The higher the number, the faster the access. BPS stands for "bits per second," a bit being a small chunk of electronic information. 28.8bps is the best way to go (for now) to reduce the waiting times associated with being on-line. The Internet is a slow creature, so, just as with computers themselves, buy the fastest modem you can afford. It will save you time and possibly your sanity!

Tip: ISDN and coaxial cable (like that used for cable TV) are two newer, faster formats that are available in some areas. If you can afford to, get them—you'll make your friends green with envy! They offer substantially faster data transfer rates than standard modem/telephone line combinations. They also may cost substantially more, so it may be a while before they reach the mainstream.

TCP/IP

Transmission Control Protocol/Internet Protocol is essentially a standard for transmitting data across the Internet in a format that can be understood by many different computers running with many different operating systems. On a typical session on the WWW, for example, you might start out on a Web page run off a UNIX server, click a link to a Sun workstation, then move to a Macintosh Web page. You will not necessarily know that these machines are different; all you can see are new Web pages popping up on your Windows 95 PC.

TCP/IP Stack

The TCP/IP stack is a file on your PC that lets your computer communicate with the Internet. Your ISP is more than likely using a powerful computer that uses a different operating system from your Windows 95-based PC. The TCP/IP stack does for you the job that the TCP/IP format does for the big computers on the Internet—it allows different computers, in this case your PC and your ISP's server, to communicate. When your modem dials your ISP, the TCP/IP stack on your computer translates the data coming from your PC to a format understandable by your ISP's server. Windows 95 comes with its own TCP/IP stack that it uses with Dial Up Networking to actually control your modem, but you may have heard of other winsock programs that are available. They all do the same thing—work with a dialer to make a connection to an ISP—so if your connection works, it's probably best to leave well enough alone. But now you know what other people are talking about!

WHAT'S AHEAD:

- Learn what makes up a Web page in Chapter 2.
- Start working with Internet Explorer in Chapter 3.
- Learn more Web surfing tricks and techniques in Chapter 4.

THE MAKEUP
OF A WEB PAGE

You've loaded Internet Explorer and started to look around. But what does it all mean? Your computer screen is full of large and small pictures, lots of words, and pointers that don't seem to point anywhere. It almost looks like the table of contents of a book or magazine. But how do you know where to go?

The book or magazine analogy is relevant and meaningful, but with some major distinctions. At least there aren't any new terms to learn, right? After all, this is called a Web *page*. Before you get too confident and skip this chapter, remember that you are using a computer, and you must learn some new terms and follow some conventions. Don't be discouraged, though! Even though you need to learn some new customs before you can really begin surfing the Web, once you are familiar with them you will be able to cover serious ground!

KEY POINTS IN THIS CHAPTER:

- What are the new terms and what do they mean?
- Why is http:// everywhere I look?
- What are all these pictures and underlined words?
- Where are Web pages actually located?

BASIC WEB TERMINOLOGY

First, you need to know some terms used in describing the Web and Web pages. For instance, if you were told to turn to Chapter 2 of this book and you did not know what a chapter was, you would be lost. Similarly, if someone tells you to point your browser at the URL **http://www.apnet.com**, you would be just as lost if you did not know what a browser or URL was or what the http:// thing meant. That said, let's learn some Web lingo.

Web Author

The *Web author* is the person (or company) who designed the Web site and programmed the code to make it work. Authors usually give credit to themselves somewhere!

Web Server

The *Web server* is the actual computer that contains all the information and files relating to a Web site. Web servers are generally fairly powerful machines that are designed to handle a large volume of traffic from the Internet and to search for and retrieve information quickly (although they do slow down noticeably when traffic is high). They have dedicated lines to the Internet, so they are always connected. Usually they are running 24 hours a day, every day, unless they are taken off-line for maintenance. When you access a Web page, you access a file running on a Web server. Web servers are sometimes called hosts.

Page

When you are on the World Wide Web, you are usually looking at a page, the basic unit of the Web. A *page* is the document displayed on your screen, but it is by no means limited to the size of your monitor. On the page are the pictures and other information contained in that site as well as ways to get to other pages. The right side usually has scroll bars that let you move up and down the page (similar to moving around in a word processing document). A collection of Web pages and associated files are called a *Web site* throughout this book.

Note: What are scroll bars? They are the little arrows at the side and some-times at the bottom of a screen that are used to move the image on screen. Take a look at Appendix C for more on this and other Windows basics.

Home or Start Page

Many Web sites are composed of several pages. To organize these pages, most Web sites have a *home page* that is used as an introduction and a table of contents and provides the means to reach the other pages contained within that site. You will usually find a brief descrip-tion of the site followed by a list of other pages to visit.

Microsoft sometimes calls the home page a *start page*, even though it is much more commonly referred to as a *home page* in Internet dis-cussions. (Don't be surprised if you see the term *start page* in Microsoft documents, although they seem to use the terms interchangeably!) Figure 2.1 shows the start page that Internet Explorer is programmed to go to every time it is launched. When it is used this way, to describe

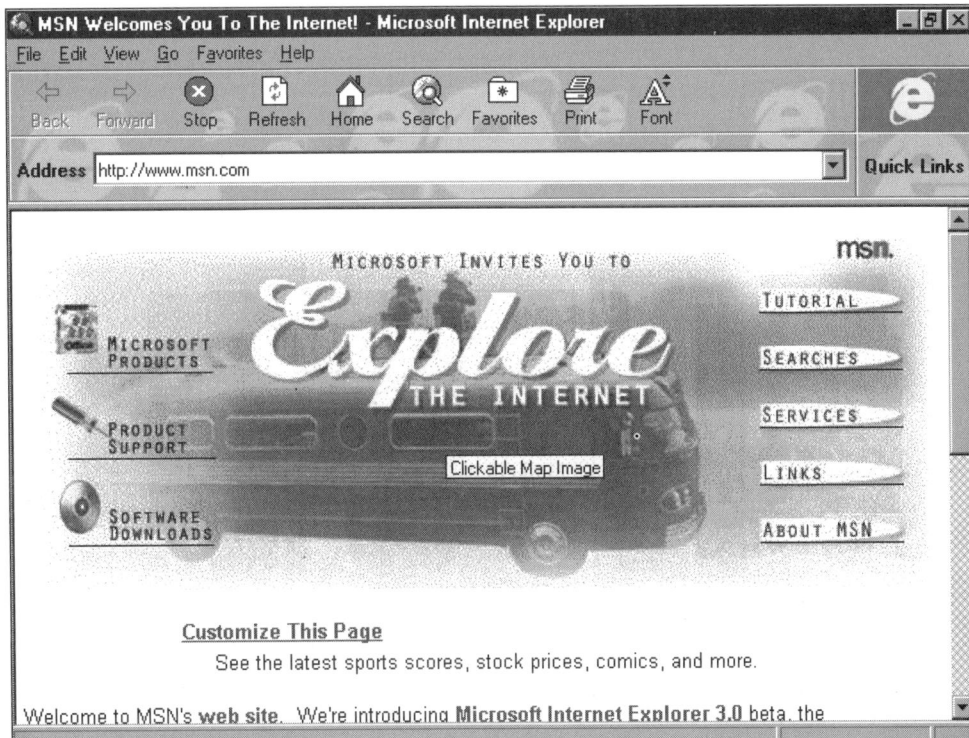

Figure 2.1: The Microsoft Network home page.

the first page you see when starting the program, the description start page is actually very accurate.

Tip: The default start page for Internet Explorer can be changed if you do not wish to visit MSN every time you surf the Net. See Chapter 3 for details.

Browser/Viewer

This is the program that is used to *browse* the Internet or *view* Web pages. Microsoft Internet Explorer is a browser. Other popular browsers are Netscape and Mosaic. They are more commonly referred to as *browsers*, but the term *viewer* does pop up occasionally.

URL

That funny bunch of words you type in to go to a site in cyberspace is called a URL. *URL* stands for Uniform Resource Locator (or sometimes Universal Resource Locator) and is an address to connect you to different sites on the Internet. The URL gives the browser the information it needs to go out and find the site on the Net. The URL for the Microsoft Network home page looks like this:

http://www.msn.com

You pronounce the URL as "h-t-t-p colon slash slash w-w-w dot m-s-n dot com."

DISSECTING A URL

Most URLs look very similar, and they all consist of the document's protocol, a host name, and sometimes the document's path and filename. Let's take a closer look at the URL "http://www.msn.com".

URL Protocol

The first part of a URL defines the type of site you are visiting. Every URL starts with a protocol, although Internet Explorer will add it automatically if you are accessing a Web site. The protocol of our example above is "http://". Some common types are:

    http://   Hypertext Transfer Protocol, or a standard WWW page

ftp://	File Transfer Protocol address
telnet://	Telnet address
usenet://	Usenet newsgroup address
gopher://	Gopher address

Host Name

The second part of the URL is the location of the host computer (or Web server). The location is divided into several parts, which are separated by periods. It often starts with *www* (although that is not always the case), followed by a name (usually a company or ISP name), and an identifier. The identifier tells you with what type of organization the author of that page is associated. The host name of our example above is "www.msn.com". Common identifiers are:

com	Commercial, usually for-profit companies (microsoft.com)
edu	Educational, colleges and universities (indiana.edu)
gov	Governmental, federal and state branches of the U.S. government (whitehouse.gov)
net	Networking, usually for-profit ISPs (iquest.net)
org	Noncommercial, usually nonprofit organizations (npr.org)

Foreign organizations have identifiers that tell you from which country they come:

jp	Japan
uk	United Kingdom
ca	Canada
de	Germany
se	Sweden
au	Australia

Path and Filename

The path and filename are not always needed in a URL. Many sites (like our example) do not use them. In these cases, the host computer is programmed to automatically display the file that the Web author wishes to be viewed. In other cases, the directory and/or filename are needed to get to specific documents. As an example, to go to the Internet Explorer home page, you would type:

http://www.microsoft.com/ie

The "/ie" is the directory. In another example, to get to a page explaining how to animate your own Web page using Microsoft PowerPoint Animation Player, you would type:

http://www.microsoft.com/mspowerpoint/internet/player/default.htm

The "/mspowerpoint/internet/player/" is the path, and "default.htm" is the filename.

Tip: Think of a URL as a phone number for the Internet. The first part (http, ftp, ...) is like an area code that tells the computer which part of the Internet to search. The second part (www.msn.com) is like the actual phone number, but with periods separating the parts instead of dashes.

Hits

Every time someone visits a Web page, it registers as a *hit*. These hits give Web authors an exact count of how often people check their page, and they are often displayed on a counter on the actual page. Figure 2.2 shows a counter measuring hits.

Hypertext and Links

Hypertext, and its ability to create links to other files, is the basis of the Web. *Hypertext* is regular text that, when clicked with a mouse, takes you somewhere else. Hypertext can be *linked* with a pop-up help menu, other parts of a Web page, a completely different Web page, an e-mail address, a file to download, or any location on the Net! Hypertext is generally shown in a different color from the rest of the text on the document, and links are usually underlined.

Frames

Frames allow Web authors to design pages with two or more independent sections. One section can be scrolled while the other remains constant. This can be used to keep navigational links on-screen at all times, even while browsing through a page. Corporate Web pages can keep a logo visible while customers look through a catalog. A table of contents can be displayed on one side, with the actual content displayed on the

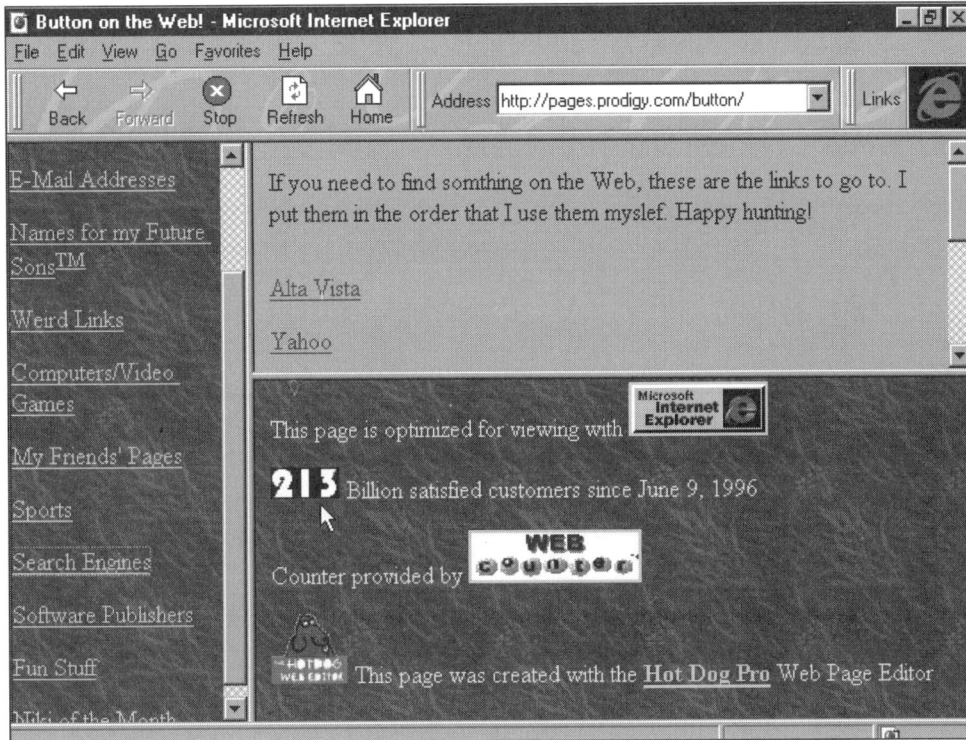

Figure 2.2: A Counter showing that this page has received 213 hits.

other. Figures 2.3 and 2.4 show frames in action. Note how the logos at the top and the buttons at the bottom remain constant while the two sections move independently of each other.

Internet Explorer supports three types of frames: borderless, nonscrolling, and floating.

Borderless frames are just as they sound, with no lines separating the sections. In Figures 2.3 and 2.4 the top and left sides use borderless frames.

Nonscrolling frames do not move, and they usually do not contain much information. They are generally used for logos (like the top section in Figures 2.3 and 2.4) or navigational buttons (like the bottom section in Figures 2.3 and 2.4).

Floating frames can be thought of as windows. They can be positioned anywhere on the page, and they are completely surrounded by the page in which they reside Figure 2.5 shows an example of a floating frame.

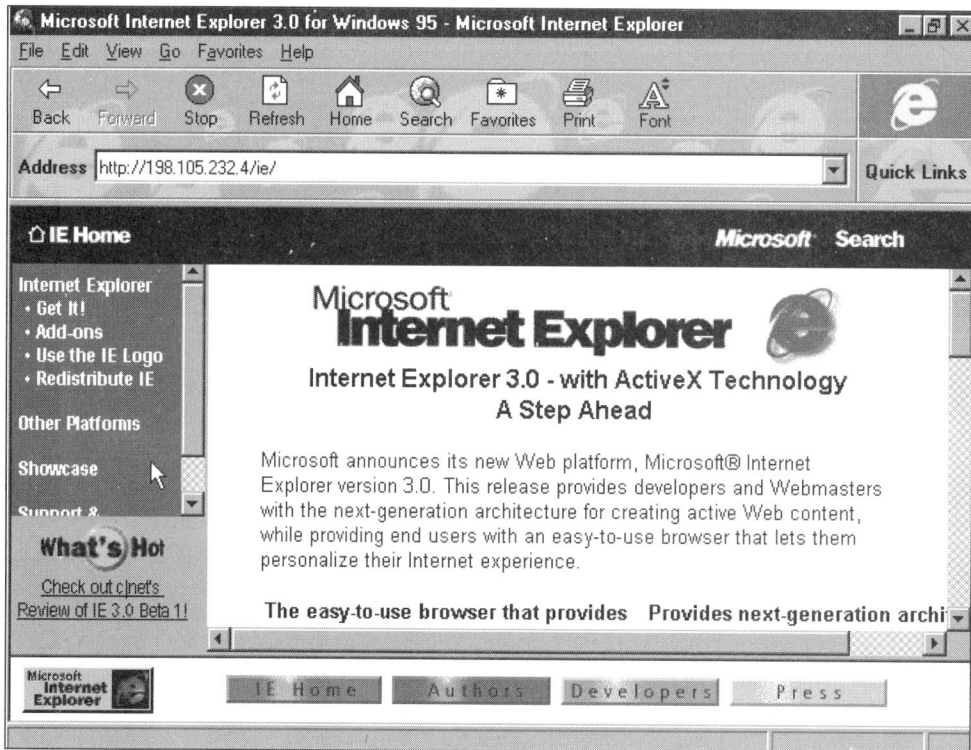

Figure 2.3: A Web page using multiple frames.

HTML, VRML

HTML stands for HyperText Markup Language; *VRML* stands for Virtual Reality Modeling Language. HTML is the programming language in which the actual Web pages are created. Some HTML programming basics are presented in Chapter 12. VRML is the language used to create 3-D Web pages, where the user does not just read text and click on links, but "walks" and "flies" through graphical representations of buildings or cities.

Some other programming languages that you will hear mentioned often (both on the Net as well as in this book) include the following:

ActiveX is a new standard used in Internet Explorer 3.0. ActiveX allows Web authors to create fully interactive pages that incorporate non-HTML files and programs. For example, users can edit an Excel spreadsheet file on-line even if they do not have Excel on their PC.

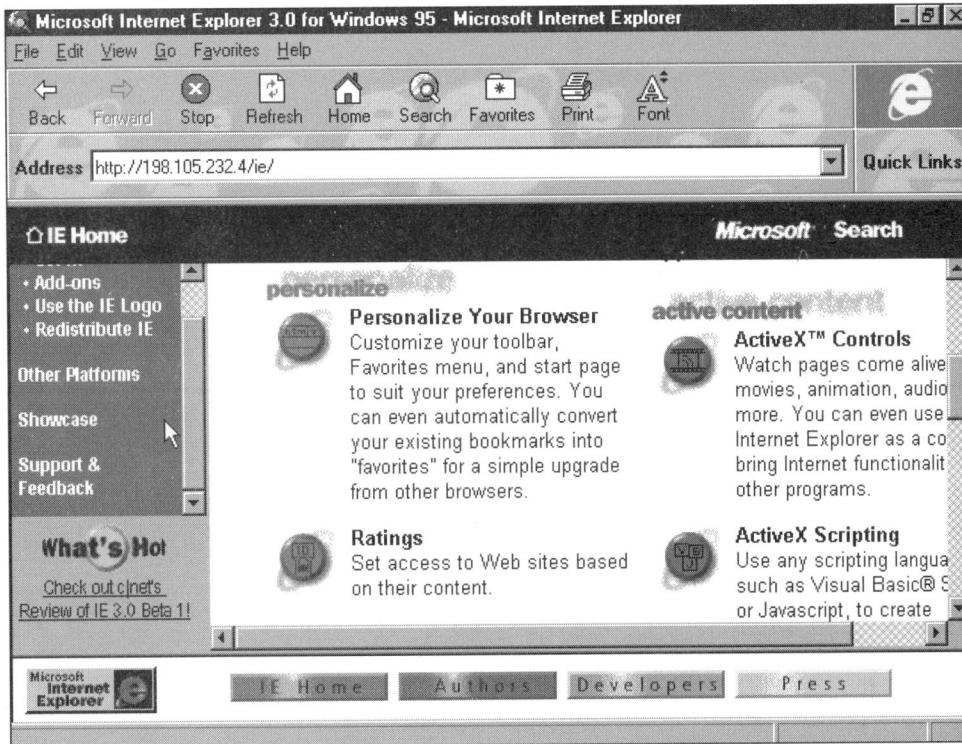

Figure 2.4: Note how the sections moved but the frames remained the same.

ActiveX is fully compatible with and can run programs written in Java.

Java is a language developed by Sun Microsystems to add interactivity to Web pages. It is not as comprehensive as ActiveX, but it has been rapidly accepted by the development community.

VBScript and *JavaScript* are mini-languages that can also be used to increase interactivity in Web pages. Common applications are small animations, calculators, and games. The main difference between VBScript/JavaScript and ActiveX/Java is that VBScript and JavaScript code is written directly into the HTML document while ActiveX/Java code works more like separate programs.

Note: Chapter 11 contains more information on VRML, ActiveX, Java, VBScript, and JavaScript.

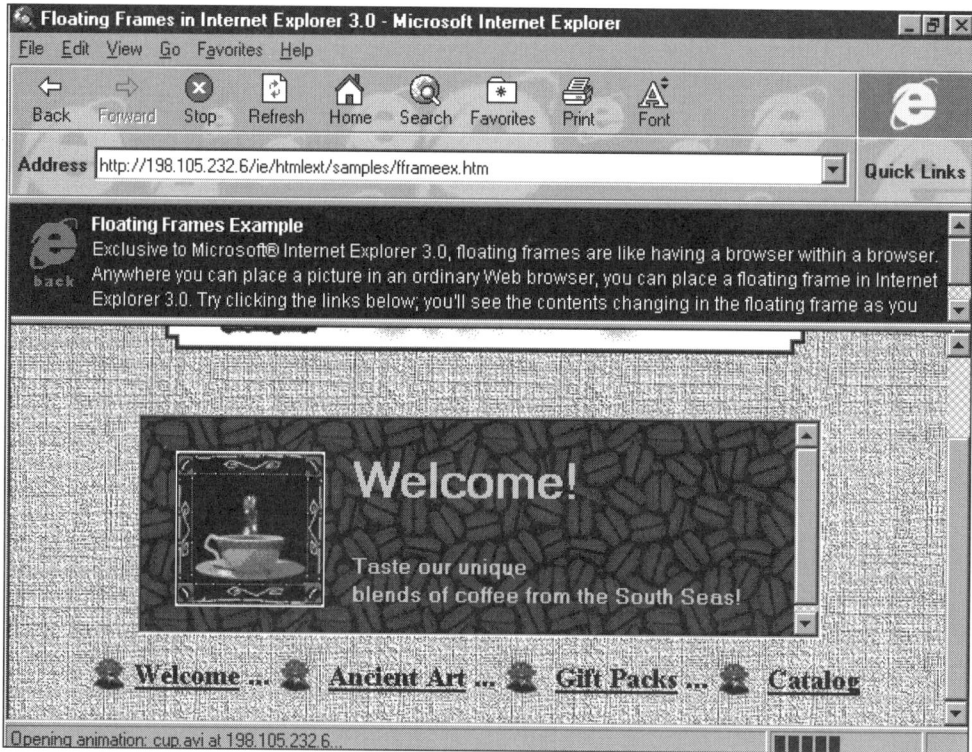

Figure 2.5: A Web page using a floating frame.

DESIGN OF A WEB PAGE

Now that you are familiar with the most commonly used terms, it is time to see how they all fit together to form a working Web page. Figures 2.6 through 2.10 show the most frequently used—and seen—aspects of a Web page.

Title

The title is simply whatever the Web author wants to call his page; see Figure 2.6.

Title   Pictures

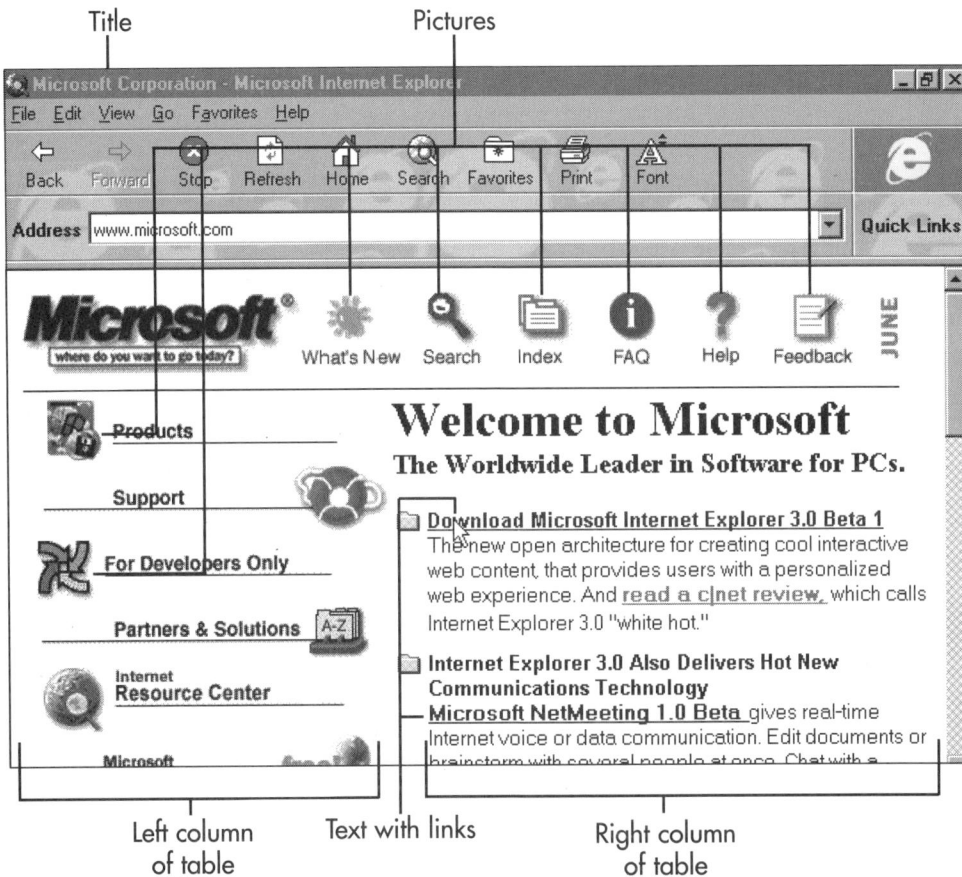

Left column   Text with links   Right column
of table   of table

Figure 2.6: Some common elements of a Web page.

Text with Links

The Web wouldn't be the Web without Hypertext links, and there are some on most pages. Note the underlining of all the text links in Figure 2.6.

Tables

A table is similar to a table in a spreadsheet. It contains multiple columns and rows filled with text, pictures, or data. The table in Figure 2.6 is a much more creative use of tables. The pictures on the left are actually in the left column of a table, and the text on the right is in the right column of the table. Although many Web pages use more traditional tables, the Web page itself can be a large table.

Pictures/Photos

Some Web authors put lots of pictures and photographs on their pages to make them fancy. Mostly this slows down access times, so responsible Web authors use pictures sparingly or use small pictures to keep loading times to a minimum. It is common for pictures to be linked just as underlined text is linked.

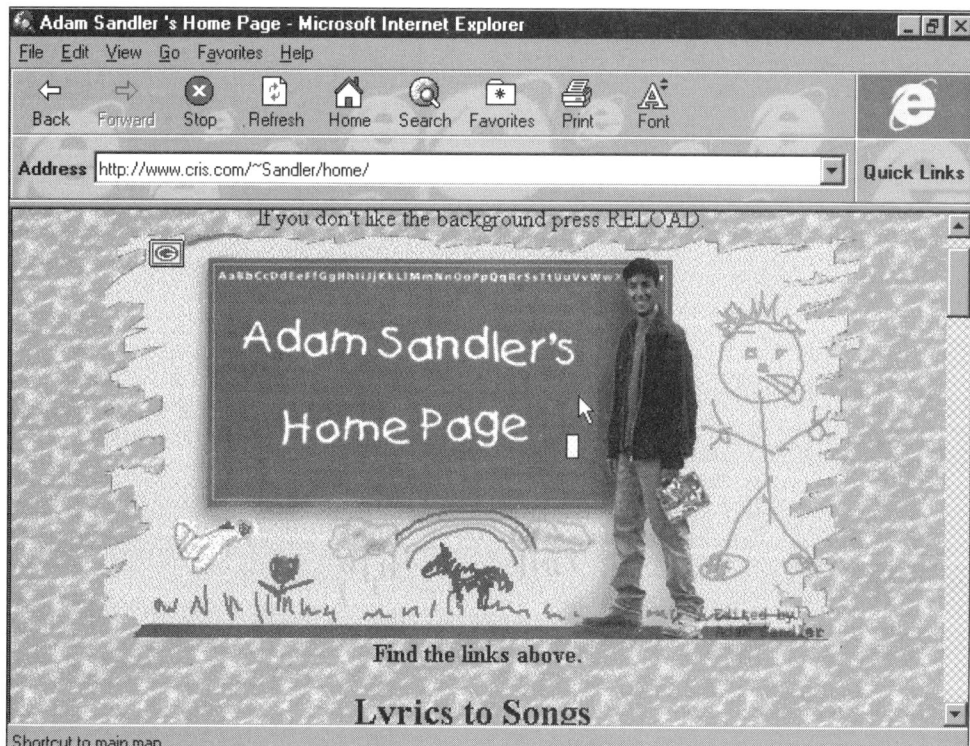

Figure 2.7: An image map.

Radio buttons

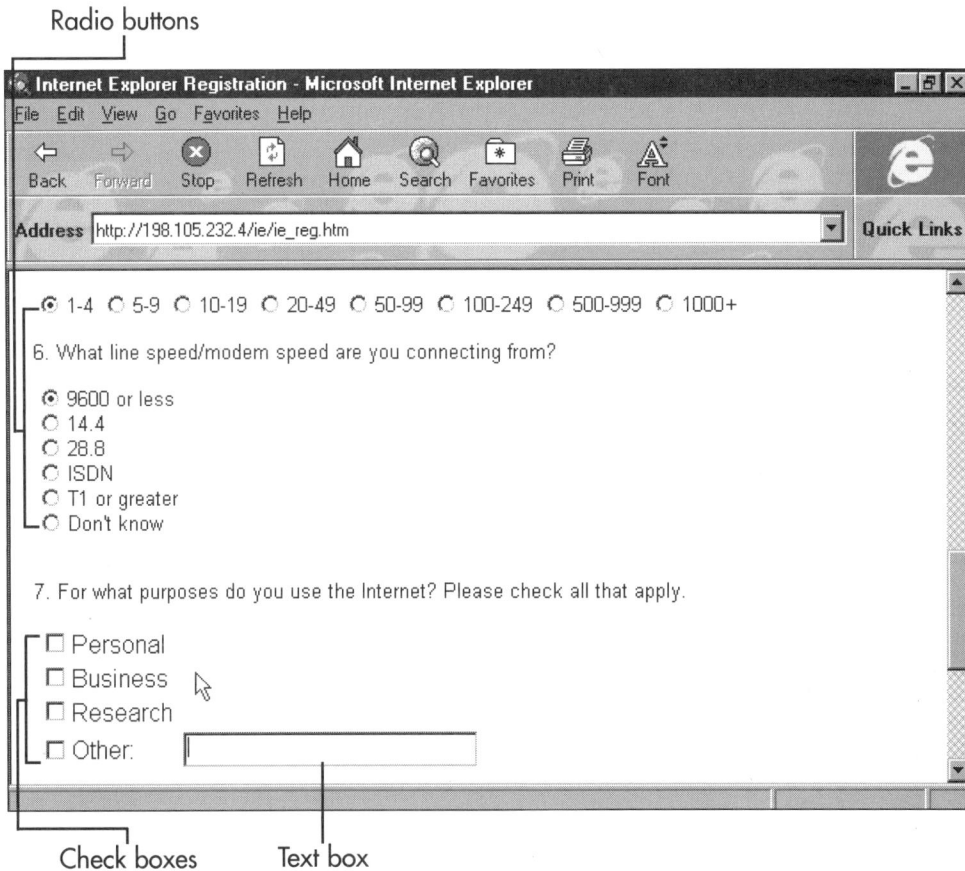

Figure 2.8: Radio buttons, check boxes, and a text box.

Image Maps

Some pictures contain many links within them and are called *image maps*. Moving your cursor around within an image map reveals different links that are associated with parts of the picture. For example, in a personal Web page, a Web author may have a family picture that is an image map. Clicking on a family member takes you to a page about that particular member. The image map in Figure 2.7 is a little sneakier, making the Web surfer find the hidden links.

Text Boxes, Check Boxes, and Radio Buttons

If a Web author requests feedback, text boxes, check boxes, and radio buttons are the most commonly used ways to get it. The Web surfer can click on a text box and type directly in it. Check boxes and radio buttons are clicked with the mouse. When a radio button is clicked, all other radio buttons in its group are automatically deselected, whereas several check boxes can be clicked without affecting each other. Radio buttons, therefore, are used for input that is mutually exclusive, like modem speed, as shown in Figure 2.8. Check boxes are used for multiple possibilities, such as Internet uses. Usually after all entries have been made and all boxes and buttons checked, the Web surfer will click on a "Submit" button or a similar button to send the information to the Web author.

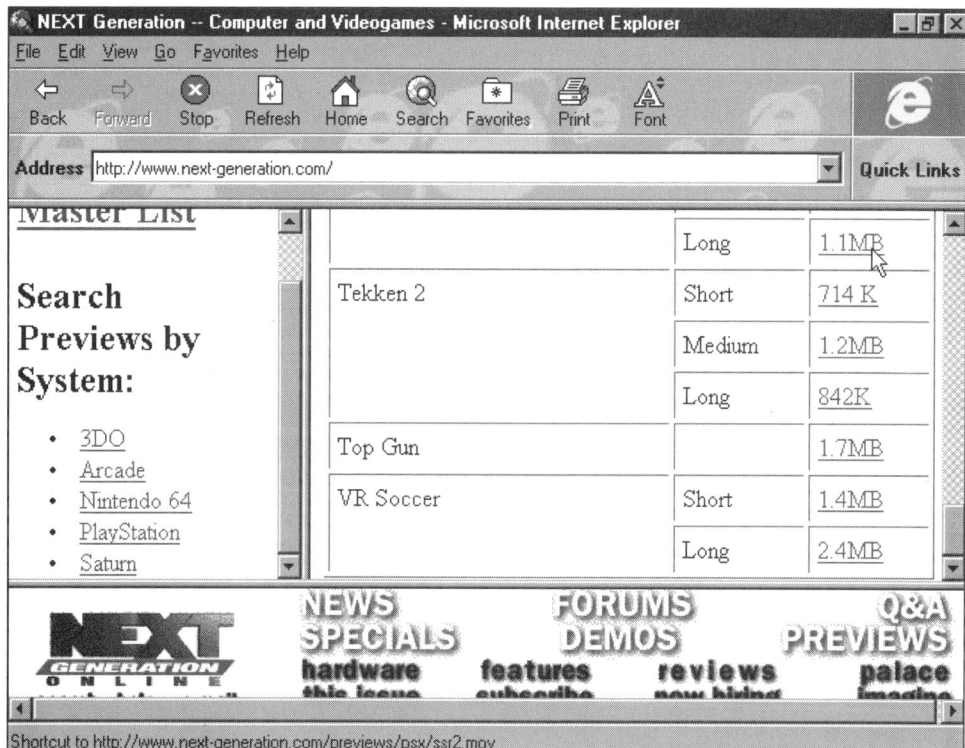

Figure 2.9: One way to represent files to download (above and below the pointer).

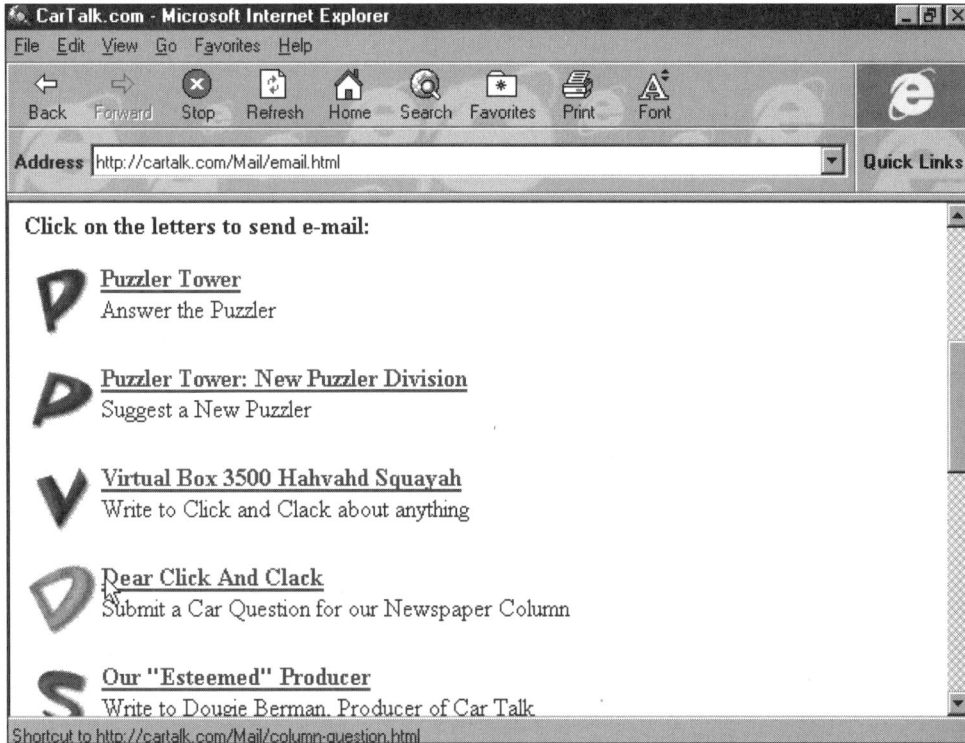

Figure 2.10: A common way to offer e-mail access.

Downloadable Files

Files that you can download are very common and can be represented by a name (underlined just like a link) or a picture (a drawing, a photo, or a small icon), as shown in Figure 2.9. Clicking on the link starts the download process (which is discussed in Chapter 6).

E-mail Addresses

An e-mail address is typically a text link (underlined, of course) that automatically launches the user's e-mail program to send a message to the addressee, as shown in Figure 2.10. As with downloadable files, an e-mail address can also be represented by a picture.

Figure 2.11: Tommy Cam at USC.

Where Are These Pages?

Speaking literally, Web sites and pages are on Web servers. But where are these servers actually located? Well, you may have gathered from the name that the Web is World Wide just like the Internet itself. Started in Europe, the Web has crept all across the globe in just a few short years, but it does not encompass the *entire* earth just yet. Currently, the majority of Web servers are in North America and Western Europe. South America, Eastern Europe, the Middle East, and the Far East are not yet well represented, but they soon will be as the Internet gains more popularity as a worldwide communications network. Internet Explorer itself is available in 23 different languages, from English to Japanese.

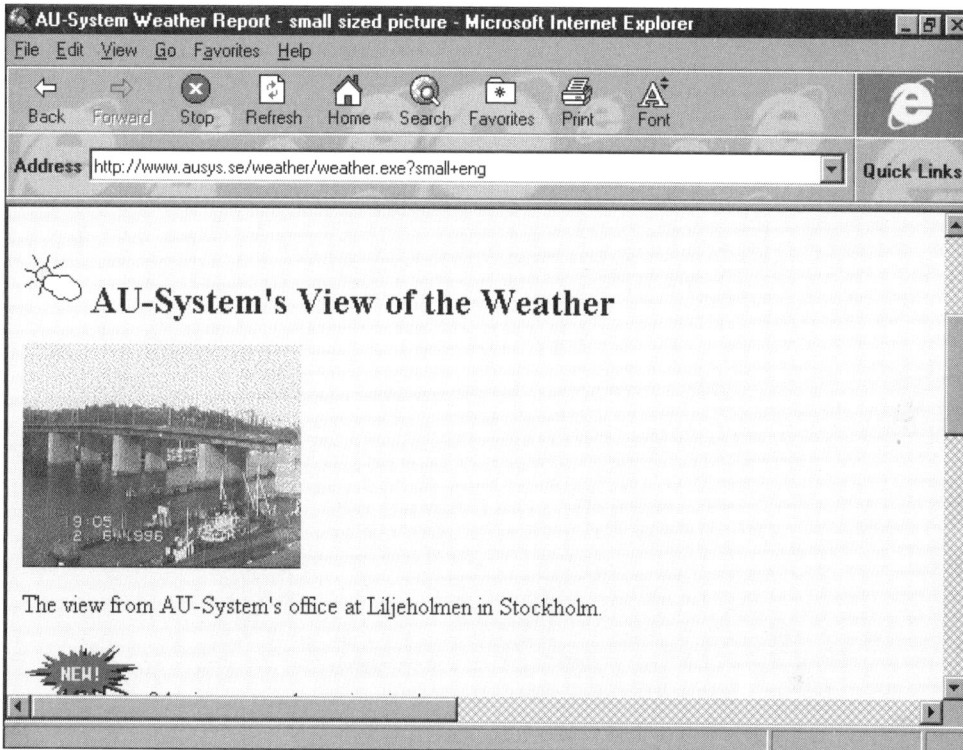

Figure 2-12: A river in Sweden.

Just in case you belong to the Flat Earth Society and think that the Web (and the Internet, for that matter) is contained in a computer locked in a garage in Silicon Valley, I offer you proof (sort of) that it is indeed all across the world! Point your browser towards these sites (Hey! You know what that means now!) that offer live photos from different locations across the world:

- **http://www.usc.edu/dept/TommyCam/**
     Live shot from the campus of USC
- **http://www.ausys.se/weather/weathre[sic].htm**
     Live picture outside an office in Liljeholmen, Sweden

For more pictures from around the world (mostly of the insides of buildings), try this URL:

http://www.cris.com/~Sandler/camera/index.shtml

For more information on entering URLs in Internet Explorer, see Chapter 4.

WHAT'S AHEAD:

- Get into Internet Explorer in Chapter 3.
- Learn how to surf the Web in Chapter 4.
- Search for information on the Net in Chapter 5.

Chapter 3

EXPLORING EXPLORER

"OK, already," you must be thinking. "Let's go do something on the Internet!" You have been briefed on the major parts of the Net and the basic layout of a Web page. I bet you have already done a bit of Web surfing on your own, and that's good! One of the best ways to discover the Internet is to just jump right in.

Now it's time for a tour of Internet Explorer itself, the tool (or surfboard, if you will) with which you will surf the Net. After all, if you are going to spend time with Explorer, it is important to know where its features are located so it can work best for you.

Key Points in This Chapter

- How do I start?
- What is this first page that I see?
- What do all these menus and buttons do?
- How do I move around once I find a Web page?
- Do I ever use the keyboard?

GETTING CONNECTED

Have you noticed that icon on your desktop labeled "The Internet"? That's the shortcut to Explorer. Click it and Explorer will load. If you used the Internet Setup Wizard to set up your ISP, you may then have to enter your password (see Figure 3.1). MSN users will also have to enter a password (see Figure 3.2). MSN users can also launch Explorer via MSNs Internet Center.

Note: If you don't have an icon labeled "The Internet" on your desktop, use the "Find" command from Windows 95 Explorer or the Start menu to search for the file "Iexplore.exe." If you don't have this file, see Appendix A to learn how to install Explorer.

THE START PAGE

The start page is where Microsoft wants you to go today! When you first launch Explorer, the start page loads automatically after a connection with your ISP is established. By default, the start page is the Microsoft Network home page. Figure 3.3 shows what you see when Explorer is launched. The Explorer start page offers links to various Web resources and information. It can also be customized for each individual user to display specific information. For example, if you

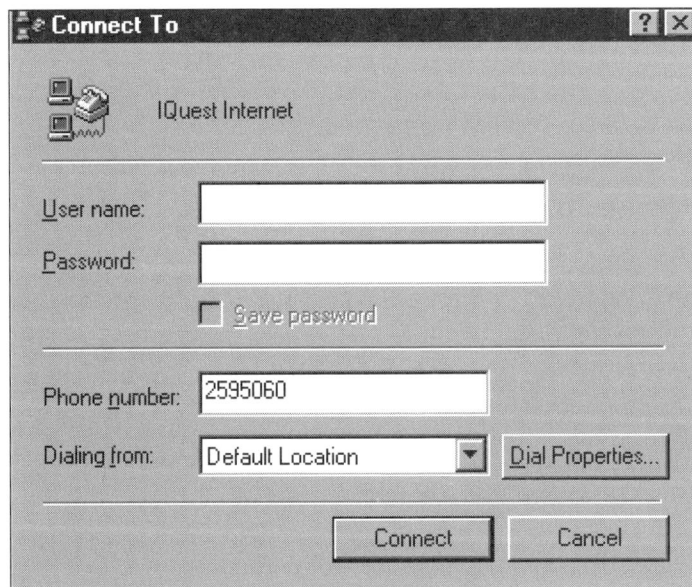

Figure 3.1: Connecting to Explorer using an ISP.

Figure 3.2: Connecting to Explorer using MSN.

always want to see the latest scores first, the MSN home page can be configured to show them at the top. Click on the text hyperlink "Customize This Page" to find out how.

Changing the Start Page

Let's say that you don't always want to go to the MSN home page when you start Explorer. After all, you pay for access time, and you would rather not pay for Microsoft's page to load. Changing the start page is easy. Because you're such a Microsoft fan, you want to change the start page to another helpful Microsoft site: the Internet Explorer home page. Here are two ways.

1. Select the Navigation tab from the View Options menu.
2. Type the **http://www.microsoft.com/ie** in the box next to Address.
3. Select OK.

or

1. Click on the address bar.
2. Type **http://www.microsoft.com/ie**.
3. Press the Enter key on your keyboard.
4. When the page is loaded, select the Navigation tab from the View Options menu.
5. Choose Use Current.
6. Choose OK.

Note: If some of these terms are unfamiliar, read ahead in this chapter and then return here to change your start page.

The next time you launch Explorer, you will be taken to the Microsoft Internet Explorer home page (a good place to check for

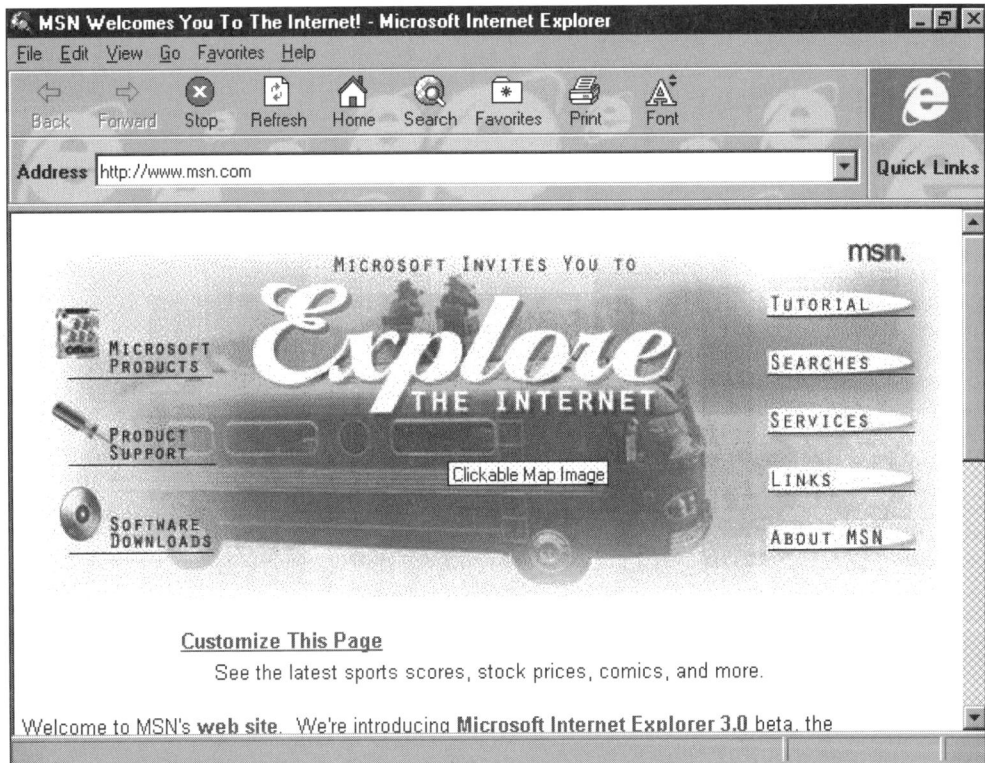

Figure 3.3: Internet Explorer's default start page.

upgrades and new add-ons). As you might have imagined, you can change your start page to any Web site. You can change your start page to visit your friend's personal Web page, your company's corporate home page, or **www.apnet.com** for great book info!

Tip: Here are some criteria to keep in mind when choosing a start page. First, make it a page with many hyperlinks to other pages. Anything that eliminates typing is good! Second, make it a page that changes frequently. There is little point in connecting to a page that is always the same. Finally, if you search the Internet for information frequently, consider making one of the popular search engines your start page (for more on search engines see Chapter 5). This will allow you to begin your search immediately.

THE MAIN AREAS OF EXPLORER

Figure 3.4 shows the basic Internet Explorer screen (without a Web page loaded). It is cleanly laid out, and it is composed of four main parts that you will use regularly. These parts are the title bar, the menu bar, the toolbar, and the status bar. The toolbar can be broken into the icon bar, the address bar, quick links, and the Explorer logo. Each of the features of these parts will be named below, and later chapters will cover them in more detail.

Title Bar

The title bar is at the very top of the Explorer screen. It identifies the name of the current Web page being viewed. Because there is no page loaded in Figure 3.4, all the title bar displays is "Microsoft Internet Explorer." If you go back to Figure 3.3, the MSN home page, you will see the title bar displaying "MSN Welcomes You To The Internet!". Note that this is the title of the page, not the URL.

Menu Bar

The menu bar is located directly below the title bar (see Figure 3.4). It contains the pull-down menus that control some of Explorer's more advanced functions for customizing and configuring. When a page is loaded, each pull-down menu provides access to features relating to its name.

Icon Bar   Title Bar Menu Bar   Explorer logo Quick Links

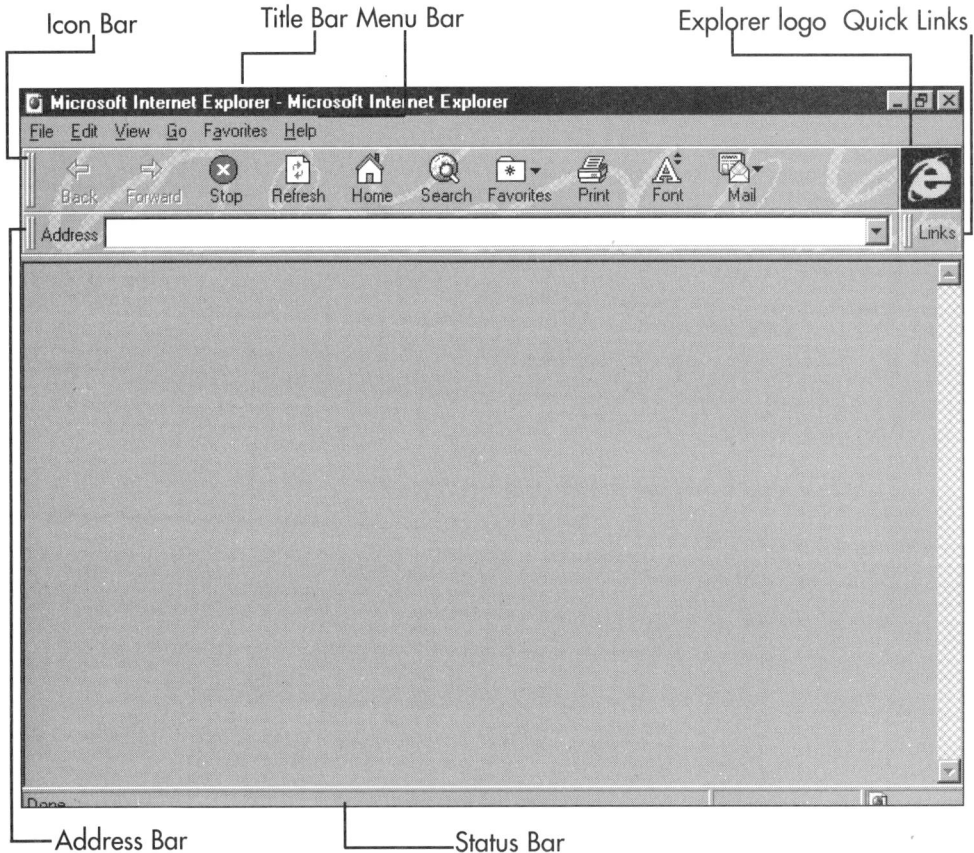

Figure 3.4: The basic parts of Internet Explorer.

The File Menu Figure 3.5 shows the File menu, which covers the basics of file management including Open, Save, and Save As. New Window allows you to open a second page while maintaining a connection with the first. Send To is used to e-mail a URL to a friend or coworker. Page Setup and Print are for creating hard copies of a Web page. Create Shortcut and Properties let you manipulate and see details of the current URL. Close closes the active window and disconnects from that URL.

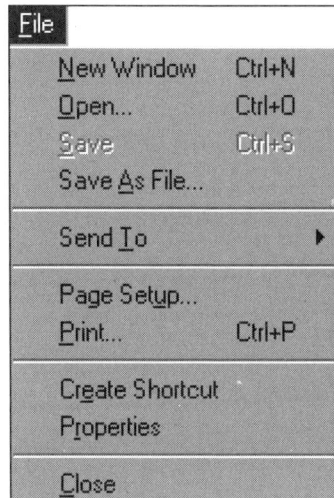

Figure 3.5: The File Menu.

The Edit Menu Figure 3.6 shows the Edit menu, which allows you to cut, copy, and paste selections from the current page. Select All highlights all the text on the page for editing. Find (on this page) searches the page for words of your choice.

The View Menu Figure 3.7 shows the View menu. The View menu lets you show or hide the toolbar and status bar, change the fonts, stop a page from loading, refresh a page that is already loaded, view the source HTML code, and pull up the Options window that allows you to change some of the settings for Explorer.

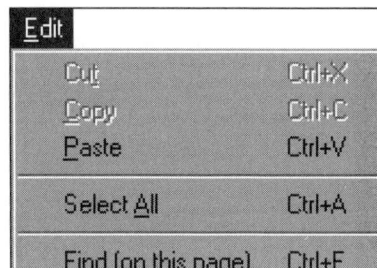

Figure 3.6: The Edit menu.

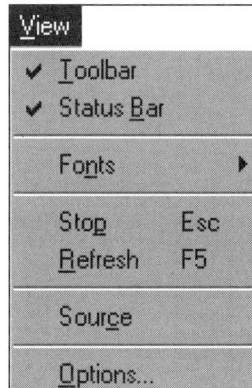

Figure 3.7: The View menu.

The Go Menu Figure 3.8 shows the Go menu, which acts as a navigational aid to move between pages. Back and Forward move you through pages already visited during the current session. Start Page takes you to your designated start page. Search the Web takes you to a preset page on the Microsoft Web site that contains several search engines. Today's Links is another preset page from Microsoft that contains links to interesting sites that are updated daily. Below Today's Links is a list of sites that have been visited during the current session. The check mark indicates the page that is currently being viewed. This part of the Go Menu would also be used to keep track of multiple windows. Finally, the Open History Folder lets you load pages that were visited in previous sessions of Web browsing.

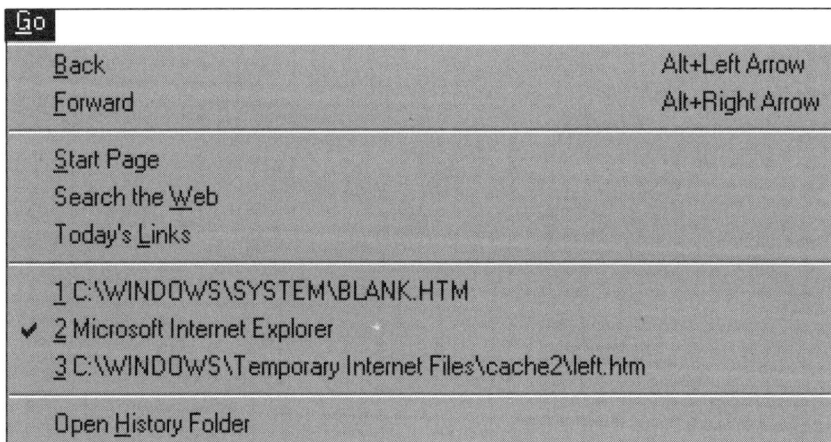

Figure 3.8: The Go menu.

The Favorites Menu Figure 3.9 shows the Favorites menu. This menu option allows you to add to your list of favorite sites and organize the way your favorite sites are stored. The bottom of this menu displays the sites you have saved (or in this case displays special folders in which my favorite sites are kept).

The Help Menu Figure 3.10 shows the Help menu, probably the most self-explanatory menu. Help Topics displays a table of contents for the help system. Web Tutorial links to a site offered by Microsoft that teaches Web basics. Microsoft on the Web is a collection of links that are maintained by Microsoft that offer support, feedback, and other services. About Internet Explorer lists the version number, copyright information, and registration information.

Figure 3.9: The Favorites menu.

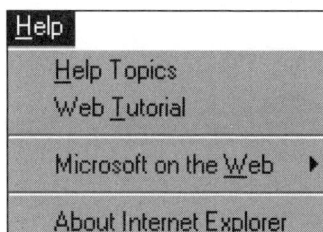

Figure 3.10: The Help menu.

Toolbar

The menu bar is great, but it is used only occasionally. Many of its features are duplicated on the toolbar, which is much easier (and more fun) to use. You will use the toolbar very often in your Web surfing. The toolbar is divided into the icon bar, the address bar, Quick Links, and the Explorer logo.

Icon Bar Located directly below the menu bar (see Figure 3.4), the icon bar is perhaps the most frequently used portion of Explorer. Each icon represents a commonly performed task or a link to a popular site.

The back icon will take you to the previously viewed page. This icon is available only after you have visited at least two pages.

After you use the Back icon, Forward will return you to the page you just left.

If you no longer want a page to load (perhaps it's taking too long or is the wrong page), Stop will force Explorer to stop loading and allow you to enter a new URL.

The Refresh icon will reload the currently displayed document.

The Home icon will take you directly to the start page as it is configured in Explorer. Why is it called a start page everywhere except here? Ask Microsoft.

The Search icon takes you to a Microsoft page with several search engines for finding information on the Web. It can be changed to a site of your choice the same way the start page can be changed.

As you find cool sites on the Web, you can save them as Favorites. The Favorites icon will open your Favorites list and display these sites' addresses.

The Print icon will print the current page.

Some people prefer different sizes of fonts with which to view Web pages. The Font icon lets you make the display fonts larger or smaller.

The Mail and News icon will launch Internet Mail, which is used to send and receive E-mail, and Internet News, which is used to read Usenet newsgroups. Not all versions of Explorer will have this icon—only the complete version contains Mail and News.

Address Bar   The address bar is clearly labeled in Figure 3.4, directly underneath the icon bar. It is the place to enter URLs manually. Simply place the cursor over the address bar, left-click, then type the URL and press Enter. Your URL will load. The arrow at the right of the address bar is used to select previously entered URLs. Click on the arrow, then click on a URL to go there!

Quick Links   New for Explorer 3.0, Quick Links are almost hidden in Figure 3.4. Figure 3.11 shows them more clearly. To unhide them, simply click where it says Quick Links and they will appear, covering the address bar. Quick Links are preset by Microsoft (or your employer if you are using a corporate version of Explorer) to take you to specific pages within the Microsoft Web site.

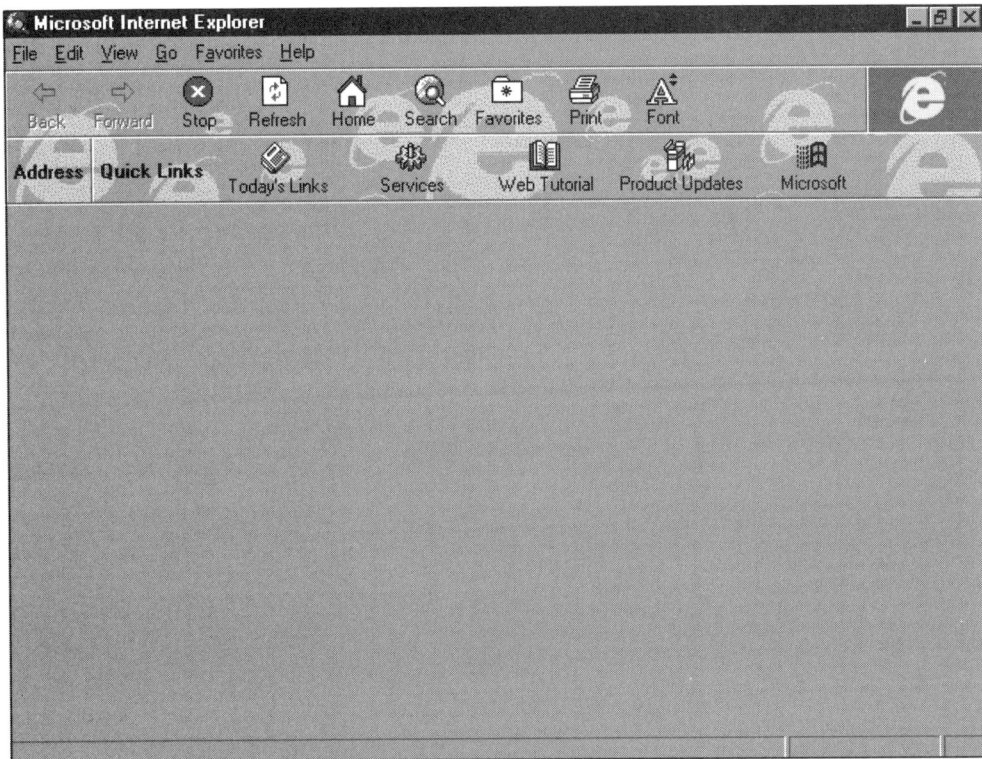

Figure 3.11: Quick Links.

The Today's Links icon will take you to a collection of interesting (but not necessarily important) Web sites that are updated daily.

The Services icon will take you to a page full of links to all kinds of services, from tax information to writer's tools to computer support.

The Web Tutorial icon will take you to a brief but informative tour of the World Wide Web. Some of the information overlaps what was presented in Chapters 1 and 2, but this still is a good way for beginners to spend 10 or 15 minutes.

Clicking the Product Updates icon will take you to the Internet Explorer home page, where you can check for new releases of Internet software and add-on programs.

Yes, these guys are just crazy about themselves. The Microsoft icon is yet another way to go to a Microsoft Web page, this time the main Microsoft home page.

Explorer Logo At the far right of the toolbar is a big "e" (check Figure 3.4). Sometimes this is an image of the Earth with a ring moving around it, and sometimes it is just an "e" on a black background. There is a reason for these special effects! The rotating Earth indicates that data is still being sent from the Web site to your computer, meaning that part of the page is still loading. When the image is still, the page is completely loaded. Pressing the Stop button (described above) cancels any data transfer, and within seconds the logo should be still.

Status Bar

The status bar (see Figure 3.4) is the text bar that runs along the bottom of the Explorer window. Most of the time it just sits there and stays out of the way, but it still performs an important function for Web surfers. It gives you the status (thus its name) of hyperlinks by displaying their target URL (called a shortcut by Explorer) when the cursor is passed over them. When connecting to a Web site, the status bar also gives connection information such as "Web site found" or "Waiting for host" to let you know how the connection is coming. The middle right of the status bar houses a group of blue bars that are used to indicate the progress of a download. In the bottom right corner of the status bar is a special place for tiny little icons that identify Explorer's current actions. These icons will tell you if Explorer is waiting for a connection, downloading a page or file, or is finished with any activity. Some enterprising programmers also use the status bar to act as a scrolling marquee by using JavaScript to post messages on their Web site.

THE POINTER OF 1,000 FACES

As you move the cursor along the Explorer window, trying out all the neat buttons on the toolbar, you will probably notice that the cursor changes depending on where it is aimed. This little guy is mutitalented, and it will change its appearance based on the function it can currently perform. Here are the most common cursors.

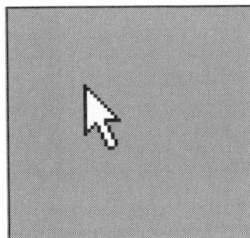

This pointer is the standard cursor for most tasks in Windows.

When a task is in progress but it is not using all of the system resources, this cursor will appear. The hourglass tells you that Explorer is working, but the pointer also lets you know that you can do other things while this task is in progress.

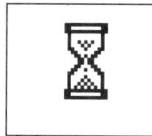

If Explorer (or Windows itself) is too busy to accept any more user input, this cursor is displayed. You will have to wait!

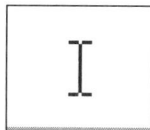

When you place the cursor over text in a Web page, your cursor changes to look like this. This curser indicates that you can highlight text in this area and copy it to the Windows clipboard.

When you move over a hypertext link (text or an image) the cursor changes to this pointing hand to inform you that a left click will take you to that link. The status bar will identify the link's URL.

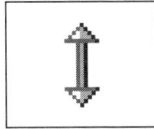

This pointer is used to resize the height of the Explorer window or a frame within the Explorer window.

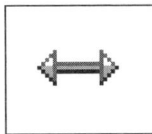

This pointer is used to resize the width of the Explorer window or a frame within the Explorer window.

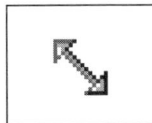

This pointer is used to resize the height and width of the Explorer window or a frame within the Explorer window.

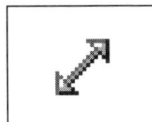

This pointer is also used to resize the height and width of the Explorer window or a frame within the Explorer window.

You may have noticed that the cursor changes into this shand tool when you moved over the toolbar. By holding the left mouse button and dragging the cursor, you can rearrange the toolbar using this cursor.

Tip: For more about customizing the toolbar, see Chapter 7.

THE RIGHT MOUSE BUTTON

You may have mistakenly pressed the right mouse button (or maybe you pressed it on purpose!) during some of your early exploring and found that some new menus popped up. These can be very helpful in opening new windows, capturing images, and more. Depending on where you use the right mouse button, the menus can be a little or a lot different. Don't be afraid to play around with these features, but for now we are going to ignore them. They will be discussed in detail in the next chapter.

MOVING WITHIN A PAGE

When you get to a Web page that your friend at work told you about, you may find that all of it does not fit on your screen. Words may be going off the left side, and the text disappears, unfinished, at the bottom of the screen. What do you do? Internet Explorer works just like any Windows document in this respect—there are several ways to move around using both the mouse and the keyboard.

Using the Mouse

To move up and down on a page that is too "tall" to fit on your monitor, use the navigation arrows located on the right side of your screen. They are rather small, black arrows with a gray line running between them. Figure 3.12 has these arrows highlighted. Simply click on the up or down arrow with the left mouse button to move one row. Hold the mouse button down to really cover some ground.

To move left and right on a page that is too wide for your monitor, use the navigation arrows at the bottom of your screen. They look just like the up and down arrows turned sideways, and they can be seen in Figure 3.12. They work the same way, too. Both sets of arrows are also used to move around a page that uses frames.

Figure 3.12 also shows the trio of tiny buttons in the top right corner of the screen. These buttons, from left to right, will hide the Explorer window, minimize or maximize the window, or close the window. These buttons are very helpful when you have several URLs in multiple windows all open at the same time.

When a window is not maximized (as in Figure 3.12), the resize cursors discussed above come into play. Moving the cursor to the edge or corner of the window will bring up a resize cursor. Left-click the edge

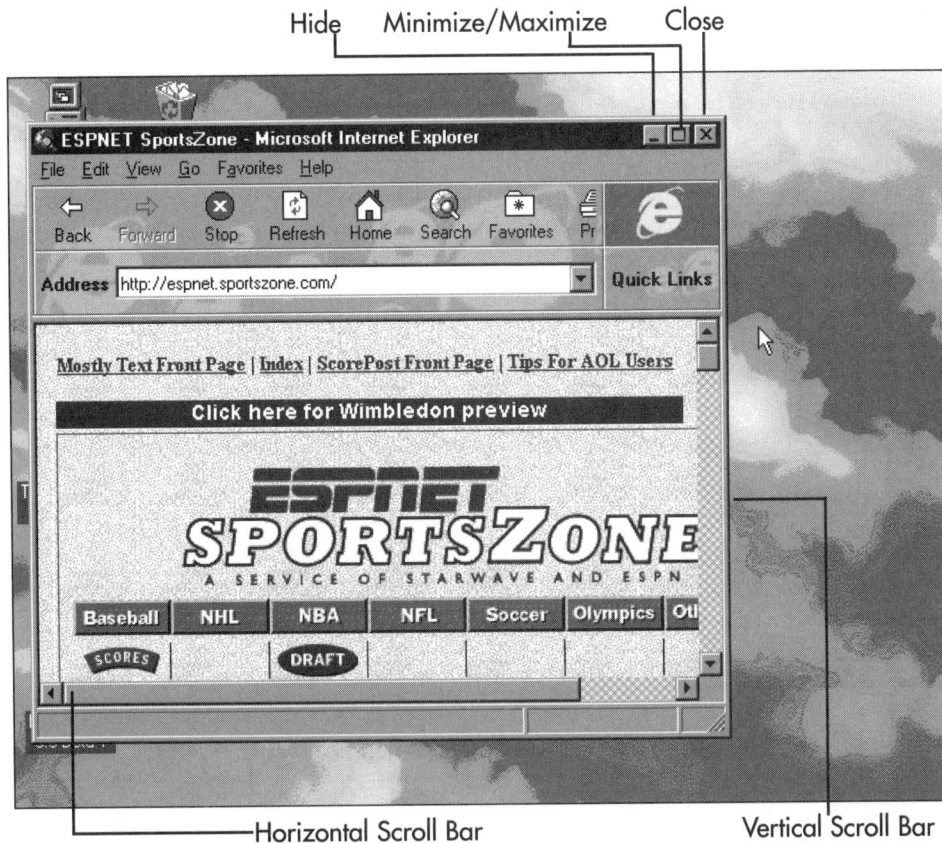

Figure 3.12: Navigation features in an Explorer window.

and drag it to the desired size. Clicking and dragging the title bar will let you move the entire window around the screen. Again, these are helpful when you have more than one window open on the desktop.

Some Web pages have links to themselves. That is, a page will have a link that does not take you to another page, but to a different part of the same page. These can be very helpful in large pages, and they work with a simple left-click, just like a standard hyperlink.

Using the Keyboard

Keyboard navigation is fairly straightforward. Pg Up (Page Up) and Pg Dn (Page Down) will move the document up and down one screen at a time, respectively. The Home and End keys will move the cursor to the beginning and end of the selected line. The arrow keys will move one space left or right and one line up or down. For you mouse haters, these keys can save you time.

KEYBOARD SHORTCUTS

For mouse lovers and haters alike, Explorer makes extensive use of keyboard shortcuts. A shortcut uses two or more keys on the keyboard simultaneously to perform a task such as saving or printing a document. While accessing the menus from the menu bar, you may have noticed that some functions have a few words next to them, such as "Ctrl+N." This means press and hold the Ctrl key then press the N key. Keyboard shortcuts may seem a bit strange at first, but they do save a little time once you know the combinations.

The keyboard shortcuts for Internet Explorer are listed in Table 3.1.

Table 3.1 Keyboard Shortcuts for Internet Explorer

Tab and Shift+Tab (Forward and Backward, respectively)	Navigate between: Image Hyperlinks Text hyperlinks Nonhyperlink Images Hyperlinks within image maps The address bar
Enter	Activate selected hyperlink
Shift+F10	Display a context menu for a hyperlink

Table 3.1 *Continued*

Ctrl+Tab	Cycle between frames
Shift+Tab	Go backward through hyperlinks
Shift+Ctrl+Tab	Go backward through frames
Alt+Left arrow	Go back to previously viewed pages
Alt+Right arrow	Go forward through pages
Alt+Left arrow	Go back to previously viewed pages
Ctrl+R	Refresh the current document
F5	Refresh the page
Esc	Cancel download of a page
Backspace	Go back to previously viewed pages
Shift+Backspace	Go forward through pages
Ctrl+O	Go to a new location
Ctrl+N	Open a new window
Ctrl+S	Save the current page
Ctrl+P	Print the current page

WHAT'S AHEAD

- Explore more Web surfing tricks and techniques in Chapter 4.
- Learn how to search the Web in Chapter 5.
- Discover the basics of downloading and file management in Chapter 6.

Chapter 4

WANDERING THE WEB

Now that you have been briefed on Internet Explorer's features and just a few of its basic tricks, it is time to get to the real use of this program—Net surfing! But with so much out there, is this chapter going to tell all there is to know?

In a word, no. There is no possible way to explain the Internet or even all there is to know about navigating the Internet in one chapter. Many people write entire books on the subject. (But isn't this a book on the subject? Hmmmm. You have me there.) The truth is, you don't need to know everything to have a good time. The majority of people can't explain how an internal combustion engine works, but most of us can still drive our cars. This is the same concept. This chapter will tell you enough about Web surfing with Explorer so you can go out and have a really good time. Then, if you continue reading subsequent chapters, you will learn quite a bit more about the art of Internet navigation.

Key Points in This Chapter

- Entering URLs
- Moving between pages using hyperlinks and Explorer features
- Saving cools sites for later visits
- Revisiting sites
- Other tips and tricks for better surfing

ENTERING URLS

Remember URLs? Uniform Resource Locators? These are the phone numbers of the Internet. Many times you will not have to type them in manually—you will just click on a hyperlink that will take you to the site. But there will be many times when you find a cool address when you are away from your computer. When you return to your PC, what do you do? How do you enter that address?

Remember the address bar? We used it in the last chapter to enter a URL for Microsoft to change our start page. That was the basic technique for manually entering a URL. Simply click on the address bar with your mouse, then type the URL. Then press the Enter key on your keyboard to go to the desired Web page. Figure 4.1 shows where to position your cursor to type.

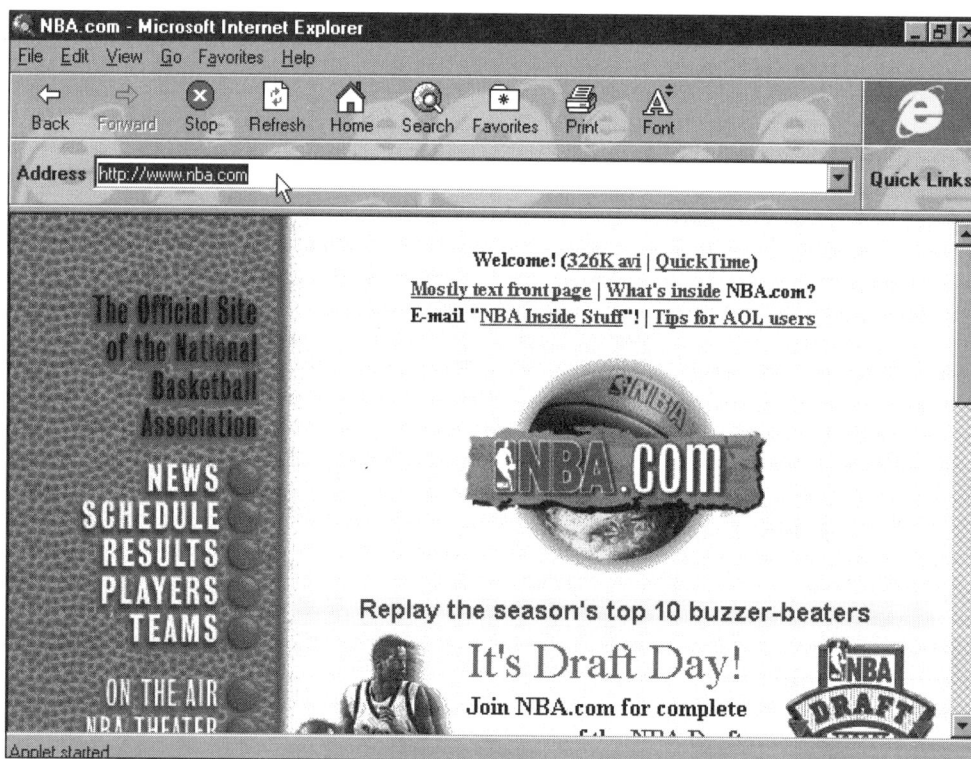

Figure 4.1: Manually entering a URL.

There are two key points to remember, however. Watch capitalization *very* carefully. No, you won't blow up any computers if you put an address in all caps, but you will get an error message. If you copy an address from somewhere, be sure to copy it identically. Second, watch for typing errors. The computer won't know you mean "nba" if you type "nab." Figure 4.2 shows the error message that is displayed if you make any kind of typo.

Tip: In Chapter 2 we discussed the URL protocol. In the case of Web pages, it is "http://". Explorer is smart enough, however, to add this part for you. Therefore, typing "www.nba.com" has the same effect as typing "http://www.nba.com". Saving keystrokes is good!

If you are wondering where to find URLs, Table 4.1 gives you some ideas.

USING HYPERLINKS FOR NAVIGATION

Hyperlinks are the key to moving about the Internet. Almost every Web page is loaded with them, and using them couldn't be easier.

Figure 4.2: If you make a typing mistake.

Table 4.1: Where to Find URLs.

Computer books	Internet guides (such as this one), WWW directories
Magazines	Basic computing and Internet specialty
Advertisements	TV, radio, magazines, newspapers
Usenet groups	Posted as message titles and contained within messages
Other Web pages	Usually as hyperlinks
Friends	Let them do the searching, then you can hit them up for all the cool sites!

Simply position your cursor over the link. When the cursor changes to a hand, left-click to go to that site. The site could be anything from a Web page to an e-mail address to an FTP site. The Earth will start to spin in the Logo window (telling you that Explorer is working), and the status bar will give you a few messages telling you what files are being loaded. The status bar will also show a series of blue squares on its right side when loading large files or when access is slow. These tell you how close the given file is to being completely loaded.

LEARNING THE SECRETS OF THE LINKS

If you want to know the URL of the site that a hyperlink represents, position your cursor over the link without left-clicking. The status bar in the lower left corner of Explorer will show you the URL. By default, it will show the URL in simplified form. To me, this can be more confusing than standard form, so I recommend changing Explorer to show standard URLs. Follow these steps.

1. Select View from the Menu bar.
2. Select Options.
3. Select the Advanced tab from the Options window.
4. Under Additional, deselect Show friendly URLs.
5. Select OK.

You may notice that when you visit a page, choose one of its links, and return to that original page, the link you chose is now a different color from the remainder of the links. This is Explorer's way of reminding you which sites have already been visited. If you are on a page with many links, you can easily lose your place and accidentally visit the same site twice. Explorer displays links that have not yet been viewed in blue and viewed links in purple. As with many of Explorer's features, this can be changed if you don't like the color scheme. Simply follow the directions above. The color options are in the General tab.

Tip: I recommend leaving the link colors alone. Many Web authors will design their pages with custom colors that match their layouts. Changing the default in Explorer may cause some links to be difficult to find amid the background image.

And just how many links can be on one page at a time? As many as the Web author can fit! Links can also take the form of pictures and photographs. Anything that changes your cursor into a hand is linked to another place on the Net. Figure 4.3 shows a typical page with several different examples of links. How many can you find on that single page?

Image maps are also a form of hyperlink. An *image map* is a picture with different sections assigned as links. In Figure 4.4, the different parts of the garage represent different links in the cartalk.com Web site. For example, clicking on the computer screen takes you to an advertisement for one of the sponsors, while clicking on the mailbox on the back wall takes you to the e-mail page. The key with most image maps is to move your cursor around while keeping one eye on the status bar. When you come upon a link, the status bar will display its URL. When you are in dead space, the status bar will be blank.

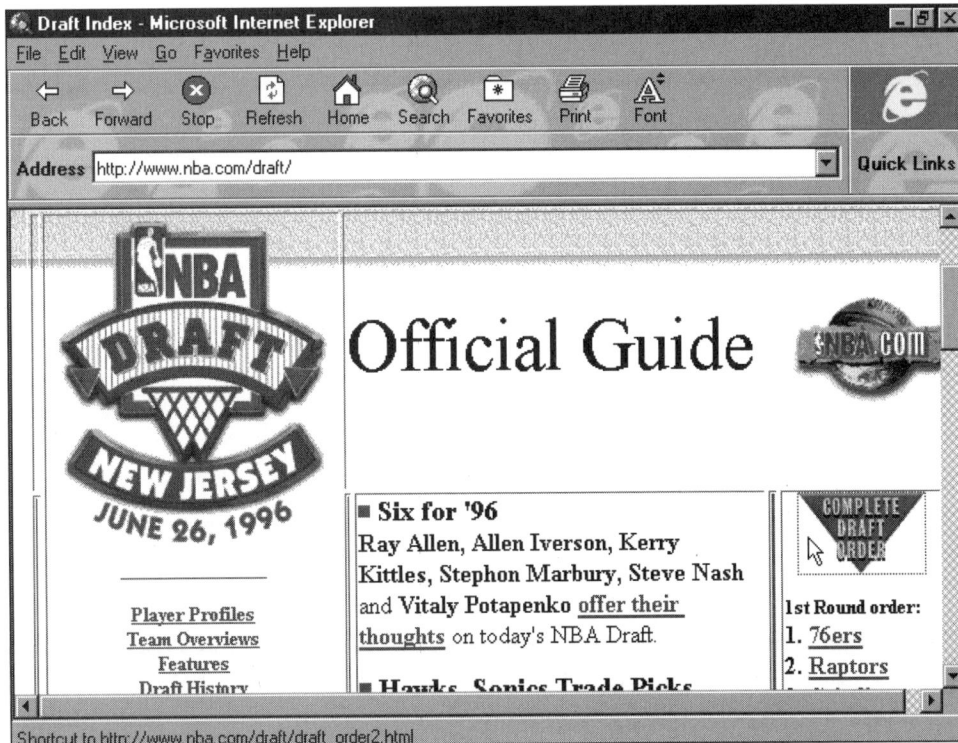

Figure 4.3: How many links are on this page? Can you find 12?

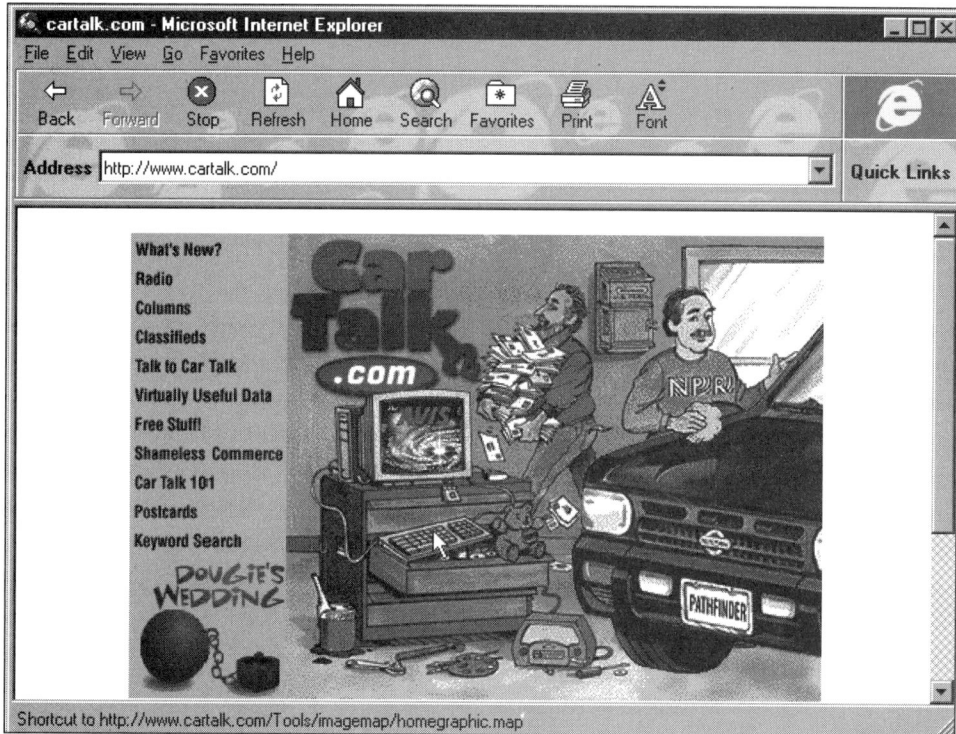

Figure 4.4: An image map filled with links.

Note: Unfortunately this doesn't work with every image map. Some will merely show you the x and y coordinates that your cursor has crossed, while others will always be blank. When in doubt, click away. Then be prepared to use the feature discussed in a later section of this chapter—the Back icon!

E-MAILING VIA A HYPERLINK

Many links do not go to another Web site but instead are designed to send an e-mail message. For instance, most Web authors want feedback on how people like their pages, so they want to make it easy for Web surfers to send their comments. Without an e-mail link, the Web author would have to post his or her e-mail address, then you would have to write it down (or copy it to the Clipboard) and then load your e-mail program to write and send the letter. If you haven't noticed already, Internet users don't like unnecessary keystrokes when faster options are available. The e-mail link (or mailto link, as it is known) automatically launches your e-mail program and addresses the message to the person named in the link. All you have to do is write the message and send it, a greatly simplified procedure.

Note: There are several options for composing e-mail through Internet Explorer. These options are explained in Chapter 9.

BACKWARD AND FORWARD WE GO

If you want to move between pages that you have visited in your current session of Web surfing, the Back and Forward icons are for you. Located on the icon bar, these buttons will whisk you between pages with one mouse click.

One click on the Back icon, and you are right back on the last page from which you jumped. Because the page was in your computer's memory from your previous visit, it will load very quickly. If you have been to several pages in your current session of Web surfing, the Back icon may still be active, indicating that you can back out of your current spot some more. When you have reached the very beginning of your session, the Back icon will "ghost" or change to gray to indicate that you have backed up as far as you can.

If you have visited several pages and then returned to one of them (by using the Back icon or by other means) the Forward icon will be available. It will take you through Web pages in the same order in which you originally visited them. When you reach the last new page that you visited in your current session, the Forward icon will ghost.

Now let's say that you visit a great site, take a link to another site, and then take another link to a third site. Then you want to go back to the first really cool site. How do you go back two sites? Well, you could click the Back icon twice. That's easy enough, but it might be a little too slow for you. (After all, it was a really cool site, and you have to go back now!) Try this: click on the little down arrow key found on the right side of the address bar. If you manually entered that URL, it will still be waiting on the address bar. Select the site to which you want to return, and Explorer will take you there nonstop! Figure 4.5 illustrates this example.

Tip: If you become really lost and can't back out of your situation, click on the Home icon on the icon bar. It will take you to your start page, where you can regroup and start again. Or you can open your Favorites window and choose from some familiar sites. Keep reading to learn more about Favorites.

USING FAVORITES

Chances are that in your exploration of the Internet, you will find many Web pages to which you would like to return—some because they contain lots of terrific links to other sites, some because they change all the time, and some because you really just can't get enough information about monkeys! Thankfully, in the electronic age you don't need to keep a notebook next to your computer and then type in each URL by hand when you want to visit. The Favorites menu allows you to save the addresses of your favorite sites for easy future visits. Once a URL is saved, it is just a few mouse clicks away.

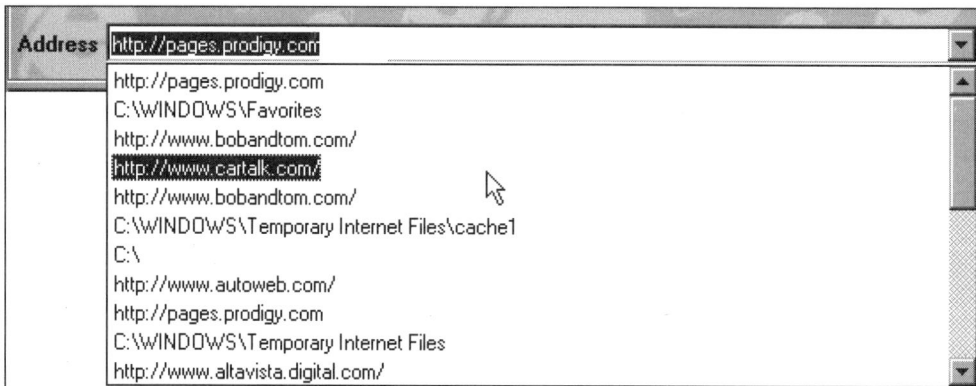

Figure 4.5: Navigating with the address bar.

Internet Explorer gives you two ways to access your Favorites menu. The most obvious is by clicking the Favorites icon on the icon bar, which will fill the entire Explorer window with your Favorites (as shown in Figure 4.6).

The second way is by clicking the Favorites menu in the menu bar. This will display a window similar to Figure 4.7.

Note: Does your Favorites window look the same as Figure 4.6? If not, keep reading to learn different ways to organize and display your Favorites.

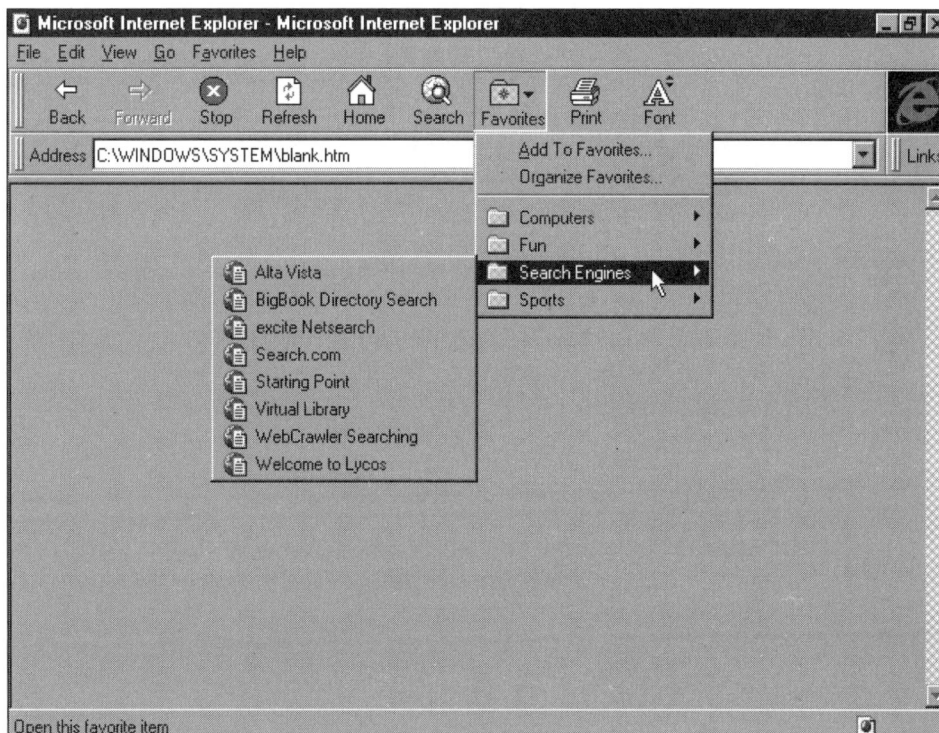

Figure 4.6: The Favorites menu from the icon bar.

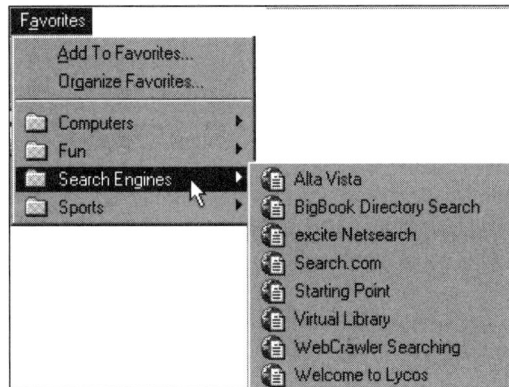

Figure 4.7: The Favorites menu from the menu bar.

Saving Your Favorite Sites

But you haven't saved any favorites, yet. Or have you? I bet you have just to see how they worked, but just for fun, here are two ways to save a favorite page.

1. Go to the Web page that you want to save.
2. Select Favorites from the menu bar or icon bar.
3. Select Add to Favorites (see Figure 4.8).
4. Name your shortcut.
5. Select Add.

1. Right-click on the background of the Web page.
2. Select Add To Favorites.
3. Name your shortcut.
4. Select Add.

Note: Keep reading for more info on right-clicking.

That page is now saved for future visits. To access that page from now on, simply open the Favorites menu as described above and click on the shortcut.

Keeping Your Favorites Organized

After a while, your Favorites will get out of hand. Most people collect so many (especially when they are new to Web surfing) that the

Figure 4.8: Creating a folder to organize Favorites.

Favorites menu becomes too full. If you find that it is faster to manually type your favorite URL rather than find it in Favorites, you need some organization. The trick is to create categories of folders in which you can store your favorites. It is much easier to find the shortcut to Microsoft when it is neatly tucked away in a "Computers" folder than when it is one of 50 links to all kinds of sites. As a general rule, it is best not to have many (or even any) pages listed on the Favorites' top level. That is, when you select Favorites from the icon bar or the menu bar, only a few shortcuts should appear. The rest should be folders.

Creating Folders

Decide how many folders you need to keep your Favorites organized. Then follow these steps.

1. Select Favorites from the menu bar or icon bar.
2. Select Add to Favorites.

3. Select Create In.
4. Select New Folder (see Figure 4.9).
5. Type a name for your new folder.
6. Click OK.
7. Repeat to create as many folders as needed.

From now on, saving your favorites will require a few additional steps, but the organizational benefits are worth it. Now when you select Add to Favorites from the Favorites menu, a window with your new folders will appear (Figure 4.8). Select Create In (Figure 4.10). Choose the folder in which to save the shortcut, and select OK. Your shortcut is right where you want it.

From time to time you may want to clean house or organize your favorites (even when they are organized in folders). You may have noticed the Organize Favorites option when you opened the Favorites

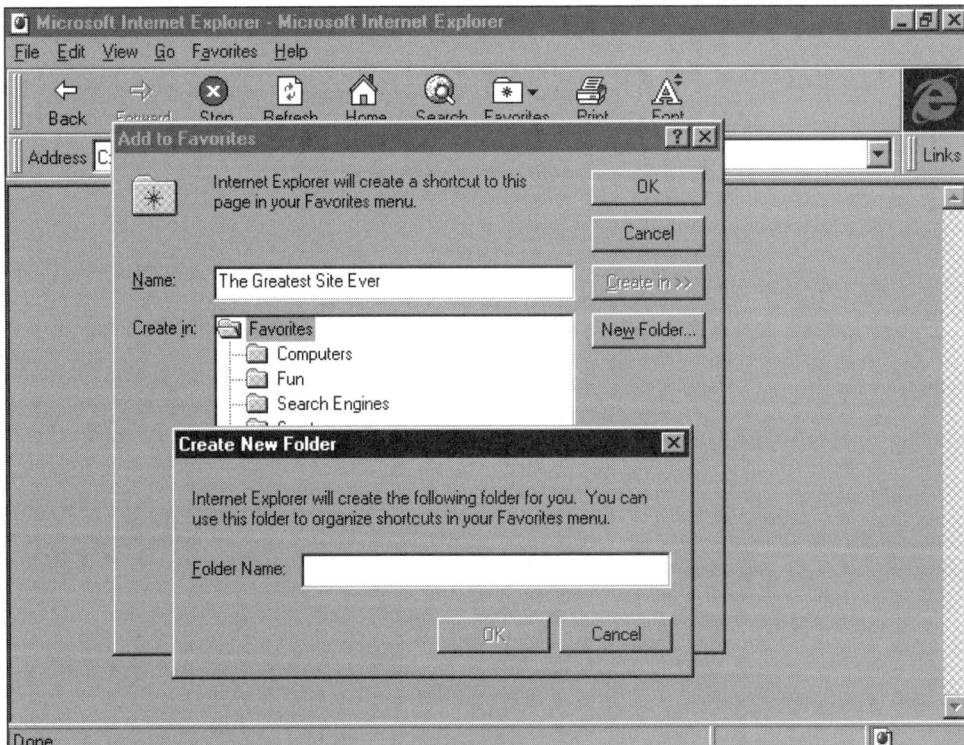

Figure 4.9: Using folders to organize the Favorites window.

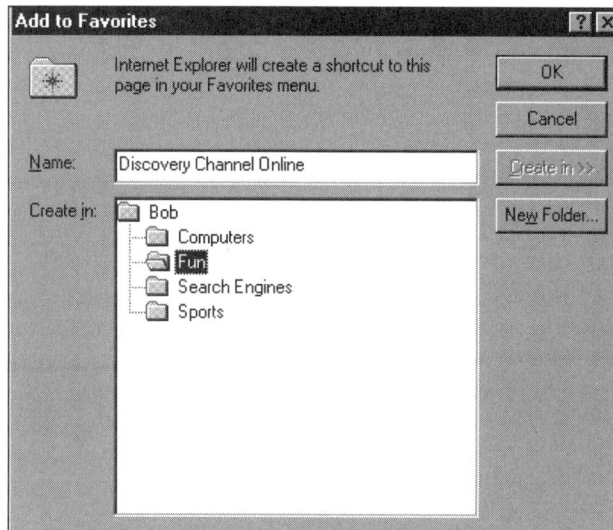

Figure 4.10: Using Folders to organize the Favorites menu.

menu. This feature, shown in Figure 4.11, allows you to move, rename, delete, and create new folders as well as open the links to which the shortcuts point.

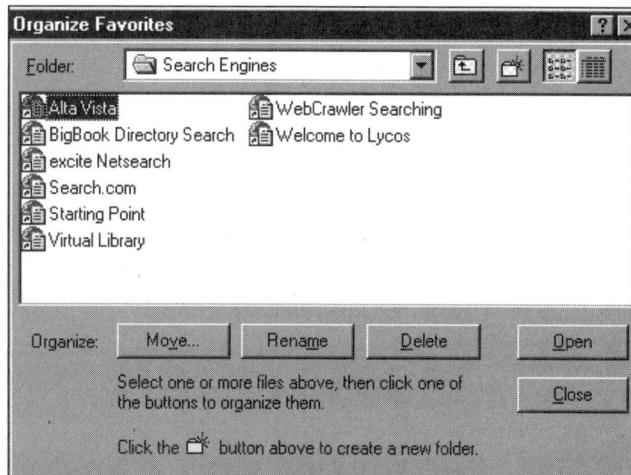

Figure 4.11: Keeping your Favorites organized.

Placing Shortcuts onto the Desktop

Internet Explorer has the very convenient ability to go to a Web site just by clicking on an icon for that site—even if Explorer is not running and your computer is not connected to the Internet. This makes placing shortcuts to Web sites on the Windows 95 desktop a great time saver. Now, frequently visited sites can be reached without ever having to visit the start page. There are three ways to place Shortcuts onto your desktop.

Method 1—From Within Internet Explorer
1. Select the Favorites icon from the icon bar.
2. Open the folder containing the shortcut you want to place on the desktop.
3. Highlight the shortcut, drag it to the desktop using the right mouse button, and drop it.
4. Select Copy Here or Create Shortcut Here.

Method 2—Without Using Internet Explorer
1. Open the My Computer window.
2. Choose the drive that contains your Favorites folder (usually the drive that also contains the Windows files).
3. Find and open the Favorites folder (usually within the Windows folder).
4. Select the folder that contains the shortcut to be copied.
5. Highlight, drag with the right mouse button, and drop the shortcut onto the desktop.
6. Select Copy Here or Create Shortcut Here.

Tip: This can also be accomplished by using the Windows Explorer instead of Internet Explorer or the My Computer window.

Method 3—Right-Clicking

1. Right-click on the background of the Web page.
2. Select Create Shortcut on the menu that appears.

Note: Keep reading for more info on right-clicking.

The result should look like Figure 4.12. Now all you have to do is double-click the shortcut and you will go straight to that site. A variation on this same idea is to place the entire Favorites folder onto the desktop. You then have access to all of your favorites without having

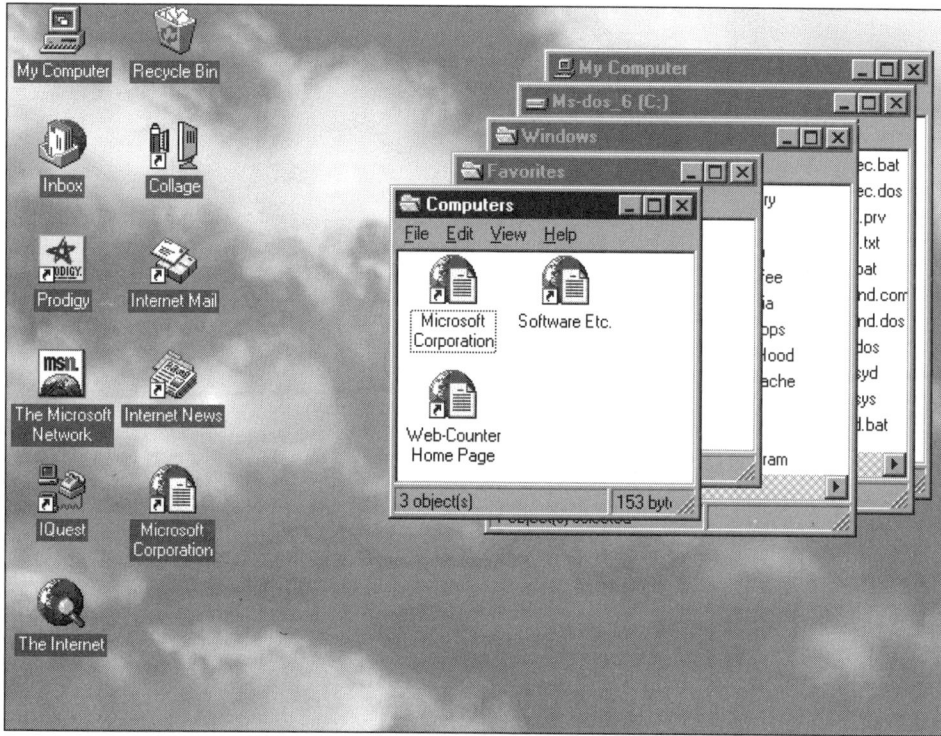

Figure 4.12: My desktop with a Web page Shortcut added.

to choose them when on-line charges might be adding up. This also reduces the clutter of placing several Internet shortcuts onto the desktop. Figure 4.13 shows a desktop with the Favorites folder.

Deleting Favorites

If a site disappears (which isn't all that uncommon) or you simply no longer want it as a Favorite, deleting the shortcut is easy. From Internet Explorer, Windows Explorer, or My Computer (your choice), highlight the shortcut and press the Delete key on your keyboard or drag and drop it onto the Recycle Bin. If you change your mind, the shortcut will remain in the Recycle Bin until you empty it. This process will also apply if you wish to delete an entire folder of Favorites.

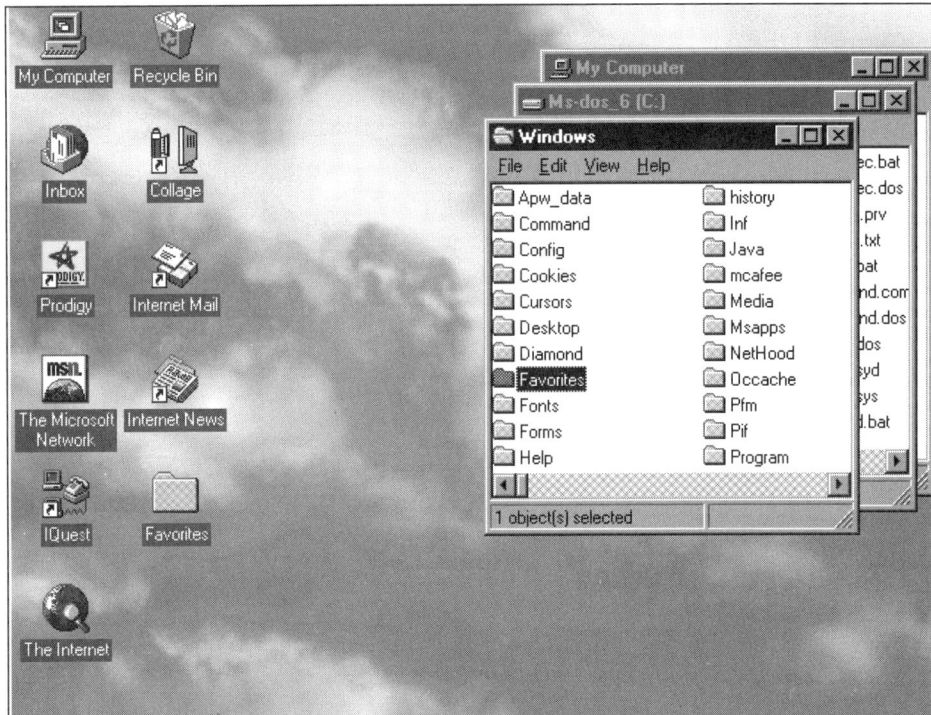

Figure 4.13: My (slightly) less cluttered desktop with my Favorites folder added.

Note: This process will also work on the Favorites folder itself. It is highly unlikely that anyone would want to delete the entire Favorites folder, so when you decide to delete be careful not to delete too much!

USING THE HISTORY LIST

The Web has so many interesting places to visit, it can be difficult to keep track of them all. The Favorites feature is a lifesaver, but what if you forget to save a page to your Favorites file? Or what if you are in too much of a hurry to save a site to your Favorites list? Are these sites gone forever? Luckily, no. Explorer has several methods for keeping track of previously visited sites. These methods all access what is known as the History List.

The Address Bar and History List

Perhaps the most obvious is the method mentioned earlier in this chapter. The address bar has a down arrow that, when clicked, will show you a list of the last sites that were manually entered. Click the down arrow and select the site to which you would like to return.

The next method resides on the Go option on the menu bar. When you click Go, a menu drops down that contains a list of the last five sites visited. A check mark indicates which site is currently being viewed. Figure 4.14 shows an example of the Go menu with five sites listed. To revisit any of these five sites, simply click on the site name to which you would like to return. Ta da!

The History Folder

If you need to go way back, Explorer has a more powerful option for you. Again, from the Go menu, choose Open History Folder. Figure 4.15 shows what you will see. Each time you visit a site (any site) it is recorded to the History Folder. To return to previously viewed sites (even sites that were visited long ago) simply find the name and double-click. There you go!

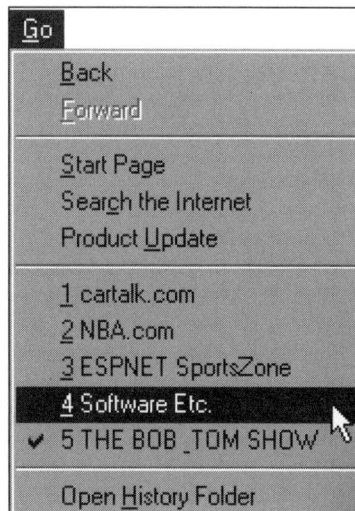

Figure 4.14: The History List.

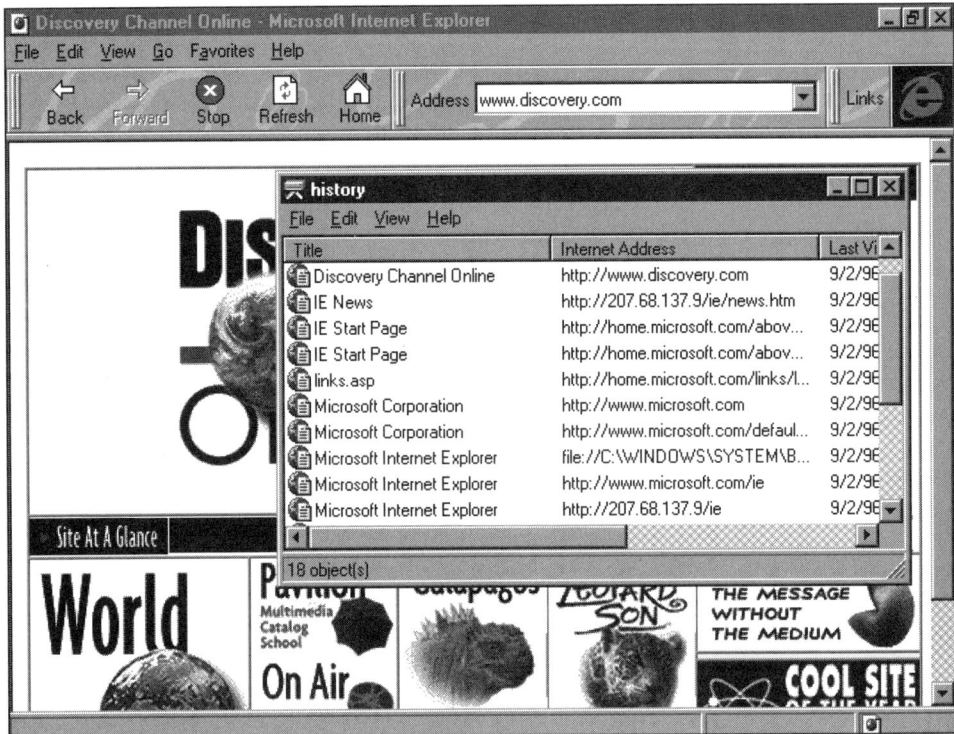

Figure 4.15: The History Folder.

DIFFERENT WAYS TO DISPLAY
THE CONTENTS OF YOUR FOLDERS

When you open the History folder and any subsequent folders, Windows 95 lets you choose from different ways to display the icons within. Right-click on the background of the window to show the View/Arrange icons menu. This menu allows you to choose the display format.

View

Large Icons The shortcuts are displayed as—you guessed it—large icons with their names underneath. These icons are arranged in rows. This is a good setting if you do not have very many icons within your folders. When too many large icons are displayed, the folder becomes difficult to read when titles overlap other icons.

Small Icons Small icons, with the names to the right, are organized in rows like the large icons. They are still not the best choice.

List The Shortcuts are displayed in a similar fashion to the small icons, but they are arranged in a list instead of rows. This is probably the best if your folders contain many shortcuts.

Details This view displays the small icons along with the size, type, and date of last modification for each shortcut. This view is unnecessary, so don't bother with it.

Arrange

By Name The icons are arranged alphabetically. This is the default, and it is probably the best view.

By Type The icons are organized by file type, with the name following. Because these are all the same type of files (shortcuts), this view is rather worthless.

By Size This view displays the icons in order of file size, which is pointless here.

By Date Here the icons are organized by the date in which they were added to the History folder. The most recent shortcuts are displayed first. This is helpful if you need to keep track of more recently saved pages.

Auto Arrange This option keeps the window organized using the method you selected above. When Auto Arrange is not checked, the icons can become cluttered and misplaced.

Windows 95 lets you change the format in which the History shortcuts are displayed. I recommend the List option with either alphabetical sorting or date sorting. Alphabetical sorting is helpful when you are searching for a specific page; date sorting is helpful if you must revisit sites that were viewed at a certain time. Date sorting places the most recently visited sites at the top of the list.

Tip: Want to keep track of your kids' or roommates' activity on the Net? Check the History Folder for a complete list of the sites they are visiting. To protect your own privacy (especially at work), delete the contents of the History Folder from time to time. That prevents anyone from checking on you.

OPENING MULTIPLE PAGES

This is probably one of my personal favorite features of Internet Explorer. Let me set up the situation. You need two pieces of information from the Web. First, you have to download that new shareware game (something about nukes in the title). But you also need to check the score of the big game. Which do you do first? The answer: both!

Well, not really, but here is what you can do. Go to the site containing the game to download. 5MB! That will take at least 15 minutes to download at 28.8. Do you just sit there or go read a book? Go ahead and start the download. Then open a second window so you can check on the score while the file downloads. Explorer will let you open as many windows as you like as long as you have enough system resources available to support them. Usually two or three will do just fine. Figure 4.16 shows an Explorer session with three open documents.

Explorer offers two ways (of course) to open additional windows. For the first method, click on File (on the Menu bar) and select New Window. A new Internet Explorer window will appear, waiting for you to tell it where to go. You can minimize the original window, maximize the new window, or arrange them however you like. Neither will interfere with the other.

The second way works if the current page has a hyperlink available that looks cool. Let's say that the game company has a link to an on-line magazine that has reviewed this new game. Right-click the link and a menu appears with the option to Open in New Window. Bingo! Select that option and you're off and loading.

RIGHT-CLICKING

Now that I have teased you with some information about right-clicking, it's time to go into detail. Right-clicking can be a terrific time-saver, and it offers some features that can't be accomplished any other way. Depending on the section of a page that is right-clicked, one of

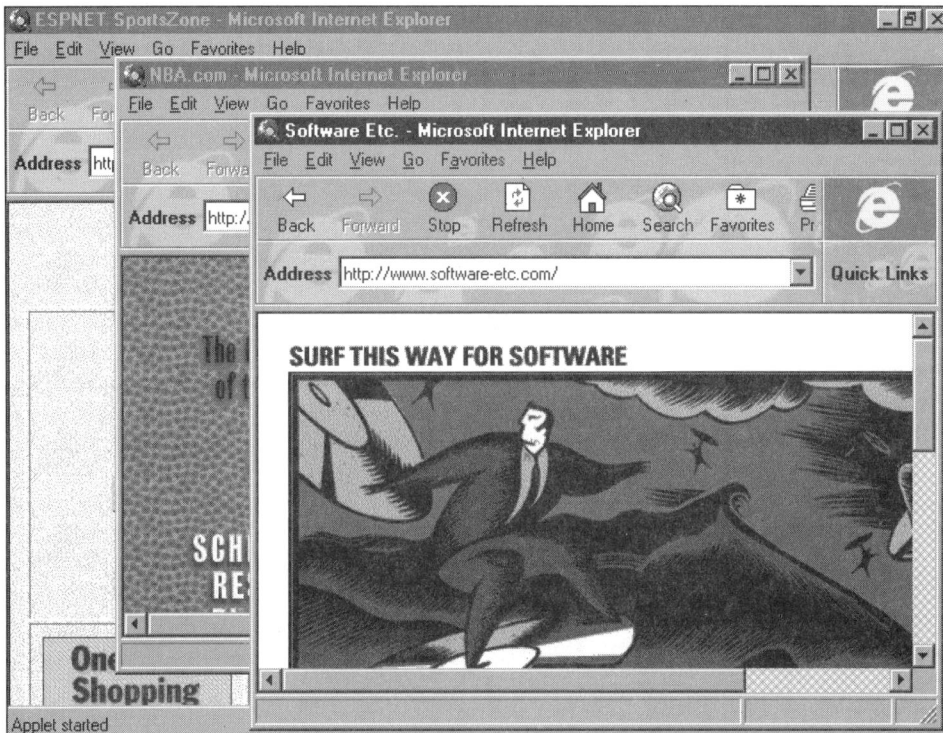

Figure 4.16: Multiple Web pages open at the same time.

five different Explorer menus will appear. The options on each menu are specific to each situation, although some options are available on more than one menu.

Background or Text

Right-clicking on a background image or nonhighlighted text brings up the menu shown in Figure 4.17. This menu provides some options that aren't available by any other means, most notably the Save Background As . . . option.

Save Background As... This option saves the background image to your computer as a graphics file. Explorer chooses a default name for the image, but it gives you the option to name it yourself.

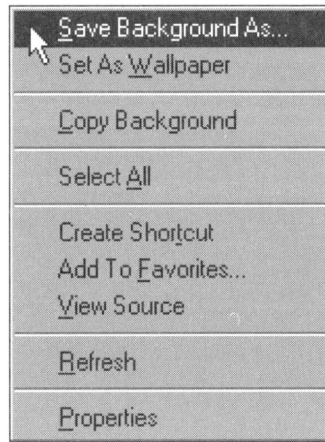

Figure 4.17: Right-clicking on the background or text.

Set As Wallpaper This option saves the background image to your computer and uses it for your background wallpaper on your Windows 95 desktop.

Copy Background This option copies the background image to the Windows Clipboard. If you want to use this image in another document, select the Edit, Paste command in that program.

Select All This option selects all the text in the document. From there you could copy it to the Clipboard and paste it somewhere else.

Create Shortcut This option creates a shortcut for this document on your desktop.

Add To Favorites This option adds the document to your Favorites list.

View Source This option displays the source code (HTML) in which the Web page was written. If you are really curious about what it all means, Chapter 12 covers the basics of HTML. If you have permission from the Web author, you can copy and paste this code to get ideas and techniques for your own page.

Refresh This option reloads the document.

Properties This option displays the properties of the document such as the URL, the file protocol, and the security information.

Caution: Copying background images, document content, and source HTML code may violate copyright laws. Always get permission from the Web author before copying any information from a page.

Images

Right-clicking on an image brings up the menu shown in Figure 4.18. If the image contains a link, all of the options are enabled; otherwise some options are ghosted.

Open This option loads the document targeted in the link. It is essentially the same as left-clicking the image.

Open In New Window As described in Opening Multiple Pages above, this option loads the document targeted in the link in a new Explorer window.

Save Target As... This option saves the document referenced in the link to a file on your hard disk.

Save Picture As... This option saves the image to the hard disk as a file. The Save Picture As . . . . option is always enabled.

Figure 4.18: Right-clicking on an image.

Set As Wallpaper This option saves the background image to your computer and uses it for your background wallpaper on your Windows 95 desktop. This option is always enabled.

Copy This option copies the image to the Clipboard, where it can then be pasted into another document. This option is always enabled.

Copy Shortcut This option copies the link (Shortcut) to the Clipboard, where it can then be pasted into another document.

Add To Favorites This option adds the targeted document to your Favorites list.

Properties This option displays the properties of the image: the protocol, file type, URL, size, and file information. This option is always enabled.

Highlighted Text

Right-clicking on highlighted text brings up the menu shown in Figure 4.19. Text can be highlighted by left-clicking and dragging the mouse over the desired area.

Copy This option copies the highlighted text to the Clipboard, where it can be pasted into another document.

Select All This option selects all the text in the document. From there you could copy it to the Clipboard and paste it somewhere else.

Text Hyperlinks

Right-clicking on a text hyperlink brings up the menu shown in Figure 4.20.

Open This option loads the document targeted in the link. It is essentially the same as left-clicking the link.

Open In New Window As described in Opening Multiple Pages above, this option loads the document targeted in the link in a new Explorer window.

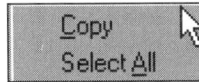

Figure 4.19: Right-clicking on highlighted text.

Save Target As... This option saves the document referenced in the link to a file on your hard disk.

Copy Shortcut This option copies the link (Shortcut) to the Clipboard, where it can then be pasted into another document.

Add To Favorites This option adds the targeted document to your Favorites list.

Properties This option displays the properties of the targeted document: the file protocol, the URL, and the file type.

Images Turned Off

When the images are turned off and the icon representing the missing image is right-clicked, Figure 4.21 is shown. For more on turning images off, see Chapter 7. If the image contains a link, all of the options are enabled; otherwise some options are ghosted.

Open This option loads the document targeted in the link. It is essentially the same as left-clicking the image icon.

Open In New Window As described in Opening Multiple Pages above, this option loads the document targeted in the link in a new Explorer window.

Save Target As... This option saves the document referenced in the link to a file on your hard disk.

Show Picture This option displays the picture that was not loaded automatically. This option is always enabled.

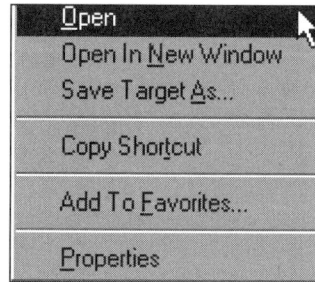

Figure 4.20: Right-clicking on a text hyperlink.

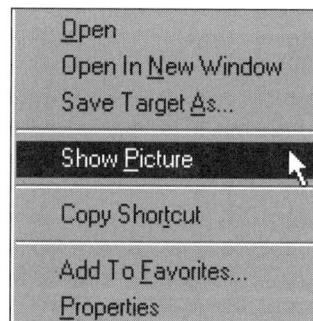

Figure 4.21: Right-clicking on a missing image icon.

Copy Shortcut This option copies the link (Shortcut) to the Clipboard, where it can then be pasted into another document.

Add To Favorites This option adds the targeted document to your Favorites list.

Properties This option displays the properties of the image: the protocol, file type, URL, size, and file information. This option is always enabled.

WORKING WITH FRAMES

Frames are a fairly recent development for the Web. They weren't even possible until the current generation of Web browsers became available, and they are starting to become more popular as a means of displaying information on the Web. The main reason for frames' popularity is their ability to display information in multiple panes on the screen. This allows related Web pages to be displayed side by side. Yes, you could just open two Explorer windows and almost have the same result, but frames make things a little simpler. Figure 4.22 shows an example of a Web page using two frames to divide its working space into three panes.

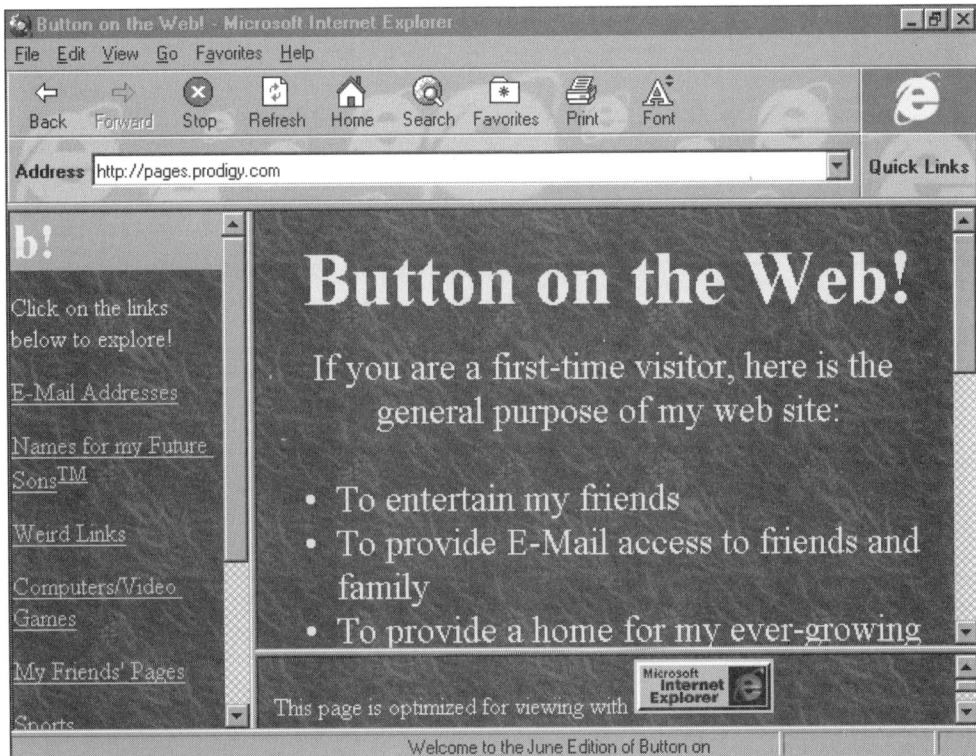

Figure 4.22: A Web page with multiple frames.

Navigating within Web pages that use frames is simple, but there are a few tips that can help. Like standard Web pages, many pages with frames use scroll bars to move up and down the window. Pages with frames, however, often have multiple scroll bars, one or two for each pane. When you use one scroll bar, it moves its pane independently of the other panes. In the example in Figure 4.22, the left pane is a menu that will change the page in the largest pane on the right side of the page. By scrolling down the menu pane, you are given different display options, but the main display pane does not change.

Many Web pages allow you to change the size of the panes to facilitate better viewing. In the example in Figure 4.22, the bottom pane can be resized by "grabbing" the frame itself and dragging it up or down. This lets you see more or less of the bottom right pane. Figure 4.23 shows resizing the frame. Note that some Web authors will design

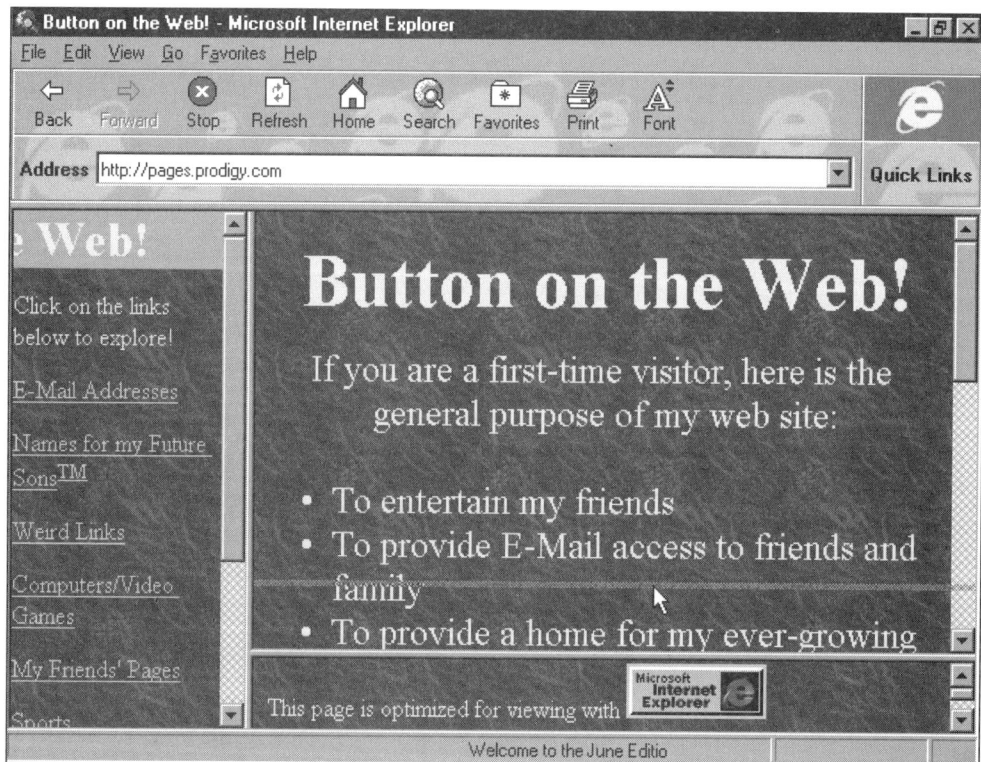

Figure 4.23: Resizing a frame.

their pages to have permanent frames that are not resizable. In the example in Figures 4.22 and 4.23, the left pane is not resizable (you could tell by moving the mouse over the frame). If the frame is resizable, the pointer will change into a resize cursor. If the frame is not resizable, the pointer will not change.

OPENING FILES FROM THE HARD DISK

Sometimes while searching the Web you may want to compare something you have seen on-line with a file that is already on your hard disk. With the multitasking capability of Windows 95, it is not difficult to load Word for Windows or Paint while still running Internet Explorer, but the process can be simplified by opening the desired file directly from within Explorer itself.

What kind of files can Explorer open? If you have saved any Web pages to your hard drive, Explorer will read them as if they were on-line. These files will have the extension .HTM, .HTML, or .SHTML. Other compatible files types are text files (.TXT), graphics files (.GIF, .JPG), and audio files (.AIFF, .AU).

So how do you get to these files? The easiest way is to go to the address bar and type the letter of the hard drive that contains the files you want to open. Figure 4.24 shows the view that appears when I use Explorer to view the contents of my C: drive. From this point, click the folders until you reach the file you want to view. This part works just like Windows Explorer. Coincidence? Definitely not! Microsoft's eventual goal is to integrate Internet Explorer with Windows Explorer so you will need only one program to browse the Internet or your hard drive. This will be a component of an upcoming release of Windows; for now, Microsoft is taking us there one step at a time.

STOP THAT PAGE!

At some point while browsing the Web, you will come across a page that you simply don't want to wait for. Maybe you clicked the wrong link, or maybe you are in a hurry and that particular page is taking too long to load. Whatever the reasons, Explorer offers you a way out.

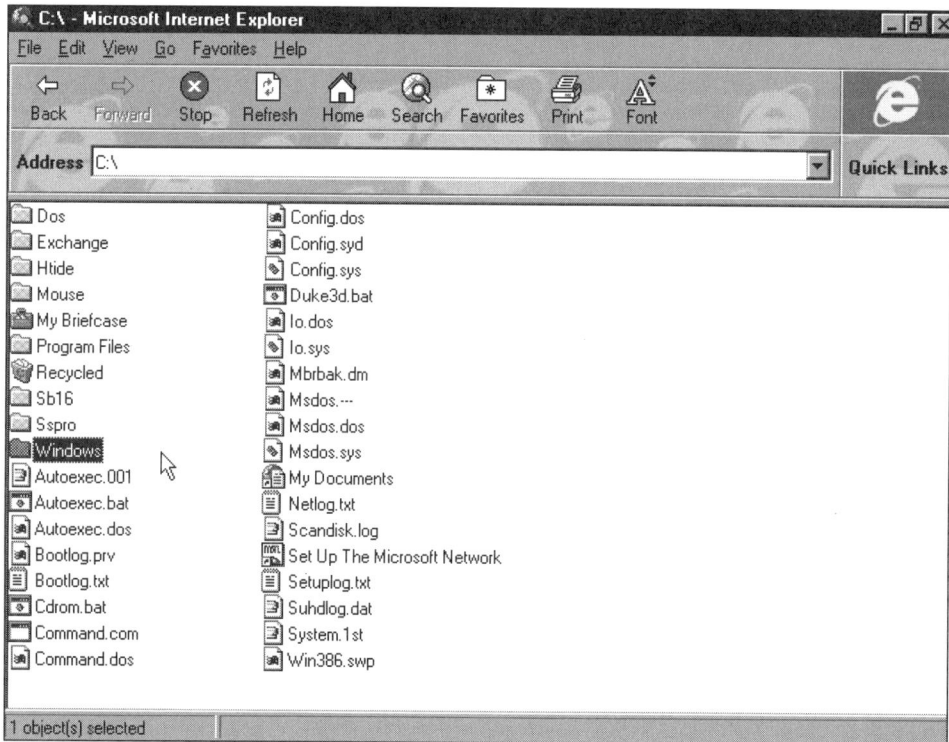

Figure 4.24: Viewing the contents of a hard drive through Internet Explorer.

The Stop icon will cancel the last page being loaded or image being displayed. It may take a few seconds to actually stop, but soon the Logo window will stop moving and the page will just sit there—even if it was only a little bit loaded. This is a good time to use the Back icon or the Favorites menu to go back to a page that you actually want to view. Another way to stop a page from loading is to select View, Stop from the menu bar, but why go through the extra steps when only one click on the icon bar is needed?

WHAT'S AHEAD?

- Learn how to search the Web in Chapter 5.
- Discover the basics of downloading and file management in Chapter 6.
- Change settings and customize Explorer in Chapter 7.

SEARCHING THE INTERNET

Even though it can be a lot of fun to aimlessly browse the Net with little or no purpose, eventually you will want or need to find a specific piece of information. Clicking on links in Web pages can take you only so far and can be rather time-consuming. Between all the worthless links that you will come across and the fascinating but totally unrelated links you will find, you can spend hours searching and never find what you're looking for.

The Internet is such a large network of computers, it's amazing that anything at all can be found. The needle-in-a-haystack analogy is perfectly appropriate here. What you need is a metal detector to help you find that needle, and the Internet has several detectors available for your use. The trick is learning how to use these tools *effectively.* Just as using a metal detector with the sensitivity turned way down will probably not find that needle, using the Internet search tools without the correct type of query will yield you either too little information or too much worthless data. In this chapter you will learn about the different search tools on the Net and how to use them so they actually work for you.

KEY POINTS IN THIS CHAPTER

- What are search engines, and do they take regular or unleaded?

- Are there places on the Web where I can just download programs?
- FTP? Don't you send flowers with them?
- Why are cartoon characters on the Internet?
- What good is Telnet if it's so hard to use?

SEARCH ENGINES

Search engines are the librarians of the Internet. You tell them what you are looking for and they go out and get it for you. Unlike a librarian who has access to every item in the library, search engines have access to just a portion of the Internet. The Net is growing so rapidly it is simply impossible for any source to keep track of it all. Search engines do, however, continuously search the Net on their own to find new information and new sources to add to their lists.

SPIDERS

Spiders are the basis for most search engines. They are not creepy arachnids, but they do crawl through the Net looking for information. A spider is an automated computer program that is designed to visit sites on the Internet (mostly the Web pages and Usenet groups). As it moves from site to site, it checks each hyperlink that it finds and reports back to a central database, or list, containing all of the previous sites it has visited. Some spiders are even sophisticated enough to make a quick summary of each site by recording common themes found there. This summary is then included in the central database. Most of the major search engines use some form of spider to do their dirty work. It would be impossible for humans to try to keep an updated catalog of Internet sites; they simply are added too fast to keep pace. Spiders can recheck previous sites for any changes and look for new sites 24 hours a day.

I am starting this chapter with search engines for several reasons. First, they are probably the most used of the Internet search tools (as compared to Gopher, Archie, etc.). Second, you will probably use them fairly regularly during the course of your Web surfing. Third, they are very often misused. That is, they are not used effectively. For example, the most common complaint I hear from people new to the Internet is that they can't find anything. When I tell them about search engines, they usually say that they got too many responses to their searches or that the results weren't related to their search. This usually happens because their searches were either too vague or too broad. Throughout this section, I will show an example of a vague, misguided search for each of the search engines described. With most engines, the results will be exactly what you would expect—overwhelming amounts of unrelated sites. I will then explain how to get the most from each search engine so this doesn't happen to you. Remember, though, that each search engine is a complete program. My tips will help you greatly, but please read the search engine help files for even more specific information. There is much that I do not have space to include here. There are also many other search engines not covered here. For some fun, try to use one search engine to find another!

Tip: Many search engines started in universities. Many were even started by graduate students who created them as projects. Most of them have now gone commercial, but their history can be rather interesting. Check out each search engine for an "About" link to learn its history. Some information is contained within help files, also.

NARROWING YOUR SEARCHES WITH BOOLEAN OPERATORS

Boolean operators are commands that you enter to give the searching computer specific instructions on how to conduct the search. There are many variations, but several standards prevail.

a and b

This means search for term *a* and term *b*. For example, "Ford and Mustang" will search for sites containing the terms Ford and Mustang. It will not find sites that contain only Ford or only Mustang.

a or b

This means search for sites that contain either, but not necessarily both terms. "Ford or Mustang" will find sites with Ford, sites with Mustang, and sites with both Ford and Mustang. This usually leads to much larger lists. In this example, the results will include (among other things) Ford Motor Company, former President Ford, Ford Mustang, and mustangs (the horse).

a not b

This will search for only one of the two terms. If you wanted information on mustang horses, "Mustang not Ford" will exclude any sites relating to the car.

a near b

This searches for sites that include the two terms in close proximity to one another. If the search engine uses 25 words as a rule, "Ford near Mustang" will include sites in which Ford and Mustang are within 25 words (in either direction) of each other in the text of the site. Not all Internet search tools will support this option.

( )

Parenthetical references allow you to mix the options mentioned above. For example, if you wanted to find information relating to the Ford Mustang Cobra, you might search for "Cobra near (Ford or Mustang)." If you wanted information on the Shelby Cobra (a different car from the Mustang that was also made by Ford), "Cobra and (Ford not Mustang)" would limit the search to Ford Cobras, but exclude Mustang Cobras and cobra snakes.

Wildcards

Some searches can include wildcards such as *, +, or − to expand or limit your search. For example, to search for any topics relating to boats, "boat*" will search for any words starting with boat. The results might include boat, boats, and boating. Plus and minus signs can have the same effect as the terms *and* and *not*, respectively. Minus signs are also used to precede other search criteria. Veronica uses the minus sign in this way, and we will discuss it later in this chapter.

Microsoft

When you click on the Search icon on the Explorer icon bar, you go to the Microsoft search page (unless you have reconfigured your search page from Explorer's Options menu). This is really not a search engine in and of itself. Microsoft has combined several search engines on this single page. You can choose which engine out of the four to use. This can be a great time saver because it keeps you from having to link to different sites. It can also cause problems because it does not allow you access to some of the advanced features available from these search engines. This may result in vague searches. Figure 5.1 shows the Microsoft all-in-one search page.

Yahoo!

Yahoo! (shown in Figure 5.2) is perhaps the best known of the search engines. It contains a catalog of sites that have been categorized by the Yahoo! staff. If you are simply looking for ideas, try one of the many categories available. This will provide you with links to sites relating

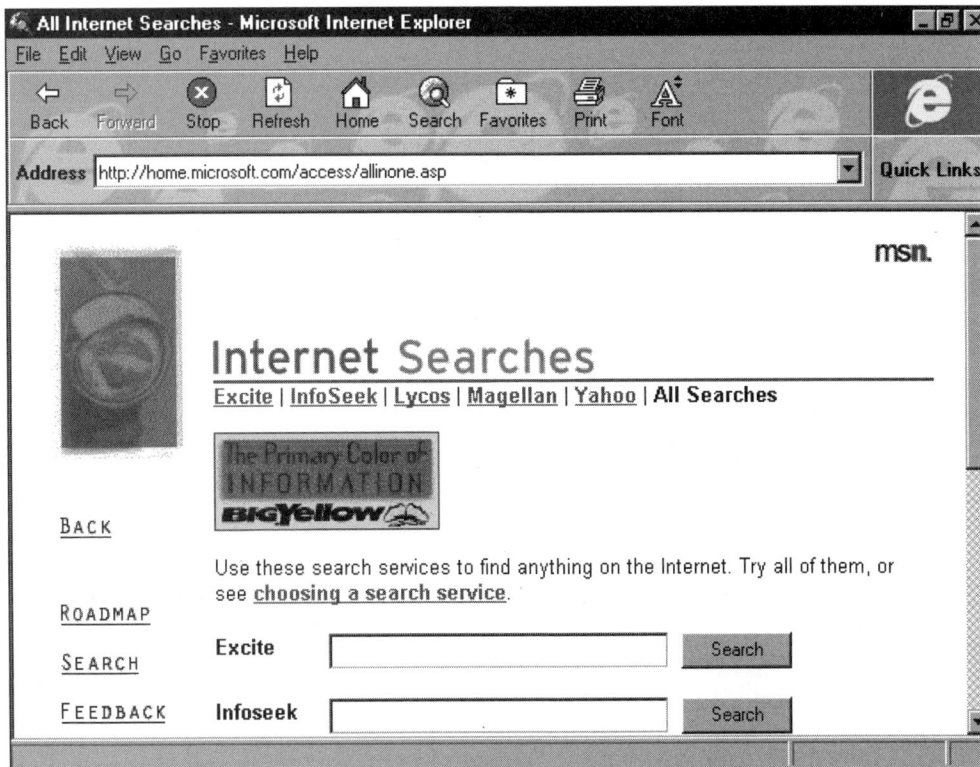

Figure 5.1: Microsoft's search page.

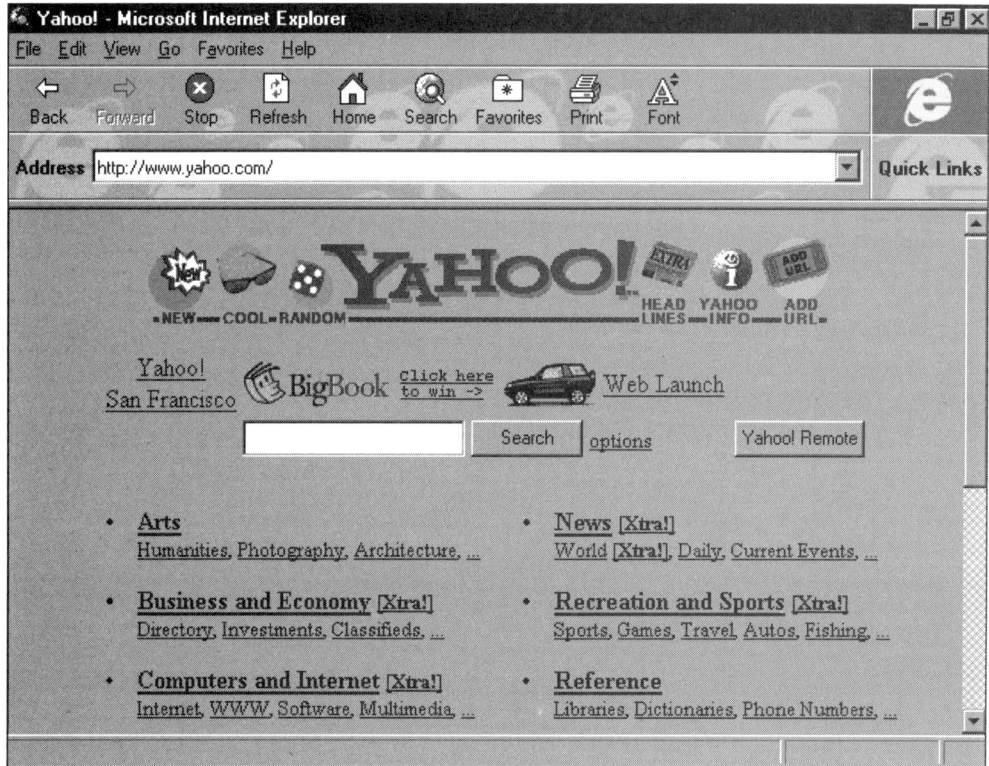

Figure 5.2: The Yahoo! intro screen.

to that topic. For more specific searches, enter your search term in the text box. Yahoo! will take this term and search its list, which contains categories, site titles, and comments regarding each site and display the first 100 matches (assuming 100 were found). Case is not important when entering your search term. In my search for "monkey" (Hey, everybody loves monkeys!), Yahoo! will search its categories for "monkey," then search a list of titles on file for the term "monkey," and then search each site's comments for the term "monkey."

As expected, the results did not bring up any matches directly related to primates (see Figure 5.3). If I wanted to limit my search, I could choose a category relating to monkeys (maybe Science) and search only that category instead of the entire Yahoo! database. Boolean *and* and *or* operators are available by clicking the Options hyperlink.

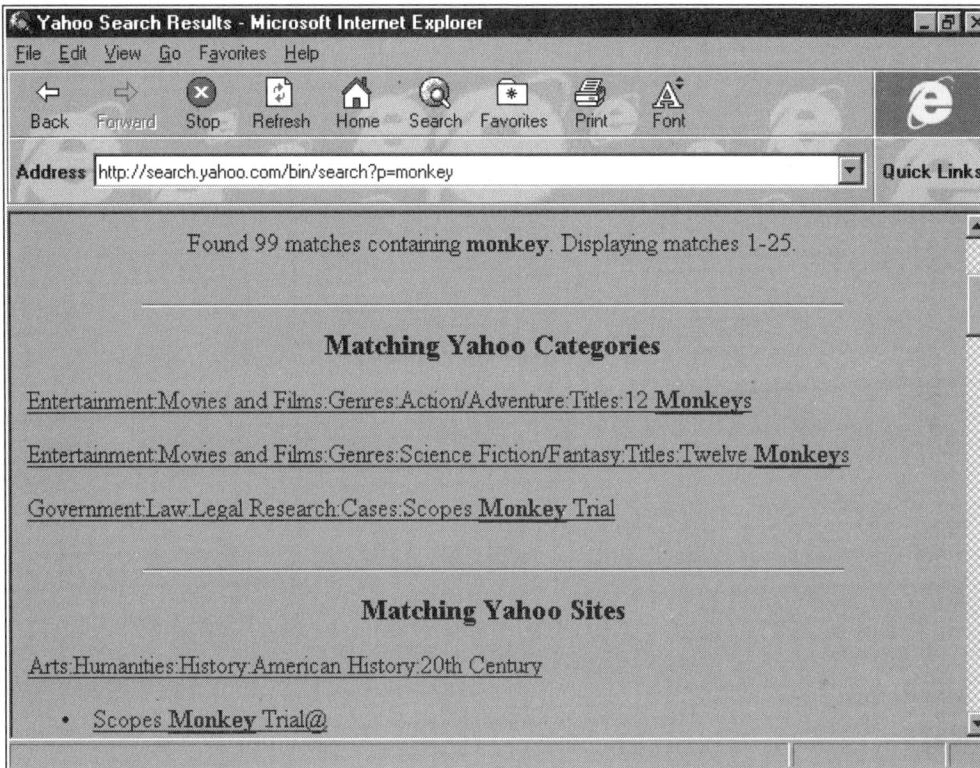

Figure 5.3: Yahoo! search results.

Overall, Yahoo! is one of the best organized search engines. With many options such as random links and cool sites (chosen by Yahoo!) as well as news headlines, Yahoo! is a good place to start a search or just find fun sites to visit. Yahoo! can be found at **http://www .yahoo.com.**

Tip: Explorer uses Yahoo! to help you find Web sites. For example, if you want to find the American Airlines Web site, just type American Airlines in the address bar (do not use http://w.com). Explorer will take you to a Yahoo! search results page showing what it has found.

Alta Vista

If you need a lot of information, Alta Vista (Figure 5.4) is a good place to start. It works with an enormous index, so many searches will result in thousands of hits from Web pages and Usenet groups. Alta

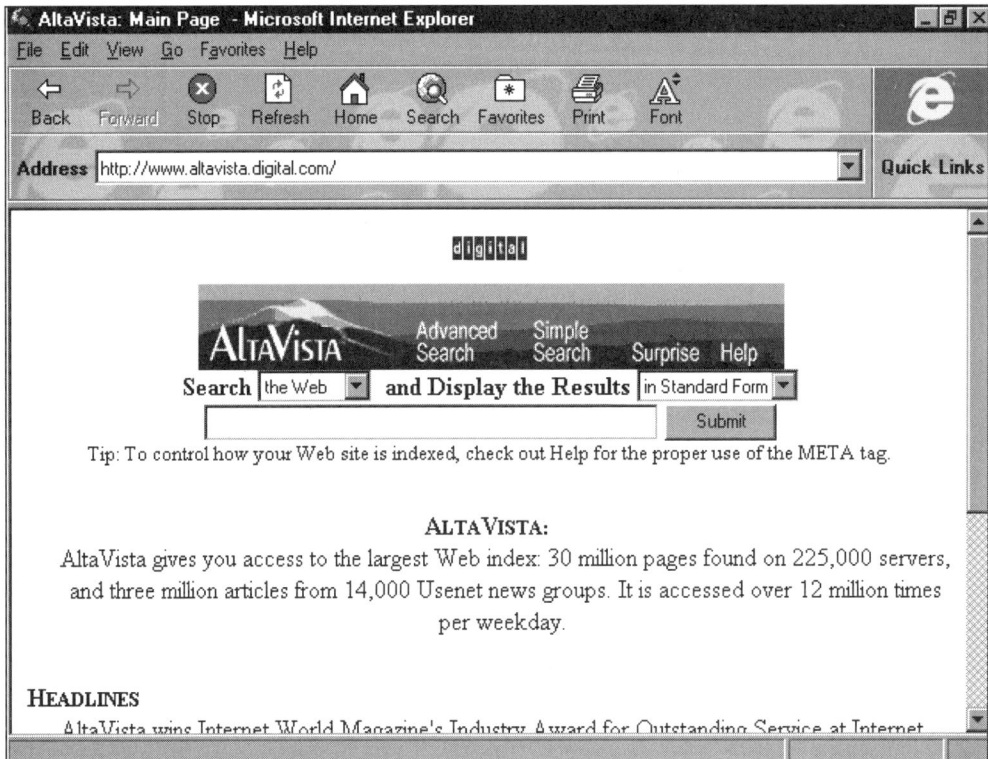

Figure 5.4: Alta Vista intro. screen.

DIGITAL, AltaVista and the AltaVista logo are trademarks or service marks of Digital Equipment Corporation. Used with permission.

Vista allows for simple or advanced searches. In both searches, lowercase will find all matching terms while uppercase will force an exact match. For example, a search for "monkey" will find all references to monkey, while a search for "Monkey" will find only those terms using a capital M.

In a simple search, + (plus) is used to require a word (just like *and*), – (minus) is used to exclude a word (just like *not*), * (asterisk) is used to find a base word and its variations (boat* and boating as mentioned above), and ; (semicolon) is used to link words together. Linking word forces them to be accepted in that order. For example, "Ford Mustang" will start a search for any site containing those words in any order. "Ford;Mustang"—with no space between the words—will find only sites containing those words in that exact order. It will ignore sites containing "Mustang by Ford." In Alta Vista, quotation marks are used the same way parentheses are used in other search engines—to combine two terms. See "Narrowing Your Searches with Boolean Operators" above for information on parentheses in searches.

Advanced searches in Alta Vista require the use of Boolean operators (*and*, *or*, *not*, *near*). Near searches within ten words in both directions of the target term. The search results can also be ordered by providing further information to the search. For example, when doing a search for "monkey and primate," you can reorder the list of results by specifying that hits containing "chimpanzee" are placed at the top of the list. You can further order your results by specifying the dates of the sites included in the list.

The search in Figure 5.5 used none of these techniques, and resulted in 40,000 matches! The first match, as you can see, has nothing to do

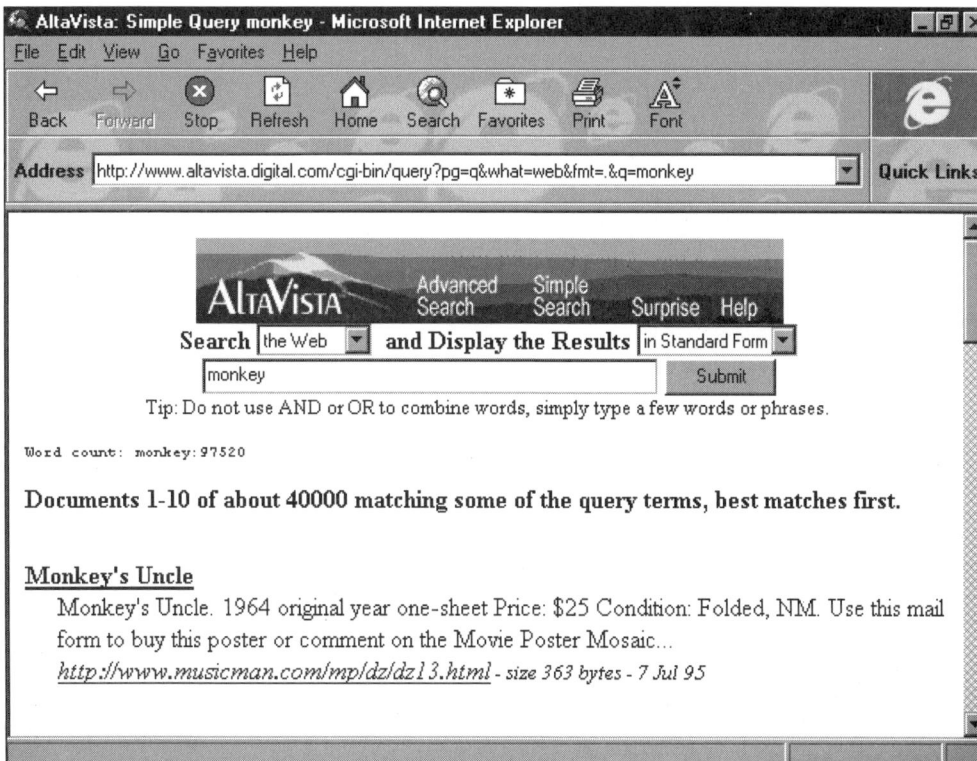

Figure 5.5: Alta Vista search results.

with animals that live in the jungle. Using + or − and other search terms would be a great help in focusing this search. Alta Vista is located at **http://www.altavista.digital.com.**

Lycos

Lycos (Figure 5.6), like Yahoo!, contains categories that you can use to browse on your own or to narrow your searches. The Lycos information is contained as abstracts of each site, which are searched using criteria that you input. The search results also display portions of these abstracts. Lycos also contains several information sections with news, reviews, and regular columns.

The standard search is fairly straightforward. The "Customize your search" link will allow you to change several search criteria such as the

Figure 5.6: Lycos intro. screen.

number of terms you wish to match. Simple Boolean searches are available, but only using *and* and *not* options, which are presented as radio buttons. Lycos provides a percentile reading to show how closely it feels the search results follow your criteria.

The results in Figure 5.7 are once again disappointing. I hope you are seeing a pattern resulting from vague searches! Try choosing a category to search or use *and* and *or*. Lycos can be found at **http://www.lycos.com**.

WebCrawler

WebCrawler (Figure 5.8) searches by titles or summaries and lists up to 100 results. WebCrawler contains categories that you can select

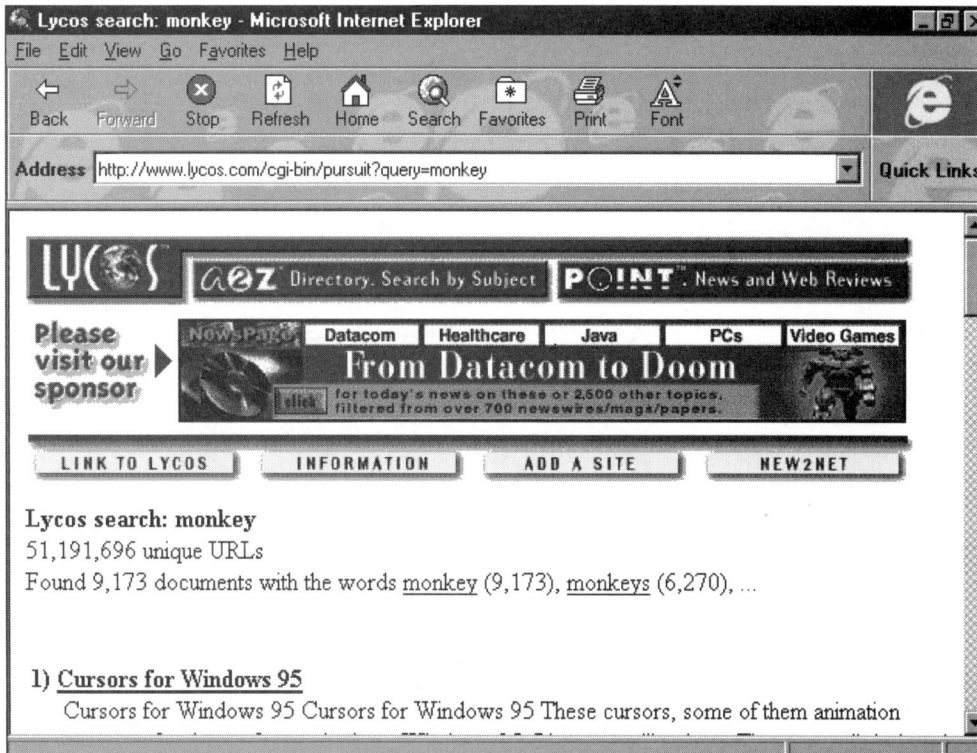

Figure 5.7: Lycos search results.

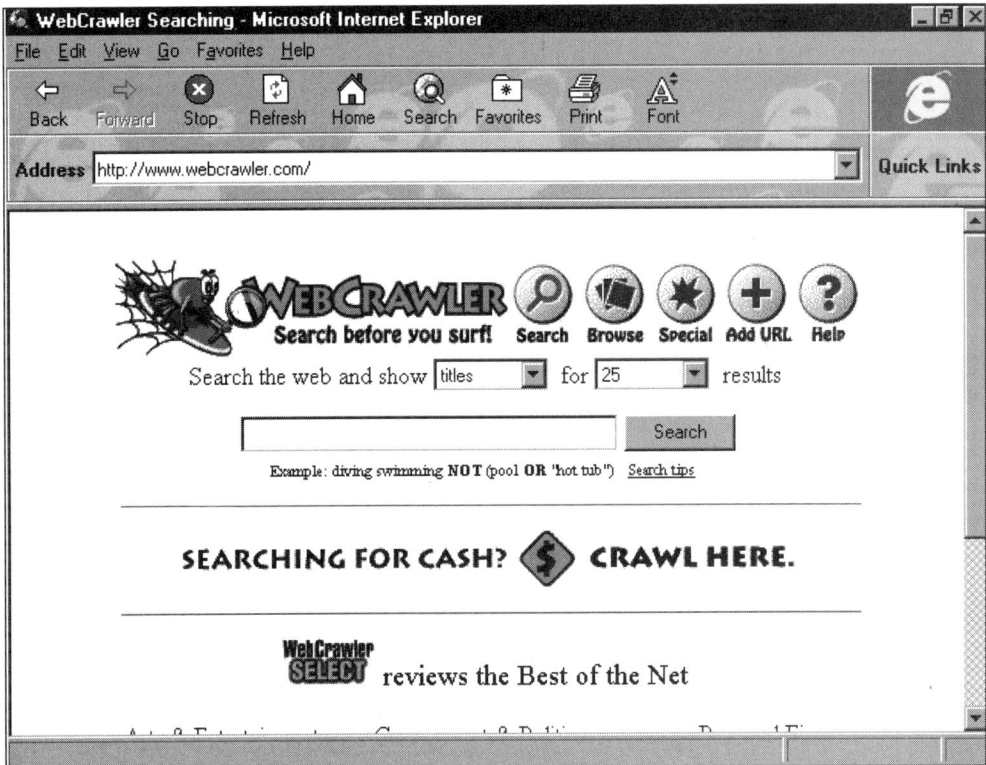

Figure 5.8: WebCrawler intro. screen.

and browse, and it has a unique feature that allows you to browse the Web "backward" to see who is visiting your Web site (assuming you've registered with WebCrawler). Boolean operators *and*, *or*, *not*, *near*, *adj* (adjacent), " " (used to link terms together just as Alta Vista uses the semicolon), and ( ) are available in a standard search. *Near* searches within 25 words in either direction. Search results are represented by icons (that look like medicine capsules!) filled with color. The more the icon is filled, the greater the confidence the results will match your search criteria. Summaries of all the hits can be displayed.

Figure 5.9 shows the results from my search. Again, nothing is a perfect match, but the second is very close. I have found that, although WebCrawler doesn't reference as many sites as other search engines, its results are often better than those of some

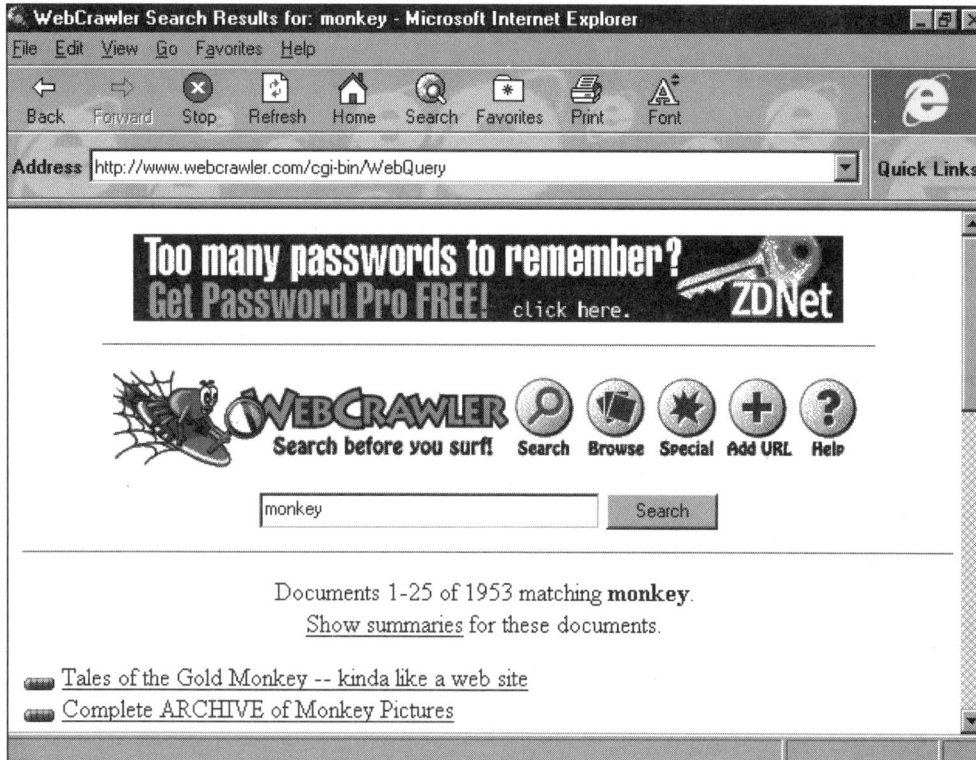

Figure 5.9: WebCrawler search results.

Copyright © 1996 America Online, Inc. All Rights Reserved.

other search engines. WebCrawler is located at **http://www .webcrawler.com**.

Excite

Excite (Figure 5.10) contains summaries of Web sites and Usenet groups, reviews (by real people, not automated spiders), and classified military secrets. No, not really. More like a classified ads portion of Usenet. Like the abstracts of Lycos, Excite contains summaries of each site. You are able to search these summaries by concept or keyword. Concepts are created by the Excite computer. As it searches, it develops concepts based on the site content. This isn't as detailed (or as accurate) as the reviews by people, but it should be obvious by now that automation is needed to track something as large as the Internet.

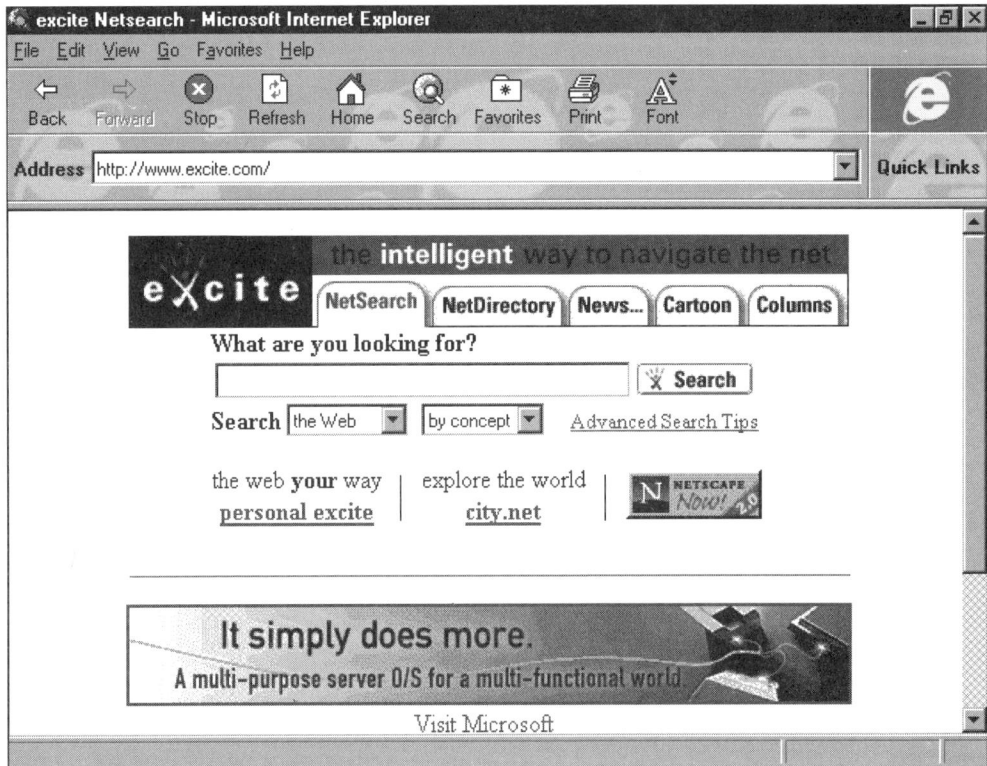

Figure 5.10: Excite intro. screen.

The default search uses a hybrid *and/or* operator. That is, "Ford Mustang" is treated as "Ford *and* Mustang" as well as "Ford *or* Mustang". Standard *and*, *or*, *not*, ( ), +, and – are also available. Result confidence is measured by percentage, and as you can see with my search (Figure 5.11), my percentages are not very good. Reading the summaries, I'm really not sure how effective this search was. I will have to check out a few of these sites for myself. Once again, using Booleans would help this search.

Combined Search Engines

Microsoft's search page is an example of a combined search engine. It is not really a search engine itself, but it contains input lines from several actual search engines. I mentioned it first because it is an option on the icon bar, but there are several other combined sites out there.

```
excite Query Results - Microsoft Internet Explorer                    _ 5 X
File  Edit  View  Go  Favorites  Help
  <=      =>      X       [c]      [home]    [Q]      [*]      [print]   [A]              [e]
 Back   Forward  Stop   Refresh   Home    Search  Favorites  Print    Font
Address  http://www.excite.com/search.gw?search=monkey&collection=web&searchType=Concept&mode=rel ▼   Quick Links
```

Documents **1-10** sorted by <u>confidence</u> [Sort by Site]
[icon] - higher confidence, [icon] - lower confidence; click icons to find <u>similar documents</u>

[icon] 77% <u>Monkey</u>
   Summary: Monkey. "Monkey"
[icon] 76% <u>Monkey mOnkey moNkey monKey monkEy monkeY MONKEY monkey!!!</u>
   Summary: Monkey mOnkey moNkey monKey monkEy monkeY MONKEY monkey! HOSE
   MONKE - another person (like myself) with too much time on their hands Lotta Monkey An
   even dumber homepage WebCrawler search Yahoo Lycos search InfoSeek Net search Barney
   homepage.
[icon] 75% <u>Home of Cyber Monkey</u>
   Summary: Eighteen months ago, a young fellow by the name of Vic made a trip to Boston to
   visit his cousin, Rick, at M.I.T. I'll leave it at that. Thank you, Frequently asked questions of The
   Monkey Stupid letter of the week (you humans are scary) Search for gifted monkeys The
   Human I Love My keeper with my Love before I stole her away.

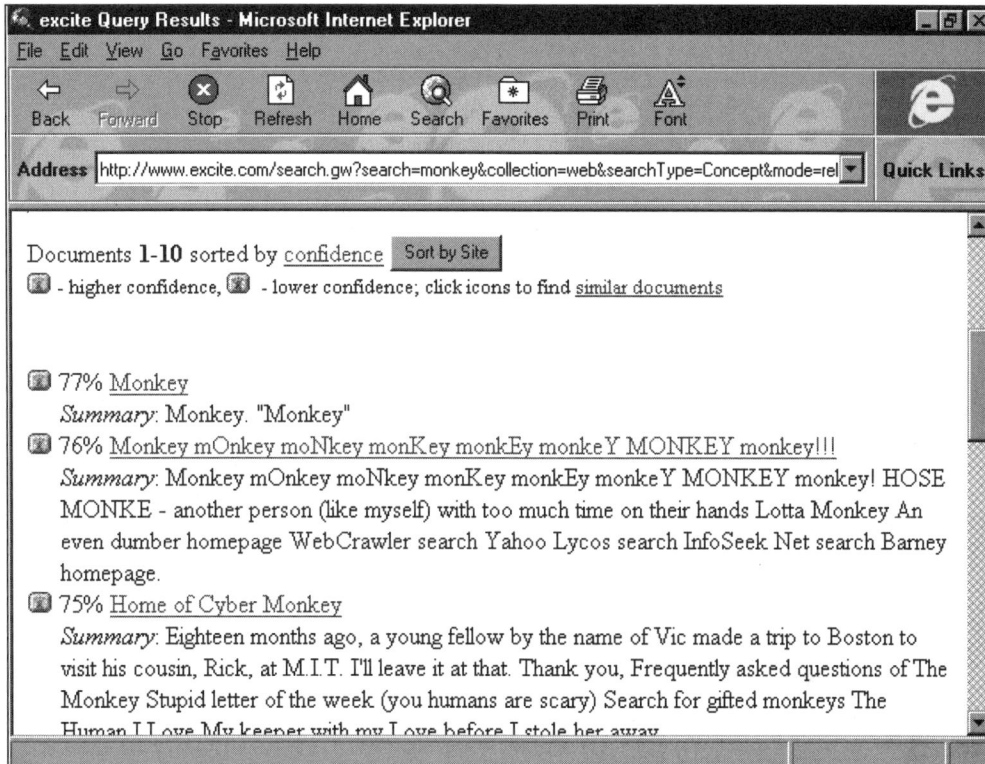

Figure 5.11: Excite search results.

Figure 5.12 shows Starting Point (**http://www.stpt.com**), which has what is called a MetaSearch, which allows you to choose from many search engines as well as Archie (described later in this chapter). Starting Point is a solid choice at the very beginning of a search when you're not sure which engine might work the best for you. Here you can try many and decide which is the best, then go directly to it to use its advanced options.

Figure 5.13 shows Search.com (**http://www.search.com**), another combined site. Like Starting Point, Search.com is a good place to try several search engines before you decide which is best for your specific search. Many standard Web pages are now including links to search engines, even pages maintained by individuals. Don't be surprised if you log on to your friend's page and find WebCrawler's spider mascot looking at you!

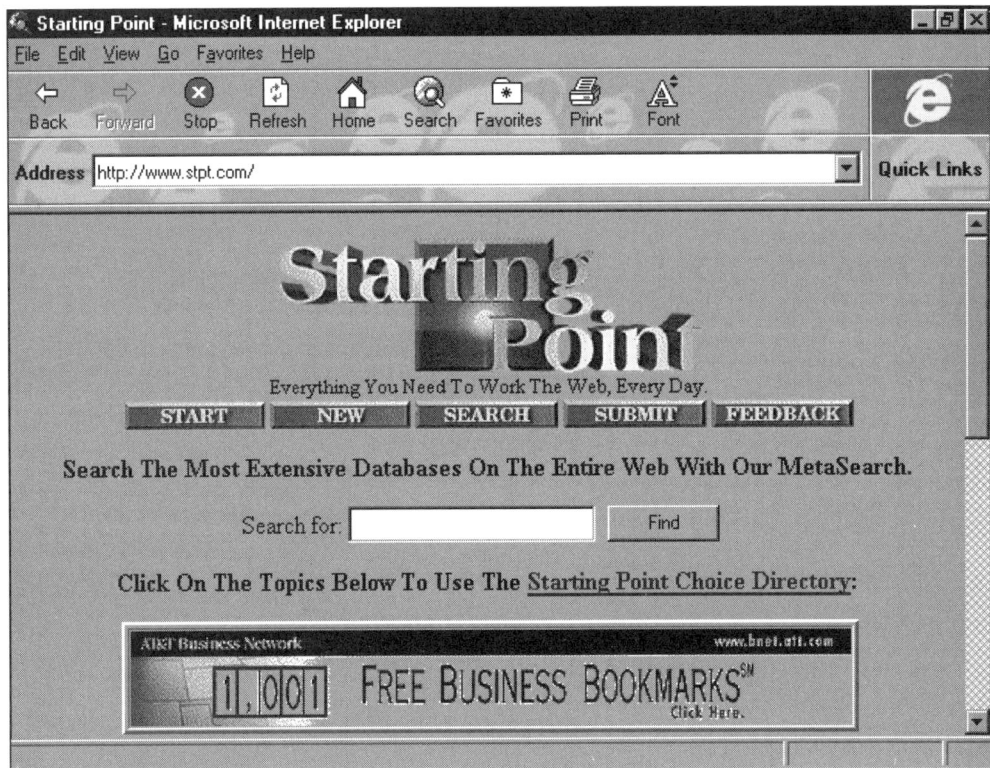

Figure 5.12: Starting Point.

Tip: If you need to see the results of a past search, but don't want to repeat the actual search, open the History Folder. It will contain the results of all your searches filed under the names of the search engines used to perform them.

Other Sources

The WWW Virtual Library (Figure 5.14) is a listing of many Web sites that is maintained entirely by individuals. Because it is human

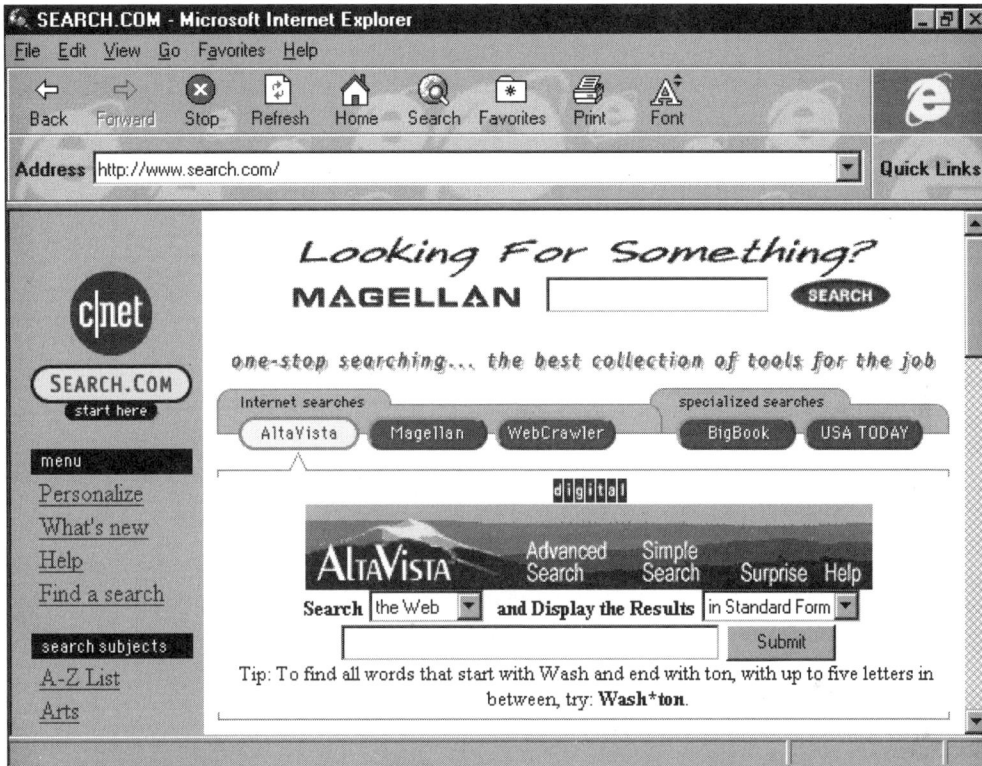

Figure 5.13: Search.com.

operated, this listing is not nearly as extensive as any search engine can provide, but the information contained within is much more detailed. The VL is organized into alphabetical categories that can be browsed by hand or searched automatically. The search covers only those sites listed in the VL. The address is **http://www.w3 .org/pub/DataSources/bySubject/Overview.html**. Be sure to watch typos and caps!

If you are looking for computer programs and files rather than information, the next section of this chapter covering FTP may prove to be very helpful. First, however, let me cover one such place on the Web. Shareware.com (Figure 5.15) is a terrific source of programs that are available to download. The programs are categorized by platform (Windows, Mac, etc.) and by category (entertainment, productivity, etc.). This site can also be searched, making it easy to

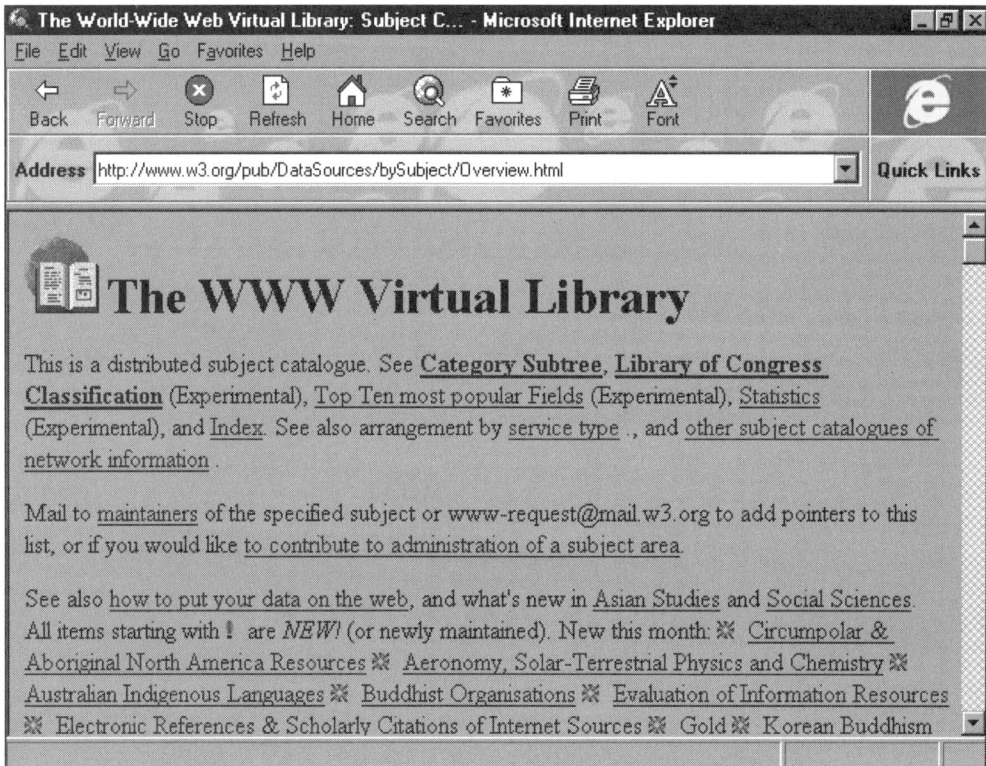

Figure 5.14: The WWW Virtual Software Library.

find a variety of titles. Shareware.com can be found at (you guessed it) **http://www.shareware.com**. Other extensive listings of files follow in the next section.

FILE TRANSFER PROTOCOL (FTP)

File Transfer Protocol (or FTP, as it is called) is a collection of computers that allows users to access remotely and transfer files and applications. Users who have access to an FTP site and who have a username and password can copy, move, delete, or otherwise rearrange the files on an FTP site. Not everybody has this kind of access, however. Most of us have access to *anonymous* FTP sites. These are the same sites that everyone can visit, but users connected anonymously can only view and download the files contained within. It is not possible through

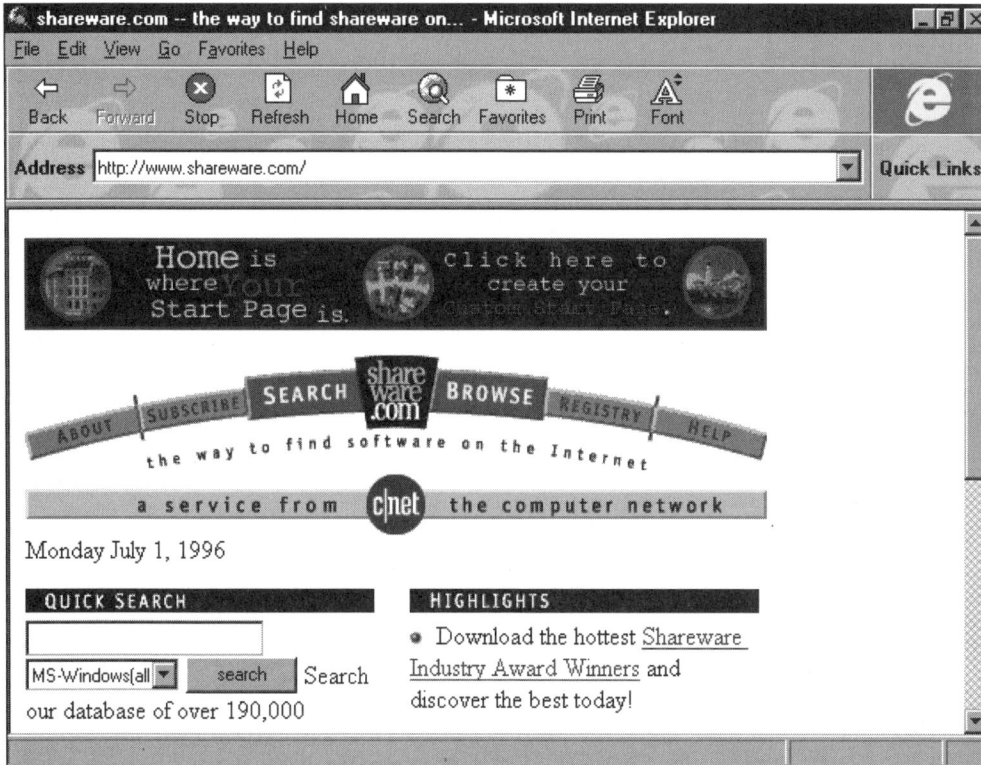

Figure 5.15: Shareware.com.

Internet Explorer or other Web browsers to upload files at this time. (Even if it were possible, the anonymous access probably wouldn't let that happen anyway.) All we really need to do is download, though, so the arrangement works out nicely.

What types of files are available via FTP? Almost everything. You can find full programs, text files, graphics files, sound files, utilities, and even lists of old Usenet discussions. Sounds a lot like a Web site, doesn't it? There are several main differences between FTP sites and Web sites.

First, FTP site have no multimedia aspects. There are no pictures to see (unless you download them), no sounds to hear (unless you download them), and not much color. Figure 5.16 shows a typical FTP site at its root page. The root page is almost equivalent to a Web site's home page in that it is a starting point that shows the other

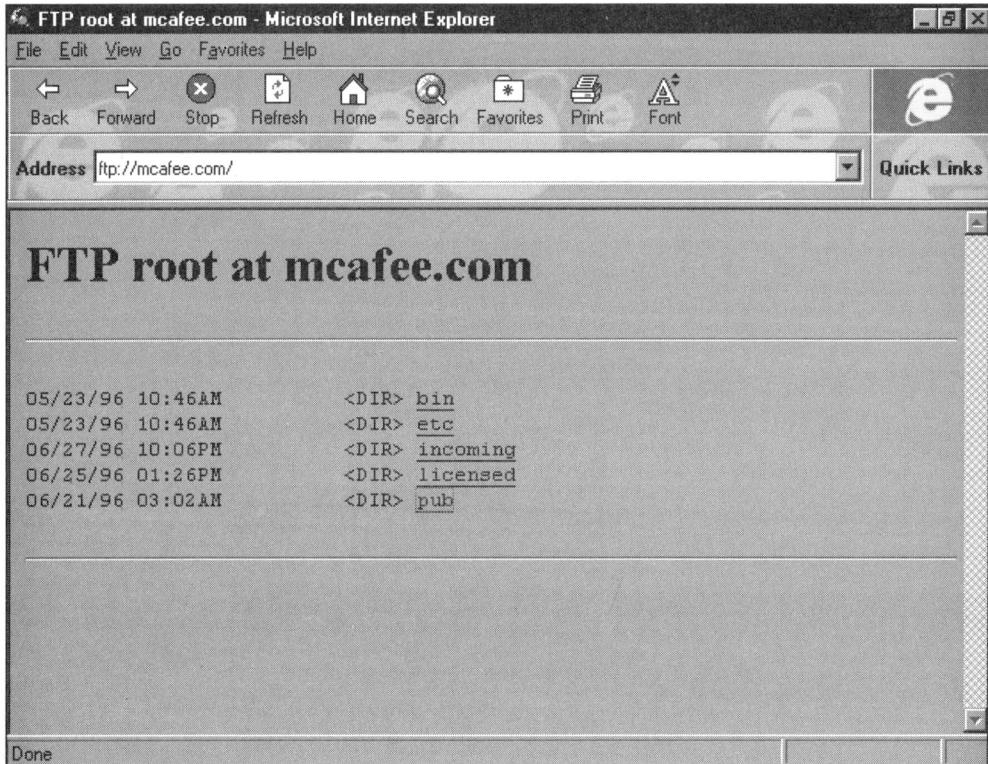

Figure 5.16: An FTP site.

parts of the site. Most FTP sites, therefore, will look basically the same.

Second, although FTP sites contain links that can be taken and files that can be downloaded with a single mouse click, there are no dedicated navigational tools. You move around using links, the scroll bars, and the Back and Forward icons from Explorer's icon bar.

Navigating FTP sites

Although it is possible to move around FTP sites with Explorer's navigational tools, learning some terminology from the UNIX world is helpful. UNIX is an operating system that uses text commands on a command prompt (the same way that DOS does). Even though you won't have access to the command prompt or need to learn UNIX commands (Explorer takes care of this for you), it is important to learn the directory structure in UNIX.

In Windows 95, files are arranged in folders, represented by icons of actual folders. Files in an FTP site are arranged in directories. These directories are represented on-screen by <DIR>. In Windows 95, folders can be stored within other folders. Clicking on a folder will open that folder and show you its contents. Directories within directories are called subdirectories in an FTP site. Clicking on the name of a directory (marked as <DIR>) will show you that directory's contents. Figure 5.17 shows the subdirectory "pub" within the McAfee FTP site. When you have "backed out" as far as possible in Windows 95, you are in the desktop (check Windows 95 Explorer to see what I mean). When you have backed out as far as you can go in an FTP site, you are in the root directory.

When navigating through FTP sites, it is important to know how far "in" the site you are. As you can see in Figure 5.17, Explorer displays the current subdirectory in the address bar, and the FTP site displays

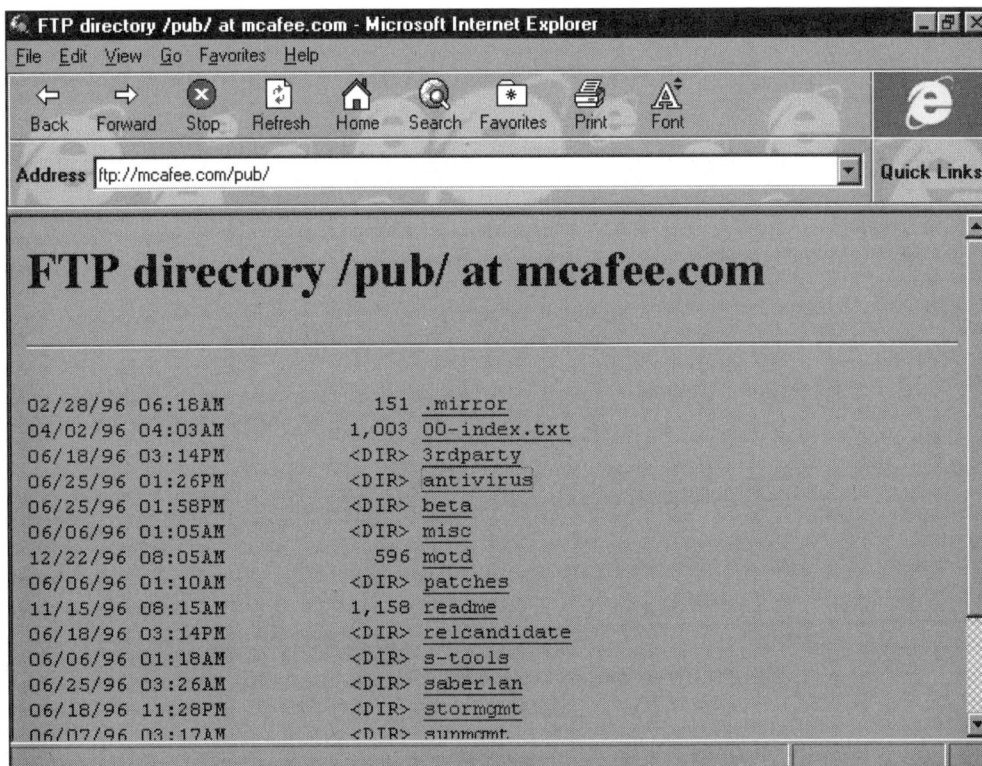

Figure 5.17: In the "pub" subdirectory of the McAfee FTP site.

it at the top of the viewing window. If you were to click on the "antivirus" subdirectory, the address bar would read "ftp:// mcafee.com/pub/antivirus/" and the FTP site would display "FTP directory /pub/antivirus/ at mcafee.com."

Tip: Rather than trying to look at every subdirectory in an FTP site (which could take hours), look for a file called "index.txt," "readme.txt," or "directory.txt." In Figure 5.17, this file is called "00-index.txt." These are plain text files that list the contents of the FTP site. Clicking on this type of file will display it on-screen and will save you much search time.

The final aspect of navigating an FTP site is downloading files. This can be accomplished by clicking on the file to download. Explorer will ask you if you want to open the file or save it to disk. You more than likely want to save it to disk (unless it's a sound file you want to hear right away). Then Explorer will ask where to put the file and what to call it. For more information on downloading files, see Chapter 6.

Caution: Downloading files involves the risk of downloading a virus. Be sure that your antivirus program is up to date and scan the file immediately after downloading.

Accessing FTP sites

There are several ways to access FTP sites with Explorer:

1. Clicking a link in a Web page
2. Typing the address in the address bar
3. Typing the address in the Windows 95 Run command

The easiest way is to click a link provided on a Web page. Just as it does with a link to another Web page, Explorer will automatically take you to that site. If you have the site address, you can manually enter it in either the address bar or in the Run command. Using the address bar is just like entering a Web page URL. Simply type the address and press Enter. The Run command can be used if you are not currently using Internet Explorer. Type the address, press Enter or OK, and Explorer will launch and take you to that site.

Tip: It is not necessary to type the ftp:// in the address bar. Explorer will add this part automatically. However, if you want to go to an FTP site that has the same URL as a Web site (except, of course, for the ftp://), Explorer will go to the Web site by default.

FINDING FTP FILES WITH ARCHIE

Boy, how does anyone ever find anything using FTP? Sure, many of the directories are named by the types of files that they contain, but there are so many FTP sites and so many directories! Luckily, someone else asked this same question. Then he or she got together with some programmers and came up with Archie. Archie is a way to search FTP lists for specific files. It is clunky and requires the user to know the exact name of the files to be located. On top of everything else, Explorer (and other browsers) can't access it directly! Wow, what a deal!

There is ArchiePlex, a service that offers a gateway to Archie via the Web. There are several ArchiePlex servers in operation around the world that can perform an Archie search. Many of these servers will also let you choose which country you would like to search. A popular ArchiePlex located in the United States is operated by NASA at **http://www.lerc.nasa.gov/archieplex** shown in Figure 5.18. This site

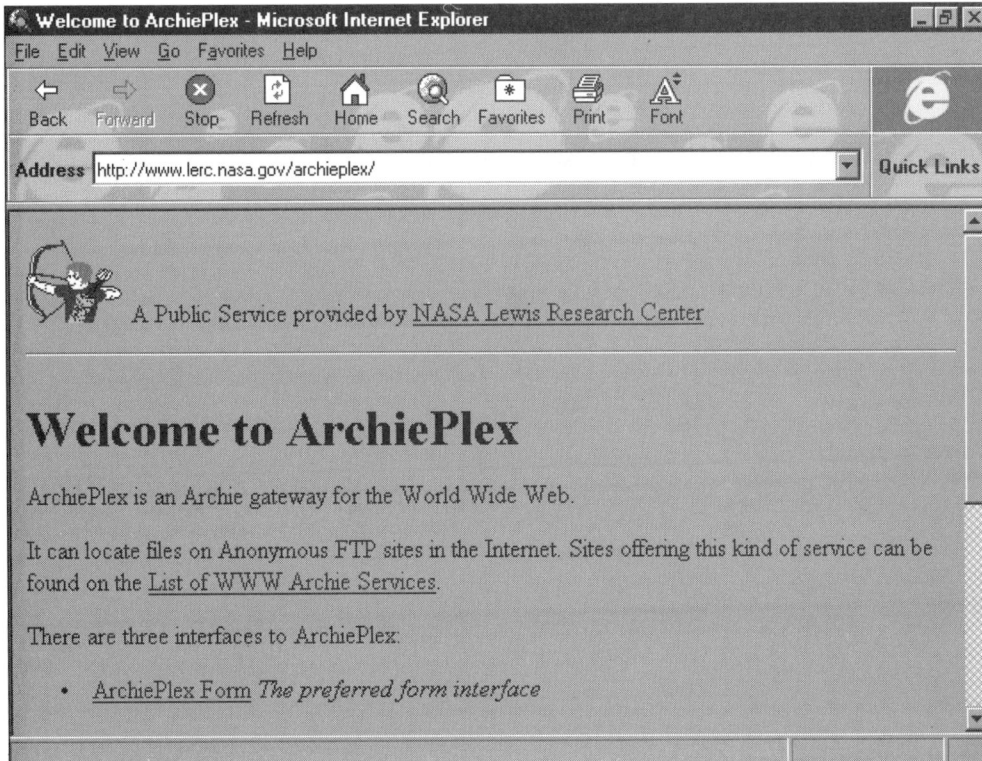

Figure 5.18: An ArchiePlex server.

lets you choose your search method. The ArchiePlex that uses a form interface (the first option) is the preferred method with Explorer. Enter the name of the file you want to find. You then choose which Archie server to search (choose the server closest to you geographically) and wait. It will take a few minutes to receive a list of sites, an error message, or a busy message.

You may have noticed if you tried the Starting Point search engine that one of its options is an Archie search. This uses an Archie server at Rutgers University, which gives a few more search options and a priority option. Figure 5.19 shows the Rutgers Archie server, located at **http://www-ns.rutgers.edu/htbin/archie** (also available at Starting Point). Figure 5.20 shows the results of a search with this server. Simply click on the link to the FTP site that contains the file, then download the file.

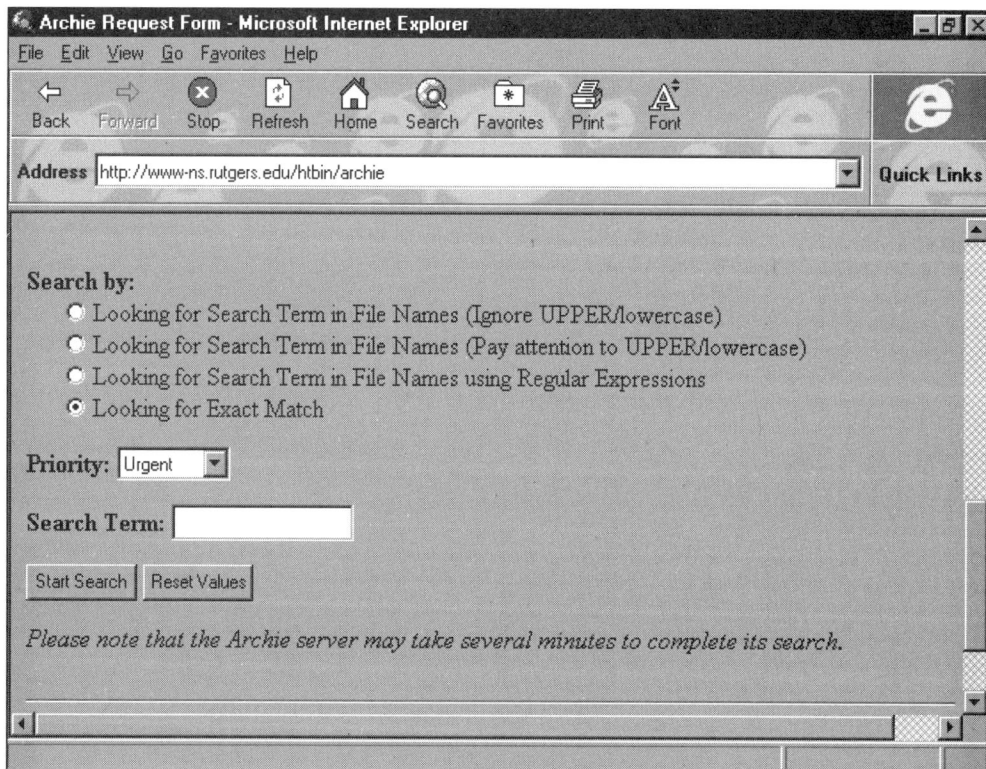

Figure 5.19: A Rutgers University Archie server.

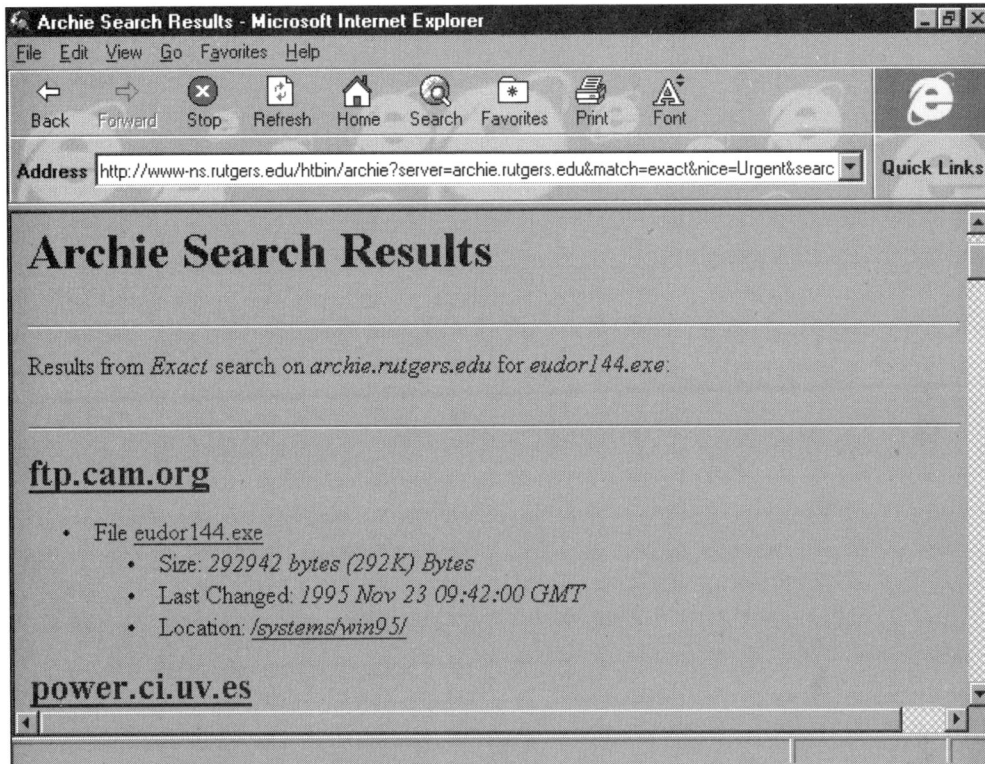

Figure 5.20: An Archie search result.

GOPHER

Gopher is another rich source of information on the Internet. Like its cousin FTP, Gopher is a bit dated in comparison with the Web, but also like FTP, it contains many resources. Gopher was created at the University of Minnesota as a way to search different computer systems for different file types. The name Gopher came from Minnesota's mascot, the Golden Gopher, and the act of "digging" through computers looking for information. Gopher sites contain documents, graphics files, and binary (encoded) files. The documents can be displayed on-screen while the graphics and binary files can be downloaded. Figure 5.21 shows a Gopher directory at the University of Minnesota (**gopher://gopher.tc.umn.edu**). Note that the URL begins with gopher://.

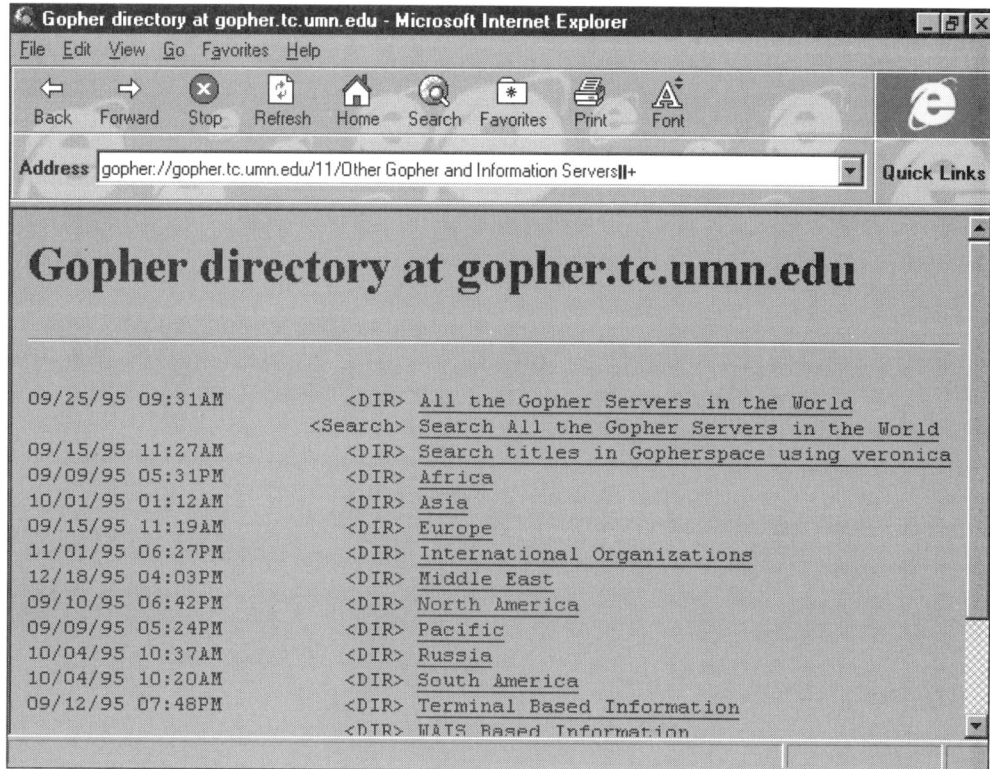

Figure 5.21: A Gopher directory.

Tip: Moving around in Gopherspace can be a little more confusing than moving within other Internet sites. Many Gopher menus are vague, and moving the cursor over them in Explorer's default mode may not tell you much on the status bar. Remember that the status bar displays the address of the linked site when the cursor is held over that link. I recommend changing the display options for the cursor from showing simplified URLs to showing full URLs to eliminate the confusion. This can be done through the View Options menu. On the Advanced tab, deselect the checkbox next to Show friendly URLs.

Navigating a Gopher site is similar to navigating an FTP site. There are no on-screen navigational aids, so Explorer's Back and Forward icons are used often. When you find a directory to search or a file to download, they are treated as hyperlinks, so a single mouse click will change directories or download files. But how do you find these files?

VERONICA

Veronica is a search engine for Gopher servers. It is designed to search a list of directory titles and document names. It is not able to search the content of any files, as some of the Web search engines do. Veronica does have two different types of searches:

- All Gopherspace
- Directory titles only

All Gopherspace will search for directory titles and filenames, while directory titles only won't look for individual filenames. Figure 5.22 shows some Veronica options. The simplified Veronica automatically chooses a server to search for you (the options in the

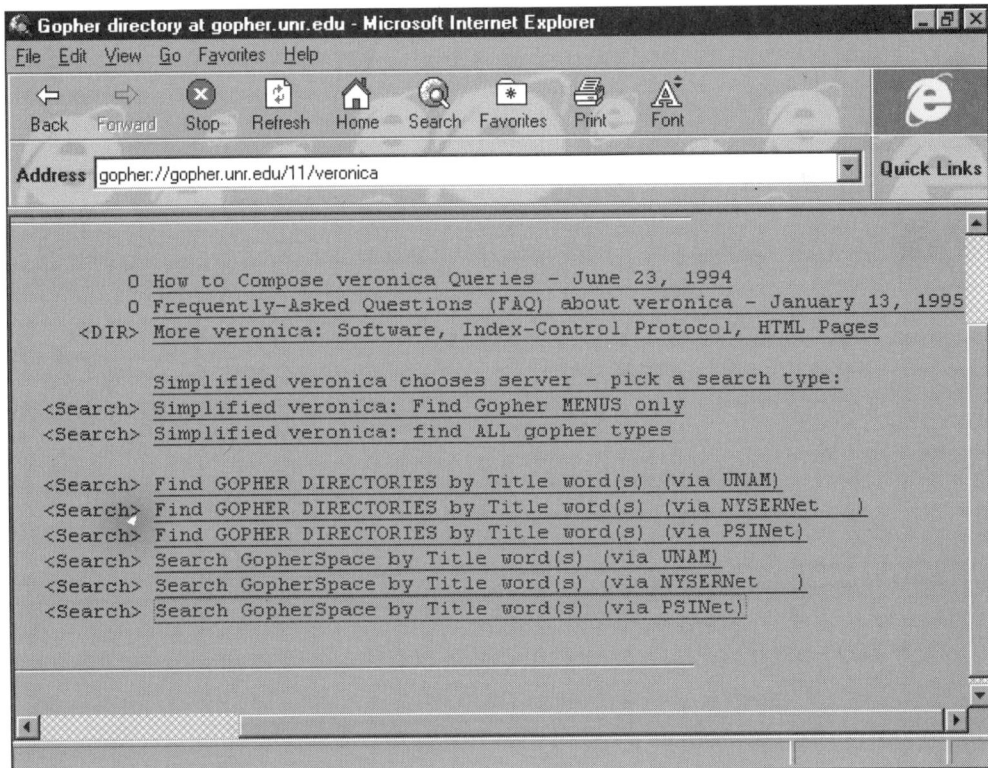

Figure 5.22: Veronica options.

middle of Figure 5.22). A standard Veronica search allows you to choose the server yourself (the options at the bottom of Figure 5.22). Veronica searches are notoriously slow, so choosing the simplified search can save you some time (being logged on at 4 A.M. is good, too!). When the search is completed, a Gopher menu is displayed containing the files found during the search. This is a standard Gopher menu with hyperlinks, and it can be navigated normally.

Veronica supports standard Boolean operators to focus your search as well as some special details. These details can be used to narrow your search to certain file types only. Table 5.1 lists these special details and their functions. They are used with the -t operator placed within the search words (at any point). For example, to search for only a GIF file (a graphic image) of Niki Taylor (a supermodel), you could type Niki Taylor -tg. Multiple file types can be searched using the same command. To expand our search to also include any text documents about Niki Taylor, you would type Niki Taylor -t0g.

Table 5.1 Special Details for Limiting a Veronica Search

0	Text file
1	Directory
2	CSO name server (a database used to locate people on the Internet)
4	Macintosh HQX file
5	PC binary file
7	Text index
8	Telnet session
9	Binary file
s	Sound file
e	Event file
I	Image file (other than GIF)
M	MIME multipart/mixed message
T	TN3270 session (Telnet)
c	Calendar
g	GIF image
h	HTML document

JUGHEAD

This is the last of the comic book characters (I promise). Jughead is another method for searching Gopher menus, although not all Gopher servers have this capability. Jughead can search only the current server; it cannot search another Gopher menu on remote machines, and it is limited to searching only directories. Because of this, Jughead searches do not cover as much information, but they are quite a bit faster than Veronica searches. Jughead can accept Boolean operators to help focus your search. Figure 5.23 shows a Jughead menu at the University of Utah.

Note: Because many Veronica and Jughead services are located on university computers, you may not have access to them unless you are affiliated with that institution. If this is the case, keep sniffing around until you find a server that grants you access.

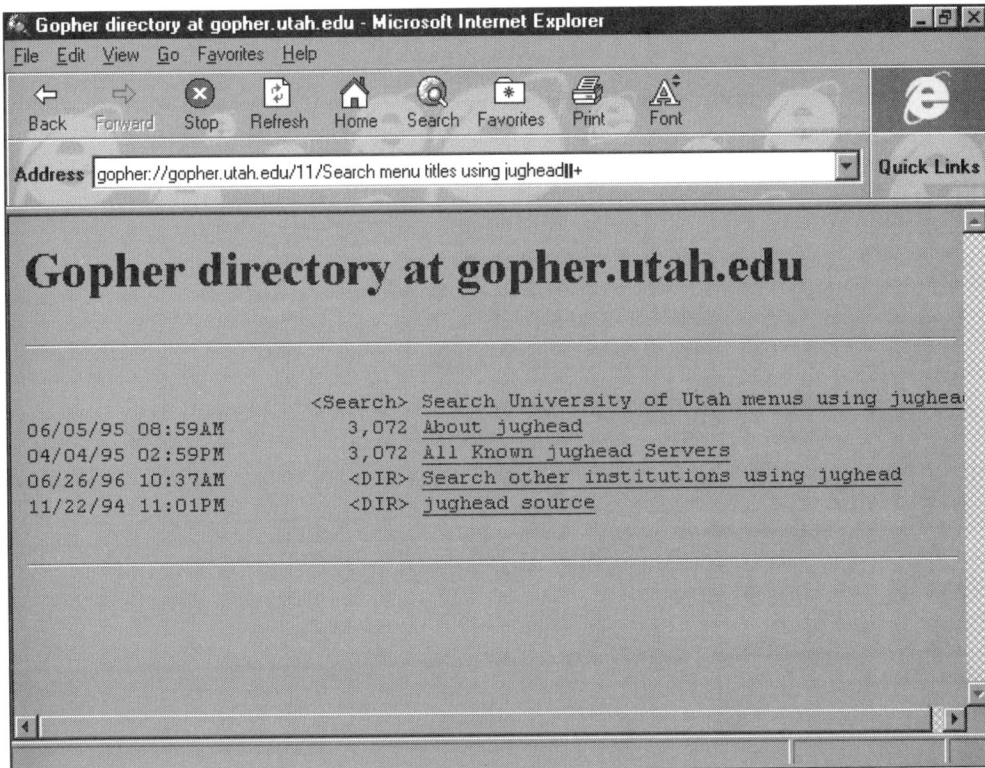

Figure 5.23: A Jughead menu.

TELNET

As you may recall, Telnet is a portion of the Net containing computers that cannot communicate with each other using the standard Internet languages. This leaves us with nonstandard, text-based interfaces that can be confusing to navigate. A Telnet session is shown in Figure 5.24. Explorer does not directly control Telnet sessions; they are accessed with a program contained within Windows itself.

Uses for Telnet

What is Telnet used for? Even though it is old and clunky, Telnet is still often used for several functions. Many libraries have catalogs on Telnet, as shown in Figure 5.24. It is still a capable way to search text

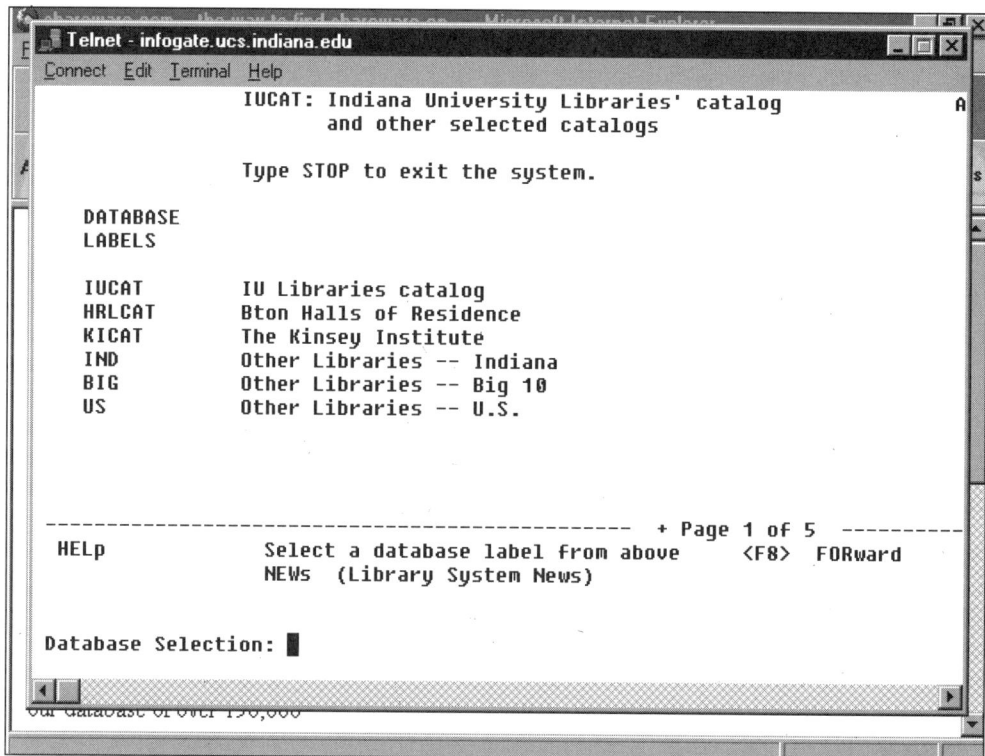

Figure 5.24: A Telnet session.

lists. Many gamers still use Telnet to play MUDs (Multi User Dungeons), as shown in Figure 5.25. These games can be intense role-playing experiences or simply socialization centers. Others use Telnet as an inexpensive alternative to full Internet accounts for e-mail access. Many businesses and universities have Telnet-based e-mail systems. Telnet is far from being a relic of the Internet past.

Note: Telnet gamers are a very picky bunch. They don't like people snooping around and slowing the system down. If you are serious about playing, most MUDs will welcome you. If you are just curious, you might consider staying away. Serious gamers have been known to gang up on newbies. Check out MUD information on Usenet to find games that may be more tolerant of new players.

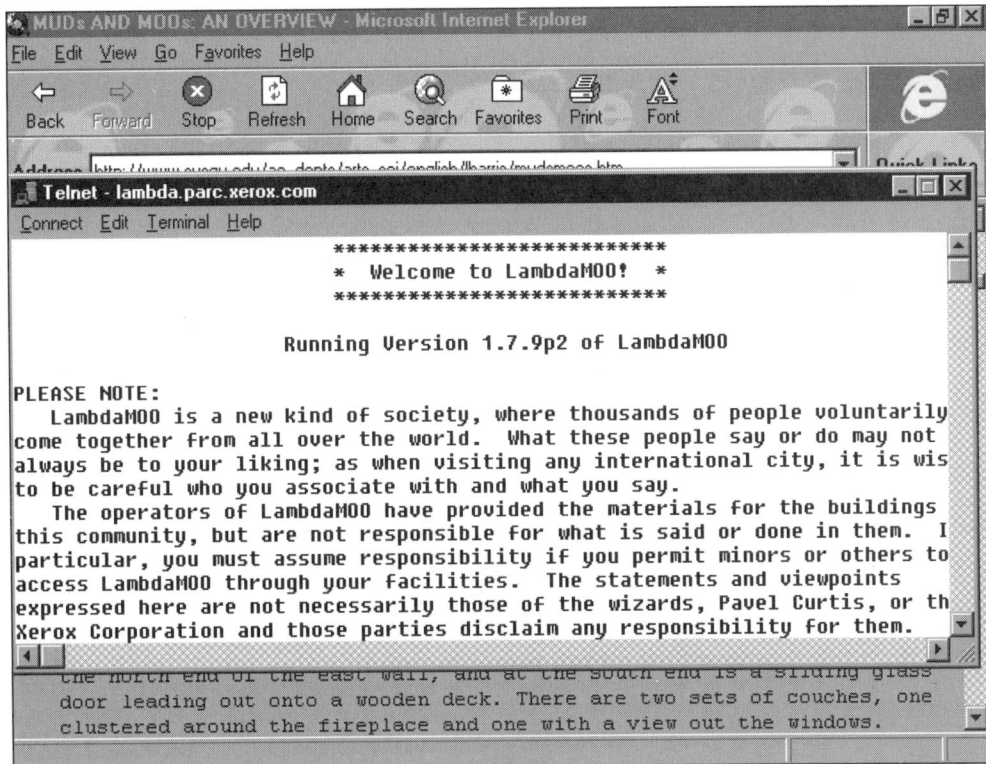

Figure 5.25: A popular Telnet MUD.

Accessing Telnet

So how do you get to Telnet? The Windows Telnet program is launched in three ways:

1. By clicking on a link to a Telnet site
2. By typing a Telnet address in Explorer's Address bar (tel-net://)
3. By using the Windows 95 Run command on the Start menu

When using the Run command, you can either input the full Telnet address preceded by Telnet:// or just type Telnet and OK or Enter to launch the program. Then choose Connect Remote System and type the address in the window followed by Connect or Enter. It is not uncommon to receive a "Connection to Host Failed" message. Telnet sites are quirky and slow, and most do not allow new users to connect when the maximum allowable number has been reached.

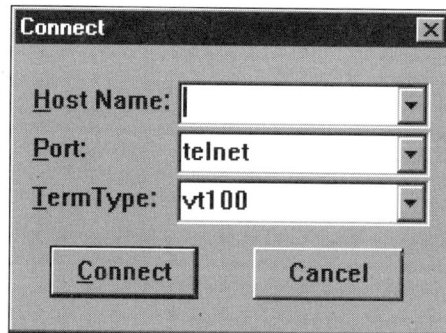

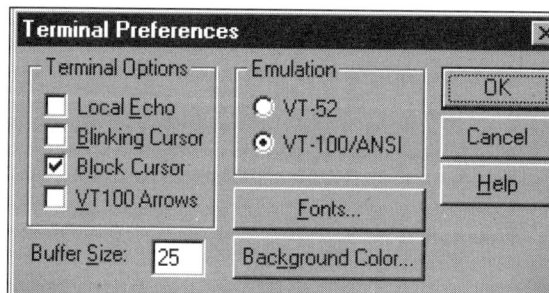

The Telnet Connect window has an option for Term Type. This is set by default to VT100, which is a popular system for Telnet servers. This is called an emulation mode because it is emulating the signals sent by a VT100 machine. The Telnet machine at the other end will not know that it's really connected to a PC. This setting can also be changed in the Terminal Preferences menu. VT52 is the other emulation possible, although it is not often encountered. Try it if you have repeated connection problems or gibberish on your screen. Local Echo should be selected if your typing does not appear on your screen. Keep in mind that your keystrokes may take a few seconds to register on the Telnet machine.

Because Telnet offers no files to download, its main attraction is information. But how do you save this information? If you find a book in a library catalog, how do you record its catalog number? Pencil and paper? In the Telnet menu bar, choose Terminal Start Logging to keep a record of your Telnet session. This option will keep a copy of everything that appears on-screen until you log off or choose Terminal Stop Logging. You can then print the results or copy them to the Clipboard.

HyTelnet

How can information be found on Telnet sites? There is a database of Telnet sites on the Web called HyTelnet (Figure 5.26). HyTelnet is a searchable list of Telnet servers accessible at several sites including **http://www.lights.com/hytelnet**. HyTelnet will let you search for keywords and will display a list of matches that include hypertext links to the Telnet sites as well as a sample of those sites.

WHAT'S AHEAD?

- Discover the basics of downloading and file management in Chapter 6.
- Change settings and customize Explorer in Chapter 7.
- Learn about multimedia on the Web in Chapter 8.

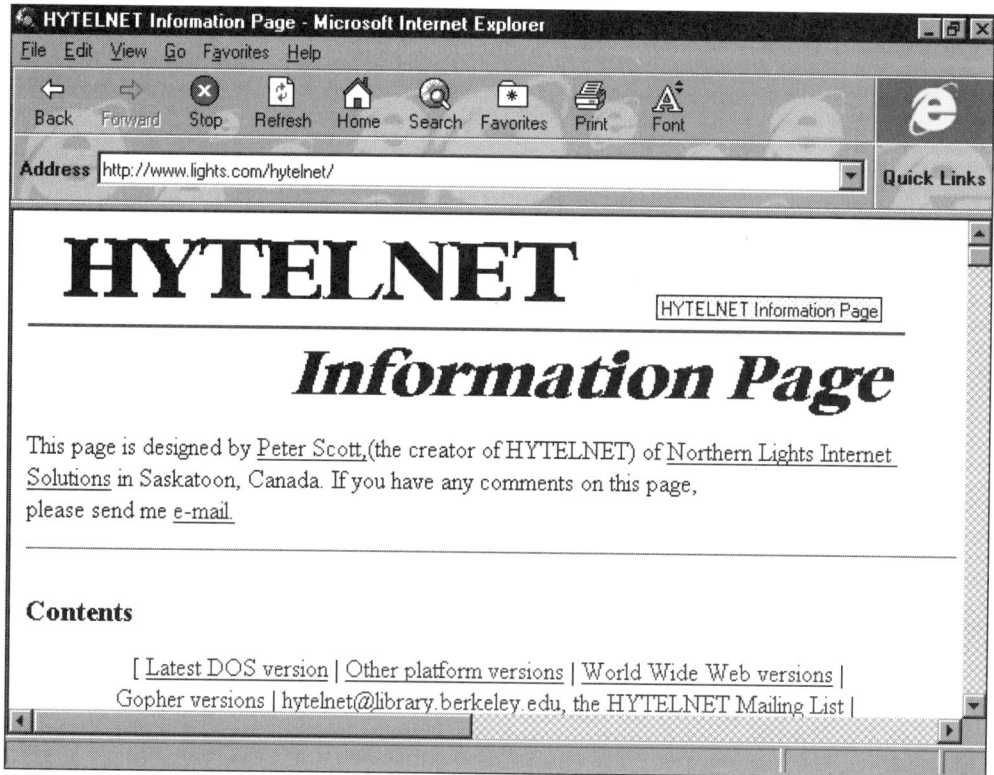

Figure 5.26: A HyTelnet site on the Web.

Chapter 6

MANAGING
YOUR DOCUMENTS

The Internet is full of great stuff. Files that can help you at work or at school or make your computer run faster or more efficiently are all within your reach. Many companies now produce their programs (both productivity and game software) as shareware and post them on the Net for everyone to access. The Internet is also full of completely worthless stuff that just happens to be a lot of fun. Games, sound files, screen savers, pictures, and movie clips are just a sample of the types of time wasters that reside on the Net. They all have something in common, though: These gems are located somewhere else besides on your computer.

That's where document management comes into play. I consider document management with respect to the Internet to be anything that involves moving files around in a way to make them work for you. Downloading, decoding, saving, copying, grabbing, and printing are all part of document management. With these skills, you can get almost anything you want off the Net.

KEY POINTS IN THIS CHAPTER

- How does downloading work?
- What exactly is a zipped or encoded file?
- Why would I want to save a Web page to my hard disk?

- Can I print a Web page? Will it look the same?
- Can I copy text and pictures from the Web?

DOWNLOADING FILES

When you find a file that you want to keep or share with friends, you download it—that is, you transfer the file from the Internet computer to your own hard drive. Why download? Well, most computer programs won't run unless they physically reside on your computer. Therefore, you must download them to be able to use them. The same is true of graphic images, movies, and sound files. There are exceptions (as there always are in this business), but this basic rule still must be followed.

Note: Many people mistakenly refer to installing a program as downloading it. For example, people buy a program such as Microsoft Word from a store and install it on their machine. They then say that they downloaded it to their computer. NOT TRUE! Downloading is the process of transferring data from a remotely located computer to a local computer, not installing software from disks or CD-ROM. If you refer to installing as downloading, you will totally confuse anyone you talk to!

Many Web pages, FTP, and Gopher sites exist as storehouses of files for people like us to download. Search engines, Archie, Veronica, and Jughead, discussed in Chapter 5, exist to help people find files. The procedure for getting any of these files once you have found them is basically the same no matter what type of Internet site you are connected to. When you click on a file to download (downloadable files are hyperlinks in Explorer), you will see the window shown in Figure 6.1, which asks you to make a decision to open or save the file.

Open It

Use the Open it option if you want the file you are downloading to be run automatically. For most files you wouldn't want to do this. In fact, for most files this is a very bad idea. Most of the time you will save the file to disk and use it later. Many files that you will download are self-extracting archives. That means that they are .exe files that contain many other compressed files. When opened, they will extract all of the

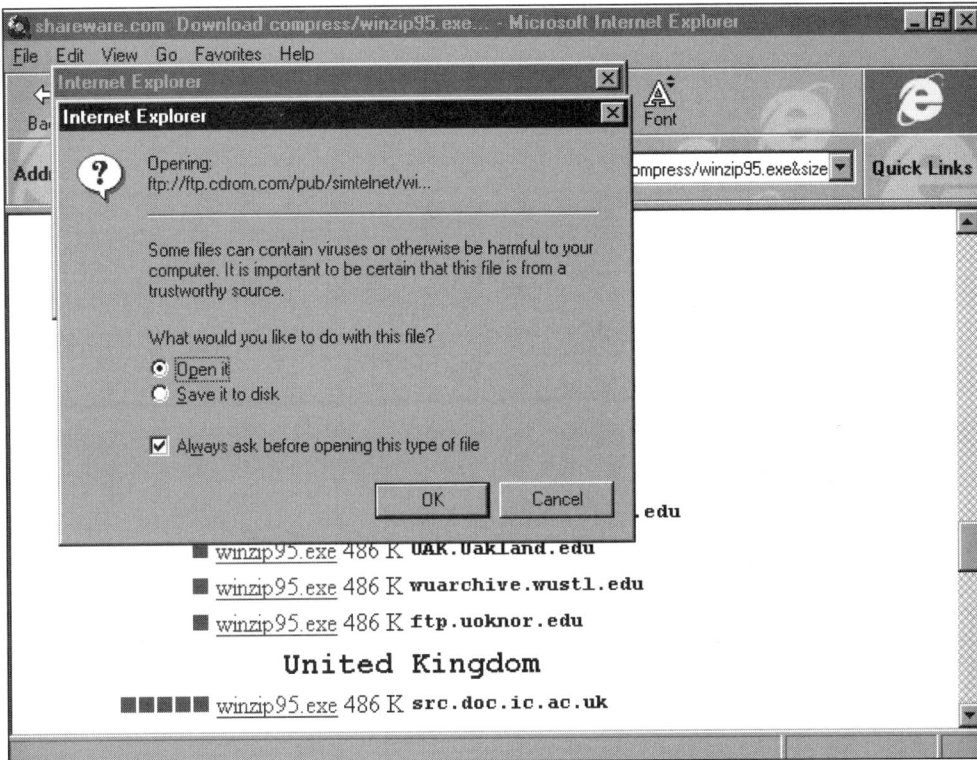

Figure 6.1: The first downloading window.

compressed files into the directory in which they are placed. Downloaded files are automatically placed in the Internet Explorer cache folder, definitely a bad place to install other programs. If anything is installed in the cache folder, you will have to find and copy each file into the correct folder (which could take quite a while if you have many downloaded files mixed in with the Explorer files). Self-extracting files should be placed in their own folder before opening them.

Viruses are another reason not to automatically open files after downloading. Unless you can be reasonably sure that the file you just downloaded is not infected, the first thing you should do after downloading is scan the file with your antivirus program. If you open the file and it is infected, you could have a big mess on your hands.

When *do* you use the Open it option? When you are sure that the file will not be infected, use the Open it option. For example, if you upgraded from Internet Explorer 2.0 by downloading the 3.0 file, you probably chose the Open it command. This automatically ran the Explorer 3.0 installation program and saved you some time. Other system files, like the Windows 95 maintenance packs, can be opened the same way. Some sound and video files are designed to play automatically after downloading. These files are not saved to disk during the download, but they are stored in RAM instead. You will know when you are downloading such files because the window in Figure 6.1 will not appear after clicking on the file.

The download status window is shown in Figure 6.2. This window tracks the progress of the download by displaying a blue bar that progresses to the right as the file is received (just like the one in the status bar that appears when a Web page is loading). Also displayed are the actual number of bytes that have been received. Usually the site from which you are downloading will show the file size next to the name. If not, the display in bytes will be rather worthless to you. If Explorer can determine the size of the file being downloaded, it will display the estimated time remaining next to the number of bytes received.

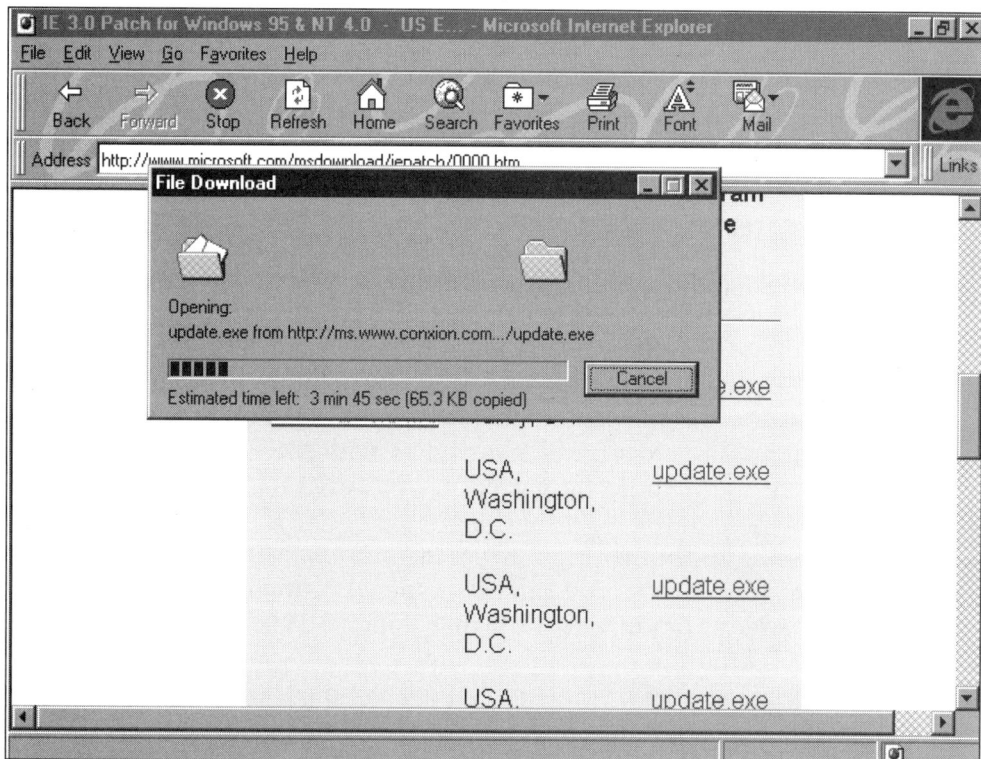

Figure 6.2: The download status window.

Save It to Disk

You will save most of the files you download to disk. This way you can choose in which folder to place the file, and you can scan it for viruses before doing anything else with it. When you choose Save it to disk, the next window you will see is the Save As window (shown in Figure 6.3), which asks you to name the file and choose a folder in which to place it. Navigating this window is similar to moving around in Windows 95 Explorer. Click on My Computer if you would like to place it in a folder on your hard drive. The other items shown in Figure 6.3 are shortcuts on the Windows desktop. These are not places to save the new file (with the exception of the Favorites folder, but that's where I keep my favorite URLs; I don't want a file in there). Figure 6.4 shows where I finally decided to place my newly down-loaded file—in my MS Internet folder. I got to this window by clicking My Computer in Figure 6.3, choosing the MS Internet folder from the list of folders on my hard drive, naming the file winzip95.exe, and choosing Save.

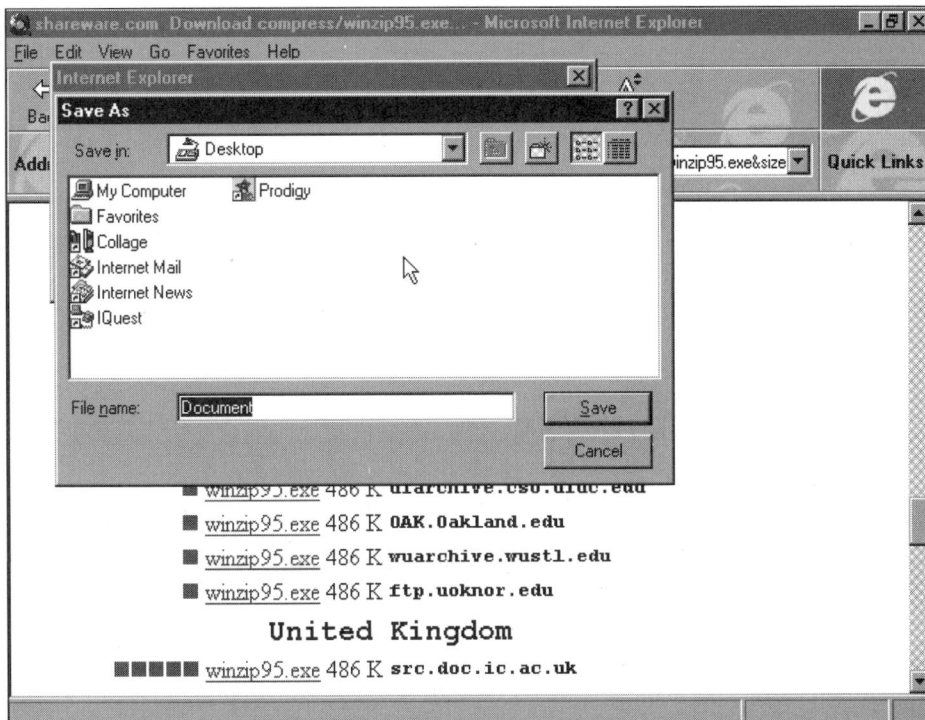

Figure 6.3: The Save As window.

Figure 6.4: My newly downloaded file in my MS Internet folder.

Remember the sound and video files that play automatically when you click their links? If you want to save these files to disk, right-click on their hyperlink and choose Save Target As. You will then see the Save As window.

Tip: What if you played these files but forgot to save them? They are actually stored in the cache folder. Choose Find Files or Folders from the Windows 95 Start menu. Search for files named *.wav (or whatever format you are looking for) in the "c:\windows\temporary internet files" folder. Be sure the option Include subfolders is checked. This will display all files with the .wav format that are in any of the cache folders. When the search is complete, double-click the name of the files to play them. When you find the file that you want, copy it to a permanent folder using Windows 95 Explorer.

Tip: When a file is downloading, you don't have to just sit there and watch the blue bar grow. You can open a second window and browse the Net some more. Click back from time to time to see how the download is progressing, but don't let it stop your exploration! For information on opening multiple windows, refer back to Chapter 4.

ZIP AND OTHER FILE TYPES

You may have noticed that the file I downloaded in the above example was called winzip95.exe. You may have also heard of zipped files. WinZip is one of many shareware programs used to zip and unzip files. *Zipping* is another word for compressing in computer lingo. *Unzipping* or *extracting* are terms used to describe the uncompressing of zipped files. Why zip a file? If you have downloaded many files, you know how slow this can be. Even at 28.8, a 1MB file takes three minutes to download in perfect conditions. Many files are much larger than 1MB, and conditions are rarely perfect, so to decrease the time it takes to download, the files are zipped. Zipping works differently on different types of files. Some can be greatly compressed while others will not shrink at all. Some zipped files are made up of many combined files while others are just single files. In most cases, zipping does reduce the size of the files, thus reducing downloading time.

What do you do when you download a zipped file? If it is self-extracting, with an .exe extension, you can simply run it after it has been saved in the desired folder. It will unzip itself so you can install the program that was contained within. If it is a .zip file, however, you need an unzip program to extract the files for you. These are fairly common on the Net. PKZip/PKUnZip and WinZip are two of the more popular choices. Get one of them or buy a commercial version (several are available). You will definitely need it.

Some files you find may be in a binary format. That is, they have been transferred, or encoded, into a format that can be transmitted over the Internet. If you try to view binary files, their content looks like gibberish. These files are most often found on the Usenet groups, but files attached to e-mail messages are also encoded. To view these files, you need a decoding program. Usenet files are encoded using a process called uuencode and decoded using uudecode. Uuencode/uudecode can also be used for e-mail attachments, but a different format, MIME, is used more often. If you wish to post a picture to a newsgroup or send a file along with an e-mail message, you need an encoding program.

As with zip utilities, there are many shareware and freeware encoding/decoding programs on the Net. The most common use for binary encoding, however, is Usenet and e-mail attachments, so you may never need a separate program from your newsreader and e-mail reader. Microsoft Internet Mail and News is a combined newsreader/e-mail reader that will automatically encode and decode binary files. This is an excellent option, and it is available from the Microsoft Internet Explorer Web site. Microsoft Exchange, which comes with Windows 95, will encode and decode e-mail attachments. Chapters 9 and 10 cover e-mail and newsgroups in more detail.

Stopping a Download

Occasionally, you may want to stop the download before it is completed (if you have to leave before it can finish, or if you realize that you are downloading the wrong file). Fear not. The Cancel button (seen in Figure 6.2) will stop the download and return you to the Web page. It may not respond instantly (it might have to finish a cycle), but it will eventually stop.

SAVING AND PRINTING WEB PAGES

Sometimes you may come across a page that is so detailed and contains so much information that you don't have the time to go through it all at once. Normally you could save it to Favorites and return to it later. Let's say, though, that you really need the information, but you have to catch a plane. Because you can't connect to the Internet on a plane (yet), how can you take the information with you? If you have a notebook computer that you were planning to take with you on the flight, you can save the Web page to disk and copy it to that computer. If you have no portable computer, you can print out a hard copy to take along.

Saving a Web Page to Disk

This is really a straightforward procedure. From the file menu, select Save As File. You will then see the window shown in Figure 6.5, which is similar to the window shown after a download is completed. From this window, you name the file and choose a folder in which to save it. You will usually give the file an .html extension, although if you will be using this file on a Windows 3.1 computer, save it as .htm just to be safe (not all Windows 3.1 programs can read a file with a four-digit extension).

When the page is saved to disk, you can copy it to a floppy and generally treat it like any other file. The page can be viewed through Internet Explorer or most other browsers. If you have an HTML editor,

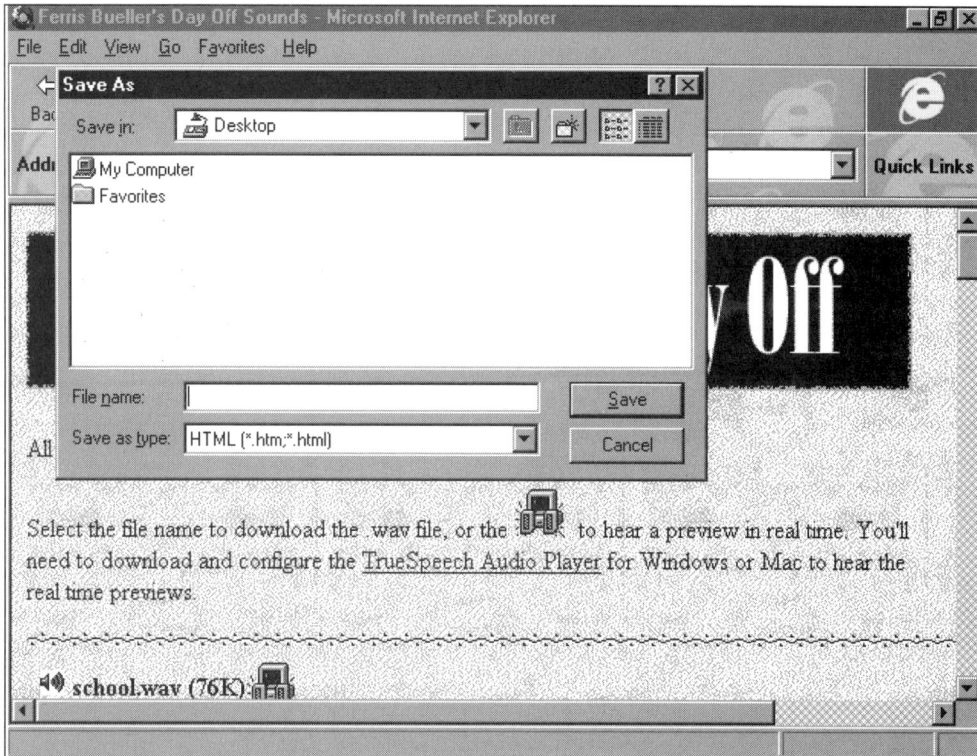

Figure 6.5: Saving a Web page to disk.

you may be able to view the page using its preview option. When working with a saved page, you can print, copy, cut, and paste items just as if you were on-line (keep reading for more info on these), view the source HTML code, and generally move about it like normal. One obvious difference, however: you cannot use the links! "Of course not," you say! But the page will act and feel just as if it were on-line, though, so don't be surprised it you try to click on one of the links! I suppose you could save all of the linked pages to disk, too!

Note: Whenever you visit an Internet site on-line, Explorer saves that site to your hard disk in the cache folder. That's why pages always load faster after the first time you visit them—they are being loaded off your fast hard disk instead of a slow Internet connection. Theoretically, you could find the file where a Web page is saved in the cache folders and copy it to disk. In reality, this causes some problems. Graphics are not saved within the HTML files in *the cache (each graphic is saved as an individual file), so if you did find the right file, it would have no pictures. Also, there are several cache folders from which to choose. You could search them by using the Windows 95 Find Files or Folders command and searching for *.htm, but this would pull up lots of files. It ends up being much easier to use the Save As File command. For more information on the cache folders, see Chapter 7.*

Printing a Web Page

If you need a hard copy of a Web page, again, it is an easy process. You can select Print from the icon bar or Print from the file menu. If you would like to change your printing options, select Print Setup from the file menu. You will see the window shown in Figure 6.6, where you can change the paper orientation, margins, and other standard Windows printing options.

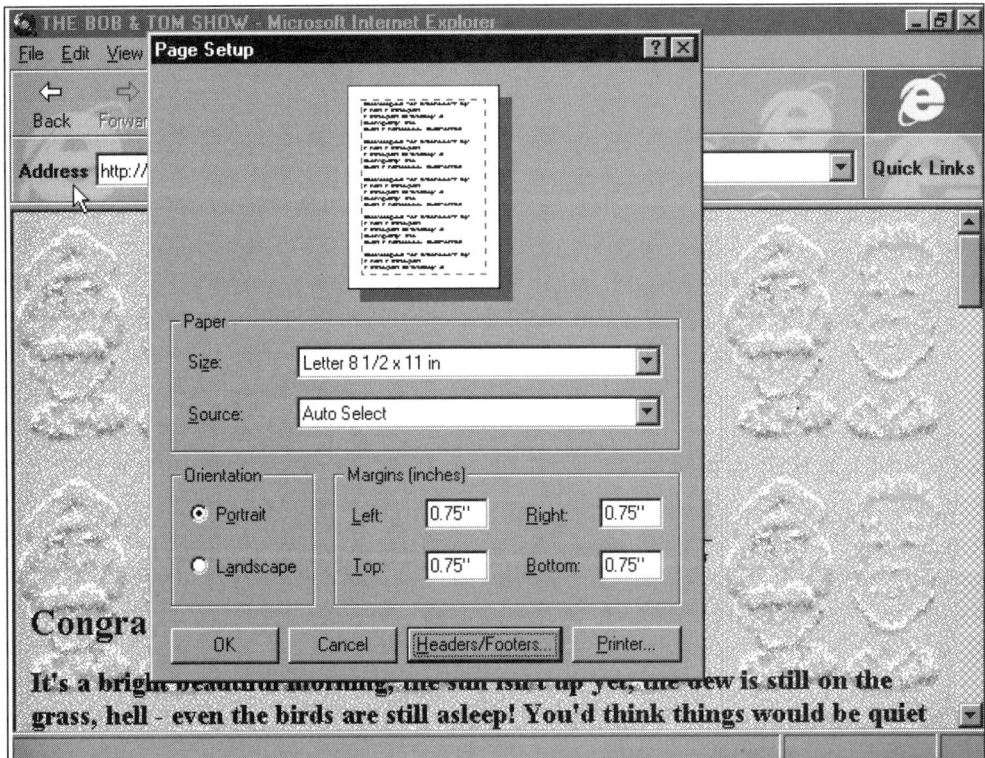

Figure 6.6: Print Setup options.

The Print icon and the File Print commands will bring up the window shown in Figure 6.7. This is a standard Windows print screen except for one difference. Notice at the bottom of the screen there is a Shortcuts section. By selecting this option, all of the links contained within the page will be listed in a table format at the bottom of the printout. This is a very convenient way to check all of the links contained within a page even if your print quality isn't good enough to display some of the graphic hyperlinks.

COPYING ITEMS FROM A WEB PAGE

If you see a part of a Web page that's useful but don't want to copy the entire page to disk or print it, you can select what you want and copy only it. This includes text and images. This is accomplished by using the Windows clipboard or, in the case of images, saving directly as a

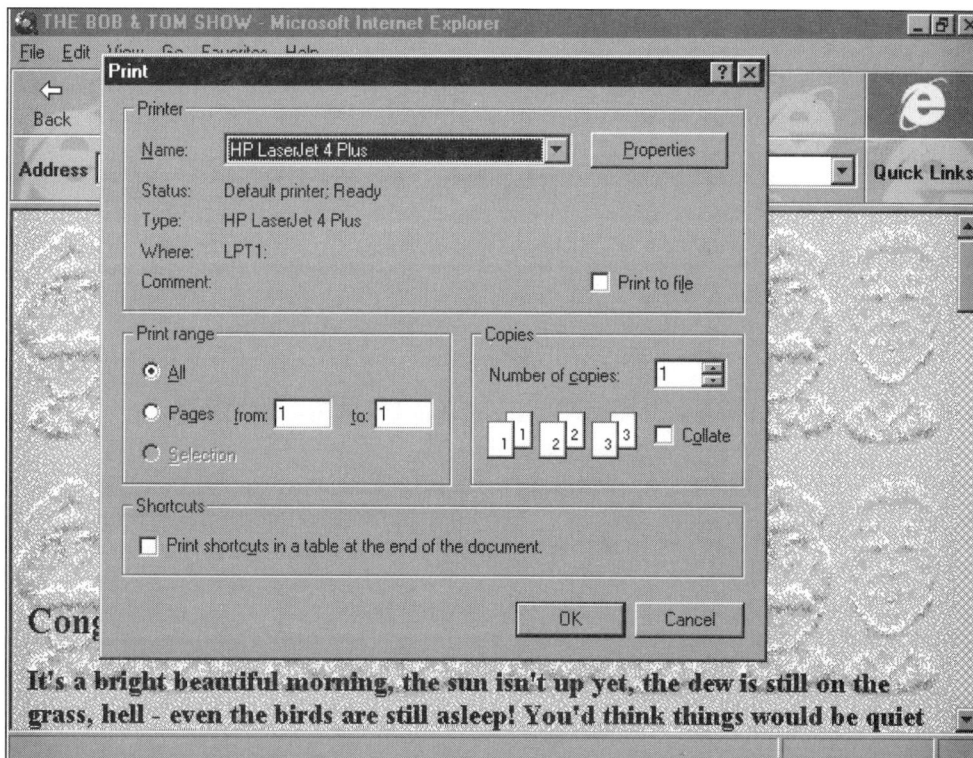

Figure 6.7: Print window—notice the Shortcuts option at the bottom.

file. Remember that much of the material on the Web is copyrighted, so always get permission before using any text or images.

Copying Text

You can copy text using the Windows clipboard. When you see a portion of a Web page that you like, highlight the text that you want, as shown in Figure 6.8. Highlighting is done by left-clicking the mouse and dragging the cursor over the text. Release the left button when you have highlighted everything you want to get. In Figure 6.8, I have highlighted some text from the Discovery Channel Web site.

Once the text is highlighted, right-click and choose Copy from the pop-up menu, or select Edit Copy from the menu bar. This copies the selected text to the clipboard, where it can be pasted (using the Paste command) into another document. If you don't know where you want to copy it, open the Notepad or Wordpad and paste it there for later use.

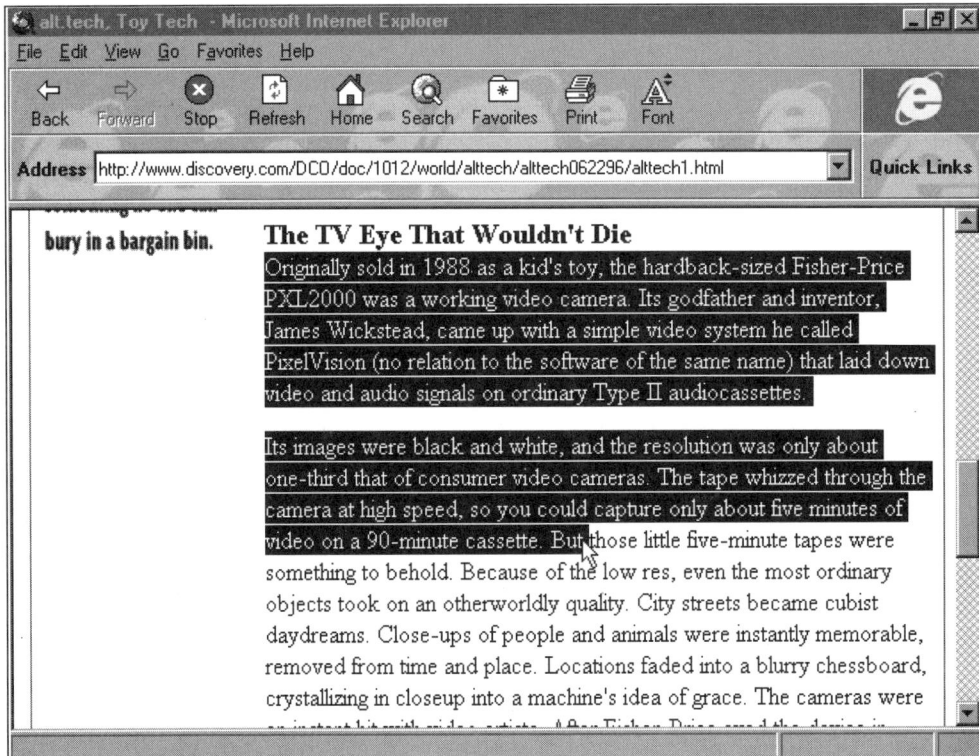

Figure 6.8: Highlighting text to copy.

Copying Images

Images (sometimes called inline images or inline graphics) that are used in Web pages can also be copied, even if the image is being used as a link. The right-clicking feature of Explorer comes in handy here. To save an image as a file, right-click that image and select Save Picture As. If the image you want to save is being used as the page's background, then select Save Background As. This will open a window that looks just like the Save As windows shown in Figures 6.3 and 6.5. Name the file and choose a folder. It is now on your hard drive!

Another way to copy images is to copy them to the clipboard. Right-click the image and select Copy (or Copy Background). This places the image on the clipboard, where it is ready to be pasted into another document.

Copying Images to Use as Wallpaper

Wallpaper is the background image on the Windows desktop. If you still have a plain background, then you haven't lived! If you see an image on the Web that you think would make great wallpaper for your desktop, right-click the image (or the background itself) and select Set As Wallpaper. This will copy the file to the Windows folder, name it Internet Explorer Wallpaper.bmp, and automatically set it up as your wallpaper. (If you don't believe me, then minimize Explorer and check for yourself!)

Note: If you see another image on the Net that you would like to make wallpaper later, be warned that it will overwrite the Internet Explorer Wallpaper.bmp file. If you want to save the previous wallpaper, be sure to rename it before you grab the new one.

Tip: Only choose simple images for your wallpaper. If you choose a fancy design with 65,000 colors, you'll never be able to find your Shortcuts!

GRAPHICS FORMATS

Three main graphic image formats are used on the Web: .gif, .jpg, and .bmp. There are many other graphic extensions in use (.TIF, .pcx, .EPS, and lots more), but they are not generally used in Web design. Internet Explorer has the capability to display all three types of files, as well as the new animated .gif format now in use. This means that not only can Explorer display these images when you are browsing the Web, but it can also be used as a viewer when you are off-line. If you need to view one of these types of files, load Explorer and type the file's location on your hard drive (for example, c:\windows\clouds.bmp) in the Address bar. Either Explorer will display the file or Paintbrush will automatically load to display the file (depending on the file type and any other program associations that file may have).

WHAT'S AHEAD?

- Change settings and customize Explorer in Chapter 7
- Learn about multimedia on the Web in Chapter 8
- Learn all about sending and receiving e-mail in Chapter 9

CUSTOMIZING EXPLORER

By now you are familiar with the basic operation of Internet Explorer. The earlier chapters have built on a foundation of day-to-day uses and techniques, and now it is time to add more specific information to the mix. Even the most casual user wonders at some point what can be done to improve Explorer's performance or to customize the experience. Perhaps security and privacy are issues as you have explored some of the virtual shopping malls. Maybe you came across some mature sites and wondered if your kids could have been there already.

Now it's time to dive into the "guts" of Explorer and make it work specifically for us. Explorer offers numerous ways to customize its basic operation, interface, speed, and security, all of which can make being on the Net simpler and more enjoyable. By the end of this chapter you will be familiar with some of the more technical details of Explorer, and you will have customized it to work better for you.

KEY POINTS IN THIS CHAPTER

- What purpose does the Options window serve?
- How can I change the toolbar?
- Make it go faster!
- Is it safe to make credit card purchases over the Web?
- How can I keep my children from accessing inappropriate Web sites?

THE OPTIONS WINDOW

The Options window (Figure 7.1) is the control center for Internet Explorer. From here you can customize settings and change some of Explorer's more technical details. Even though some of the features of the Options window have already been discussed (such as changing the start page), this chapter will cover all of the features briefly and some of the features in depth. You can get to the Options window by selecting View Options from the menu bar.

The first detail you will notice is the layout of the menu. It is divided into tabs that represent each section of the menu. To go to the Security section, for example, click the Security tab to display that section on the screen. Another noticeable detail is the Apply button in the bottom right corner of each section. Press this button if you want to see the effects of a change immediately, but you do not want to leave the window. Apply will save any changes you have made and leave the window open; OK will save any changes you have made and close the window.

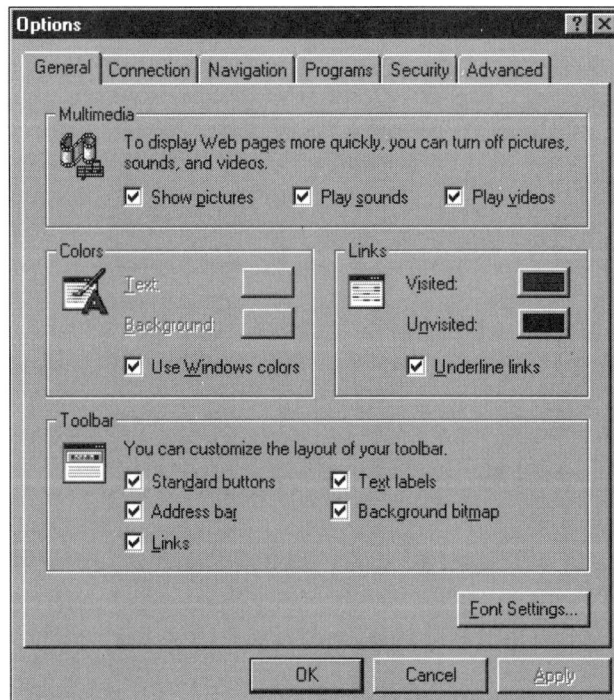

Figure 7.1: The Options window.

General

Figure 7.1 shows the General tab, where the display settings for Web pages are customized. The multimedia section dictates which multimedia aspects of Web pages are loaded. These will be discussed later in this chapter. The Colors and Links sections allow you to change the colors of pages and links, and even let you choose if you want hyperlinks underlined. Making color changes will also be discussed later in this chapter. The Toolbar section is used to change the appearance of Explorer's toolbars (icon bar, address bar, etc.).

Connection

Figure 7.2 shows the Connection tab, which is used to verify and change settings dealing with your Internet connection. If you connect using different ISPs at different times (if you have a work account and a personal account, for example), you can switch between default services.

1. Click on the down arrow near "Use the following Dial-Up Networking connection."
2. Select the service from the list that will appear.
3. Click Apply or OK to save your choice. The next time you launch Explorer, you will use the ISP that was last selected.

Note: In order for this to work, you must already have more than one ISP configured in the Dial-Up Networking section of Windows 95 itself. See Appendix A for information on how to do this. The Add button, described below, will also configure a new ISP.

The Add button lets you add information for a new account or a new modem. The Properties button lets you change access phone numbers for your ISP as well as change your modem type. The Disconnect check box is fairly self-explanatory—it can save you access time if you forget that you are logged on. The "Perform system security check before dialing" check box is used if you share files over a network. It checks to make sure that file sharing is not enabled before connecting to your ISP. If file sharing is turned on, a window will warn you that your files could be accessed by other people on the

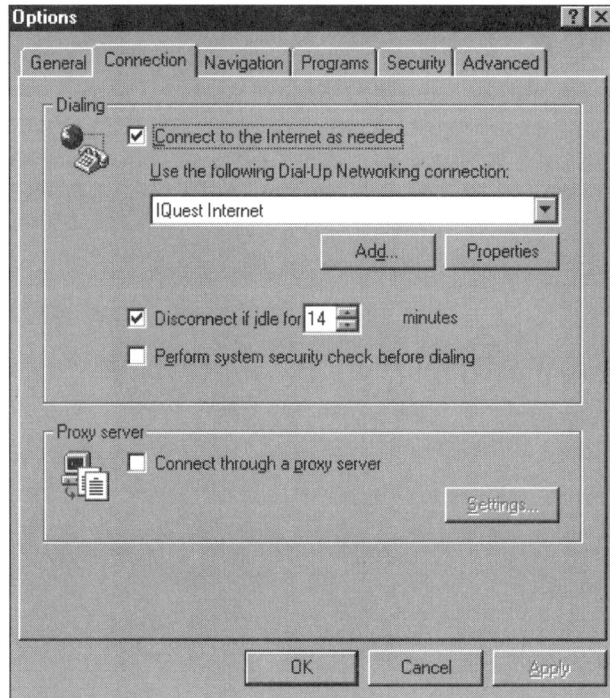

Figure 7.2: Connection tab from the Options window.

Internet! Definitely disable file sharing before connecting. This is not necessary on a stand-alone PC. Finally, Proxy server may be used if you are connecting to the Internet over a local area network. If this is the case, you need to get network settings from your network administrator. If you don't know what proxy means, this probably doesn't apply to you, so leave it alone!

Navigation

The Navigation tab, shown in Figure 7.3, is used to customize your start and search pages and your Quick Links. It is also used to configure your History folder.

Explorer allows you to customize just about everything, and the preset links are no exception. If you don't like where the start page takes you, set your own start page. If you don't like the preset search

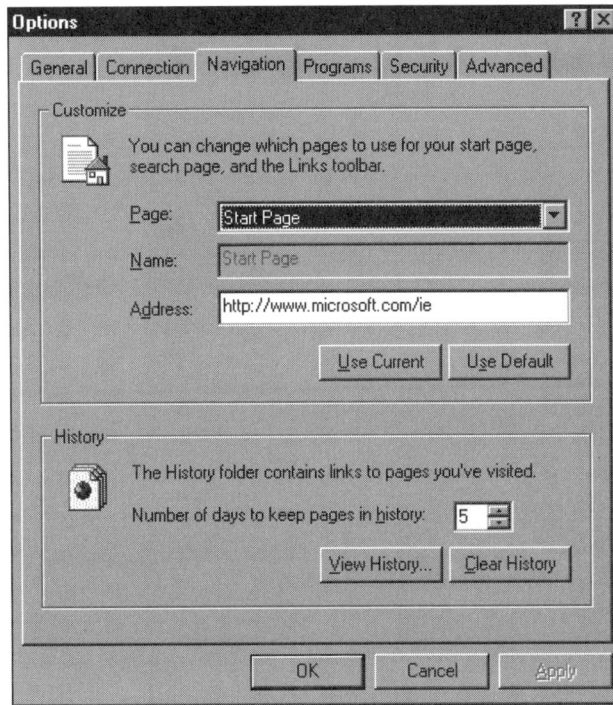

Figure 7.3: Navigation tab from the Options window.

page, reset it to go to a different search engine. And if you find that you never use the Quick Links, make them link to other sites.

To change any of these preset links, click on the down arrow next to Page (as shown in Figure 7.4). Here you can select exactly which link to change. When you have chosen the link to change, you can select the Use Current button if you are already viewing the page you want to be active for that link. If you are not currently at that page, you can type the URL for that page in the Address line. Although the start and search pages cannot be renamed, you can rename the Quick Links to whatever you like on the Name line. If you find that you liked the original preset link better, select the Use Default button to reset the link to the original setting.

The History folder keeps track of the sites you have previously visited. You can change the number of days that the History folder is

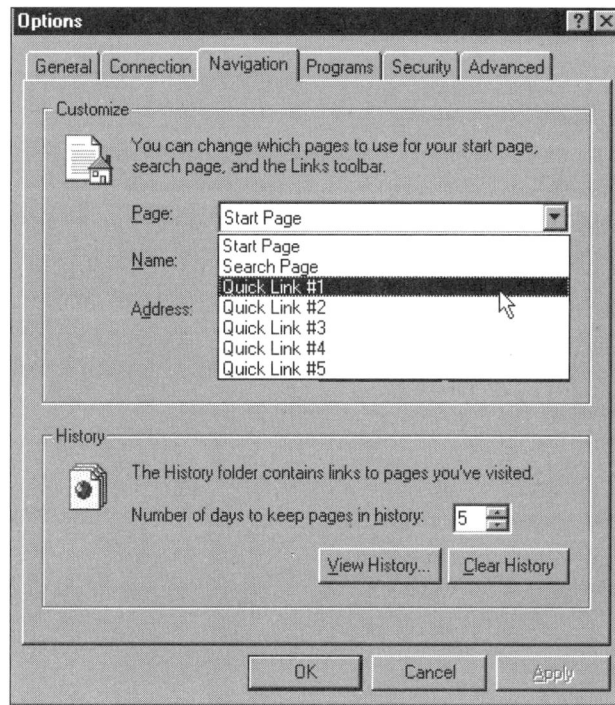

Figure 7.4: Changing Explorer's preset links.

stored in the History section underneath the Customize section. You may want to keep items stored in History for fewer days for security or privacy reasons, or you may be low on hard drive space. View History opens a window showing the sites stored in your History folder. Clear History erases the contents of that folder.

Programs

The Programs tab, shown in Figure 7.5, is used to set the default e-mail program and newsreader. If, for instance, you have a program that you prefer over Internet Mail and News (or if you are required to use a different program at work), you can specify that Explorer launch that program when clicking on a mailto or news link instead of launching Internet Mail and News.

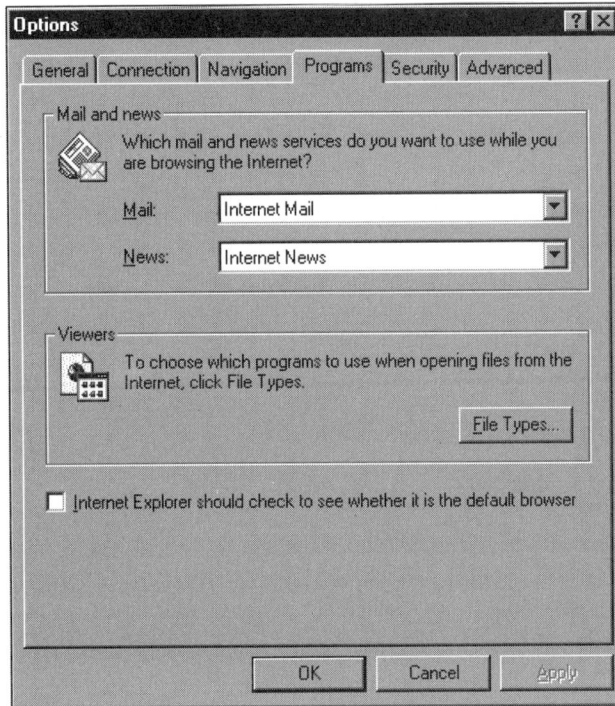

Figure 7.5: Programs tab from the Options window.

The Viewers section is used to configure file associations. For example, when you see a JPEG image, this is the section that defines what program is used to view that file. Chapter 8 will discuss this in detail.

Finally, "Internet Explorer should check to see whether it is the default" should be checked if you have another Web browser installed on your system. This keeps the two browsers from interfering with each other's operation.

Security

Figure 7.6 shows the Security tab. This is the place to change Explorer's settings that will protect your privacy when receiving and viewing information from the Web. These features will be discussed in the Security section later in this chapter. Content Advisor is the ratings system of Explorer and is also covered later in this chapter.

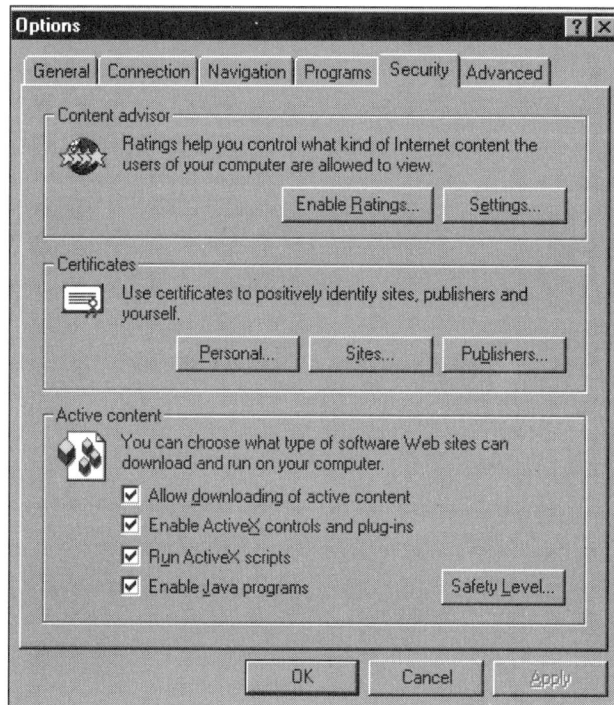

Figure 7.6: Security tab from the Options window.

Advanced

Figure 7.7 shows the Advanced tab. Sounds impressive, doesn't it? The Warnings section allows you to alter the level of security that is offered when you send information over the Internet and set warnings as you encounter possible security threats.

The check boxes at the bottom of the window offer ways to change the methods Internet Explorer uses to display certain pages. Cryptography Settings allow you to change the security protocols used by Explorer. The Temporary Internet files section lets you view the files that are stored in the cache folders with the View Files button. If you see a file that you want to load, you can drag and drop it onto Explorer to load it. The Settings button allows you to specify how often the cache files are updated (and thus how often new versions of Web pages are loaded), how much hard drive space is allotted to the cache, and where the cache is located on your system. These will be discussed in more detail later in this chapter.

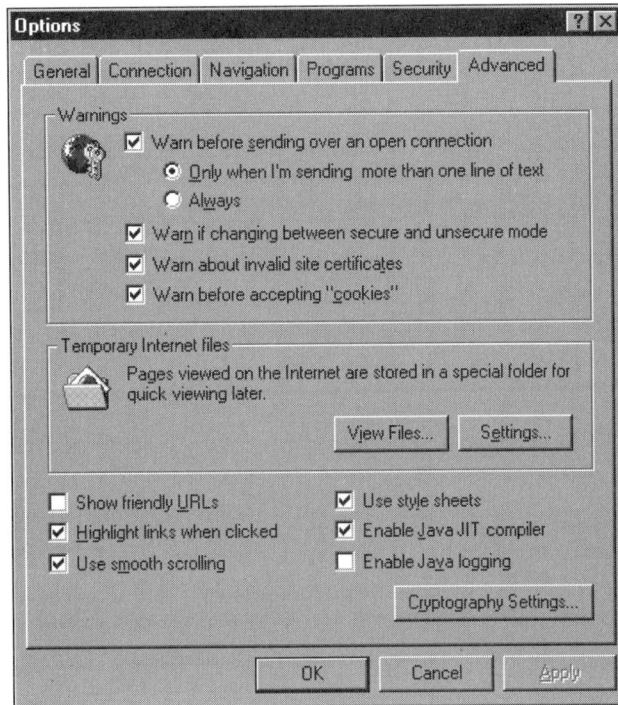

Figure 7.7: Advanced tab from the Options window.

Properties

Figure 7.8 shows the Properties menu. This is not a part of the Options window, although the information contained within is the same. This menu is accessed by right-clicking on the Internet Shortcut on the Windows 95 desktop and selecting Properties from the pop-up menu. This allows you to change Explorer settings without running Explorer.

CHANGING THE APPEARANCE OF EXPLORER

Microsoft made Internet Explorer customizable in many ways to enhance the Internet experience for as many people as possible. Naturally, there are people who don't like the look of the toolbar or

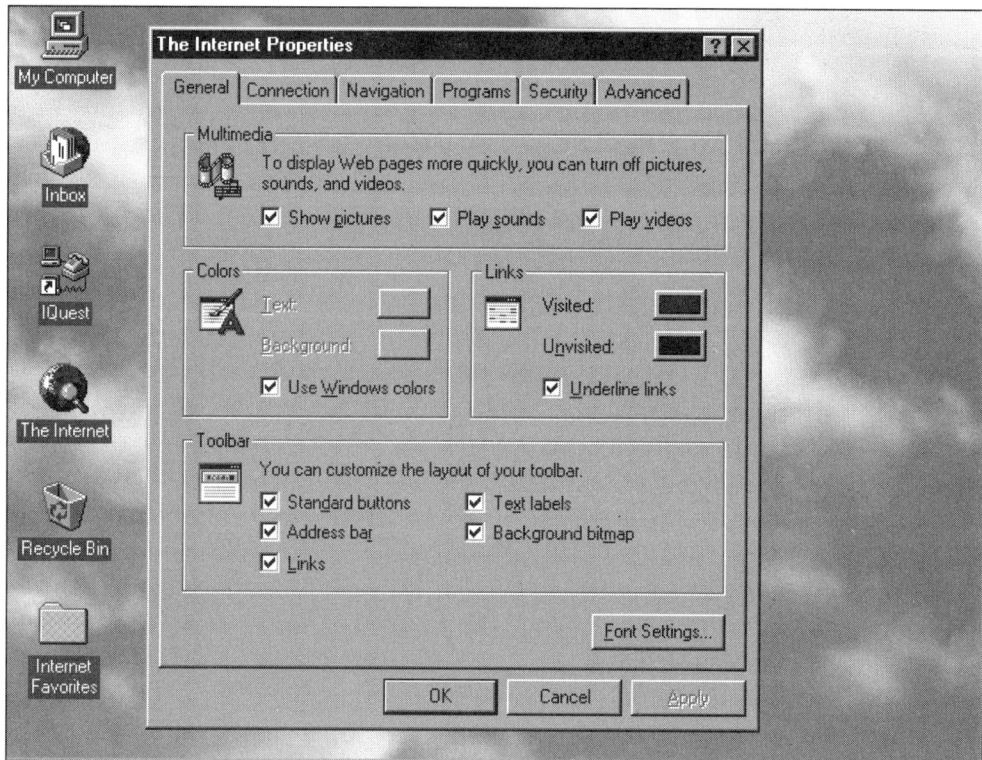

Figure 7.8: Properties menu.

who don't like the layout of the address bar or Quick Links. Explorer is designed to do its best to keep everyone happy!

Customizing the Toolbar

This unique feature allows users to drag portions of the toolbar to different locations. Don't like how the Quick Links are hidden by the address bar? Move them over! Want more room in the viewing window? Move the address bar and Quick Links up with the icon bar! To move a part of the toolbar, position the cursor over the part to be moved. The cursor will change into a hand. Click on the part, drag it to the desired spot, and drop it! Experiment to create your own best toolbar. Figures 7.9 to 7.16 show many of the custom combinations that can be created by moving parts around.

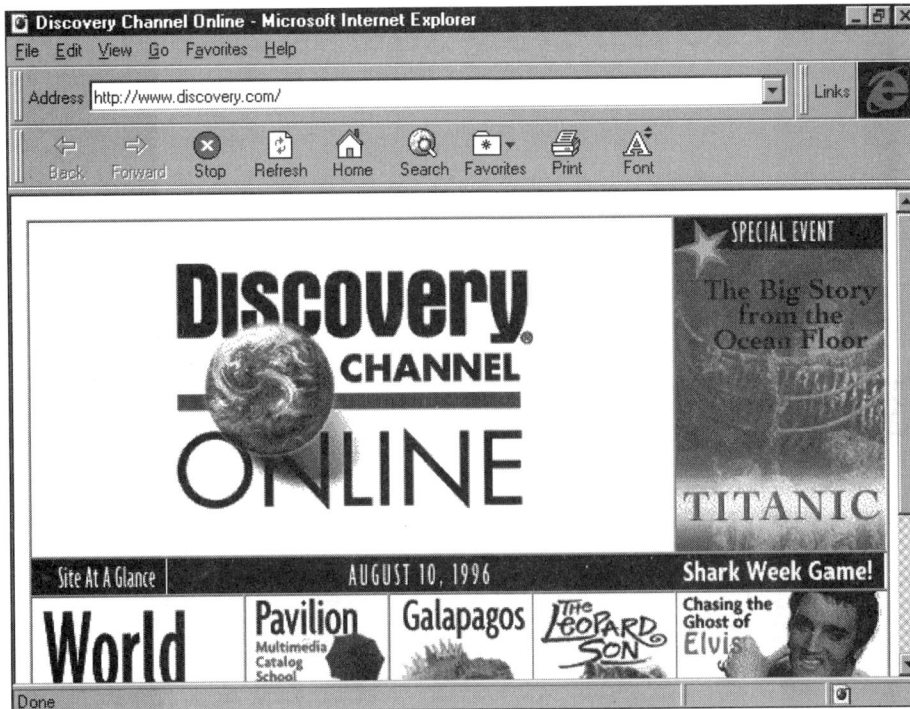

Figure 7.9: Customizing the toolbar—Icon bar down.

The icon bar can be moved if you don't like its original position. In Figure 7.9 I have swapped the places of the icon bar and the address bar.

Figure 7.10 shows one of the first obvious changes in the toolbar: moving the Quick Links over the address bar. If you find yourself using these links more often that manually entering URLs, this is a good choice.

Figure 7.11 shows the address bar sharing space with the Quick Links. Either side can be dragged farther to show more.

The arrangement in Figure 7.12 allows for more viewable room in the viewing window by pulling the address bar and Quick Links up to the icon bar.

Figure 7.13 is a variation on Figure 7.12, with the address bar showing. This does hide some of the icons in the icon bar, but the address bar can be moved around when need be. This is my favorite configuration because it gives more viewing room while still allowing access to what I consider to be the most used features.

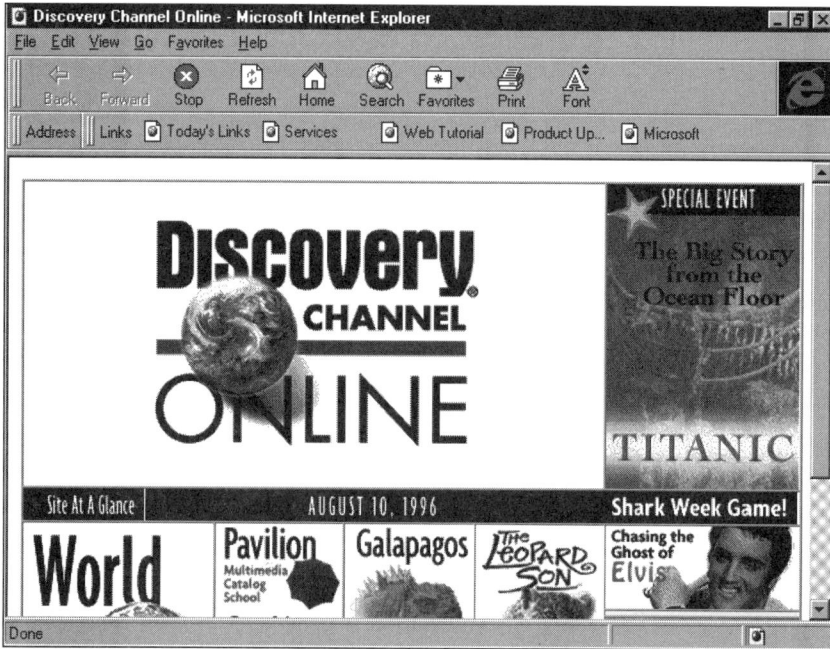

Figure 7.10: Customizing the toolbar—Quick Links over.

Figure 7.11: Customizing the toolbar—half and half.

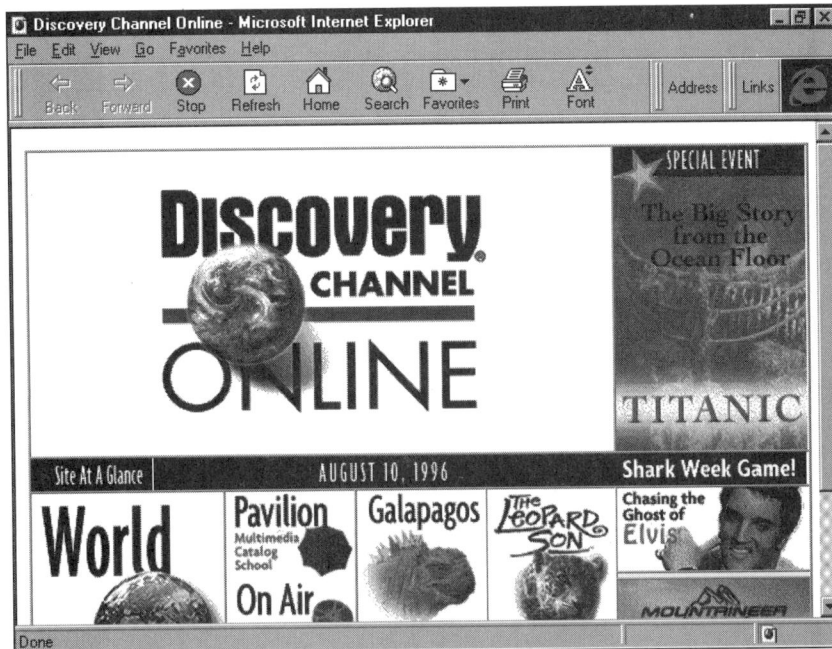

Figure 7.12: Customizing the toolbar—everybody up.

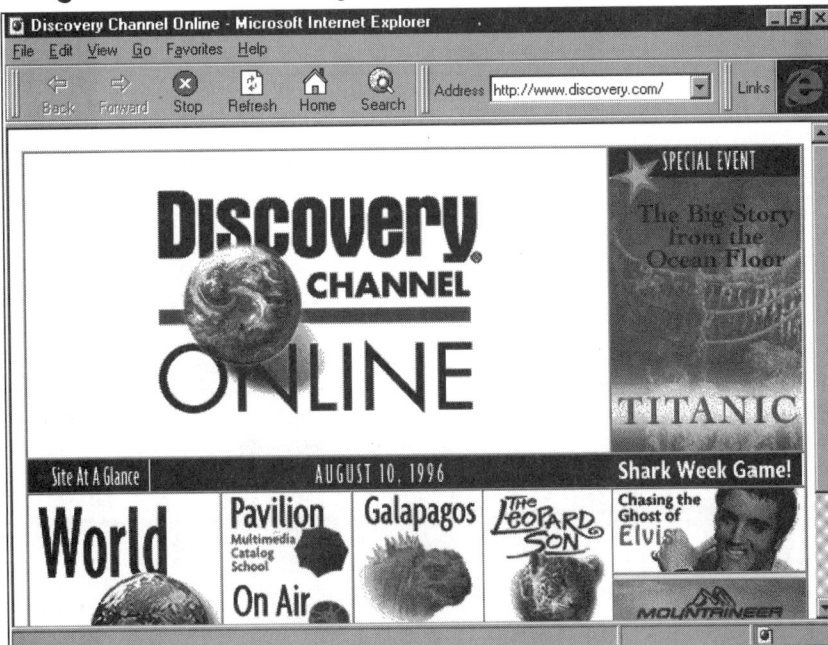

Figure 7.13: Customizing the toolbar—my personal favorite.

Figure 7.14 is another variation, this time with the Quick Links showing. Personally, I find this one rather awkward.

Figure 7.15 works well for people who use the Quick Links often and still need to see the address bar.

Figure 7.16 is for people who want it all! All portions of the toolbar are completely visible, although the viewing area is diminished slightly.

Allowing for More Viewable Space

Explorer also offers several more radical ways to increase the viewing window: removing the toolbar and removing the status bar. Removing the toolbar eliminates the need for rearranging the address bar and Quick Links because they disappear entirely! This actually opens up a lot of space for viewing Web pages, although most of Explorer's functions must then be accessed through the menu bar. Removing the status bar frees up a little space at the bottom of the screen. Removing the toolbar and address bar is done with the View menu. Click on

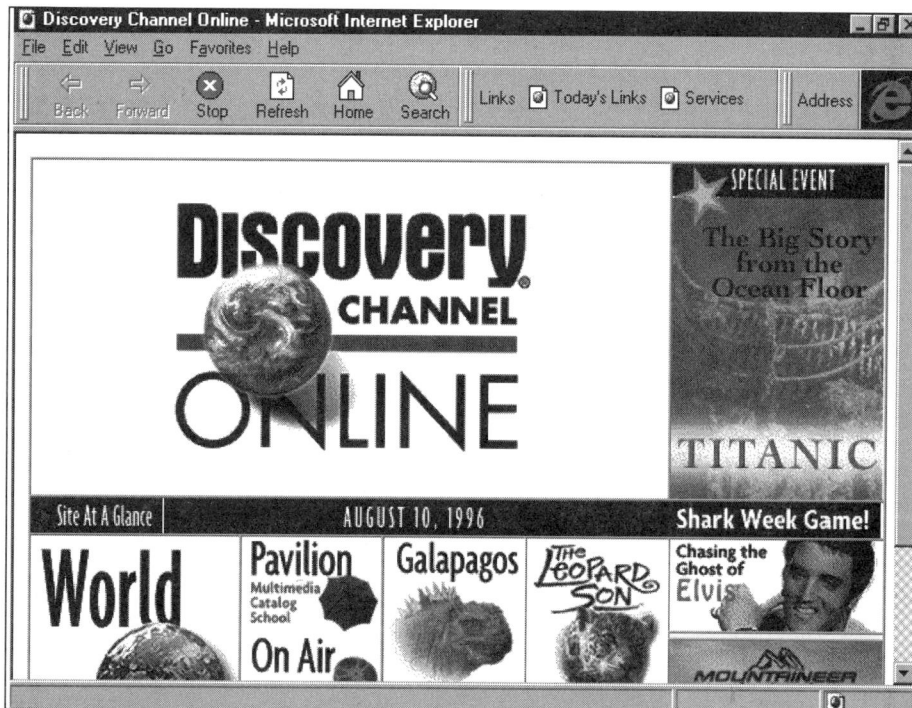

Figure 7.14: Customizing the toolbar—another variation.

Figure 7.15: Customizing the toolbar—address high, Quick Links low.

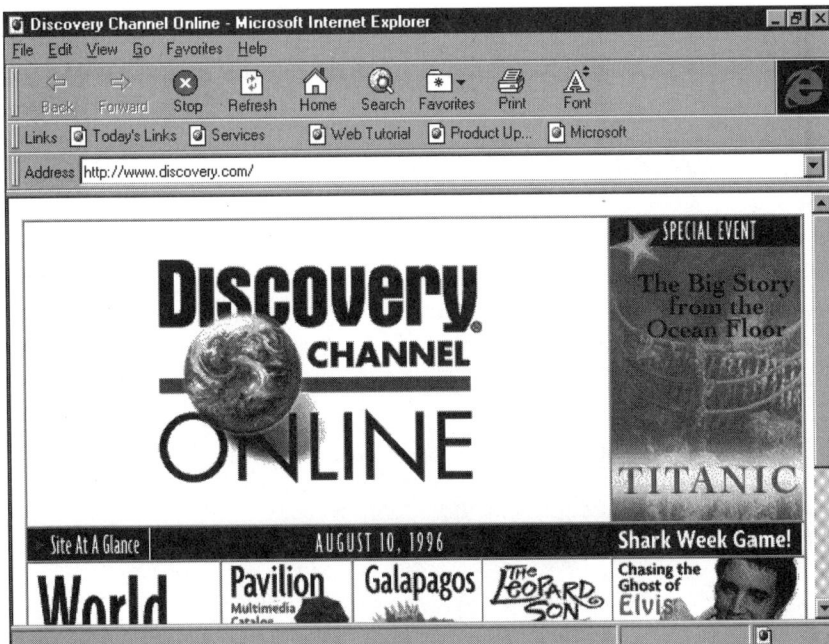

Figure 7.16: Customizing the toolbar—three tiered.

toolbar or status bar to remove them. A check mark shown next to them indicates that they are displayed. The check mark will disappear when they disappear.

Tip: I wouldn't recommend removing either the toolbar or the status bar. By eliminating them, you are eliminating many of the features that make Explorer so easy to use. One less radical option is to remove the Windows 95 taskbar (the gray bar at the bottom of the screen with the word Start in the left corner).

1. *Right click on the Taskbar to open a pop-up menu.*
2. *Select Properties to open the Taskbar Properties window.*
3. *Check the box next to Auto hide.*
4. *Click OK.*

The taskbar is now hidden from view. It will appear only when you move your cursor to the very bottom of the screen, thus saving a bit of viewing area for Web pages.

CHANGING THE APPEARANCE OF WEB PAGES

Besides changing the toolbar, Explorer gives you the option of changing the way pages themselves are viewed. Font size and color selection can be changed—font size through the icon bar's Font icon, and color selection through the General tab in the Options window (View, Options, General).

Changing Font Size

Why change font size? For a number of reasons, actually. For instance, if a page is too large to fit into your viewing window, reducing the size of the fonts will allow you to see more of that page without having to

use the scroll bars. If the Web author has chosen a font that is too small to be comfortably viewed, increasing the size may improve visibility.

The Font icon is the tool used to change font size instantly. The standard setting is Medium. Clicking the Font icon once changes to Large. Twice changes to Largest. Three times skips down to Smallest. Four times changes to Small. Five times returns to Medium. If you have changed your toolbar to cover the Font icon, you can access font size from the View Font menu. Change font size by clicking on the desired size. A check mark will appear next to the selected size in the Font menu.

Color Selection

As I mentioned in Chapter 4, I believe it is best to leave the color settings alone. Web authors try to match the colors of their links to the background images, and if you change the defaults in Explorer, you could make some links very difficult to see. For those of you who must change the colors anyway, here's how.

1. Select the General tab from the View Options window.
2. Uncheck the box next to "Use Windows colors."
3. Click the boxes for Text, Background, Visited links, and Unvisited links. When each box is clicked, another window appears, this one showing color options.
4. Click a color and select OK.
5. Select Apply or OK from the General tab when your color selection is complete.

SPEEDING THINGS UP

We all want more speed when it comes to the Internet. The main problem with being on-line, it seems, is the amount of time it takes for pages to load and files to download. As with everything else, Explorer offers several options for improving speed.

Upgrade

This is a word that everyone hears at some point in the life of his or her computer system. And it's always good advice (cost notwithstanding).

If you are using a 14.4kbps modem, get a 28.8. Some 28.8 modems can actually do 33.6kbps, although that depends on the quality of connection and the remote modem being accessed. If you want a dramatic improvement in speed, upgrade to an ISDN line. This is a newer type of line that has much higher speed capability than standard phone lines. Of course, it will cost extra to have your phone company install the ISDN line, not to mention the monthly charges that will apply. Coaxial cable modems (using the same type of line that cable TV uses) are even faster than ISDN, downloading in seconds files that take minutes on ISDN! But they are not widely available yet.

Removing Pictures and Sounds

For those of us for whom it is not possible or practical to upgrade, Explorer does offer several options for speeding things along. The first option to change is the page contents. Referring back to Figure 7.1, there are three options on the General tab of the Options menu: Show pictures, Play sounds, Play videos. Removing the check next to any or all of these will improve the speed of surfing noticeably.

Pictures Figure 7.17 shows a typical Web page with all pictures loaded. But these pictures take time to download, and if you are in a hurry, you might not want to wait. Large pictures like the one of the basketball players take an especially long time to load, even with Explorer's progressive drawing feature that loads images in low resolution and updates them gradually. (Not all Web pages use images that support this feature, anyway.) One obvious way around this problem is to avoid loading the pictures in the first place.

Deselecting Show pictures in the General tab prevents any image from being displayed. In their places are small boxes that represent the missing images. These boxes can be seen in Figure 7.18, which is the same Web page as in Figure 7.17, only without the pictures. Notice that even the background is absent. As plain as this page seems, it takes about a quarter of the time to load.

If you need to see any of the pictures that were left out, you can right-click on the boxes that appear in their places and select Show Picture from the pop-up menu. This will load that single selected image. This is demonstrated in Figure 7.19.

Note: Things get a little weird when you turn pictures off and visit a site that you had previously viewed with the pictures on. Because that site is stored on

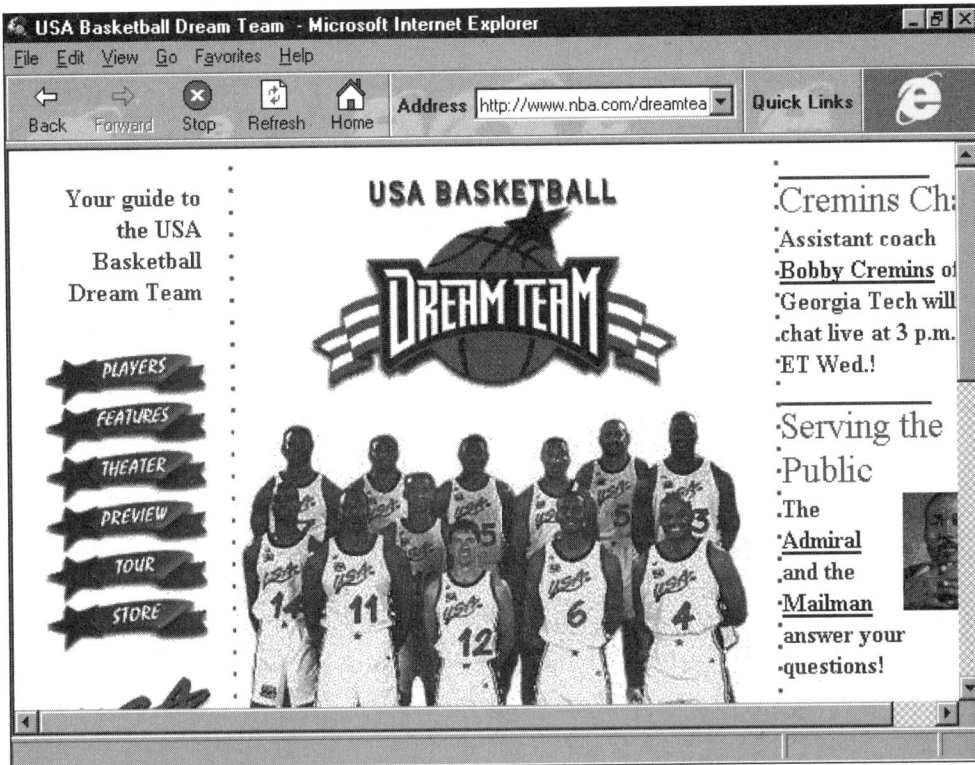

Figure 7.17: An average Web page with all images loaded.

your hard drive (read ahead about the cache for more info), the pictures will load even when they are supposed to be turned off. This is okay, though. These pictures will load much more quickly from your hard drive than from the Net, so Explorer shows them no matter what your settings say.

Sounds and Video Sounds and video images are becoming more commonly used as Web authors try to make their sites more enjoyable and memorable. As with pictures, loading these elements can also significantly slow down page access time. Videos especially take a tremendous time to load, and they can still be loading even after you've read everything else on the page! Turning these off, using the same steps as for turning pictures off, can speed the loading process along nicely.

The question that is most important when deciding which aspects of multimedia not to load is what kind of experience are you after? If

USA Basketball Dream Team - Microsoft Internet Explorer

File Edit View Go Favorites Help

Back   Forward   Stop   Refresh   Home   Address http://www.nba.com/dreamtea   Quick Links

Your guide to
the USA
Basketball
Dream Team

Follow the
USAB Women's
National Team

Cremins Ch:
Assistant coach
Bobby Cremins of
Georgia Tech will
chat live at 3 p.m.
ET Wed.!

Serving the
Public
The
Admiral
and the
Mailman
answer your
questions!

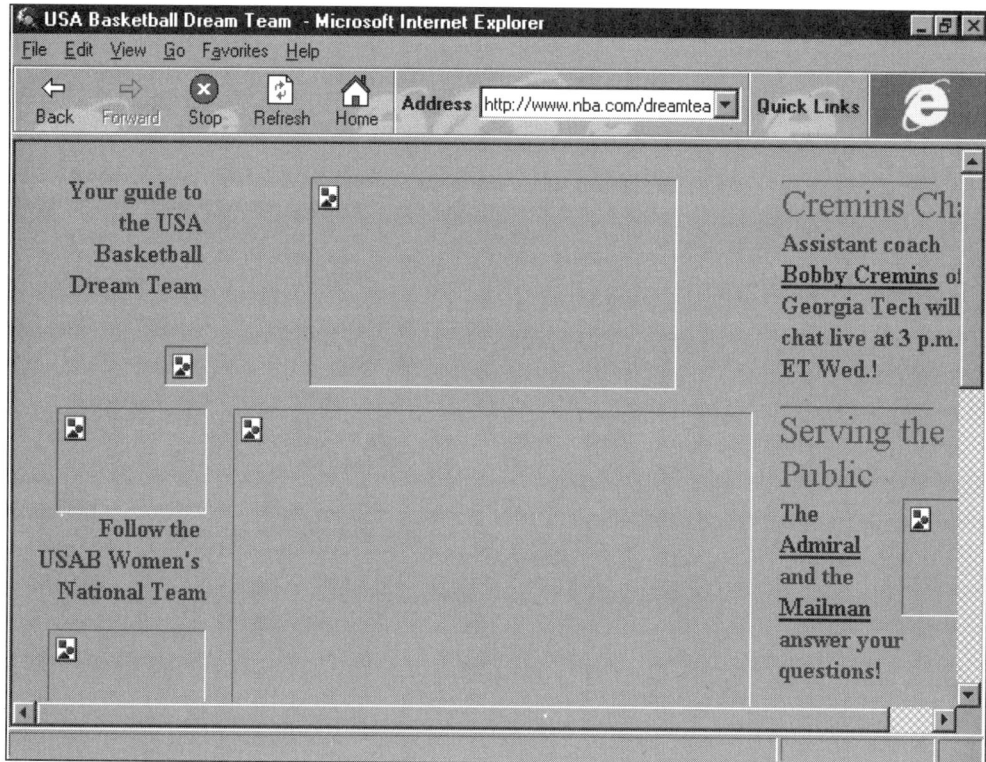

Figure 7.18: The same Web page with pictures turned off.

you are on an all-out mad dash to collect information, you may never miss that cool video clip or the picture of a company's headquarters. On the other hand, if you are browsing the Web to experience the multimedia side of the Internet, then you may find that an extra minute is worth the wait.

Cache Only, Please

A cache (pronounced *kash*), as defined by *Webster's Ninth New Collegiate Dictionary*, is a secure place of storage. Explorer uses a cache as a storage place for copies of all the files that are viewed and downloaded during your browsing. Its main purpose is to improve speed. A file loaded from your computer's hard drive will load significantly

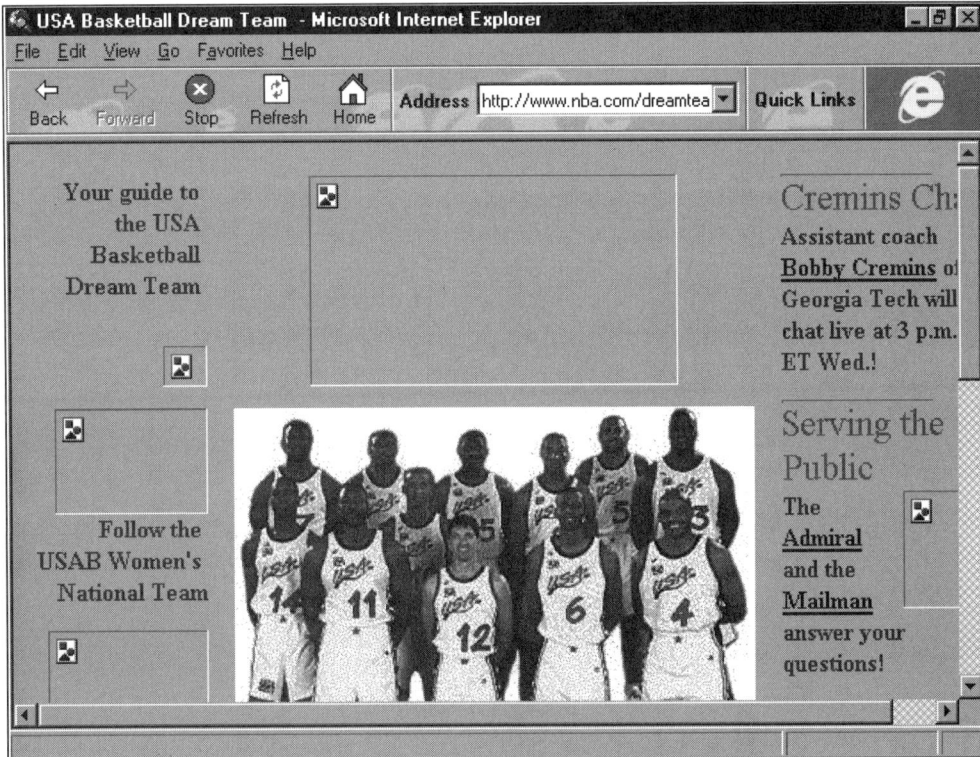

Figure 7.19: The same Web page with one picture selected.

faster than from a remote server's hard drive transmitted over an Internet connection. You have probably noticed during your browsing that pages that you have visited previously load much faster than the first time you saw them. You may have also noticed that if you launch Explorer for a second time without turning off your computer that the start page will load (as will any other pages that were visited on your last Net outing) without making a connection with your ISP. Both are a result of the cache, which has stored the HTML files, the images, the sounds, and every aspect of the pages you visit. When you access a site, Explorer checks to see if the cache contains that site's files. If it does (and if those files have not changed), it loads the files from the cache rather than from the Net.

The cache, by default, is located on your c: drive in the Windows folder. It is a group called Temporary Internet Files, and it is made up of five folders: Temporary Internet Files itself and cache1 to cache4. Figure 7.20 shows the contents of the Temporary Internet Files folder on my computer as viewed through the Advanced tab of the Options window.

One of the options you will see in Figure 7.20 is the Move Folder button. If, for instance, you are running low on hard drive space, you can move the location of the Temporary Internet Files folder to a second hard drive to avoid having to decrease the amount of storage space allotted to your cache. This will result in better performance when returning to previously viewed pages. Figure 7.21 shows the window that is displayed to help you move the Temporary Internet Files folder.

Tip: You can also view files in the cache folders by double-clicking on them in Windows 95 Explorer (which will launch Internet Explorer or a viewer program) or by entering c:\temporary Internet files\cache1 in the address bar of

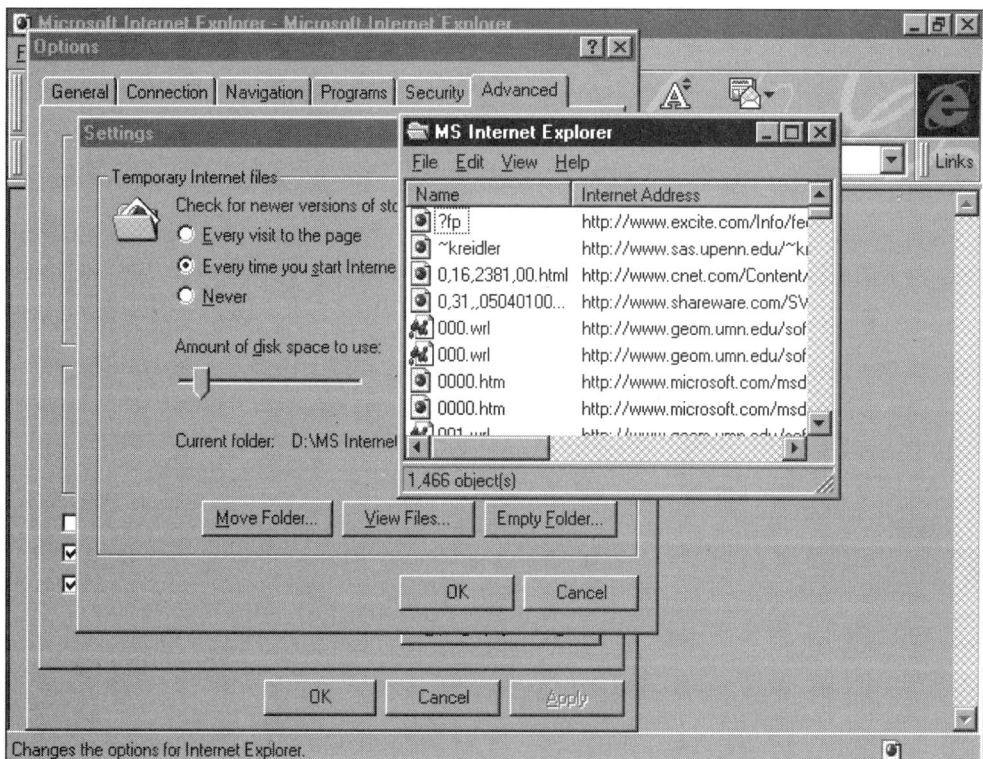

Figure 7.20: The Temporary Internet Files folder.

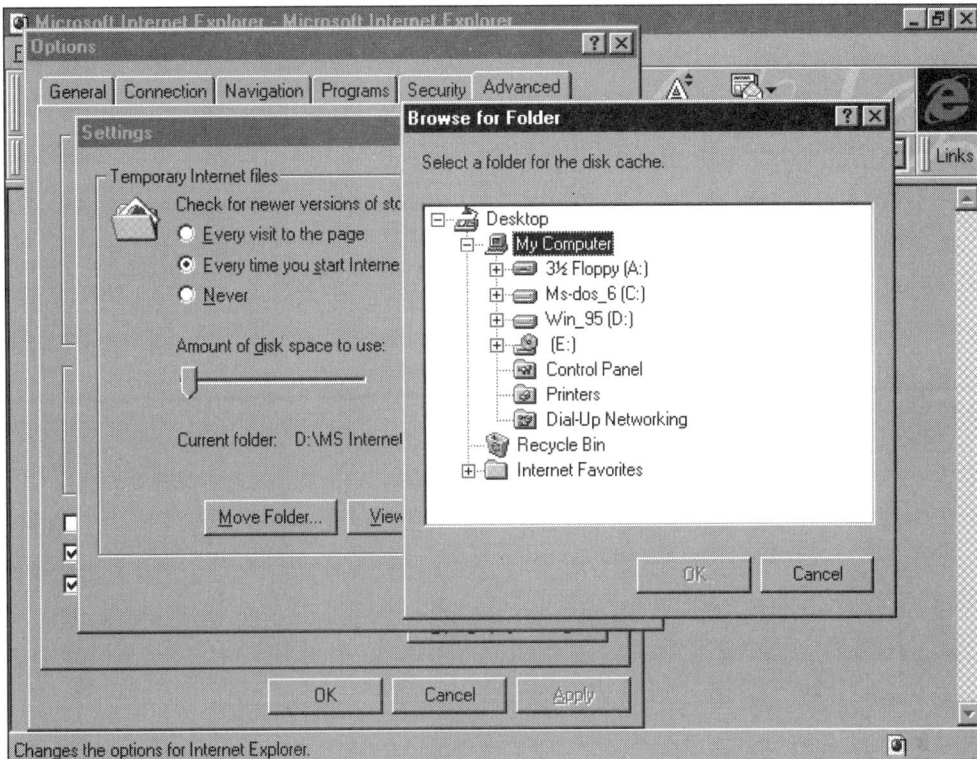

Figure 7.21: The cache1 folder.

*Internet Explorer and double-clicking on the file to load. In fact, this is some-
times a good way to find files that you forgot to save while on-line. Finding
the correct file is just a matter of separating the file types and checking the
dates they were last modified. The Find command from the Windows 95 Start
menu is good for this. If you load an HTM or HTML file from the cache, bear
in mind that it will load without any pictures or sounds. The cache breaks up
all files, so all of the images are stored separately from the main HTML file.*

Changing Cache Size Changing the size of the cache will affect the
speed of Net surfing. As the available cache space is filled, old files are
replaced with new files. Decreasing the size of the cache will decrease
the chances of having files from previously viewed sites available,
thus slowing down access time. Therefore, decreasing the cache below

the default 10% is not recommended unless you really need the space. As a general rule, using 10% of your available hard drive space for the cache is standard, but if you have a large drive with lots of space, you may wish to increase the cache size further to improve the chances of having files ready to load.

To change the amount of space reserved for the cache, refer back to Figure 7.20 or Figure 7.21. Slide the bar found in the middle of the window. Here you also have the option to view the files in the cache, move the cache folder (maybe to a bigger drive), or empty the cache folder (to hide where you've been or to really clean out your hard drive). Remember that emptying the cache folder will mean that every page will have to load from the Net until the cache is built up again.

Updating Pages Because Web pages are being changed constantly, Explorer needs to know if it should compare the version of the page on the Net with the version in the cache so it can pick the newer of the two. By selecting one of the options under "Check for newer versions of stored pages" in Figure 7.20, you tell Explorer to do this. But how often? "Every visit to the page" means that Explorer will make this comparison each time you log on to a page. If the version of the file on the Net is the newer of the two, it will load it. Otherwise, it will load the file from the cache.

"Every time you start Internet Explorer" will compare pages when you first visit them in a session. If you return to that page during the same session, it will load from the cache and not from the Internet. If you visit pages that are updated frequently (such as news or sports pages), you may have to manually reload them using the Refresh icon.

"Never" tells Explorer just to ignore the whole process, forcing it to load the files from the cache. This is much faster, but you must remember to click the Refresh icon on the toolbar whenever you think that a page has been changed. If you forget, then you could be looking at old information. For example, if you choose "Never" and log on to a sports page on Monday, you will see the very same scores when you connect again on Friday—unless you click Refresh.

Refresh, as you may recall from Chapter 3, forces Explorer to reload the current page from the Web server. When pages aren't updated automatically, this can become especially important to ensure that you are viewing the current page.

SECURITY ON THE NET

As more people look to the Internet as a place to buy goods and services, Internet security becomes more important. Consider this scenario: you find a music CD that you want to buy from an on-line merchant. To place your order, you must enter personal information (such as your address and phone number as well as your credit card number and expiration date) on a form and send it across the Net to the merchant. Much as people with scanners can intercept information passed over a cellular phone network or even conversations held with a cordless phone, devices exist that scan Internet messages for certain patterns such as credit card numbers. When this information is discovered, the file is copied or intercepted and the thief has your personal and financial information.

Because of this problem, Internet security protocols have been developed to make it difficult to observe and intercept Internet messages. These protocols encrypt the message so that only the receiver can decrypt and understand it. Internet Explorer has several safeguards built in that increase the security of on-line transactions, both to insecure and secure sites.

Insecure Sites

An insecure site is identified by the lack of two pieces of information. First, there is no lock icon on the status bar in the bottom right corner of the screen. Second, the merchant has no security certificate, or the certificate is invalid. The lock is easily spotted on screen. The security certificate can be checked, automatically by Explorer or manually. Select File Properties from the menu bar, which will open the Properties window. Click on the Security tab to display security information. Figure 7.22 shows the security information for an insecure site. It is probably best not to send sensitive data to this location.

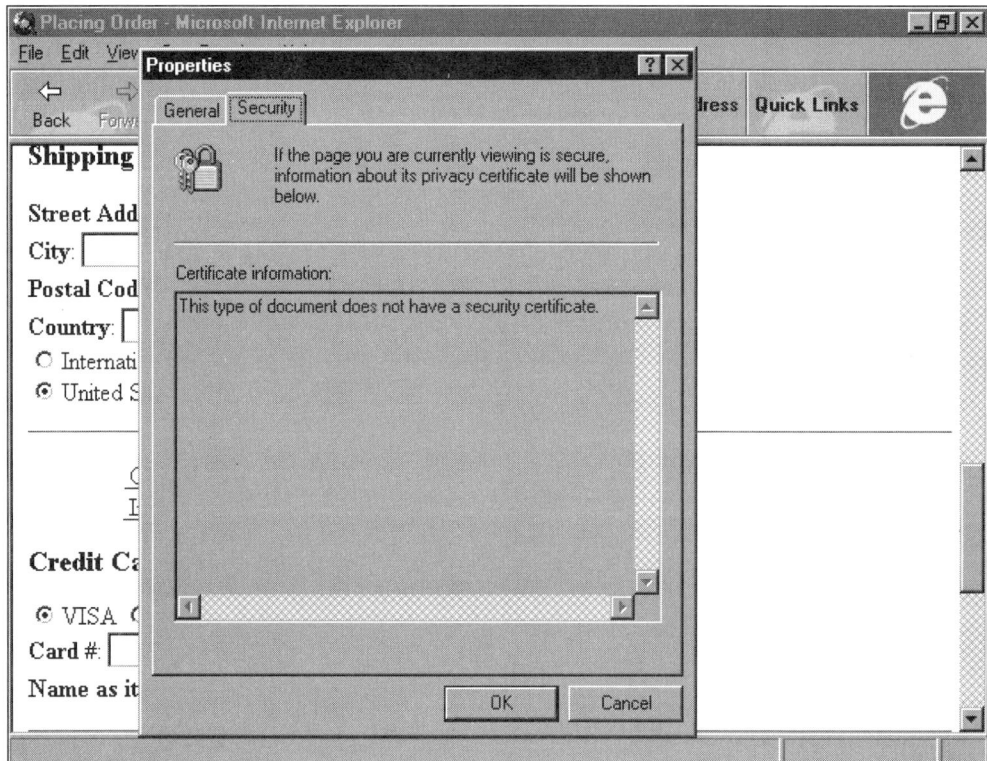

Figure 7.22: An insecure site.

SECURITY CERTIFICATES

Security certificates are a big piece of Internet security. They confirm that you have reached the site that you think you have. For instance, if you want to buy a CD from Acme CD Company, how do you know if you have reached its Web site or an impostor's site? Checking for a security certificate will verify that you have reached Acme and not an impostor.

To have Explorer automatically check for the authenticity of the security certificate and bring any inconsistencies to your attention, refer back to Figure 7.6. The Sites button lists the authorities who issue security certificates. The Publishers button allows you to choose certain companies for which you do not wish to check the certificates. If you trust Microsoft, you may choose to accept anything from them without verifying their certificate. Remember, sites with invalid certificates should be avoided, just to be safe.

Many Web pages have forms that ask for personal information.
Many software and hardware vendors want you to register when visiting their Web sites, and they provide you with a form to fill out and
send. When you send this form to an insecure site, however, other people may be able to see your message. Although there is little that can
be done to prevent this when you are connected to an insecure site,
Explorer can be set to warn you before the message is sent, as shown
in Figure 7.23. Depending on the circumstances, you may reconsider
sending the information.

Refer back to Figure 7.7 to see the Advanced tab on the Options window. This is where you set the standards that Explorer uses to warn
you when sending lines of text over the Net. In general, it is good to
have the "Warn before sending over an open connection" option
checked with "Only when I'm sending more than one line of text"

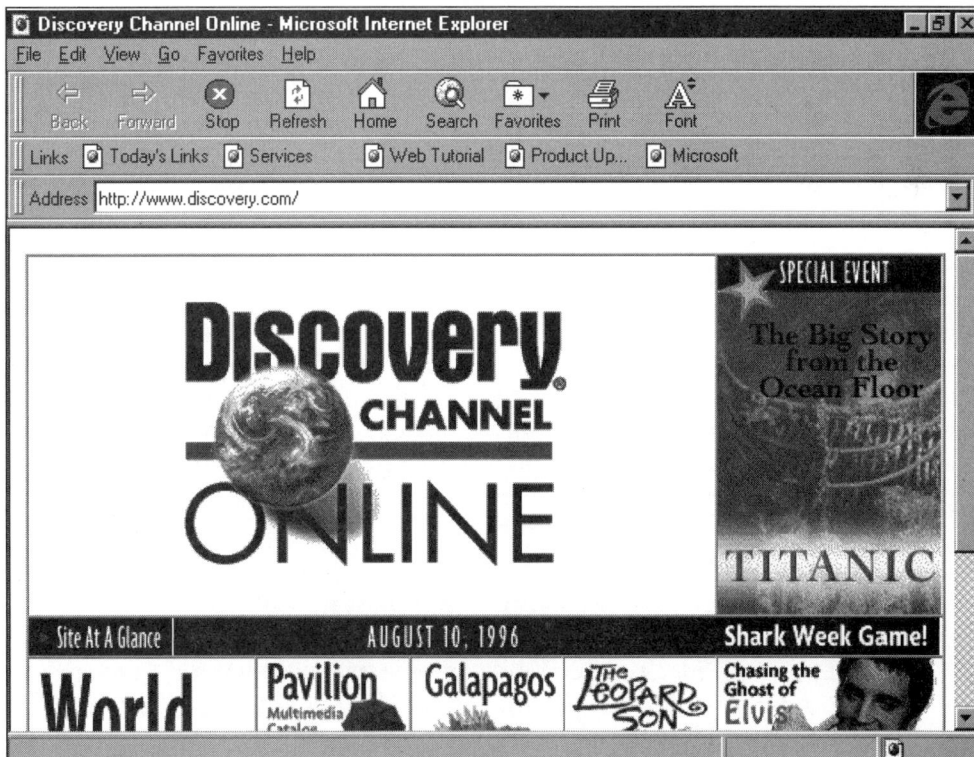

Figure 7.23: Sending a text message to an insecure site.

selected. If you choose Always, Explorer will warn you even if you just enter a password to log on to a site, which can be rather annoying.

It is best to keep the boxes next to "Warn if changing between secure and unsecure mode." "Warn me about invalid site certificates," and "Warn me before accepting 'cookies'" checked. You may have to deal with a few extra dialog boxes, but the security is worth it.

Caution: A "cookie" is a file that a Web site sends to you that gives it information about your system. Generally, this is used just to help the Web site more efficiently display its contents, but the concept could allow for some security concerns. You may want to be cautious when accepting cookies from unfamiliar sites (don't accept candy from strangers!).

Secure Sites

Figure 7.24 shows a standard Web order screen with the lock icon in the bottom right corner of the status bar. Checking for this lock icon is the first step in verifying the security of the site. Step two is done automatically if you followed the directions above for checking security certificates, but you can still check the certificate manually if you wish. Figure 7.25 shows an authentic security certificate. This, in combination with the lock icon, means that this is a secure site, one with which it is safe to do business.

Note: Don't look for a merchant's security certificate on its home page. If you do, you will never find any place safe to shop! The certificate will usually be present only on the actual order screen, as shown in Figure 7.24.

Just as wired phone lines can be tapped, these Internet security measures can be broken, but it is becoming more difficult to do so. Even with secure transactions on the Net, you must be sure to follow common sense rules just as if you were ordering over the telephone or through the mail.

THE TECHNICAL SCOOP ON SECURITY

Explorer supports three sets of Internet security standards to ensure that your communications over the Net are not interfered with: Secure Sockets Layer (SSL) 2.0, SSL 3.0, and Private Communication Technology (PCT) 1.0. These standards encrypt all communications

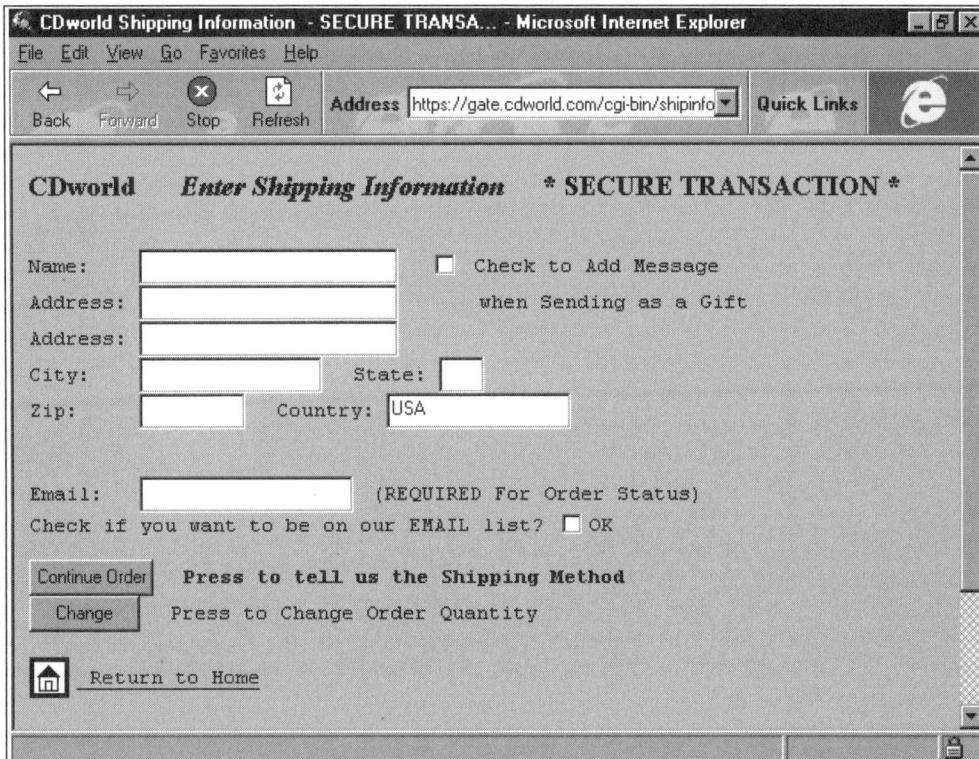

Figure 7.24: A secure site—note the lock icon in the bottom right corner of the status bar.

between supported sites and create a secure channel between computers to limit the access by potential thieves. They also permit either the client or the server to request authentication of the other. This ensures that you have reached the intended site, and it assures the receiving site that the message originated from you and not an impostor. The receiving site can also tell if the message was altered while in transit.

Other Security Considerations

With the new active content of the Web since the introduction of Java and ActiveX, a new possibility exists for this active content to expose you to insecure situations. In the Active Content section of the Security tab (originally shown in Figure 7.6), select Safety Level to display the window shown in Figure 7.26. This allows you to set Explorer's level

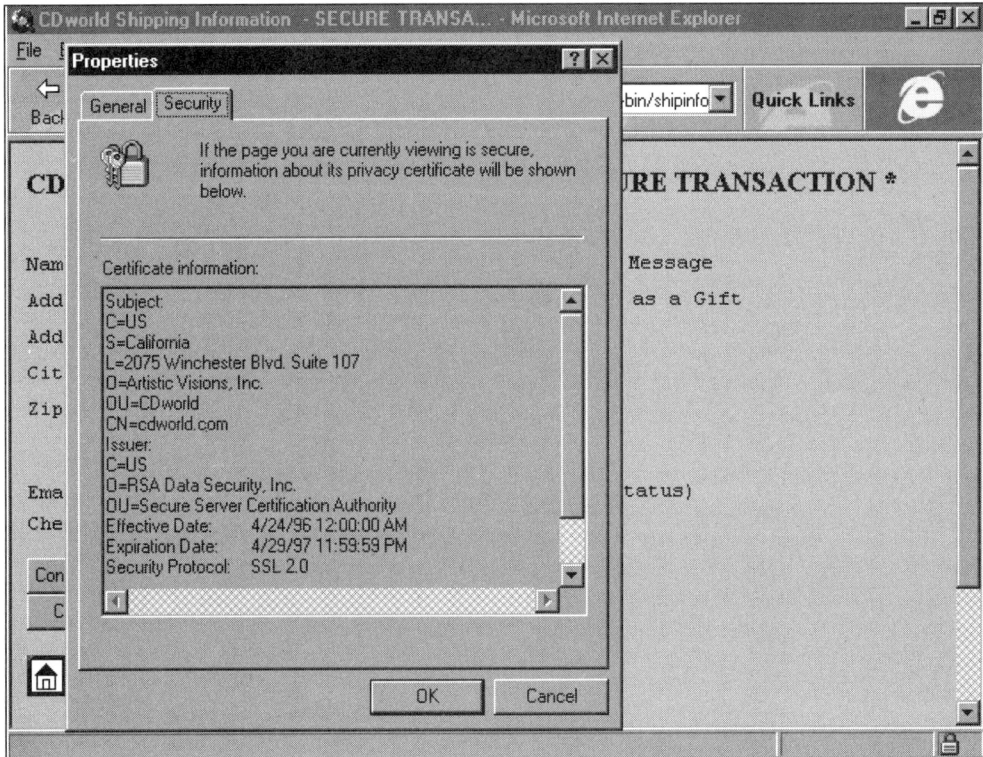

Figure 7.25: An authentic security certificate.

of participation in protecting you from active content that could lead to security problems.

You may also want to review the check boxes shown in the Active Content section of the Security tab. By deselecting these options you are making the Web a less interesting place to visit, but you are also keeping your computer safe from renegade active controls.

Microsoft has also built in capability to verify the source of a file before you download. Although this standard is not yet widely accepted, it has the potential for making downloaded software just as secure as software purchased in a store. Before downloading you can verify a certificate that shows the originator of the file so you can be sure it was not altered or tampered with.

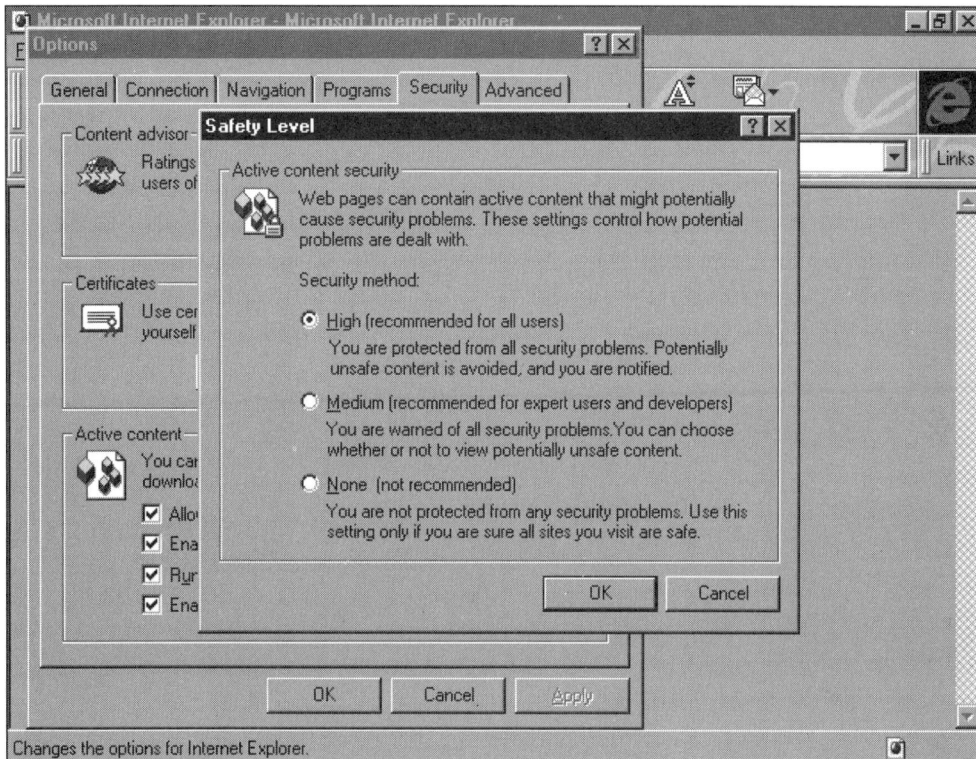

Figure 7.26: Setting active content security levels.

WHICH SECURITY METHOD IS BEST?

This section has a lot of options, so here is what I think the average user should use as security measures. Keep in mind that setting everything to the maximum secure level will overwhelm you with warning messages, and setting everything too low could leave you vulnerable. I take a middle-of-the-road approach. In the Warnings section of Figure 7.7, choose "Warn me before sending over an open connection," and "Only when I'm sending more than one line of text." Always have Explorer check security certificates before viewing and sending. In the Safety Level section of Figure 7.6, I recommend the Normal (Recommended for general use) selection. This eliminates the worry of potentially damaging active content, and it keeps most warning messages away. In the Active Content section, keep all of the boxes checked. Just be sure that you are familiar with the sites you visit that contain active content.

INTERNET RATINGS

The Net gets a bad rap when it comes to adult sites. Sure, there are many out there, but they are sort of like TV channels. If you stumble across one by mistake, you can just as easily go somewhere else. And, as with TV channels, though, kids can try to find these sites on their own when nobody is around to stop them.

Because of the bad publicity the Net has gained, many people are trying to regulate what is displayed and transmitted over the Internet. In order to prevent further legislation limiting information on the Net, some of the largest proponents of the Internet have proposed a set of self-imposed standards: a ratings system and software to limit access to adult-rated sites. Explorer has the capability to detect the rating of a site and limit access to that site accordingly.

Setting Ratings

Figure 7.6 shows the Content Advisor section in the Security tab of the Options window. This is where ratings are first set, then subsequently activated and deactivated. Click on Enable Ratings to begin. The first time Enable Ratings is selected, the Create Supervisor Password window

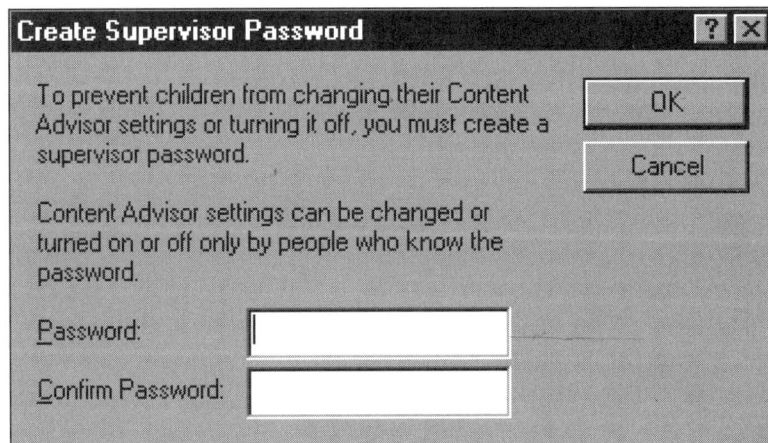

Figure 7.27: Creating a password for ratings.

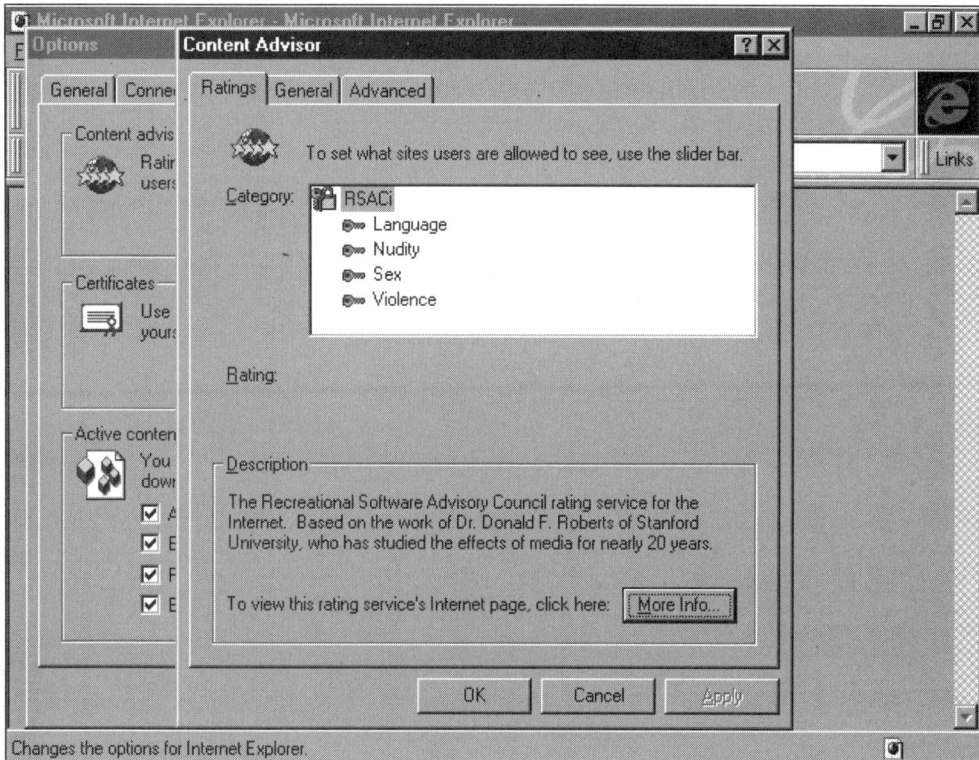

Figure 7.28: The Internet Ratings window.

is displayed (Figure 7.27). Here you enter your password, which will be used to activate and deactivate the ratings and set the levels.

Internet Ratings After creating your password, you will see the Internet Ratings tab of the Internet Ratings window, shown in Figure 7.28. Clicking on a category (Language, Nudity, Sex, or Violence) will bring up a slide bar with which to set the allowable levels for that category. For example, if you leave the slide bar for language all the way to the left, sites with any offensive language will be blocked. At the other extreme, if you move the slide bar all the way to the right, any site with offensive language will be viewable. Mix and match categories to your desire, then press Apply or OK to save those settings.

General The general tab shown in Figure 7.29 allows you to further customize the level of screening provided by Explorer. Checking the

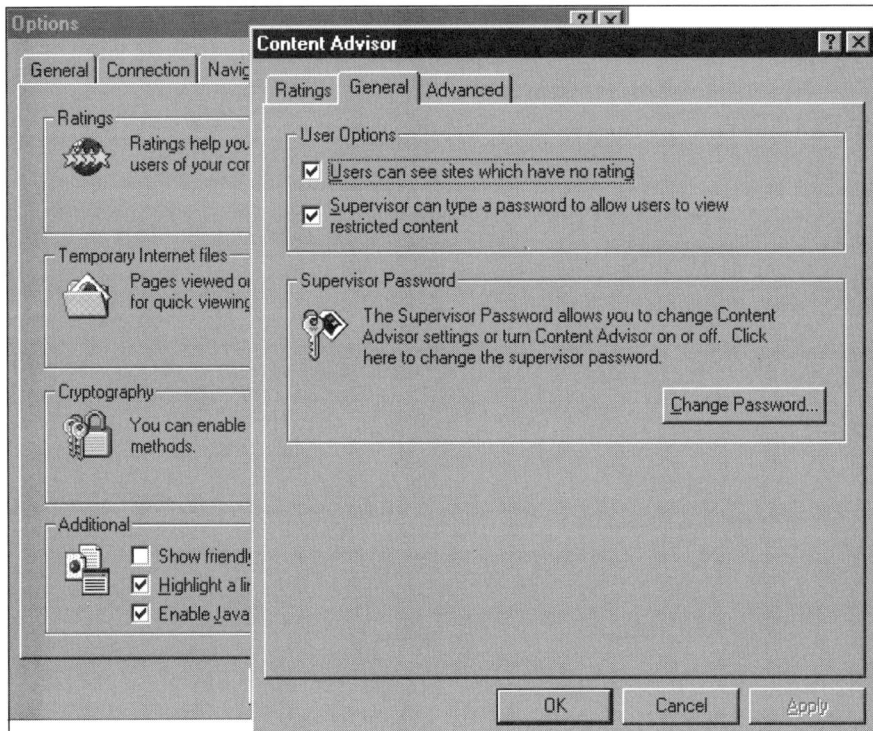

Figure 7.29: The General tab of the Internet Ratings window.

"User can see sites which have no rating" will allow any site that has not adopted the ratings system to be viewed. Because the rating system is new, the majority of sites have not yet converted, so deselecting this option (which would block any unrated sites) would severely limit the number of sites available to view. From another point of view, many of the adult sites are operated by individuals, not by companies, who may never adopt the ratings system. With that in mind, deselecting this option is the safest way to prevent access to questionable sites.

By selecting "Supervisor can type a password to allow users to view restricted content," you allow yourself to access sites that are normally locked out. When this occurs, a window (shown in Figure 7.30) appears that allows you to enter your password to gain access to that particular site.

Note: This window will appear for every page within a site that you visit. Each time you will be required to enter your password. If you plan on

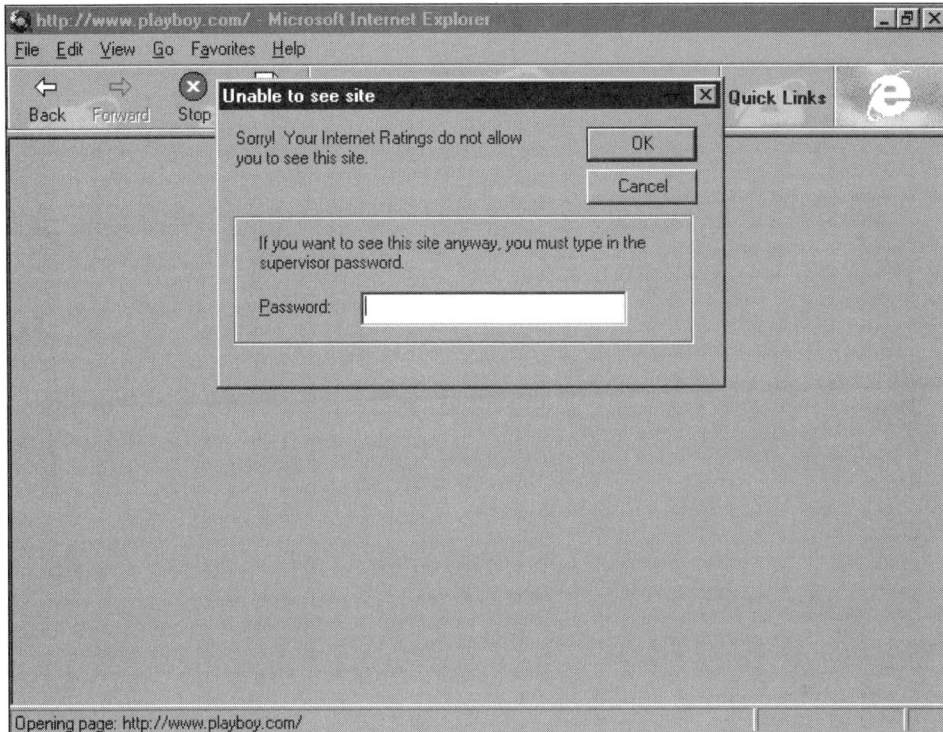

Figure 7.30: Blocked access using the ratings feature of Explorer.

spending a lot of time on these sites, it would be easiest to simply turn off the ratings using the Enable Ratings button shown in Figure 7.6. Just remember to turn them back on when you are finished browsing!

The Change Password button takes you to a window in which you can change your password if your kids are getting close to cracking the code!

Advanced The Advanced tab shown in Figure 7.31 allows you to change the ratings system or access a ratings bureau. The Ratings Systems button takes you to a window in which you can choose from the ratings system used by Explorer. Currently, the only system included is the RSAC, developed by the Recreational Software Advisory Council. In the future, other ratings systems using different criteria may be developed and supported by Explorer.

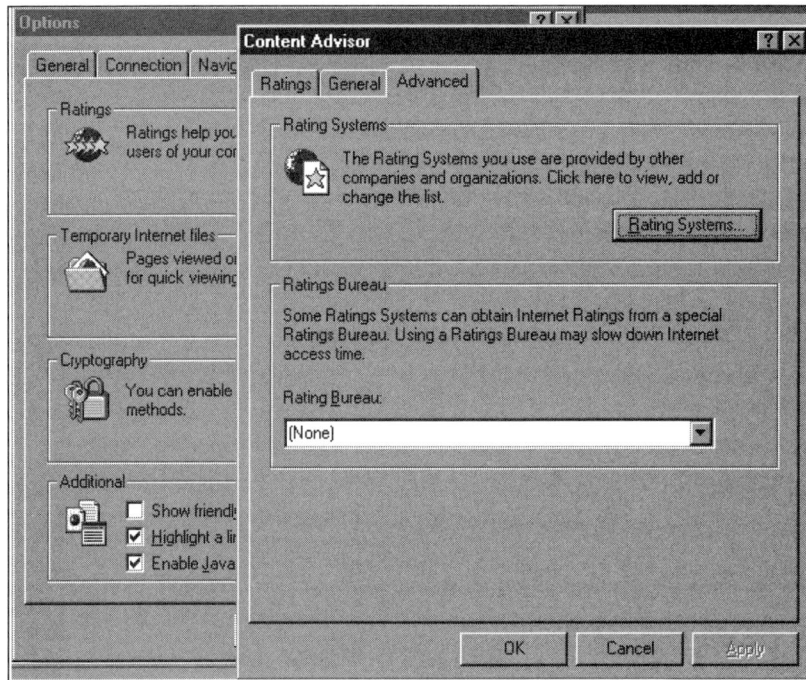

Figure 7.31: Advanced tab of Explorer's ratings feature.

The Ratings Bureau is an option that will check ratings from an Internet site other than the one being accessed. This option is not yet widely supported.

PICS

The Platform for Internet Content Selection (PICS) is an organization that is working to define standards for ratings systems on the Internet. PICS does not set the ratings system itself, but rather defines standards for the use and integration of these systems into Web programming. Without a clear standard, different ratings systems might not be compatible across platforms (PC, Mac), systems (HTML, Java, ActiveX), or even browsers (Internet Explorer, Netscape). For more information, visit its site at **http://www.w3.org/pub/WWW/PICS**.

WHAT'S AHEAD?

- Learn about multimedia on the Web in Chapter 8
- Learn about sending and receiving e-mail in Chapter 9
- Read and post messages in Usenet newsgroups in Chapter 10

Chapter 8

MULTIMEDIA ON THE WEB

If you ask most people what makes the Web more fun than any other part of the Internet, you will get two answers: hyperlinks and multimedia. Hyperlinks we know, but what exactly is multimedia? For our purposes, *multimedia* is the ability of Explorer to play sounds, videos, and animations on-line. It is very cool to log on to a Web page and be greeted by a welcome song or watch a video clip of a new video game that has not been released yet.

Explorer has many built-in features that allow multimedia files to be played with very little effort. There are so many different file types in use on the Net that Explorer can't play them all, however. Explorer does support many add-on programs—programs that will play files that are not directly supported—but these add-ons require downloading and a bit of configuring to get them to work. Keep reading to find out how to get the most from Explorer's multimedia features and the most popular add-ons.

Caution: Downloading any file—sounds, videos, and animations—involves the risk of contracting a virus. As always, download cautiously, and keep your antivirus program up to date.

KEY POINTS IN THIS CHAPTER

- What does Explorer support automatically?
- How do I play and save audio and video files?

- What if I find other types of files?
- What are add-ons, and how can I configure them?
- I'm not very athletic. Can I use Adobe Acrobat?

WHAT DO YOU NEED TO TAKE ADVANTAGE OF MULTIMEDIA?

You do need several things to really get the most from this chapter. First, you need a sound card and speakers with your computer, preferably a 16-bit sound card and some really kickin' stereo speakers. If you recently purchased your machine, these were probably included. If you have been playing the upgrade game over the years, get to the store and upgrade some more! If you are using a machine at your place of business and cannot upgrade it, skip to Chapter 9; there is nothing of value to you here. (Well, not much, anyway, but you might keep reading just so you are informed about the latest and greatest.)

You'll also need a program like PKZip for Windows or WinZip. Many of the files you will come across will be compressed, and these programs will decompress just about anything.

Next, you need a few add-on programs to play the audio and video files Explorer does not support. These can be found at many Web sites or by using a search engine. Don't know what these are? Keep reading to find out more.

Finally, you need a reliable (and new or newly updated) antivirus program. I can't stress this enough for any Internet use, but you will be downloading a lot of files, and you place your computer at risk any time you download.

EXPLORER COMPATIBLE FILE TYPES

Explorer supports many types of files by default. That is, you do not need to download any extra programs to support many of the graphic, audio, and video files that you will encounter on the Web. Table 8.1 lists all the file types that Explorer is capable of supporting automatically. Well, sort of automatically. As you will see, even some of these file types need some input by you before they will work.

Table 8.1: File Types Automatically Supported by Explorer

.gif and animated .gif	Graphics files used as inline images
.jpg .jpeg	Graphics files used as inline images
.xbm	Graphics file
.bmp	Graphics files sometimes used as inline images
.pcx	Graphics file
.wav	Audio file
.mid	MIDI music file
.aif .aiff .aifc	Apple audio files
.au .snd	Sun/NeXT audio files
.ra	RealAudio file
.mp2	MPEG audio files
.mpg .mpeg .mpe	MPEG video files
.avi	Microsoft Video for Windows file
.mov, .qt	Apple Quicktime Video files

Displaying Graphics Files

The most common graphics files found on the Web are JPEG (.jpg or .jpeg extension) and GIF (.gif extension). These files are most commonly used as inline images, so naturally Explorer supports them. Some Web pages also have pictures available for downloading (of course, you can grab any picture you want by right-clicking it) that are not displayed on the page. These also come in JPEG and GIF formats, but they are sometimes joined by bitmap (.bmp), PC Paintbrush (.pcx), and XBM (.xbm) images. To download these files, you simply click their links. JPEG, GIF, and XBM files will be displayed in a new Explorer window, while Bitmap and PC Paintbrush files will be displayed in Windows Paint (which will launch automatically). Occasionally you will see bitmap images used as inline images in a Web page. Explorer will support them when they are used this way, but it is not common.

ActiveMovie

As part of the new ActiveX technology supported by Internet Explorer, ActiveMovie is responsible for the playback of most audio and video files found on the Web. In the past, browsers only supported a few multimedia file types without needing extra, or add-on, programs. Internet Explorer, through ActiveMovie, can automatically play all of the audio and video file formats shown in Table 8.1 without the need to configure extra software components. ActiveMovie automatically takes control over playback of all multimedia files from the Internet. If you would like to change control to a different player, you may change the settings manually. The ActiveMovie Settings window, shown in Figure 8.1, is launched by selecting Start, Programs, Accessories, Multimedia, ActiveMovie File Types.

When you click on a link to an audio or video file, the Active Movie player opens. A new ActiveMovie feature is the download status bar,

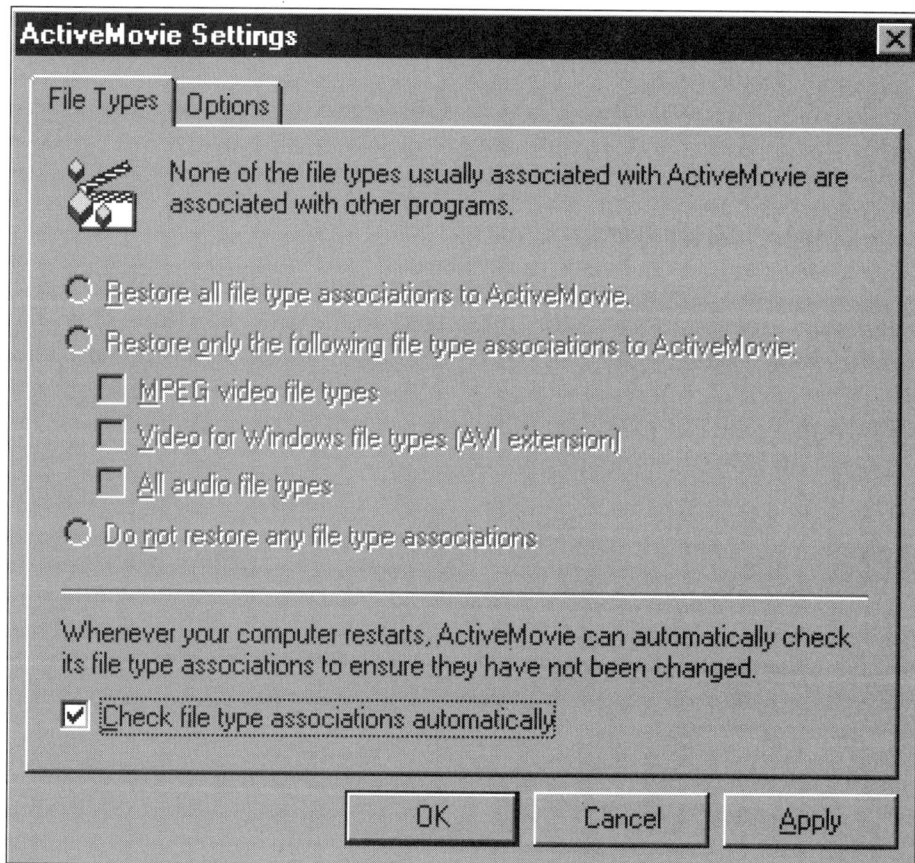

Figure 8.1: The ActiveMovie Settings window.

shown in Figure 8.2, that tracks the progress of the download so you can see how much longer it will take before playback starts. ActiveMovie also offers a standard interface for the control of the files as they are being played.

Playing Audio Files

WAV and MIDI WAV (.wav) and MIDI (.mid) are two of the most common audio formats that are used on the Web. To hear a WAV or MIDI file, simply click on its link to download. ActiveMovie will start, and the file will play after it has been downloaded. Figure 8-3 shows the playback of a WAV file through ActiveMovie. The controls for playback are standard, with Play and Stop buttons in the bottom left corner. The Play button is also used to pause playback. The slide bar moves as the file is played, and can be used to advance and rewind the file. Time is tracked on the large digital display, while the smaller digital display

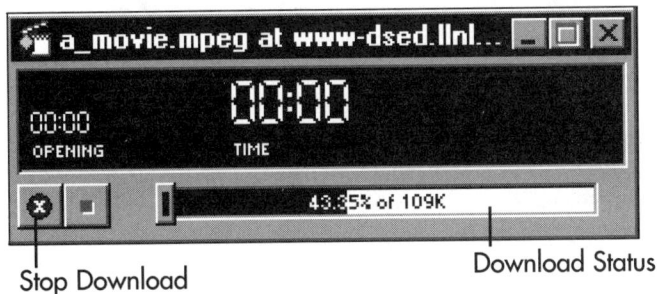

Figure 8.2: The ActiveMovie player as it downloads a file.

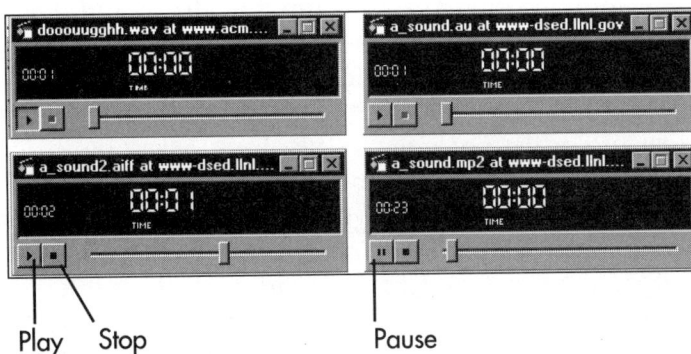

Figure 8.3: Some of the common audio file types as seen through the ActiveMovie player.

shows the total time of the file. You will find that many Web pages are designed to automatically play sounds when you visit. These sounds are usually WAV or MIDI, but you will not see the ActiveMovie control when they are played.

Apple AIFF and Sun/NeXT Apple AIFF (most commonly seen as .aif and .aiff) and Sun/NeXT (most commonly seen as .au) files are played automatically after download by Internet Explorer's built-in sound player. Click on the link to the sound to download it. The controls are identical to playing a WAV or MIDI file.

MPEG-2 Audio MPEG (Motion Picture Experts Group) is a committee made up of the International Standards Organization and the International Electro-Technical Commission. These guys sit around and come up with standards for multimedia formats. You may have heard of their video standards, but MPEG-2 audio (.mp2) is a high-quality stereo format available from many sites on the Net. An .mp2 file is shown in Figure 8.3, and the controls are the same as with other audio files.

Some files are recognized and played automatically by Windows or by Explorer, as you have just seen. Other files are supported and can be played, but Explorer needs to confirm this with you before it does anything. These file types bring up the window shown in Figure 8.4. This is Explorer's way of confirming what you want done with the file. The virus warning is important, but Explorer really just wants to know if you want to play the sound or video file or save it for playing later.

RealAudio RealAudio is a format that allows you to listen to a file as it is being downloaded to your computer; all other files make you wait until the download is completely finished before you can listen. The main drawback to this technology is poor sound quality. You wouldn't confuse these files for your CD player, but that's not what they're for. RealAudio files are for voice playback. Many radio and television networks offer RealAudio simulcasts of their news and sports programs. With this technology, you don't have to miss the big game if you are forced to work late. Hop onto the Web, start Explorer's built-in RealAudio player, and find the site with the game! You can even find news and sports highlights if you tune in late. Many programs are now regularly scheduled to be broadcast for RealAudio listeners.

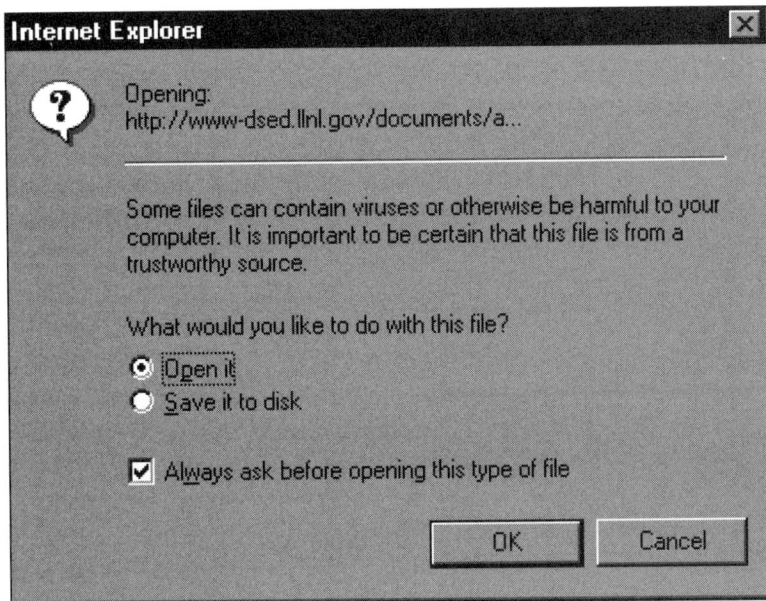

Figure 8.4: Explorer needs to know if you want to play or save this file.

Check out the RealAudio Web site for listings of current RealAudio files at **http://www.realaudio.com**. For sports simulcasts, also check **http://espnet.sportzone.com**.

To play RealAudio sound, click the link to its file. When the window shown in Figure 8.4 appears, choose Open and click OK. The RealAudio player, shown in Figure 8.5, will appear, and the sound will play automatically. The RealAudio player has Play/Pause, Stop, Back, and Forward buttons. It also has two slide bars—one to advance or rewind the file; the other, with a picture of a speaker on it, to change the volume. The speaker inside the text balloon is a link to the RealAudio home page. When you are finished, click the Close button in the top right corner.

A new service has also recently been started to keep track of all the regularly schedule RealAudio programs. This service not only plays the requested sound file through the RealAudio player, but it also opens a second Explorer window to display a related Web site. You can browse the Web site while the RealAudio plays in the background! This site is located at **http://www.timecast.com**, and it is shown in Figure 8.6.

Play/Pause   Stop   Back   Forward   Close

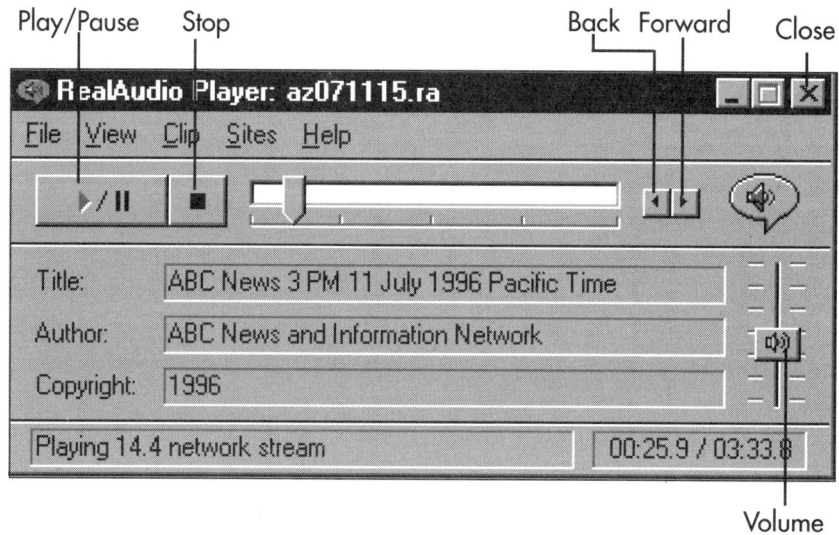

Figure 8.5: The RealAudio sound player.

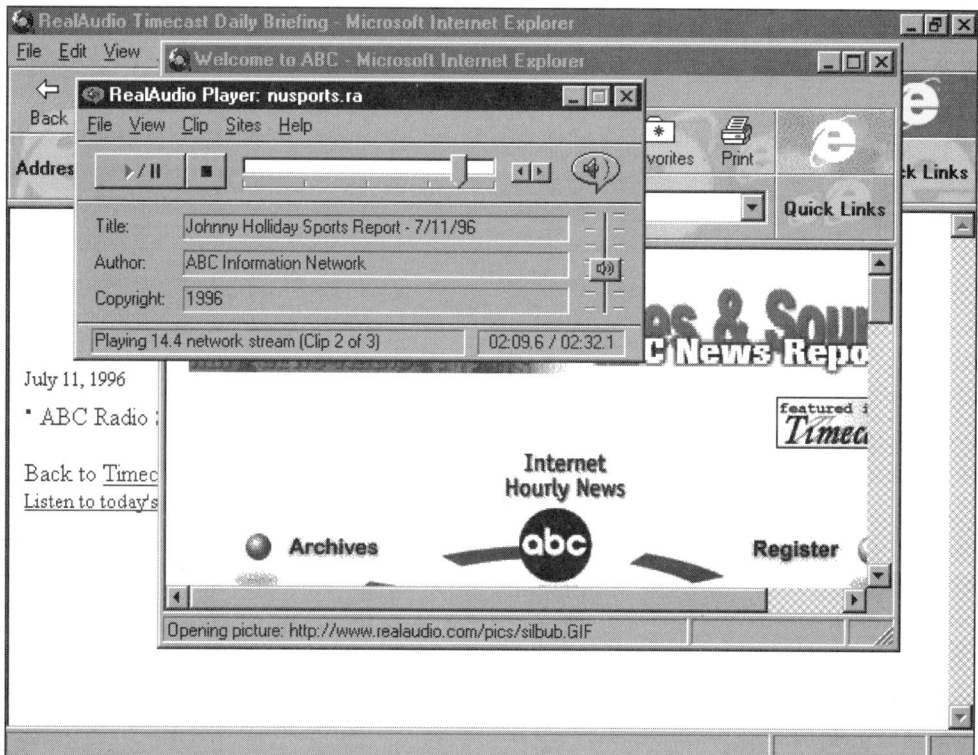

Figure 8.6: RealAudio timecast playing an ABC sports update with accompanying Web site.

Playing Video Files

One of the more common video formats you will find is Video for Windows (.avi). This format produces a small image with decent video and surprisingly good audio quality. One warning: be prepared to wait around while the large video files download. It can take several minutes to download just a few seconds of video, and the smallest files you will likely encounter will be over 1MB in size.

To play a Video for Windows file, click its hyperlink. (Then go read a book or make some coffee.) When the file has finished downloading, it will play automatically, as shown in Figure 8.7. You can stop playback with the Stop button, restart playback with the Play button, and move around in the video with the slide bar. The window can also be resized by grabbing the bottom right corner and dragging (the image quality decreases as the window size increases). Click the Close button in the top right corner when you are finished viewing the video.

Figure 8.7: An AVI file played through Media Player.

Quicktime Video

Apple computer created the Quicktime video standard (.mov and .qt) and ported it over the Windows. Its video and audio quality is perhaps a bit lower than that of MPEG or Video for Windows, but you can find these files everywhere. A Quicktime video is shown in Figure 8.7. Click on a link to download.

MPEG Video MPEG video is what the MPEG guys are most widely known for. MPEG video files (.mpg, .mpeg, and .mpe) are a bit smaller than comparable formats, and they offer about the same quality video and audio as the other formats. An MPEG hardware attachment is offered on many video cards that boosts the images to full screen, near TV resolution. MPEG video clips, as shown in Figure 8.7, play back in a larger window than Quicktime or AVI videos, and download a bit faster. Click on a link to download.

ADD-ONS

When you click a file to download and you see the window shown in Figure 8.8, it means that Explorer doesn't recognize the kind of file you are asking it to download. It can still save the file to disk, but either you don't have the correct add-on program or it is not configured properly.

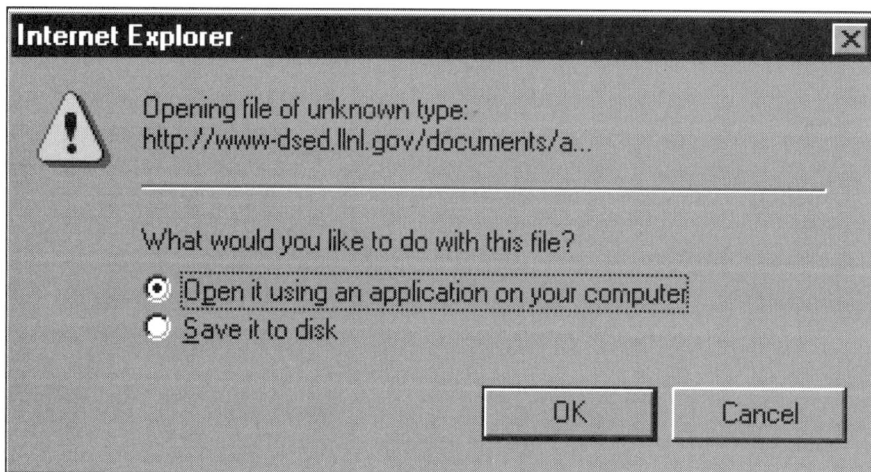

Figure 8.8: When Explorer doesn't recognize a file type.

Add-on programs (also called plug-ins or helpers) work with Windows and Internet Explorer to display file types that are not recognized natively. There are so many different file types in Internet land that I could not possibly cover them all. There are two that are especially noteworthy, and I will cover them here.

Macromedia Shockwave

Macromedia publishes two popular programs that are used to create animation: Director and Authorware. The work created by these programs can be spectacular, but the file sizes are too large to effectively incorporate into a Web site. That's where Shockwave comes in. Files from Director and Authorware can be converted to Shockwave format, which is much more compact and can be easily viewed over the Internet. Shockwave files can mix animation and video with special effects, sounds, and music. This doesn't look very good in a book, so I did not provide an example here. For a firsthand look, go to the Shockwave site, located at **www.macromedia.com/shockwave**, and download the Shockwave add-on for Internet Explorer.

Adobe Acrobat Reader

Viewing a text file can be rather bland. Even text files with pictures are still not the same as looking at, say, an original copy of the Bill of Rights. Adobe developed the Acrobat Reader (.pdf—Portable Document Format) to allow viewing of documents in their original format on many different machine types (thus the portable part). Figure 8.9 is a scanned image of one of the original copies of the Bill of Rights. Through Acrobat, you can move around the image, zoom in and out, and search for text. It is capable of viewing full page (as shown in Figure 8.9), full screen, or close-up at your discretion.

CONFIGURING ADD-ON PROGRAMS

Many of the newest add-on programs will be designed as ActiveX controls. For more on ActiveX, see Chapter 11. For our purposes here, ActiveX simply means that the program will install and configure itself automatically. There will be nothing for you to do other than click on the control to download. You won't even have to reboot your computer! If you find a program that offers both ActiveX and standard

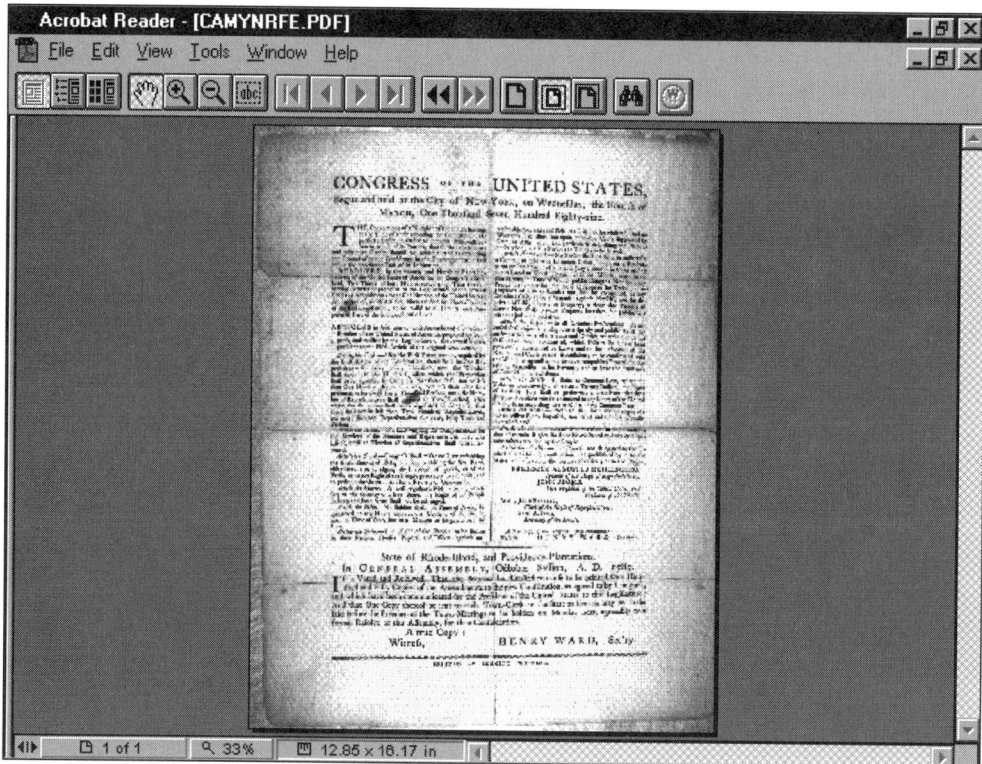

Figure 8.9: The Bill of Rights as displayed in Adobe Acrobat.

add-on technology (such as Adobe Acrobat), definitely choose the ActiveX version. Your life will be much simpler. If you choose the standard add-on format, you may have to follow the directions that follow.

When you find add-ons for Explorer that aren't ActiveX Controls, installing them on your computer isn't enough. You must configure them so that Explorer (and Windows itself) understands the relationship between certain file types and the add-on programs themselves. To do this, you need to know a little information about the add-on programs and their supported files.

First, you need to know the three-digit extension used by the files associated with the add-ons. Next, you need to know the file's MIME type, which is a way of categorizing files on the Internet. Both pieces of information for many of the popular file types you will encounter are displayed in Table 8.2.

Table 8.2: MIME Type, Data Type, and File Extensions of Popular Files on the Net

application/pdf	Adobe Acrobat	.pdf
application/x-zip-compressed	PKZip compressed	.zip
audio/basic	Sun/NeXT audio	.au .snd
audio/mp2	MPEG audio	.mp2
audio/x-aiff	Apple AIFF audio	.aif .aiff .aifc
audio/x-wav	Windows WAV audio	.wav
image/gif	GIF image	.gif
image/jpeg	JPEG image	.jpg .jpeg .jpe
text/html	HTML	.html
text/plain	Plain text	.txt
video/mpeg	MPEG video	.mpg .mpeg .mpe
video/quicktime	Apple Quicktime video	.mov .qt
video/x-msvideo	Microsoft Video for Windows	.avi

MIMES ARE OUR FRIENDS

MIME, which is short for Multipurpose Internet Mail Extension, was originally developed for encoding graphics, sound, and video files so that they could be transmitted over the Internet via e-mail. It has since caught on in other areas as well, and it is now used as a way to differentiate file format types on the Net. MIME allows associations to be made between files and their programs (for instance, clicking on an .mov file automatically launches the Quicktime viewer). By the way, it is still used for e-mail purposes.

To configure Internet Explorer to launch a program automatically when a file is downloaded, follow these instructions.

1. Select the Programs tab from the View Options menu (shown in Figure 8.10).
2. Click the New Type button. The Add New File Type window will open, as shown in Figure 8.11.
3. Next to Description of Type, type a description of the add-on you are configuring (such as Acrobat Reader). This is the name that will appear in the File Types list.
4. Next to Associated Extension, type the three- or four-letter extension that is associated with the program's MIME type. Refer to Table 8.3 as needed.

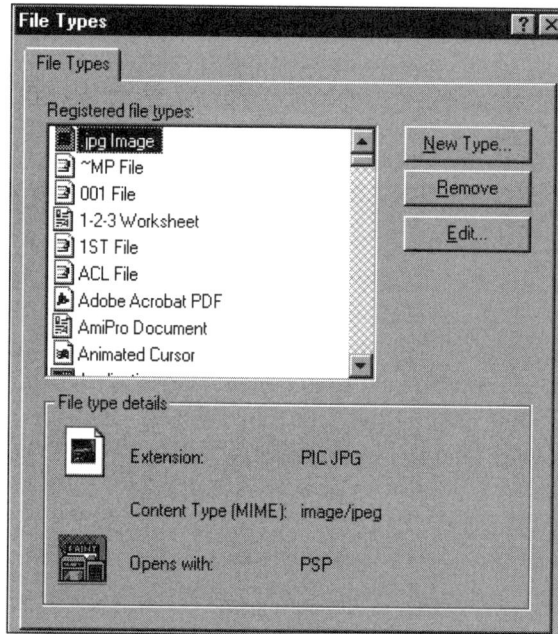

Figure 8.10: The File Types tab of the Option window.

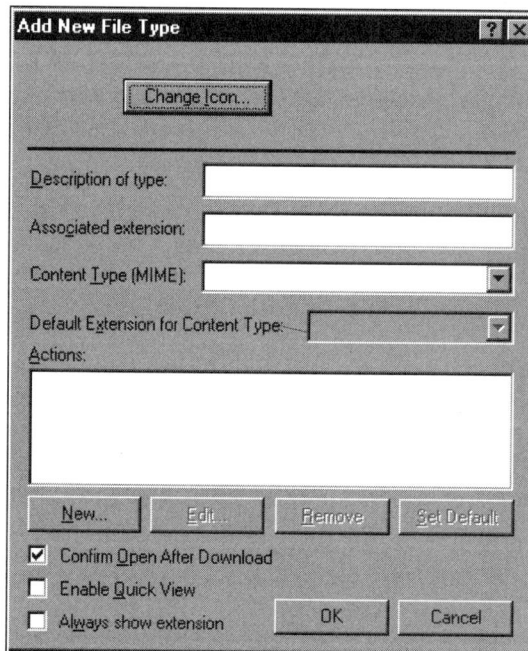

Figure 8.11: The Add New File Type window.

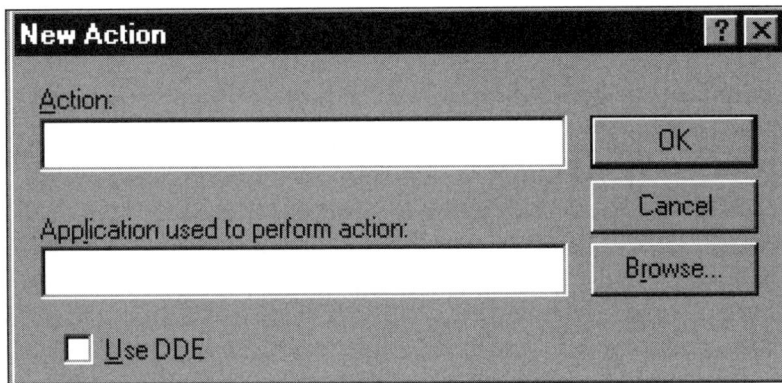

Figure 8.12: The New Action window.

5. Next to Content Type (MIME), type the MIME type. The down arrow contains a list of MIME types that are currently being used. Refer to Table 8.3 as needed.
6. Click the New button, underneath the Actions box. The New Action window, shown in Figure 8.12, will open.
7. In the blank under Action, type the action that you want to appear on the right-click pop-up menu for that application. For example, for Acrobat, you will want to open the file. Type Open. For most applications, Open or Print is appropriate. For multimedia applications, Open is usually used.
8. Click Browse to open the Open With window. This is where you find the program that you want to perform the indicated action. With Acrobat, locate the Acroread.exe file.
9. Highlight the file and click Open.
10. Click OK in the New Action window.
11. Click Close in the Add New File Type window.
12. Click Close in the Options window.

The add-on program and its files are now automatically associated with each other. When a file is downloaded, the add-on program will automatically display it. If you save the file to disk, you can display it by right-clicking the filename and selecting Open from the pop-up menu that will appear or by double-clicking it. Repeat these steps for any other add-on programs that you download. You are now in a great position to enjoy multimedia on the Web!

*Tip: If you want to find one Web site that can test your add-ons to make sure that they are configured properly, go to **http://www-dsed.llnl.gov/documents/WWWtest.html**. This site has samples of many file types that you can download to test your viewers.*

Tip: One final tip about downloading any sound or video file. Many Web pages are designed to play their files automatically when downloaded, but they do not provide an option to save the file to disk. As you have seen with non-native Windows files (like RealAudio), Explorer will ask if you want to open or save the file to disk. But what if you want to save a WAV file or AVI file? They will play and close automatically, so how do you save them? There are two options.

First, remember the right-click! Right-clicking the file's hyperlink displays a pop-up menu that has a Save option (Save Target As). Second, each file that is viewed is saved in one of the cache folders. Using the Windows 95 Find program (on the Start menu), search for all of the files that have the same extension (like .wav or .avi) as the file you are looking for. When Find gives you a list, check the dates and times on each file to narrow your search. When you see a possibility, double-click it and it will play. If it is the correct file, move it to another folder where it won't be erased.

WHAT'S AHEAD?

- Learn about sending and receiving e-mail in Chapter 9
- Read and post messages in Usenet newsgroups in Chapter 10
- Look into the future of Web browsing in Chapter 11

Chapter 9

COMMUNICATING USING E-MAIL

When you consider all of the possibilities that the Internet presents to us, what part do people use the most? E-mail. Whenever a new friend gets on the Net, one of the first questions I ask is, "What's your e-mail address?" E-mail lets you communicate almost instantly with people all over the world. I use e-mail to keep in touch with people who might normally slip away. Personally, I am a terrible letter writer, and I call people even less. But I can write up a storm when it's sent over the Net!

Some people dislike e-mail because it seems so impersonal. I agree that a message displayed on a monitor is less personal than a note handwritten on a piece of stationary, but I believe that an e-mail message every week sure beats one or two letters a year—not writing at all is extremely impersonal. I don't know if it's the actual physical process of writing and sending a letter that I dislike, but I don't have to deal with the funny stamp taste when my letters are delivered electronically!

For many businesses, e-mail is a must. E-mail within corporate headquarters has been commonplace for years. Now with the Internet, traveling representatives can keep in touch with home base from anywhere in the world for less than the cost of a phone call. Internet e-mail is almost instantaneous, too. A message will often be received only seconds after it is sent. Files and documents can be attached, saving the cost of using fax machines and shipping companies, and several people can be set up to receive the same message with only a few extra keystrokes.

E-mail isn't perfect. Messages can be intercepted and, if not encrypted, information can be stolen. Also, the recipient must know to check for new mail, otherwise e-mail will just sit unannounced in a mail box. These limitations are easy to overcome, though, and this chapter will talk about two different ways to send and receive e-mail with Explorer: Internet Mail and News and Exchange.

KEY POINTS IN THIS CHAPTER

- Is e-mail part of Explorer?
- Should I use Internet Mail and News or Exchange?
- Using Internet Mail—features and ease of use.
- Using Exchange—power and flexibility.

E-MAIL WITHIN EXPLORER

E-mail is integrated into Explorer using what used to be a separate program called Internet Mail and News (IMN). The mail part of this program is now the default setting for sending e-mail through Explorer and for reading and composing messages off-line. Plus it has a Usenet newsreader (covered in Chapter 10) to access the newsgroups on the Net. IMN will be discussed first as it is the primary mail program for Explorer.

You still have the option of using Exchange as your primary e-mail program if you like. Exchange is the more powerful cousin of IMN, although it doesn't have a newsreader. It does offer compatibility with networks and provides file sharing and fax capabilities, so it is the choice of many corporate users. Exchange is currently the only option for MSN members, although that will change soon when IMN is integrated at some point in the future.

Internet Explorer also allows you to configure other e-mail programs to be the default choice if you are obligated to use your company's program or you just prefer another. If this is the case, you may want to skip this chapter unless, of course, you want to see what you are missing!

ANATOMY OF AN E-MAIL ADDRESS

The e-mail address is divided into parts just like an Internet address. Each part identifies where and to whom a message is to be sent.

Tip: If you remember how Web page addresses are designed, the e-mail format will be obvious to you. Just like Web sites, think of an e-mail address as a phone number.

The first part of an e-mail address is the name. This is your user name from your ISP. Using John Smith as an example, a username might be jsmith.

The second part is always an @ (at) sign. This separates the user name from the last part, the domain name.

The domain name is usually the name of your ISP. Using John Smith again, his address if he were a member of the Microsoft Network might be jsmith@msn.com. This full name is pronounced "J Smith at m-s-n dot com." As with Web addresses, watch for capital letters. If the address is typed incorrectly, your mail will be returned to you.

USING INTERNET MAIL

Because many of us don't need the extra features of Exchange for sending electronic mail, Microsoft created the Internet Mail feature of Explorer. This isn't just a stripped down version of Exchange, though. It has many features that make creating, managing, and sending e-mail easier and faster than with Exchange.

Internet Mail can be launched in three ways: from the toolbar in Explorer, by clicking on a mailto: link in a Web page, and from the Start Programs menu on the Windows 95 task bar. The last method lets you check your messages or write new ones without having to launch Explorer at all.

Basics

The "look" of IMN echoes that of Explorer itself, with a toolbar, "E" logo, and status bar. The toolbar is even customizable, just like its counterparts in Explorer. The main screen is divided into two windows, as shown in Figure 9.1. The top section provides a list of

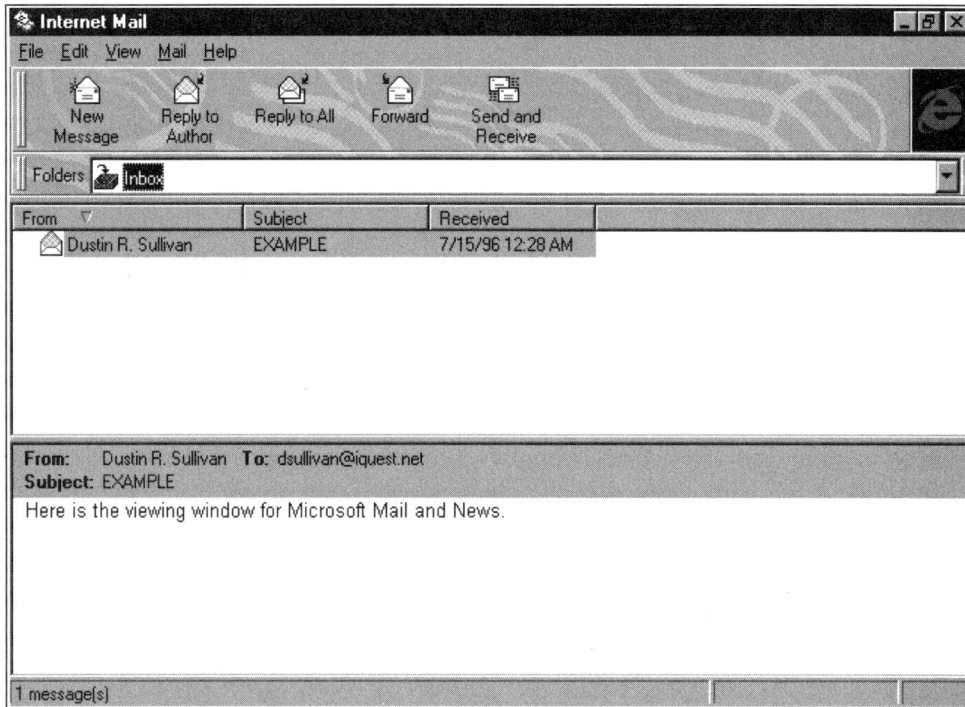

Figure 9.1: The main screen of Internet Mail.

messages that are kept in storage folders (discussed later), and the bottom section displays the text of the selected message.

Note: The windows can be displayed side by side, if you prefer, by selecting View Preview Pane from the menu bar.

The toolbar is the main control area of the program, so it will be discussed in detail. The menu bar's options are duplicated on the toolbar, so less detail is needed in describing its functions.

Toolbar The toolbar provides quick, single-click access to commonly used functions. Table 9.1 illustrates the features of the icon bar.

Table 9.1: Internet Mail Toolbar Functions

Icon	Title	Function
New Message	New Message	Opens the New Message window for writing mail messages
Reply to Author	Reply to Author	Creates a new message that is automatically addressed to the author of the highlighted message
Reply to All	Reply to All	Creates a new message that is automatically addressed to all recipients of the original message
Forward	Forward	Sends a copy of the highlighted message to an address of your choice
Send and Receive	Send and Receive	Used to send new messages from the Outbox folder and check for new messages

Tip: The icon bar can be customized by right-clicking on a blank spot. Choose Customize Toolbar from the pop-up menu. You can add and delete icons as you like.

Folders Folders are used to store received messages and previously sent messages. IMN comes preset with four, and you can create new folders to help organize your messages.

When you delete messages from other folders, they are moved here rather than being deleted. When you delete messages from here, they are not moved to the Recycle Bin, but are erased permanently.

Tip: To automatically delete all messages in the Deleted Items folder when Internet Mail is closed, select the Mail Options Read tab from the menu bar. Check the box next to "Empty messages from the 'Deleted Items' folder on exit."

All incoming messages are initially placed here. They are kept here even after they have been read until you move or delete them.

When an item is sent, it is placed in the Outbox before it is actually delivered. "Sent" items are not actually placed on the Internet and sent to the recipient (I know, this is kind of weird). See "Sending a Message" later in this section for more details.

When a message is delivered to its Internet address, it is moved from the Outbox to the Sent Items folder.

Creating New Folders If you keep e-mail messages for long periods of time, you may find it helpful to create new folders in which to store them. New folders can also be helpful to separate work messages from personal messages. Creating new folders is easy. From the menu bar, choose Folder Create. A window will prompt you to enter a name for your new folder. It is then created and placed in alphabetical order with the other folders. Figure 9.2 shows the new folder that I created called Work Stuff.

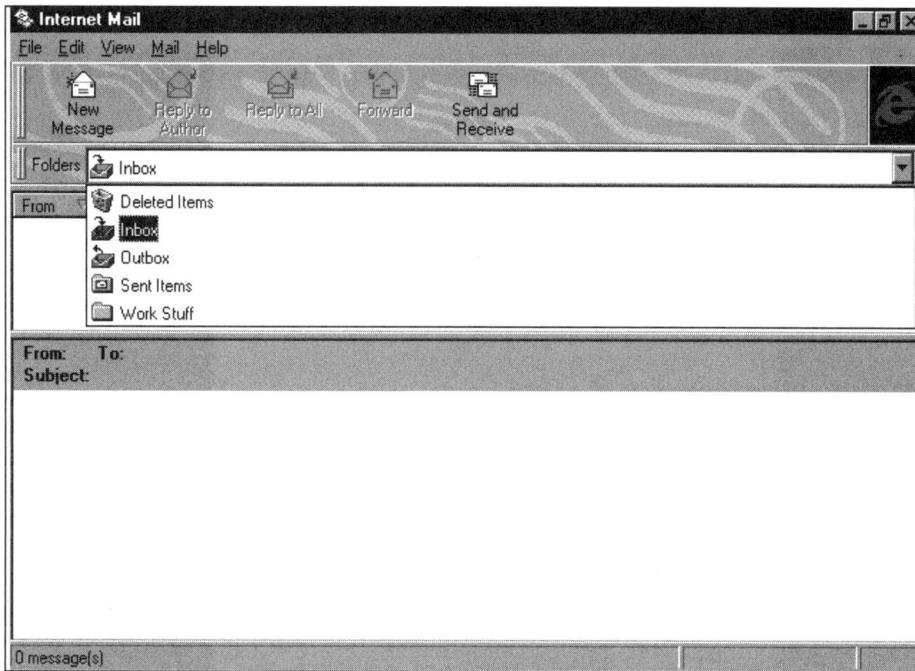

Figure 9.2: A new folder, Work Stuff, has been created.

Writing New Messages

To start writing a new message, click on the New Message icon on the toolbar. The New Message window, shown in Figure 9.3, appears. Move the cursor over the To: area and click in the box. This is where you type the e-mail address of the person to whom you are sending this message. If you don't know any e-mail address yet, just type your own (you can send a letter to yourself for practice). If you want to send a copy of this letter to anyone else, write that e-mail address in the CC: line below To:. Click in the Subject: area to enter the subject of the letter. To actually write the letter, click in the big area under Subject and start typing.

Tip: To activate automatic spell checking (if you have Microsoft Office), select the Mail Options Spelling tab. Check the box next to "Always check spelling before sending."

To send the message, click on the button that looks like an envelope on the left side of the toolbar. While we're talking about the toolbar,

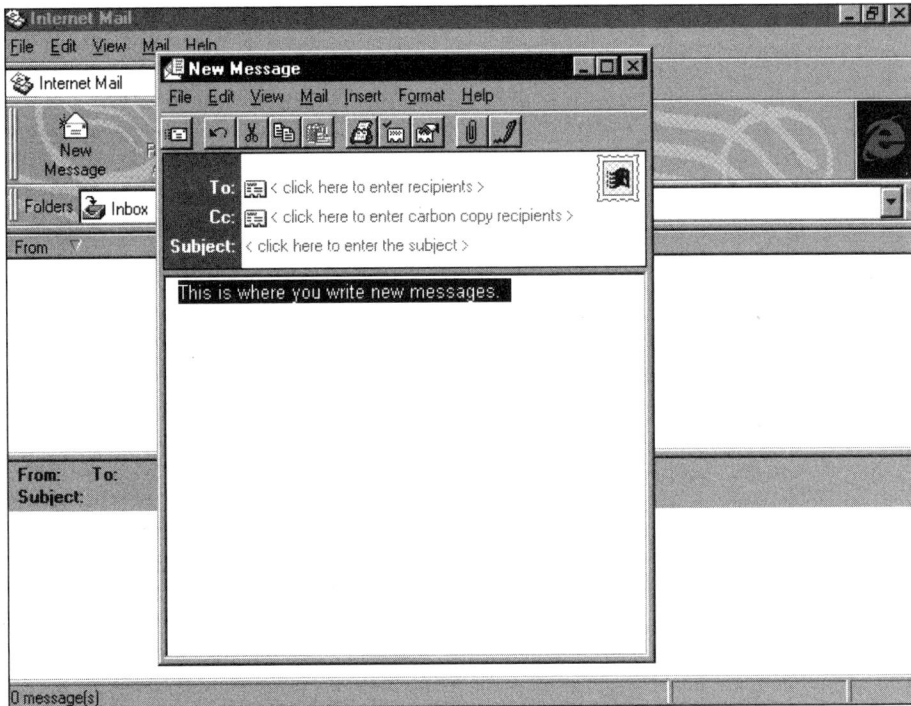

Figure 9.3: The New Message window.

check Table 9.2 for new message toolbar functions. There are also a few more buttons scattered throughout the new message window that I will cover here.

Formatting

Unlike all other e-mail programs that can send only plain text messages, Internet Mail can send and receive messages in HTML format, which allows for rich formatting. This includes color, multiple fonts, and text formatting such as bullet points. To create a message in HTML format, select Format HTML from the menu bar of the new message window. A new toolbar with font, color, and bullet options appears. You can now design your message pretty much any way you want! When the message is received (using Explorer and Internet Mail), it looks like Figure 9.4.

Table 9.2: New Message Icon Bar Functions

Icon	Title	Function
	Send	Press this button to "send" the letter to the Outbox
	Undo	Press this button to undo any previous action (such as typing)
	Cut	Cuts any highlighted text out of the letter and places it in the Windows 95 Clipboard
	Copy	Copies any highlighted text from the letter and places it in the Windows 95 Clipboard
	Paste	Pastes the contents of the Clipboard into the letter
	Address Book	Opens the address book
	Check Names	Compares the name in the To: category to names in the address book. If a match is found, that entry's e-mail address is used for the letter
	Pick Recipients	Allows you to choose names from the address book
	Insert File	Attaches a file to transmit with the message
	Insert Signature	Allows you to add a predetermined signature to the end of the message
	Choose recipients from a list	Instead of typing in names or addresses in the To: or CC: sections, these buttons open the same window as the Pick Recipients button, allowing you to choose names from your address book
	Click to set the priority of this message	This button allows you to set a high, normal, or low priority for the message

Note: You can also set the format to HTML or plain text from the Mail Options Send tab on the main screen.

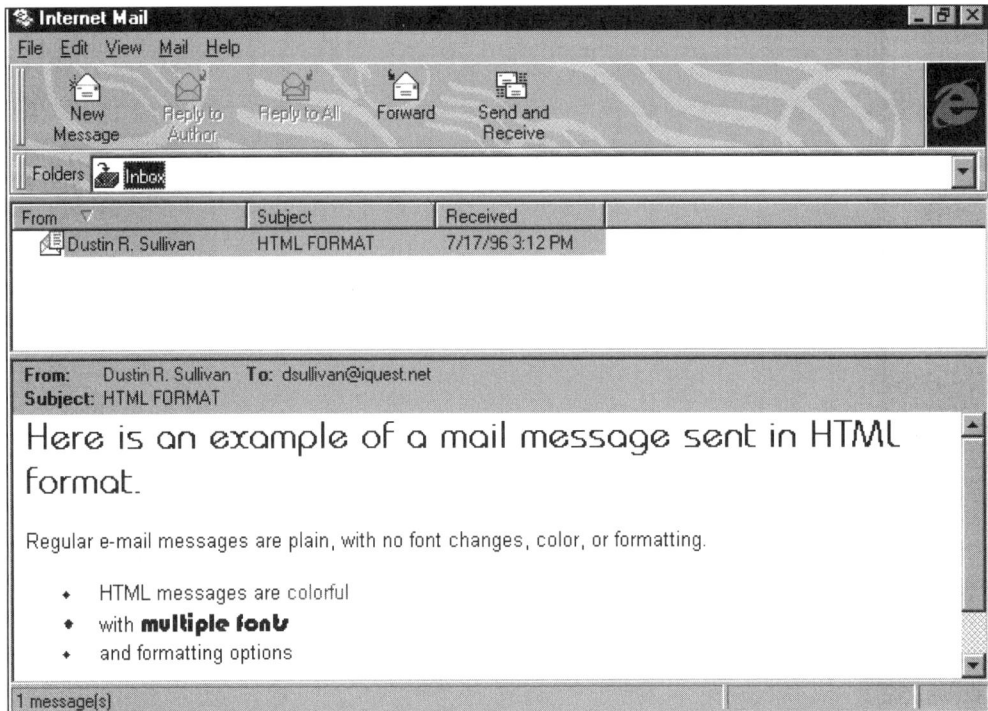

Figure 9.4: A message in HTML format.

Using the Address Book

The address book offers a convenient way to store frequently used names and e-mail addresses. Not only can you store names, but you can also store personal information about each entry. It is almost like having a mini contact manager! To add a name to the address book,

1. Click the Address Book button on either the main screen or the new message window. The window shown in Figure 9.5 will appear.
2. Click the New Contact icon from the address book icon bar.
3. Enter personal information and the e-mail address in the Personal Tab.
4. Use the Home, Business, and Notes tabs as needed.
5. Click OK when finished.

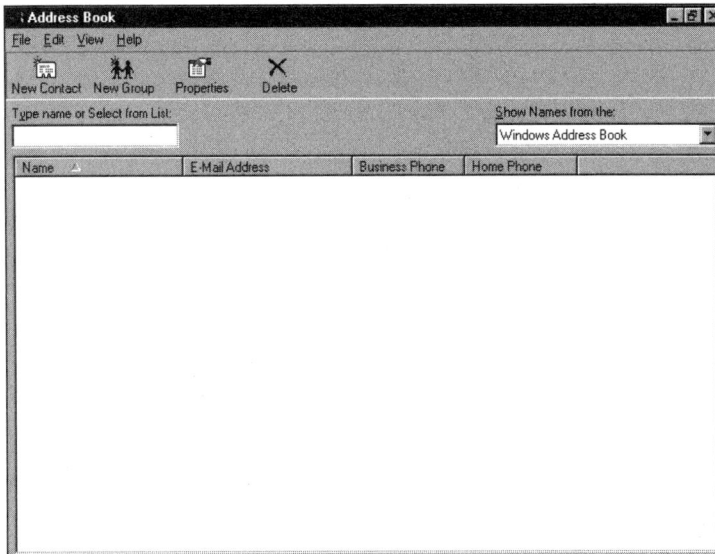

Figure 9.5: The address book.

The name will now appear on the address book list. If you need to classify your addresses into different categories, use the New Group icon. The Properties icon will show you the Personal, Home, Business, and Notes tabs for the highlighted individual. The Delete icon will delete the selected address from the address book. If you have many names, the area under "Type name or select from list" allows you to type the name of the person whose address you wish to find. The name will then be highlighted for you. The View Sort By menu lets you organize the list in many different ways.

Delivering Messages

When you are finished writing a message and wish to send it, click the Send button on the new message toolbar. This does not actually send the message, however. You are greeted by the message in Figure 9.6, which explains that the message was moved to the Outbox. In order to actually deliver the message to the Internet address, you must click the Send and Receive icon in the main window.

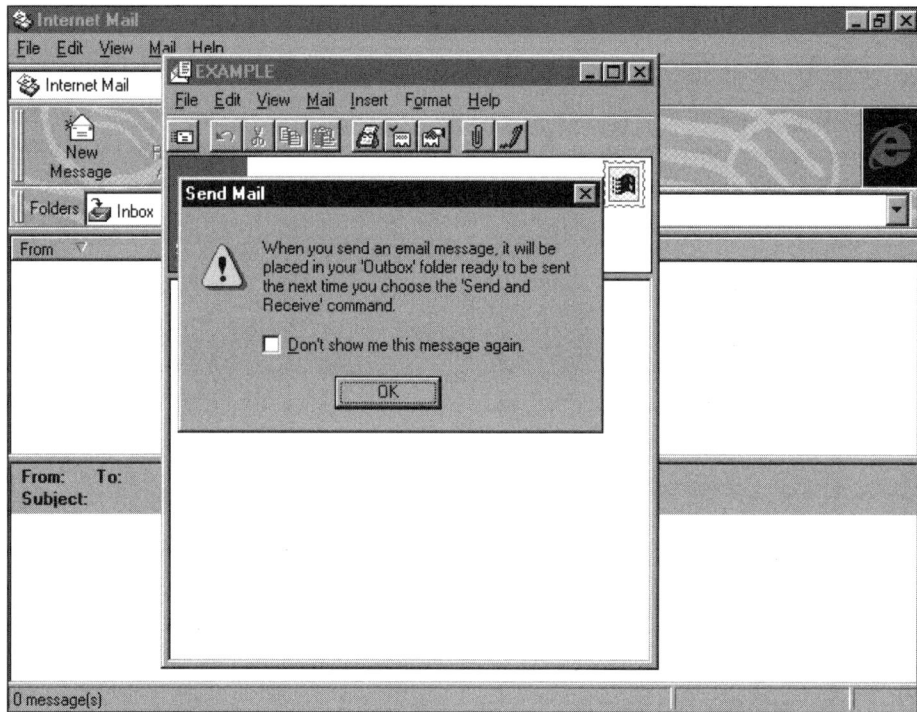

Figure 9.6: Sending mail is really not sending anything!

The Send and Receive icon will deliver the message if you are already on-line. If you are not on-line, a connection with your ISP will be established automatically, and your message will be delivered.

You can disable the extra step involved in delivering messages if you choose. When this step is eliminated, your messages will actually be delivered to their Internet addresses immediately when you click the Send button. To eliminate the extra step

1. Choose Mail Options from the menu bar.
2. On the Send tab, check Send Messages Immediately.
3. Choose OK to finish or Apply to change other settings.

Receiving and Replying to Messages

When you click the Send and Receive icon, any messages in the Outbox will be delivered. Internet Mail will also check your Internet mailbox for new incoming messages. If it finds any, it will automatically download them while displaying the message shown in Figure 9.7.

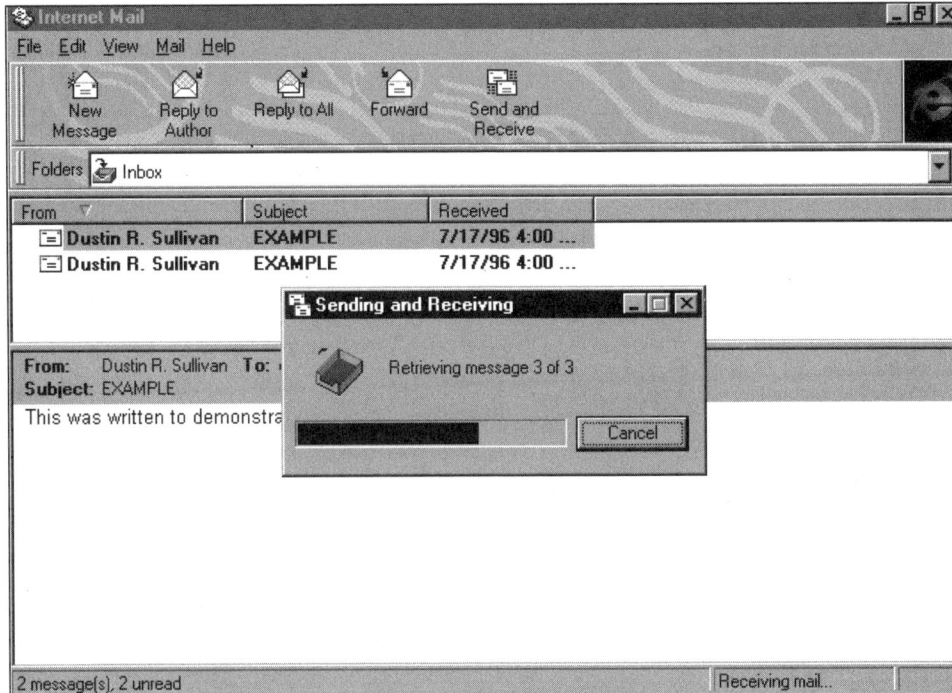

Figure 9.7: Receiving new mail messages.

Just as when you are delivering messages, if you are already on-line, Send and Receive will check for new mail. If you are not on-line, a connection with your ISP will be established automatically, and your mailbox will be checked.

When you receive new mail, the messages are placed in the Inbox. To read them, click on the message in the top pane of Internet Mail. The contents of the message will be displayed in the bottom pane, as shown in Figure 9.8. Also notice in Figure 9.8 that one message has a closed envelope next to it, while the other has an open envelope next to it. The closed envelope means that the message has not yet been read, and the open envelope means (you guessed it) that the message has been read. These indicators help in deciding which messages need to be read and which can be deleted or filed. Messages that you wish to place special emphasis on can be marked as unread by selecting Edit Mark as Unread from the menu bar. This may help remind you to read an important message.

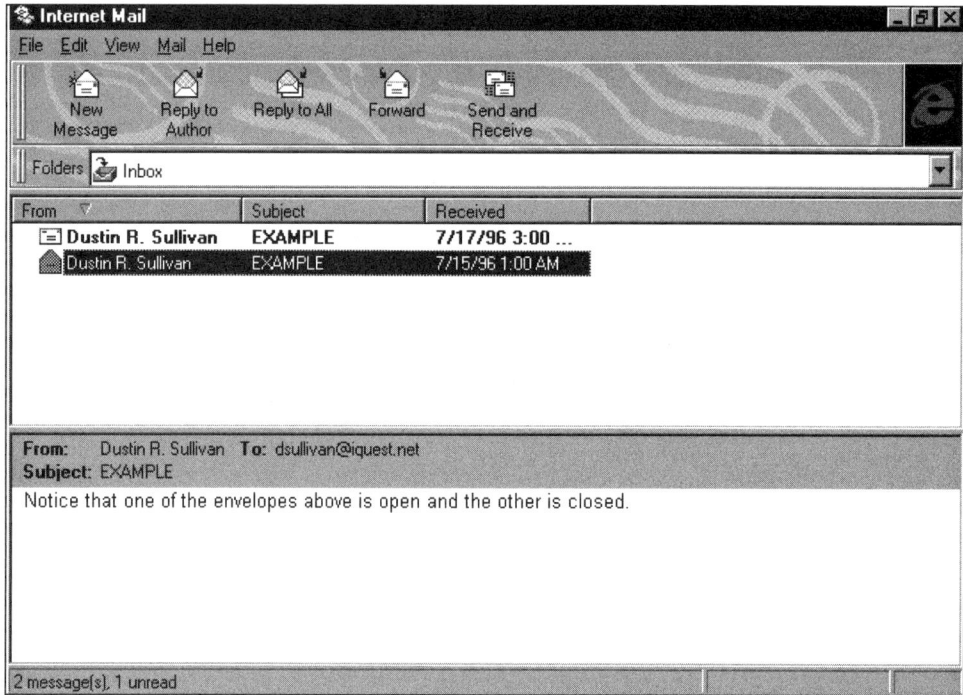

Figure 9.8: New mail in the Inbox.

Tip: Another way to read a message is to double-click the message title in the top pane. Rather than displaying the message in the bottom pane, a window opens (which looks similar to the new message window) that contains the text of the message. The toolbar and menu bar for this window are duplicates of the main Internet Mail window, but there is one nice feature on the menu bar. Add to Address Book allows you to add the sender's e-mail address to your address book without having to type it in manually.

Replying to messages is simple. Choose either Reply to Author or Reply to All from the icon bar. A window looking remarkably similar to the new message window appears (shown in Figure 9.9). The address of the original author is automatically placed in the To: section. The original message is placed in the reply. It is preceded by ">" to distinguish it from your reply. Type your reply and send the message the same way you send a new message.

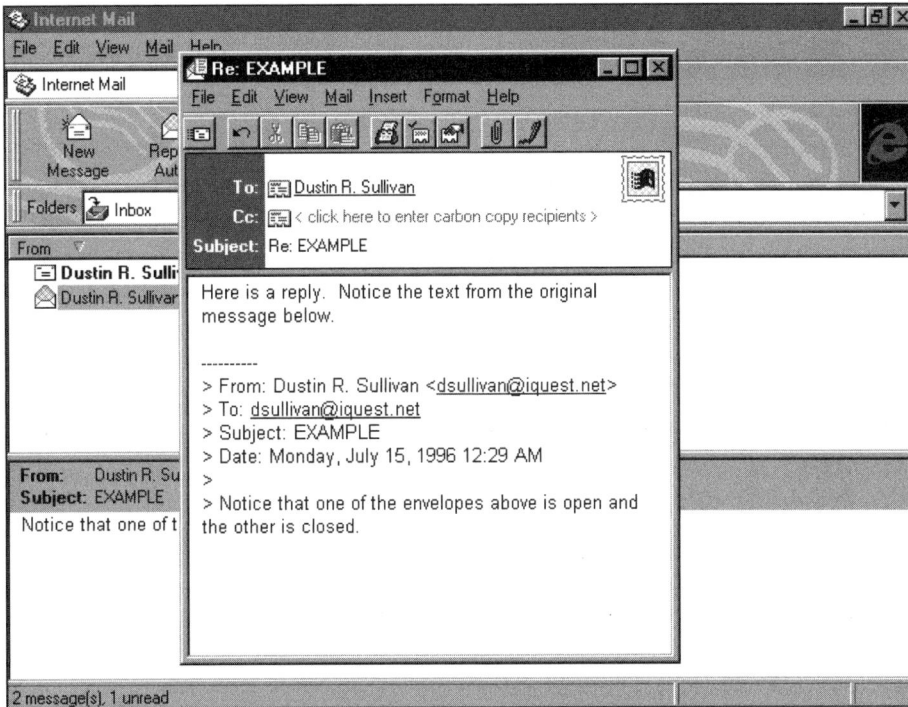

Figure 9.9: Replying to a mail message.

Attaching Files

You can attach files to send along with your message. This is great if
you want to show a friend a really cool picture instead of just describing it. Or you can send a spreadsheet containing the budget instead of
just referring to it in your message. Internet URLs can also be sent as
Windows 95 shortcuts. To attach a file to your message, click on the
Insert File button on the new message toolbar (the one that looks like
a paper clip). A standard Windows 95 menu will appear, letting you
choose the file you want to attach. When you have selected the file, it
is displayed in a separate pane at the bottom of the new message window, as shown in Figure 9.10. You can send the message as normal,
and the attachment will accompany it.

When you receive a message that has an attachment, it will be displayed like any other new message, but with a small paper clip to the
left of the message in the top pane, and on the right side of the screen

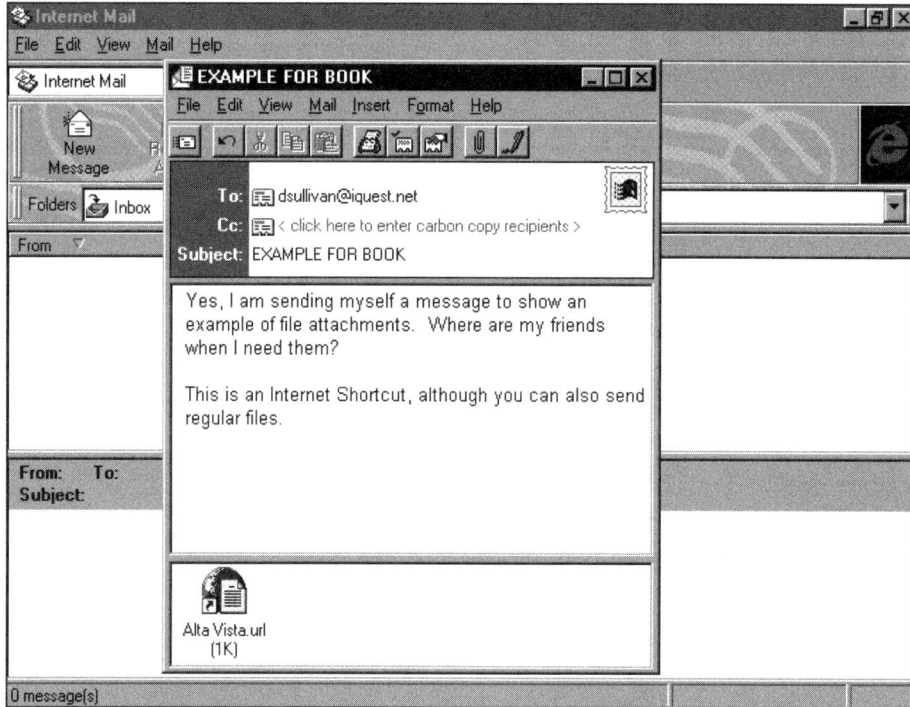

Figure 9.10: A file attached to a mail message.

in the bottom pane (shown in Figure 9.11). To open the attached file, click on the larger paper clip on the right side of the screen. The file-name will be displayed. Click the name to open the file.

Note: Remember that file attachments could contain viruses, so be sure to scan them before you use or open them.

To save an attachment to your hard disk, press and hold the Ctrl button on your keyboard as you click on the attachment's filename.

Other Really Cool Features

Internet Mail is loaded with features designed to make sending and receiving messages easy and quick. Many of these features (such as the

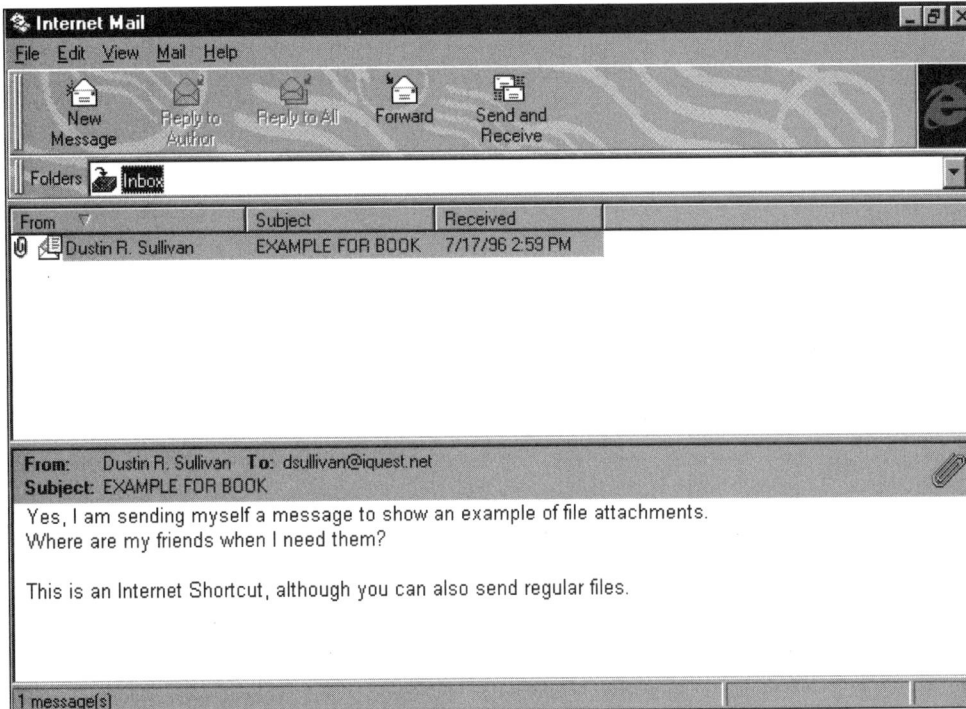

Figure 9.11: A message that includes an attached file.

HTML formatting, described above) are not currently available on other mail programs. Here are some other cool and helpful features.

Automatic Addressing of Messages This isn't entirely automatic, but it does save you some steps. In the To: area of the new message window, type the name of the person who will be the recipient of the message (usually just the first name is good enough). Continue to write and send the message as normal. When you send the message, Internet Mail will compare the name you typed with the names in the address book. If it finds a match, it will show you the match and ask if this is indeed the correct person to send the message to. If the name is not found, the program will ask if you want to add that person to your address book.

Hyperlinks Any Internet or e-mail address included in the text of a message will automatically be made into a hyperlink. Internet Mail automatically searches for groups of text beginning with http:, ftp:, telnet:, file:, and mailto: and makes them links. When you click on an Internet address, Explorer will launch and automatically go to the listed site. When you click on an e-mail address, a new message windows, preaddressed to that person, loads.

Signatures Signatures are short, prewritten sentences usually placed at the ends of messages to personalize them. Signatures are often a name and street address, although witty quotes and sayings are popular, too. To make your signature, select Mail Options from the menu bar and choose the Signature tab. You can even attach a file for your signature. To place your signature in a message, click the Insert Signature button on the new message toolbar.

Customizable Toolbar and Folders Just as in Explorer itself, the toolbar and the folder bar can be dragged and dropped in different spots to create a customized work area. Also, by right-clicking on the icon bar and selecting Customize Toolbar, you can add icons to be displayed on the icon bar. For example, if you find that you print messages frequently, you may want to add a print icon directly to the icon bar.

Import/Export If you use Exchange for work and Internet Mail for home, you can move files back and forth using the File Import and File Export from the Internet Mail menu bar. You can import both messages and address book entries from Exchange, and you can export messages to Exchange.

Searching Messages If you have many messages saved, finding a specific one can be difficult. Internet Mail has a Find button on its main toolbar to search within folders. You can search by name, recipients, subject, or by the date that the message was received.

Moving Messages You can move messages from one folder to another using the Mail Move to command. This allows you to better organize and keep track of important mail.

Sounds You can have Internet Mail play a WAV file when new messages are received. Set the WAV file up in the Sounds folder of the Windows 95 Control Panel. Activate the sound within Mail by selecting Mail Options Read. Check the box next to "Play sound when new messages arrive."

Using Exchange

Exchange is configured when you run the Internet Setup Wizard (see Appendix A if you have yet to do this). If you are a member of the Microsoft Network, Exchange is configured automatically when you install MSN software. As mentioned before, Exchange is an all-in-one solution for Windows 95, providing Internet e-mail as well as network mail and fax capabilities. For our purposes, though, we are only interested in the Internet e-mail capabilities.

If you are a member of the Microsoft Network, you must use Exchange for e-mail, but some bonuses like automatic setup and configuration are provided. Also, when you log on to MSN, the service tells you automatically if you have new mail, as seen in Figure 9.12. Go to MSN Central and click on E-mail. Exchange will launch and display any new messages that you have received. If you use an independent ISP instead of MSN, you must log on and manually check for new messages by clicking the Inbox icon on the Windows 95 desktop.

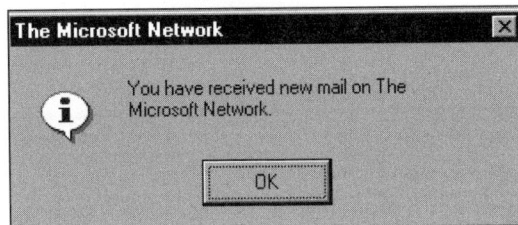

Figure 9.12: New mail on the Microsoft Network.

The Inbox icon is used whenever you want to check your e-mail or write a new message. New messages can be written at any time, even when you are off-line. If you are paying for connect time, you can download your e-mail while on-line and read it all off-line.

Exchange Basics

Figure 9.13 shows the basic Exchange screen. Notice how it is set up similarly to other Windows programs with a menu bar and a toolbar. The left pane is used for changing between mail folders (discussed a little later), and the right pane is used to display messages. Because most operating functions can be accomplished using the toolbar, it will be discussed in more detail than the menu bar. See the Windows 95 documentation if you need more specific information regarding the menu bar of Exchange.

Note: If your Exchange does not have two panes as shown in Figure 9.13, click the second icon from the left on the toolbar or make sure that Folders is checked in the View menu.

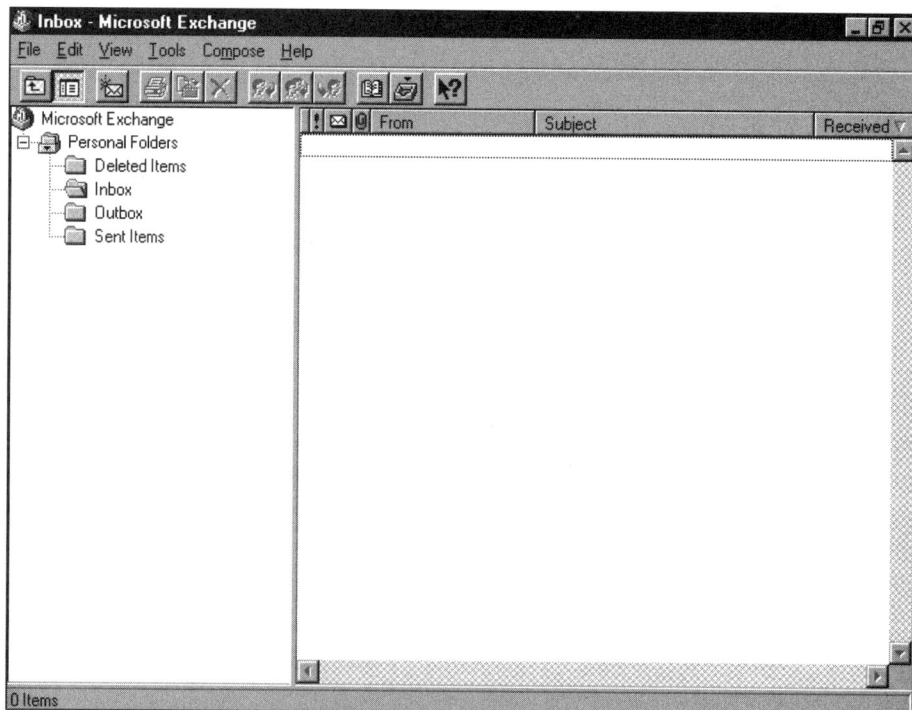

Figure 9.13: The standard Exchange screen.

Toolbar The toolbar in Exchange works just like toolbars in other programs such as Internet Explorer. Simply click a button to activate that command. Toolbar functions are displayed in Table 9.3.

Tip: Instead of using the Move Item icon, it is faster to move items between folders by dragging and dropping the message in the desired folder.

Folders The folders that are displayed when the Show/Hide Folder List button is depressed are used to separate and store both incoming and outgoing messages.

Personal Folders

This is the main folder, which contains the four secondary folders.

Deleted Items

Table 9.3: Exchange Toolbar Functions

Icon	Title	Function
	Up One Level	Used to change folders
	Show/Hide Folder List	Used to display/hide the Personal Folders in the left pane of the Exchange window
	New Message	Press this button to start writing a new e-mail message
	Print	Press this button to print the current message
	Move Item	Moves the highlighted message to a new folder
	Delete	Sends messages to the Deleted Items folder; when used in the Deleted Items folder, messages are permanently deleted

Table 9.3: Continued

	Reply to Sender	Creates a new message that is automatically addressed to the sender of the highlighted message
	Reply to All	Creates a new message that is automatically addressed to all recipients of the original message
	Forward	Sends a copy of the message to an address of your choice
	Address Book	Displays the address book
	Inbox	Takes you to the Inbox folder
	Help	Pressing this button and then clicking an item in Exchange will bring up a Help menu describing the item

When you delete messages from other folders, they are moved here rather than being deleted. When you delete messages from here, they are not moved to the Recycle Bin, but are erased permanently.

Inbox

All incoming messages are initially placed here. They are kept here even after they have been read until you move or delete them.

Outbox

When an item is sent, it is placed in the Outbox before it is actually delivered. See "Delivering Messages," later in this section, for more details.

Sent Items

When a message is delivered to its Internet address, it is moved from the Outbox to the Sent Items folder.

Creating New Folders Creating new folders is recommended if you receive e-mail from different sources that you want to keep separated. Rather than all of your messages cluttering up your Inbox or Deleted Items folders, you can create new folders to store messages from work, friends, or whomever. To create a new folder, click the folder in which you want the new folder to be placed. For example, if you want a new folder on the same level as the four original folders, click Personal Folders. Then choose File New Folder. Type the name of the new folder, and Windows will place it in alphabetical order with the other folders. In Figure 9.14, I have created a new folder called "Work Stuff." If you want to create a new folder within another folder (within the Inbox, for example), click that folder and then choose File New Folder. The new folder will appear within Inbox.

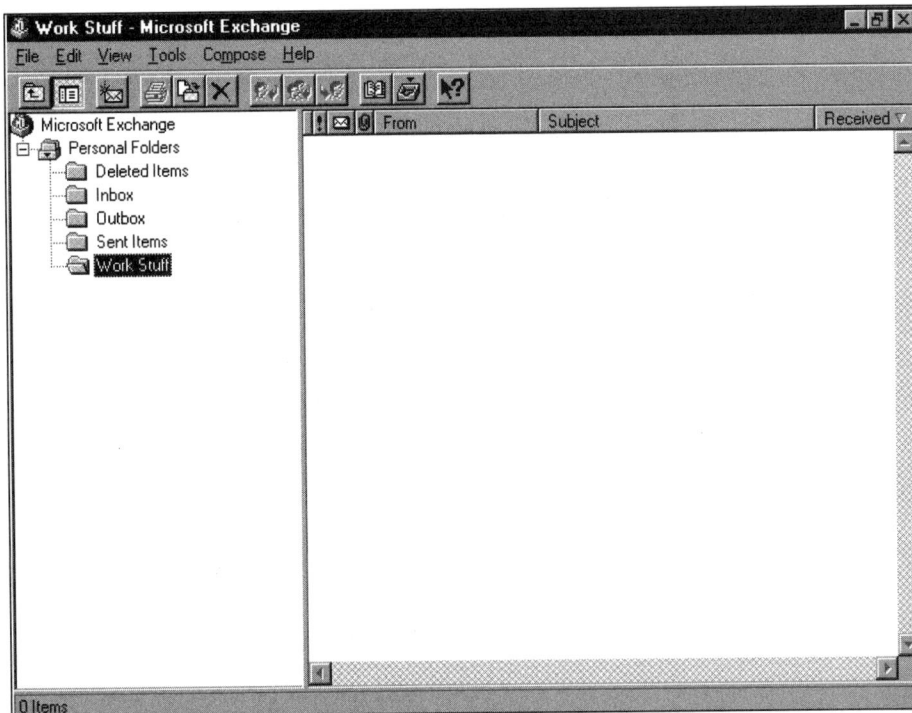

Figure 9.14: A new folder, Work Stuff, has been created.

Writing New Messages

To write a new message, click the new message button on the toolbar. The New Message window will appear (shown in Figure 9.15). The first thing you may notice is the toolbar—it's bigger than the main Exchange toolbar! Don't worry! We will cover it shortly. First, let's write the letter.

Move the cursor over the To area and click in the box. This is where you type the e-mail address of the person to whom you are sending this message. If you don't know any e-mail addresses yet, just type your own. If you want to send a copy of this letter to anyone else, write that person's e-mail addresses in the CC line below To. Click in the Subject area to enter the subject of the letter. To actually write the letter, click in the big area under Subject and start typing.

Note: Don't waste your time with the font and formatting options that are above the To area. Exchange does not convert messages to HTML as IMN can. Any special formatting that you do here will be lost when the message is received.

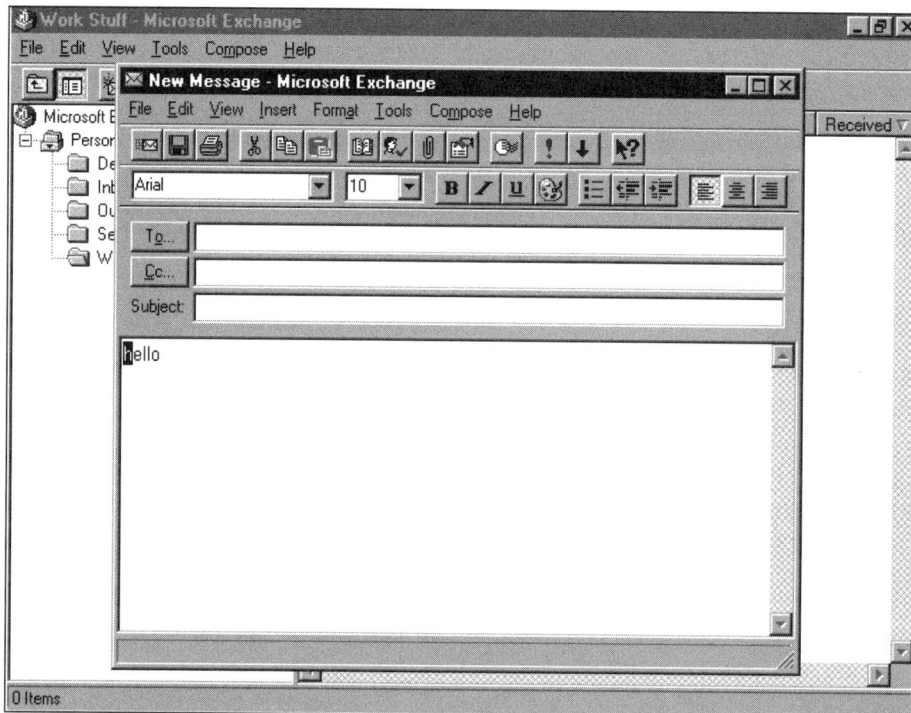

Figure 9.15: The New Message window in Exchange.

Tip: If you have Microsoft Office on your computer, you can use its spell checker on your letter before it is sent. From the Tools Options menu, choose the Spelling tab. Then check the box for "Always check spelling before sending."

When you have finished the message, press the Send button on the far left side of the toolbar. The message will then be placed in the Outbox, waiting to be delivered. Before we go there, look at the toolbar for the New Message window, shown in Table 9.4.

Table 9.4: New Message Toolbar Functions

Icon	Title	Function
	Send	Sends the letter to the Outbox
	Save	Saves the letter to disk
	Print	Prints a copy of the letter
	Cut	Cuts any highlighted text out of the letter and places it on the Windows 95 Clipboard
	Copy	Copies any highlighted text from the letter and places it on the Windows 95 Clipboard
	Paste	Pastes the contents of the Clipboard into the letter
	Address Book	Opens the address book
	Check Names	Compares the name in the To category to names in the address book
	Insert File	Attaches a file to transmit with the letter
	Properties	Displays file information about the current letter
	Read Receipt	Requests or cancels a read receipt(used mainly on networks)
	Importance: High	Places or removes a high-priority status on the message

Table 9.4 Continued

	Importance: Low	Places or removes a low-priority status on the message
	Help	Pressing this button and then clicking on an item in Exchange will bring up a Help menu describing the item

Using the Address Book

The address book is a helpful place to store the names and e-mail addresses of people with whom you correspond frequently. To add a name to the address book, follow these directions.

1. Click the Address Book button on the Exchange toolbar or the New Message toolbar.
2. From the Exchange toolbar, click the button called New Entry. From the New Message toolbar, click the New button.
3. Choose your Internet mail service from the list that appears and click OK.
4. In the windows that appears (shown in Figure 9.16), enter the information needed on the Internet Address tab and click OK. The Business, Phone Numbers, and Notes tabs are provided to store extra information about that person if you wish.

In this wonderful world of the Internet, there is yet another easy way to add a person to your personal address book. When you receive a message from someone you would like to include in your address book, right-click on the name in the From area. A pop-up menu will appear. Choose the Add to Personal Address Book option.

That person is now in your address book. From now on you can go into the address book and choose that person's name as the recipient of a new message, but there is an even quicker way. While in the New Message window, type part of the name of the person to whom you are sending the message. Then press the Check Names button on the toolbar. It will check your address book for matching names. When it finds the name, it will automatically address the letter to that person's e-mail address. If the name is not in the address book, Exchange will ask if you want to add it. If you want to send the letter to more than one person, type each person's name separated by a semicolon. This is

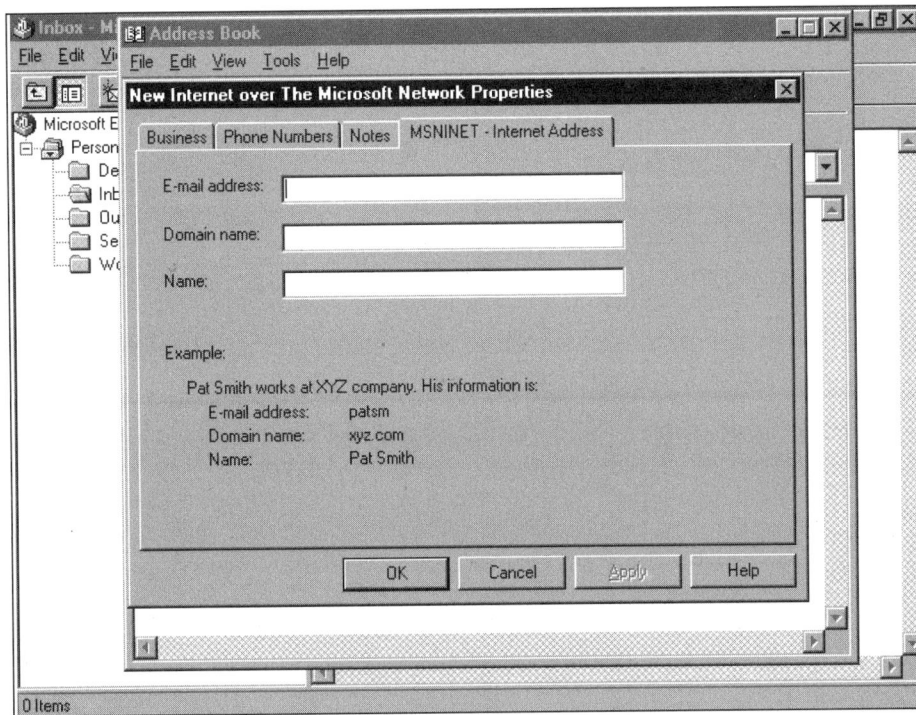

Figure 9.16: Adding a name to the Exchange address book.

a great feature if you don't want to go through the rather tedious process of pulling the name from the address book manually, or if you don't want to type the e-mail address by hand.

Note: The To line will not display the e-mail address after the check names function is used. It will only underline the name that you typed. This is normal—your message will be sent correctly, assuming that the information was previously entered in the address book correctly.

Delivering Messages

As you may have noticed, pressing the Send button does not actually send your letter. It only copies it to the Outbox folder, which is used as a storage folder for messages waiting to be delivered. To actually deliver your letter, choose Tools Deliver Now Using All Services from the menu bar. If you are not already logged on, Exchange will make the connection and deliver all messages that are in the Outbox. After these messages are delivered, they are moved to the Sent Items folder.

Receiving and Replying to Messages

There are several ways to check for new mail, depending on whether you are already on-line and already working in Exchange.

1. If you are using MSN, go to MSN Central and click E-mail.
2. If you are already working in Exchange, use Tools Deliver Now Using All Services.
3. If you are not already using Exchange, double-click on the Inbox Shortcut on the Windows 95 desktop. Exchange will automatically launch, log on to your Internet service if needed, and check for new mail.

Tip: You can configure Exchange to play a WAV sound when new messages are received by selecting Tools Options General from the menu bar. Then check the box next to "Play a sound" under the "When new mail arrives" heading.

When Exchange is checking for new messages, Figure 9.17 is displayed.

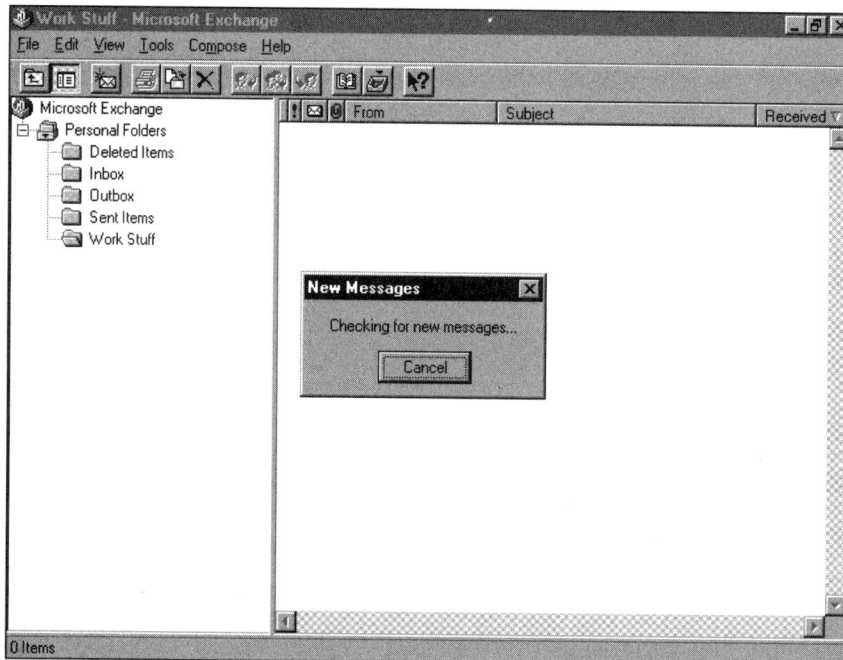

Figure 9.17: Checking for new messages with Exchange.

The Inbox folder will contain a list of new messages that were received. Messages can be marked as read or unread by selecting Edit Mark as Read or Mark as Unread from the menu bar. To read one, double-click on it. A new window appears (shown in Figure 9.18) with—you guessed it—another toolbar! This one is a bit simpler than the rest. The toolbar is described in Table 9.5.

Replying to the message is just a matter of choosing the correct Reply To button from the toolbar. Notice in Figure 9.19 that the original text is included in the reply for reference. If you do not want this to be included, you can delete it all or parts of it. It is treated as just another part of the letter. When you are finished writing your reply, send it the same way you send a new message.

Table 9.5: Toolbar Used When Reading a New Message

Icon	Title	Function
	Print	Prints a copy of the letter
	Move Item	Moves the message to a new folder
	Delete	Sends the message to the Deleted Items folder
	Reply to Sender	Creates a new message that is automatically addressed to the sender of this message
	Reply to All	Starts a new message that is automatically addressed to all recipients of the original message
	Forward	Sends a copy of this message to an address of your choice
	Previous	Displays the previous message in the folder
	Next	Displays the next message in the folder
	Help	Pressing this button and then clicking an item in Exchange will bring up a Help menu describing the item

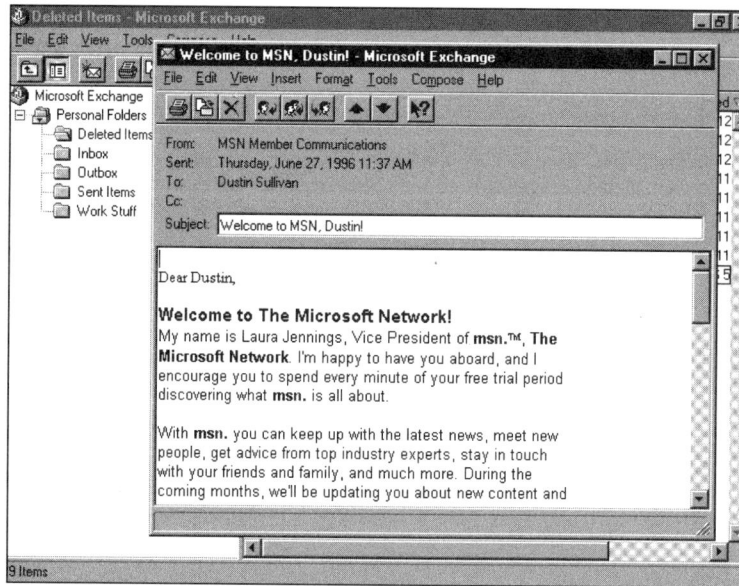

Figure 9.18: Reading a new message with Exchange.

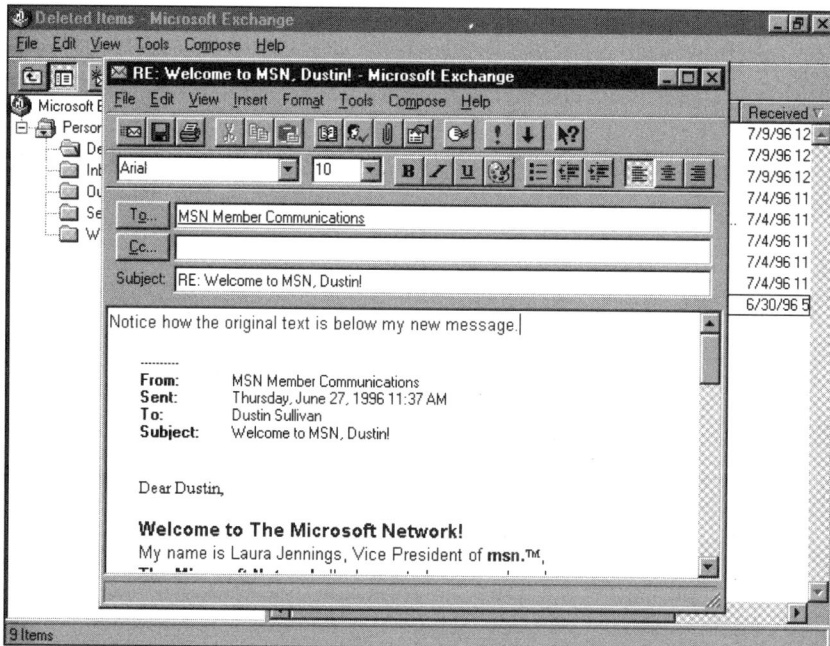

Figure 9.19: A reply with the text of the original message included.

Attaching Files

Just as with IMN, files can be attached and sent with a message. To attach a file:

1. Click in the part of the message where you want the file to be placed (Exchange will place files anywhere in a message, whereas IMN places all attachments at the bottom of the message).
2. Select the Insert File button (the one shaped like a paper clip) on the toolbar. The window shown in Figure 9.20 will appear.
3. Locate the file on your hard drive, highlight it, and select OK.

The file will appear in your message as an icon. The message can be sent as normal, and the attachment will go with it. You can also attach the text of a file or, using Insert Image from the menu bar, attach a graphics file (such as a JPEG image) that will be displayed in your message.

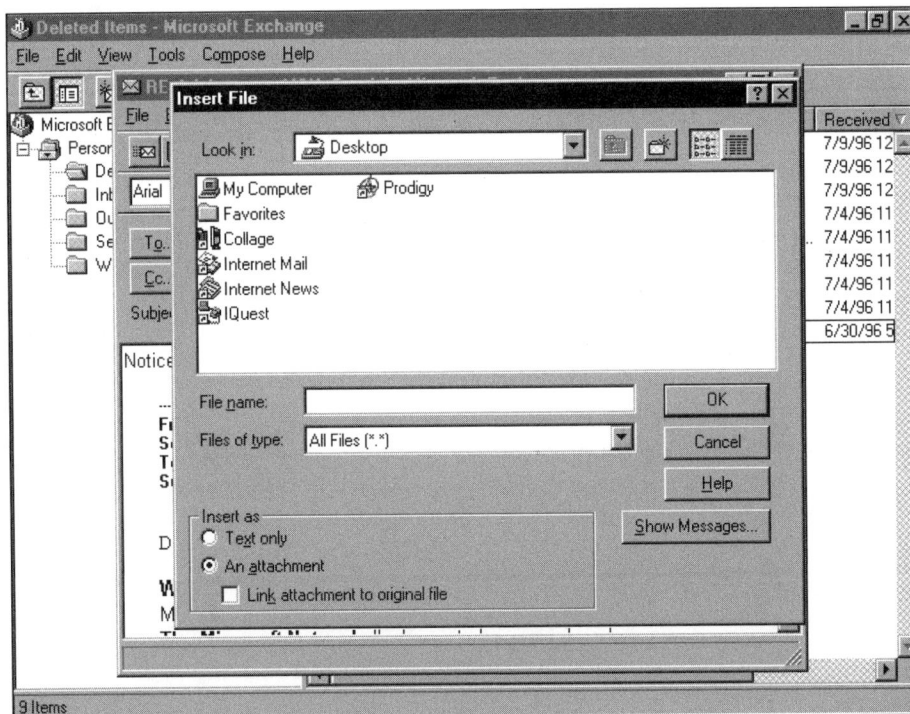

Figure 9.20: Finding a file to attach.

You can tell by two ways if a message that you have received includes an attachment. First, there will be a paper clip next to the message in the file list, as shown in Figure 9.21. Second, you will see the icon in your message (it's really difficult to miss them). To open your attachment, simply double-click its icon. To save it for later use, you can either right-click and choose Save As from the pop-up menu, or drag it and drop it onto the desktop or into a folder.

Note: Remember that file attachments could contain viruses, so be sure to scan them before you use or open them.

FLAMING

Flaming is the practice of sending many useless or harassing messages to an e-mail address. How many are many? It is not uncommon for a

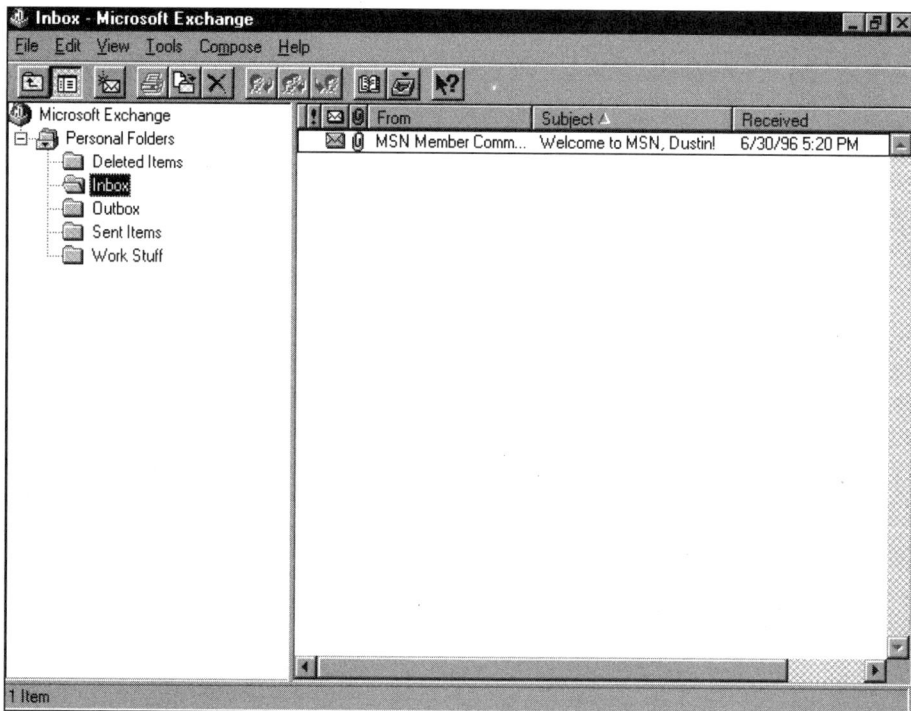

Figure 9.21: The small paper clip denotes a file attached to this message.

recipient to have several hundred messages and sometimes even more. Why do people do this? Flaming is usually in response to something that the user did to annoy (intentionally or unintentionally) a group of Net surfers. This can be anything from asking too many questions when there is a list of frequently asked questions (FAQ) available, to distributing unsolicited advertisements, to insulting another user. Flaming not only hurts the recipient, but it also ties up data lines with useless traffic and slows down Internet access for the rest of us. Please do not participate in this practice, and use courtesy and common sense when on-line so this doesn't happen to you.

WHAT'S AHEAD?

- Read and post messages in Usenet newsgroups in Chapter 10
- Look into the future of Web browsing in Chapter 11
- Learn how to create your own Web page in Chapter 12

Chapter 10

USING USENET

A tremendous amount of information is transferred across the Internet daily. Files, programs, and ideas are all exchanged as a regular course of business. Ideas? How do you transfer an idea? One of the busiest areas of the Internet are the Usenet newsgroups. Think of Usenet as a forum for exchanging opinions and ideas.

But how are the ideas publicized? How is this forum managed? Usenet is similar to a message board that anyone on the Internet can read (assuming they have the right software). E-mail-like messages are posted for public review. Everyone can read them, and anyone can post a reply. Usually the exchanges that take place are unedited, uncensored, and unrestricted. To keep the messages from being too overwhelming, the discussions are divided into many different interest groups, which also have subgroups within.

In this chapter we will discuss the way to read, reply to, and post new messages on the Usenet newsgroups. We will also discuss downloading and decoding pictures and images, as well as subscribing to groups that are interesting to you. Although many newsreading programs can be used with a PPP Internet account, Explorer includes a very powerful and very easy to use program as part of Internet Mail and News (this is the News part, if you hadn't made the connection yet). We will deal mainly with IMN, with a brief look at the Microsoft Network to start things off. Skip the MSN section if you have a different ISP. Even if you do use MSN, I think Internet News warrants consideration as your primary newsreader.

KEY POINTS IN THIS CHAPTER

- How do I get to newsgroups?
- How do I read messages and post replies?
- How do I write new messages?
- How do I download and decode pictures from Usenet?
- How do I subscribe to newsgroups?

WHAT EXACTLY IS USENET?

Let's say that you were having a discussion about basketball via e-mail with your friend. You think that $100 million is too much to pay an athlete, and your friend thinks that the players are worth whatever the market brings. In order to have this discussion, you send an e-mail message, your friend replies, you reply to the reply, and so on. Now imagine including a few other friends in the discussion. Each e-mail has a To: list of several people, and pretty soon everybody loses track of who was writing and replying to whom.

To help solve this problem, let's say that one of your friends finds a way to post messages to a spot on the Internet that everyone can access. The replies to this message are listed sequentially underneath the main message, and the author of each message is easily identifiable. Now many people can participate in the discussion, and everyone can see all of the other responses.

Now imagine that one of your friends wants to start another discussion about football, so he places this message right next to the basketball discussion. Pretty soon all sorts of discussions are taking place on all sorts of topics, and many people are involved. This is a much simplified explanation of Usenet newsgroups. Essentially, *newsgroups* are messages and replies to these messages posted in a public place. Anyone can post a new message, and anyone can reply to an existing message.

KEEPING TRACK OF THE DISCUSSIONS

You might wonder how all of these discussions can be kept separate from each other. Usenet newsgroups have very specific patterns for organizing discussions, so it is impossible to mistakenly jump to the wrong group. Newsgroups are broken into hierarchies, with each group having several subhierarchies to identify itself. Every group has what is known as a *top-level* hierarchy, which indicates the overall topic of discussion. Groups then have other parts to their names to further identify the subject matter. Table 10.1 lists some of the most common top-level hierarchies that you will find on the Net.

Let's break down a typical group name for a newsgroup dedicated to discussing the Sony Playstation, a home video game console. The group name is **rec.games.video.sony**. Notice how the more names are added, the more specific these names become. Also notice that the names are separated by periods. Another group similar to this one covers the Sega Saturn video game system, **rec.games.video.sega**. See that pattern? I'll give you a few more examples. A group dedicated to playing chess is called **rec.games.chess** (notice that this group only has three parts to its name; there are no rules for how long or short a name has to be). One more group that doesn't cover games is **misc.jobs.resumes**, which covers resume creation and general job-hunting tips.

Table 10.1: Some Common Newsgroup Topics

Top-Level Name	Subject Matter
alt	"Alternative" subject matter
biz	Business-related discussions
clari	Clarinet groups containing UPI stories and columns
comp	Computer-related discussions
K12	Primary school discussions
misc	Miscellaneous stuff that doesn't fit anywhere else
news	Information on Usenet newsgroups themselves
rec	Recreational discussions—sports, hobbies, etc.
sci	Scientific discussions
soc	Social issues and general socializing
talk	Anything controversial—religion, politics, etc.
de	German newsgroups (you will also find other countries)

*Note: Just because a group exists doesn't mean that there will be notes posted to it. Some newsgroups have been abandoned, or some are duplicates that are not used as much as the original. For instance, the Sony Playstation has another group—**alt.games.video.sony-playstation**—that is not used as often as the **rec.games.video.sony** group. Some groups exist that are completely empty, so don't blame your computer if it doesn't display any messages for some groups.*

HOW ALTERNATIVE ARE THE ALT GROUPS?

Many people assume that every group that exists in the alt category is full of sex stories. There are many, but that is not all that alt is about. In fact, the alt group is almost another Usenet in and of itself, with discussions ranging from music to movies to automobiles to science. The alt groups do traditionally take a different approach to these topics than the standard newsgroups, but the discussions can be livelier at times because of the unique views that are expressed. The sex groups are there, but remember: You can't get to a group by accident, so unless you specifically type **alt.sex.exhibitionism**, you won't go there!

HEADERS

Not a soccer term, a *header* is the piece of information that identifies a message. Once you get into a newsgroup, each message is identified by a header. The header usually contains a description of the message, the author's name and/or e-mail address, the date that the message was posted, and the length (usually in lines of text) of the message.

ACCESSING NEWSGROUPS WITH MSN

The Microsoft Network contains many newsgroups that are accessible without using Internet Explorer. From MSN Today or MSN Central Categories, you can open the Internet Center. Inside the Internet Center is the Internet Newsgroups section of MSN. This screen is shown in Figure 10.1.

From this window, you can access many newsgroups in alphabetical order or browse a list of what Microsoft considers to be the most

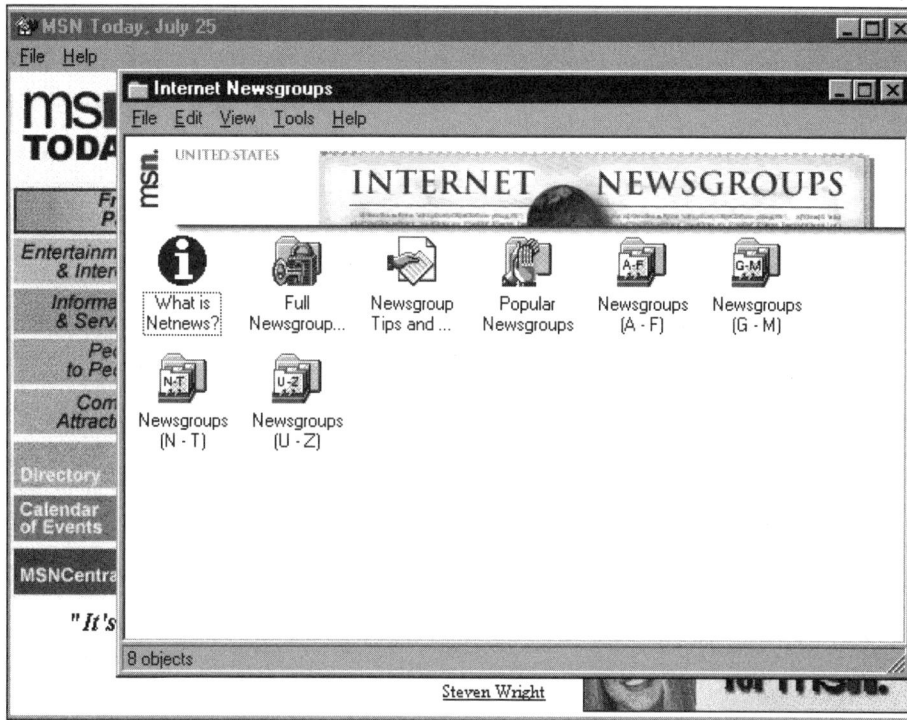

Figure 10.1: Internet Newsgroups section of MSN.

"popular" groups available. To go to a group, click on the letter that begins the top-level name ("a" for alt, for example), scan through the list of available newsgroups, and double-click that group.

Tip: In order to prevent access to "adult" material, MSN cuts out many newsgroups from its regular offering. To gain access to these groups, click on the Full Newsgroups & Adult Access Shortcut in the Internet Newsgroups window. Inside you will find a form that will give you access to all news-groups that MSN carries.

Reading and Replying to Messages

When you reach a group, your screen will look like Figure 10.2. Each line, or header, in Figure 10.2 is a separate discussion of topics relating to the Sony Playstation (that video game thing I mentioned earlier). These individual discussions are known as threads or sometimes as conversations. When a thread is preceded by a plus sign (as most in

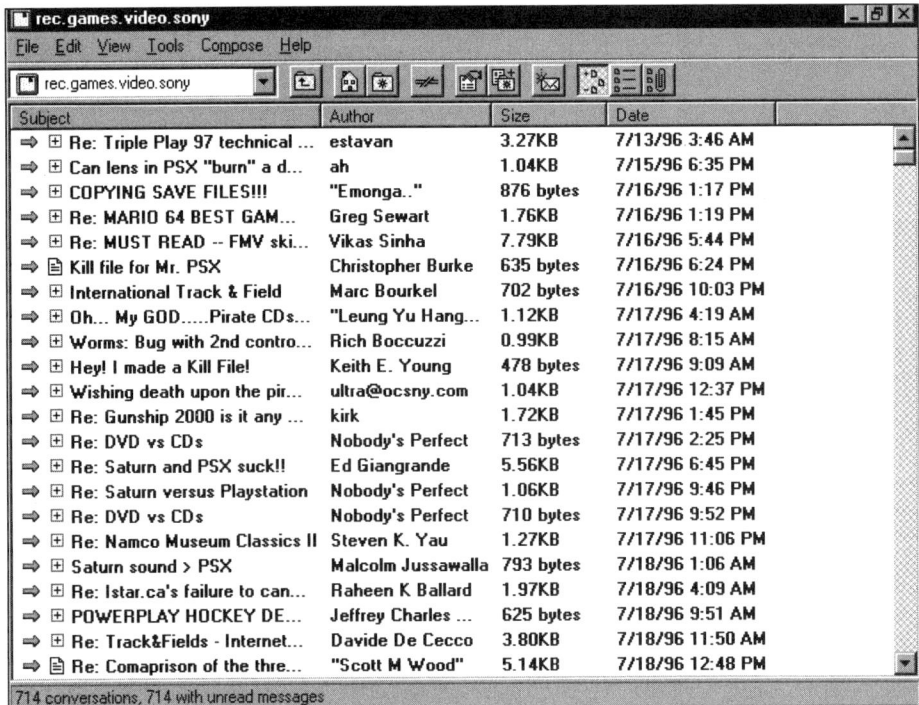

Figure 10.2: rec.games.video.sony viewed through MSN.

this group are), that means that there are several responses to the original message that can be viewed. Clicking on the plus sign will reveal the responses, as shown in Figure 10.3. The responses are slightly indented from the original message, making them easier to distinguish. There can be a reply to a reply, although mostly the replies are made to the original posted message. The toolbar at the top of the screen offers quick ways to move between threads, messages, and newsgroups. Just like e-mail, messages and entire threads can be marked as read or marked as unread by using Tools from the menu bar.

To read a message in the thread, double-click on the header. A window appears (as shown in Figure 10.4) displaying the contents of the message as well as information on the author and the time and date of posting. The toolbar for this window allows you to write a reply to this message, cut and paste sections of the message, and navigate to other messages and threads.

Replying to messages is very similar to replying to e-mail messages. When you click on the New Message button on the toolbar, a new

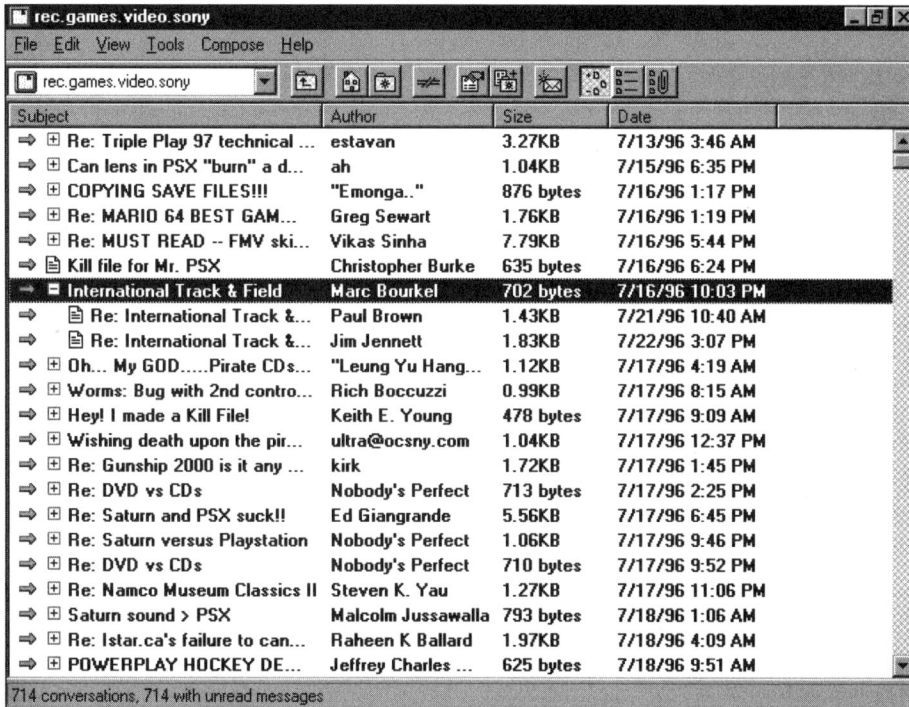

Figure 10.3: Displaying all messages in a thread.

window appears for you to use to compose your reply. The text of the original message will appear in your reply; many people use this to cite specific examples from the message to which they are replying. When you are finished with your reply, press the Post button to send it to the group. If you are not sure that your reply is worth posting to the entire world, you can reply privately by sending an e-mail message to the author by selecting Compose Reply by E-mail from the menu bar. You can also write a completely new message to post on the newsgroup. For example, if you had a question about a game that was not being discussed, you could post a brand new message that is open for others to reply. Compose New Message on the menu bar will enable you to start your own thread.

Tip: Before posting a public reply or a new message, read the section on Netiquette later in this chapter.

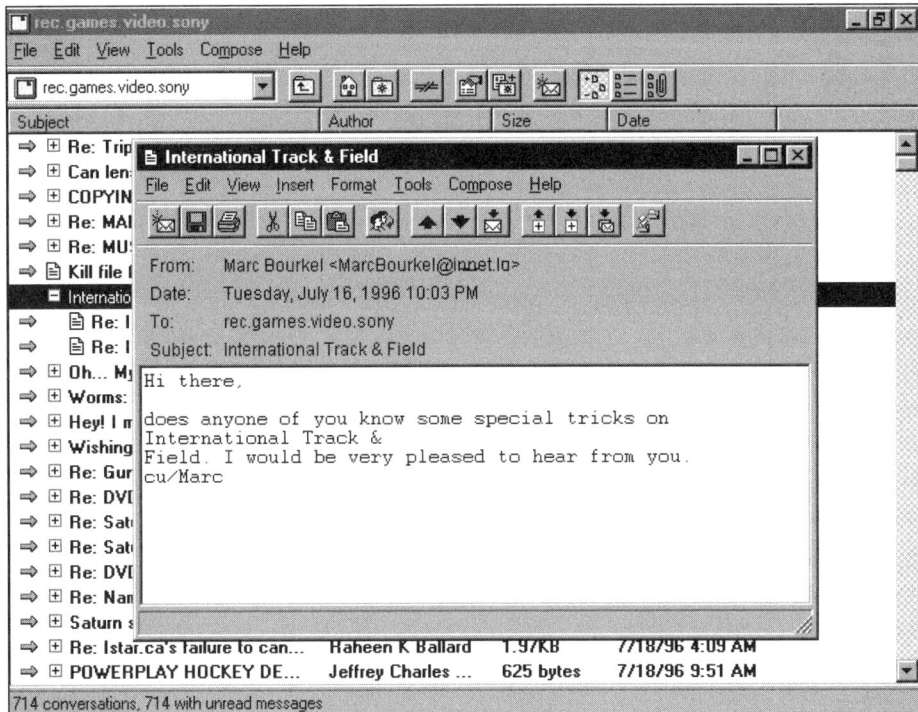

Figure 10.4: Reading a message with MSN.

Downloading Files

Many newsgroups have files, usually GIF or JPEG images or WAV sounds, included in the posted messages that can be downloaded to your computer. Unlike downloading from FTP or Web sites, these files are not immediately ready to be viewed or played after downloading. To include these files on the Usenet, they must first be encoded to a form that can be recognized by the Usenet computers. This means that until they are decoded, the files look like a bunch of useless gibberish. Files on Usenet newsgroups are encoded using a method called UUEncode.

To download a file from MSN, all you need to do is click the message header. If a file is included in that message, it will be downloaded automatically. MSN does not decode the message for you, though. To do this, you need a separate decoding program. There are several shareware and freeware programs available to do this; one of the most popular is a freeware program called Wincode (you can use a search engine to find this program). After downloading a file, save it and run it through your decoder. It is now restored to its original state and ready to be viewed or played.

Conversely, to upload a file to a newsgroup, you simply encode a file (which turns it into a text format) and include the text in the body of your message. It is usually polite to either write a very descriptive name for your message or write a separate note that people can read without downloading. This way people will know what your file is before they spend time downloading it.

ACCESSING NEWSGROUPS WITH INTERNET NEWS

The default newsreader for Explorer is Internet News. This program offers more features than MSN and is much easier to use. Internet News can be launched from Explorer by typing a news: link in the address bar, by clicking on a news: link in a Web page, or by clicking the Mail and News icon on the toolbar.

The first time you log on to the news server of your ISP, News will have to download the list of newsgroups available on that server. The actual download process can take a while, even at 14.4bps. This process is shown in Figure 10.5. Notice in Figure 10.5 that 1146 groups have been received. This number actually increased to more than 20,000 before my download was completed! Maybe now it is clear why newsgroups names have to be so specific! Once you have down-loaded groups, you shouldn't have to do this again. News is set by default to automatically check for and download new groups as they are added to your ISP's server, but these updates usually don't take long to download.

To see the list of newsgroups that was just downloaded, click the Newsgroups icon on the icon bar. This will open the Newsgroups win-dow, as shown in Figure 10.6. From this window you can scroll down through the alphabetical list of available groups. You can also type the name or part of the name of a group that you would like to see in the space below "Display newsgroups which contain:". If you are inter-ested in all of the groups that contain "video games" in the title, for example, type video.games or games.video. For an even more broad search, you can just type video or games. Internet News will then

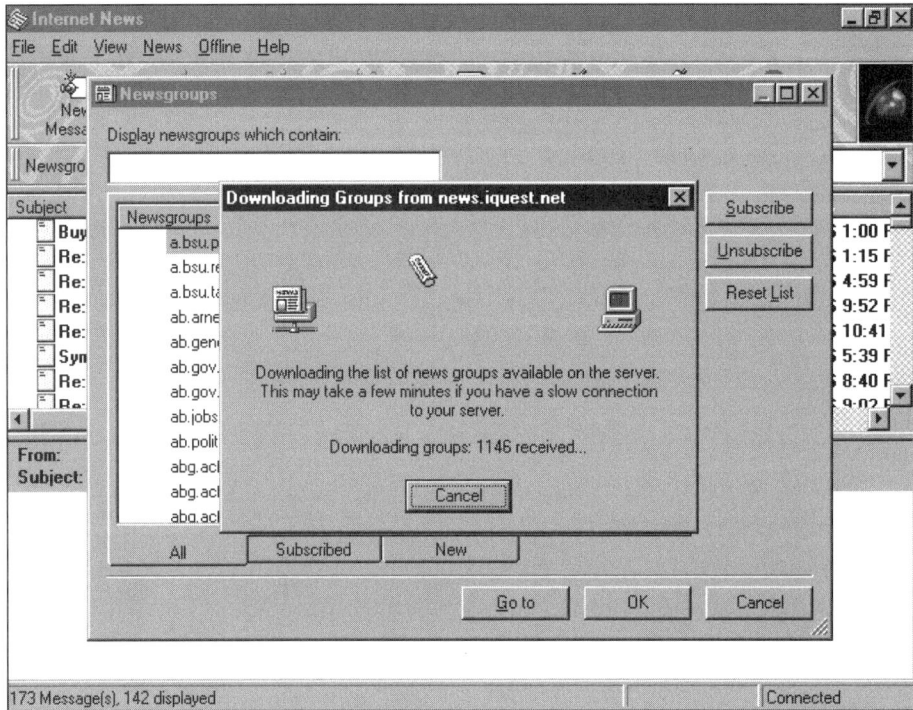

Figure 10.5: Downloading groups from an ISP.

display every group that contains those words in its title. When you see a group worth visiting, highlight its name and click Go to.

Basics

As you are familiar with the customizing features of Internet Explorer and Internet Mail, I won't go into detail about this feature with Internet News except to say that the toolbar area is customizable by dragging and dropping and right-clicking. The entire look is familiar. News is designed just like Mail and Explorer itself, with a toolbar, icon bar, "E" logo, and status bar. The main News screen, shown in Figure 10.7, will be the basis for discussing the layout and functions of the toolbar as well as the threads themselves.

The main screen is divided into two panes. The top pane is used to display the threads (individual discussions within the newsgroup identified by headers and subheaders), while the bottom pane is used

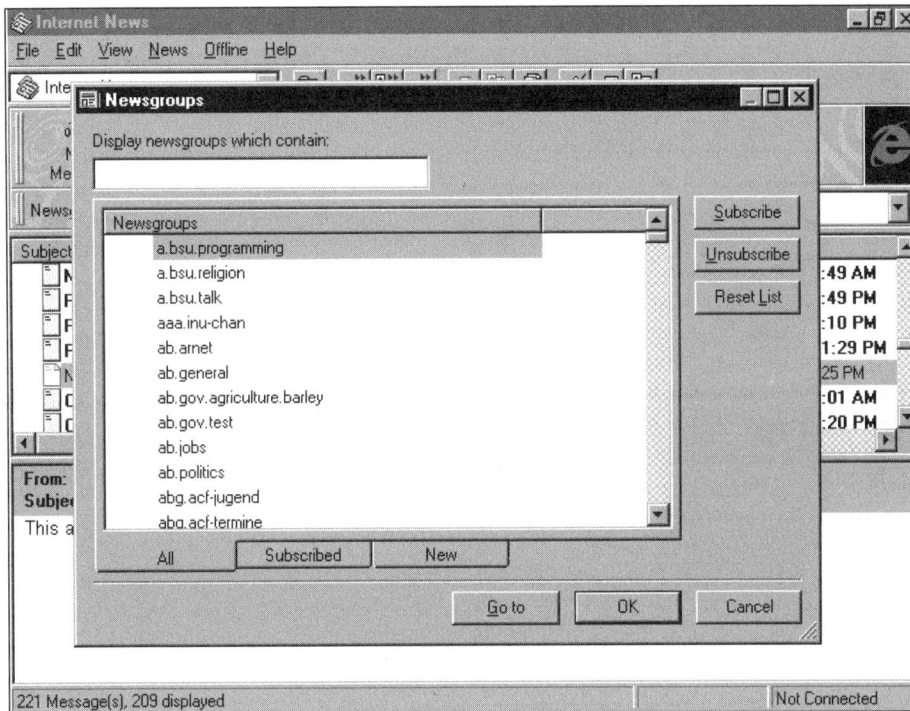

Figure 10.6: A list of available newsgroups.

to display the content of the messages themselves. The status bar displays information relating to downloads, the total number of threads in a newsgroup, and connection status.

Note: The windows can be displayed side by side, if you prefer, by selecting View Preview Pane from the menu bar.

Toolbar The toolbar works in standard Windows fashion. Simply click a button to activate its function. The toolbar functions are described in Table 10.2.

Newsgroups

The Newsgroups section of Internet News is analogous to the Folders section of Internet Mail. It is where messages that you have written or saved are stored. Newsgroups that you have subscribed to (subscribing will be discussed later in this chapter) are also stored here for easy access.

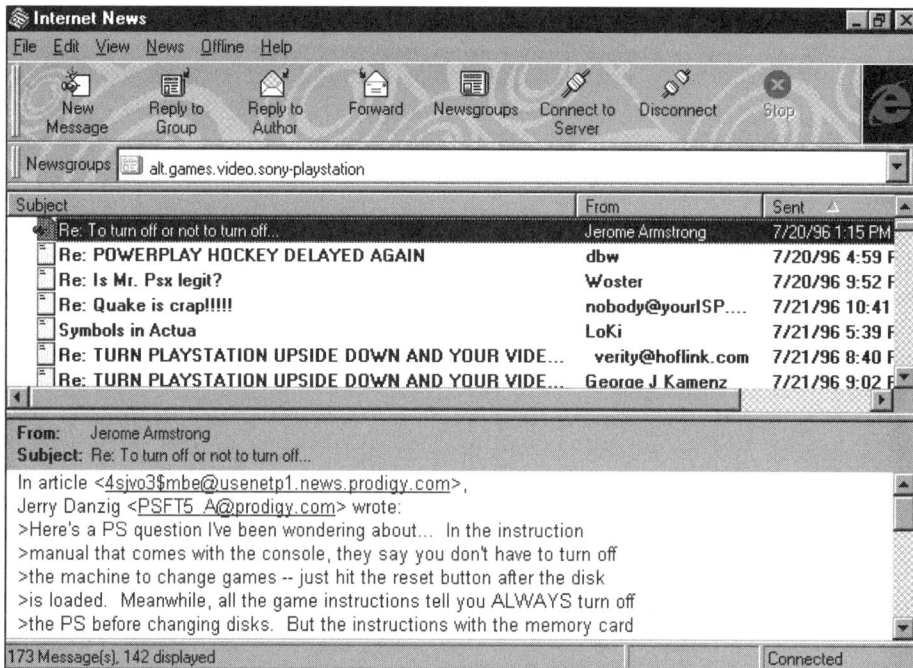

Figure 10.7: The standard Internet News screen.

Table 10.2: Internet News Toolbar

Icon	Name	Function
	New Message	Create a new message to post on the newsgroup
	Reply to Group	Write a reply to post publicly on the newsgroup
	Reply to Author	Write a private e-mail reply to the author
	Forward	Forward the newsgroup message via e-mail
	Newsgroups	Display the list of available newsgroups
	Connect to Server	Establish a connection with your ISP's news server

Table 10.2: Continued

	Disconnect	Break the connection with your ISP's news server
	Stop	End current function

rec.games.video.sony

In my example, I have subscribed to the newsgroup rec.games.video.sony. Any other groups to which I have subscribed would also appear here with the icon of a newspaper next to the group name.

Outbox

If you compose a new message or a reply while off-line, this is where they are stored until they are posted.

Posted Items

After messages or replies are actually posted on the newsgroup, they are stored here.

Saved Items

If you save a message that you see, it is stored here.

THE INTERNET NEWS CACHE

Remember the cache for Internet Explorer? It provided a way for Web pages to be stored in your computer for faster retrieval and off-line viewing. Internet News also has a cache that allows for faster viewing and off-line viewing of newsgroups. When you are on-line, the groups that you visit are placed in the cache. All of the messages are not always cached, though. Usually just the message headers, or titles, are cached. This allows you to view the subjects of the threads while off-line, but not view the actual messages. The messages can be saved in the cache if you wish to view them off-line, but it is much more reliable to manually save any messages that you are interested in.

Why does Internet News not cache everything? This would take up huge amounts of space on your hard drive. Internet News is aware of this, and even compresses, or compacts, the cache files after a session so space is not wasted. If you are in need of space, you can manually empty the cache by choosing News Options Advanced from the menu bar and selecting Clean Up Now to purge old files from the cache.

Reading Messages

Figure 10.7 shows the basic way to read a message. Highlight the message you want to read, and the text is displayed in the bottom pane. In Figure 10.8, the messages shown with plus signs next to them are threads with replies posted to the original message. To view the replies, click on the plus sign. In Figure 10.8, the highlighted message contains only one reply, which is indented slightly from the original message. To read the reply, click on its header, and the contents will be displayed in the bottom pane.

Note: You can also view messages by double-clicking their headers. This will display the message in its own window with its own toolbar. You gain one extra piece of information when viewing a message in this manner: The message header contains a list of all newsgroups that this particular message has been posted to. These newsgroups can be reached by clicking their names.

Just as Internet Mail treats every Internet address and e-mail address as a link, Internet News also automatically turns any text describing an Internet site or address into a link that can be selected.

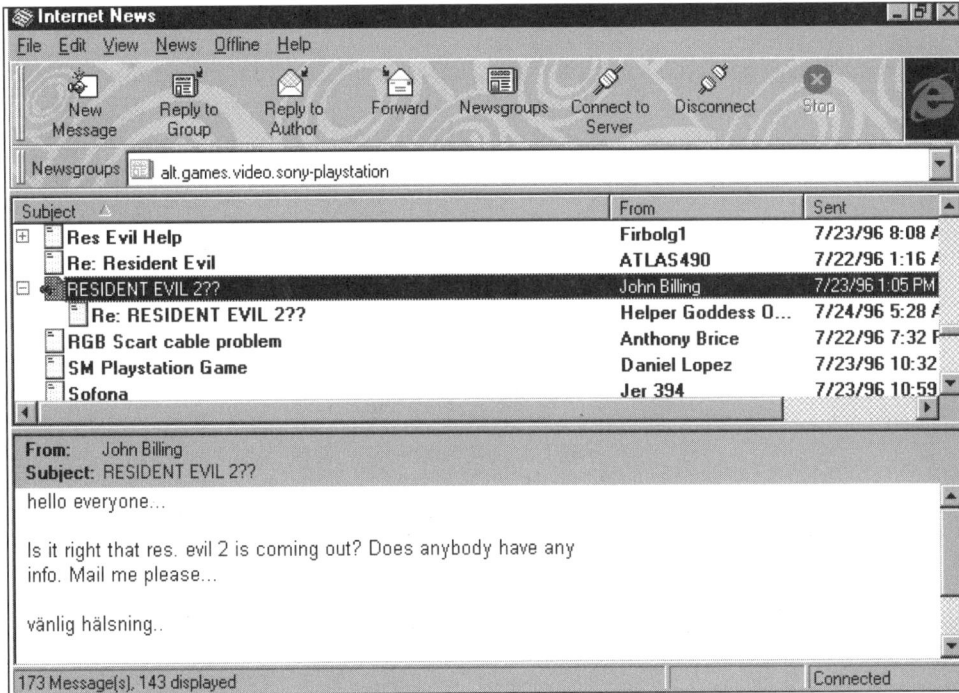

Figure 10.8: Viewing replies to messages.

Marking Messages as Read

Unread messages have a yellow paper next to the header. When a message has been read, the paper changes to a white page with a folded corner next to the header. This can be a very helpful cue to keep you from reading the same message twice. The buttons in the toolbar, Mark Message as Read, Mark Thread as Read, and Mark all Messages as Read, are used to force a read status on messages you want to ignore. Highlight the message or thread you want to mark, then press the desired button. Internet News can be set to display only unread messages so that you are not bombarded with old messages the next time you visit that group. To do this, select View Unread Messages Only from the menu bar.

Replying to Messages

Replying to a message on a newsgroup is just as simple as replying to a received e-mail message. When the message header is highlighted, select the Reply to Group icon from the icon bar. The window shown in Figure 10.9 appears. The original message appears, distinguished from your new text with ">" in front of each line (just as in an e-mail reply). The toolbar is all familiar stuff except for one icon.

After you have typed your reply, pressing this button will send it to the news server for posting. Unlike Internet Mail, which does not send your messages immediately, the Post Message button will send your message right away.

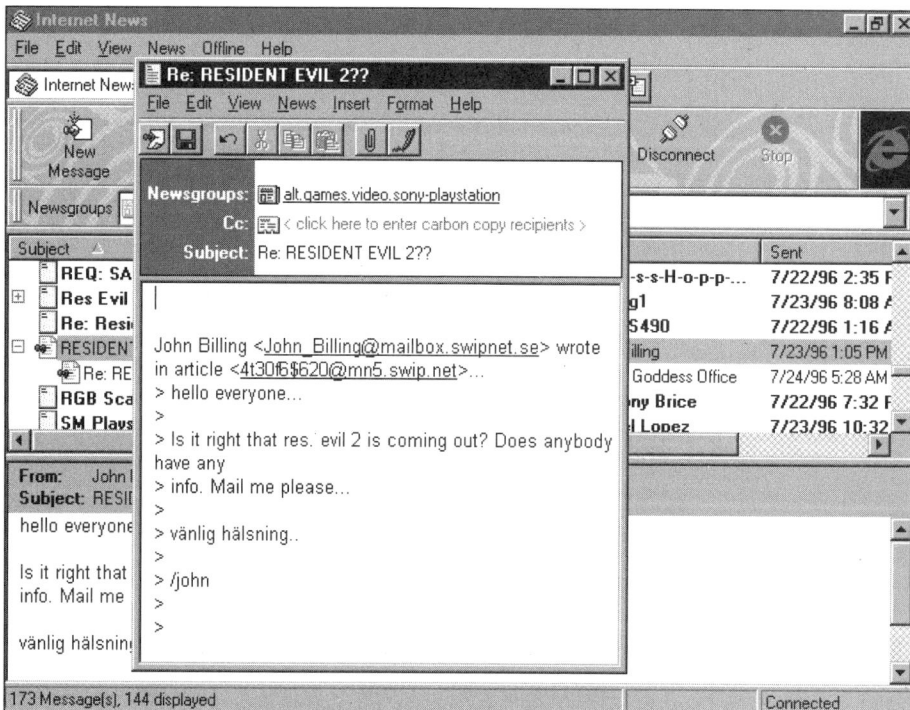

Figure 10.9: Internet News' reply to window.

Tip: Make sure you really want to send your message before you press the Post Message button. Once you have done that, you cannot change or get your message back. Read the section on Netiquette (later in this chapter) before posting any replies or new messages.

You can also send a private reply to the author of the message by e-mail. To do this, select the Reply to Author icon from the icon bar. The rest is just like sending any other e-mail message. Replying by e-mail can be much "safer" than posting a public reply because you do not expose yourself to the critiques of the Internet masses! You may also have a more personal response that you do not wish to display in public.

Composing a New Message

If you have been looking through the newsgroup for a tip to your favorite game and just can't find it, you might consider posting your own message. This could be in the form of a "Help!" or a "Request." When you post a new message, you are creating a new thread. Your message will not be listed under any other messages; it will be in plain sight on the main list of topics. When people reply to your message, you will know by looking for the plus sign displayed next to the header or the avalanche of e-mail that you might receive. Or, if nobody cares about your favorite game, you could be completely ignored!

To write a new message, select the New Message icon from the icon bar (real brain surgery here). The New Message window, shown in Figure 10.10, will appear. Again, there is no new stuff on the toolbar here. Write your message and press the Post Message button. You are now published!

Note: When you reply to a message or post a new message, your message will not immediately be displayed (Internet Mail notifies you of this when you post). The Internet news servers do not constantly update their lists, so it may take several minutes to display. Even then, you will have to leave the current group and return to see any updates, or choose Refresh from the View menu.

You can add a personalized "signature" to the end of your messages. If you have set this up in Internet Mail, you do not need to reenter it for Internet News. If you have not created a signature, go to the Signature tab of the News Options window. Signatures usually consist of an address or phone number or sometimes a clever phrase or saying. If you do not want to have your signature added to your messages

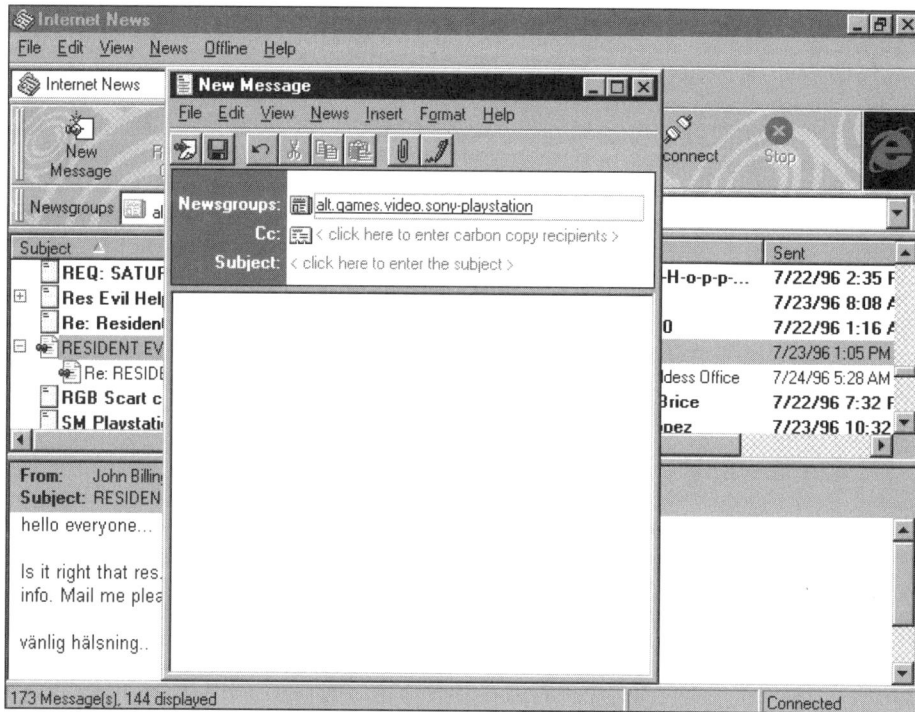

Figure 10.10: The New Message window in Internet News.

automatically, you can add it manually from the toolbar of the New Message or Reply to Group windows.

You can set Internet News to check spelling automatically before you post a message or reply if you have Microsoft Office installed on your computer. To check spelling manually, select Check Spelling from the News menu on the New Message or Reply to Group toolbar. If you want Internet News to automatically check your spelling before posting a message or reply, select the Spelling tab from the News Options window and check "Always check spelling before sending."

Tip: You can write replies or compose new messages while off-line. When you are finished, connect with your ISP, then select Offline Post and Download from the menu bar. A connection will be established with your news server and your messages sent.

Downloading Files

Many people like to exchange files as well as ideas through Usenet. Many graphics images (usually GIF and JPEG) as well as sound files (usually WAV) can be downloaded from newsgroups. Usenet newsgroups cannot display graphics or play sound files the way Web pages can, however. In order to post these files to Usenet, they must first be encoded into a text format (known as ASCII). On top of this, file size must be limited, so many files are split. For instance, a large graphic file may be divided into four parts. These parts will be listed in the header of the messages that contain them as 1/4, 2/4, 3/4, and 4/4. This informs you that you must download each part for the file to be complete.

Unlike MSN, Internet News automatically decodes messages as they are downloaded. This eliminates a rather annoying step. When a file is downloaded, it is ready for viewing or playing. To begin the download, find a message that contains a file. They are usually easily identified in the header. For example, Figure 10.11 shows a download in progress for a JPEG file of a golfer. It is identified in the header as "golf.jpg (1/1)." This means that the title of the file is golf.jpg, and it is made up of only one part (1/1). When you find a file that is interesting, highlight the header. Internet News will automatically start downloading it. The progress of the download is displayed on the status bar at the bottom of the screen. This is represented as a percentage and a blue bar (both shown in Figure 10.11).

To view the file after downloading is completed, click on the paper clip that appears in the bottom pane on the right side (just like a file attachment in Internet Mail). The filename will be displayed. Click on the filename to open the file. Figure 10.12 shows this paper clip along with an important virus reminder that pops up when viewing files. If you choose Open, the picture will be displayed. If you want to scan the file for viruses before viewing it (not a bad idea), you must first save the file to your hard drive. To save the file, hold down the Ctrl key on your keyboard as you click the paper clip and then click the filename. The usual Windows 95 Save File screen will appear.

If you want to download a file that is divided into several parts, a few extra steps are required to download and decode. Hold down the Ctrl key on your keyboard and select all parts of the file. Each message header will stay highlighted even as the others are selected. Select News Combine and Decode from the menu bar. A window will appear

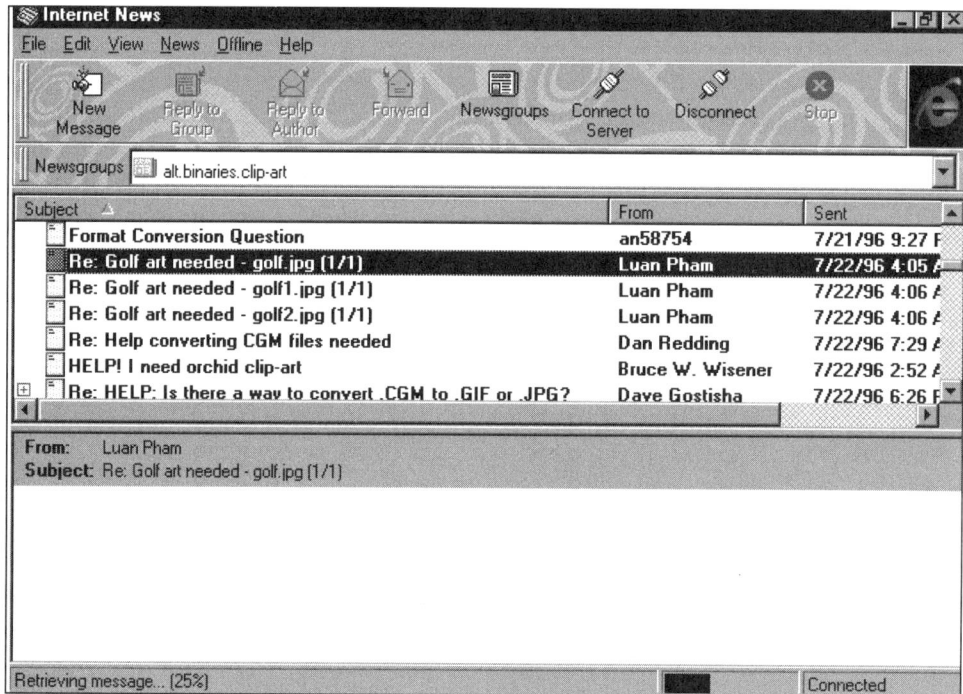

Figure 10.11: Downloading a file in Internet News.

that will allow you to adjust the order of the files (just in case 2/4 is before 1/4), and the file will be downloaded and automatically combined. When the download is complete, the file and any text in the messages will be displayed in a new window. The file itself is represented by a shortcut at the bottom of the window, and it can be opened by double-clicking. If this looks familiar, that is because this is the same way file attachments are received in Internet Mail.

Note: If you close the window and move on to another message, the file will still be stored in memory until you exit Internet News. If you return to the message that contains the downloaded file before exiting, you can still access it by clicking on the paper clip in the bottom viewing pane.

Uploading a file is accomplished using the same technique as attaching a file to an e-mail message. The easiest way is to click on the Insert File button on the New Message or Reply to Group toolbar.

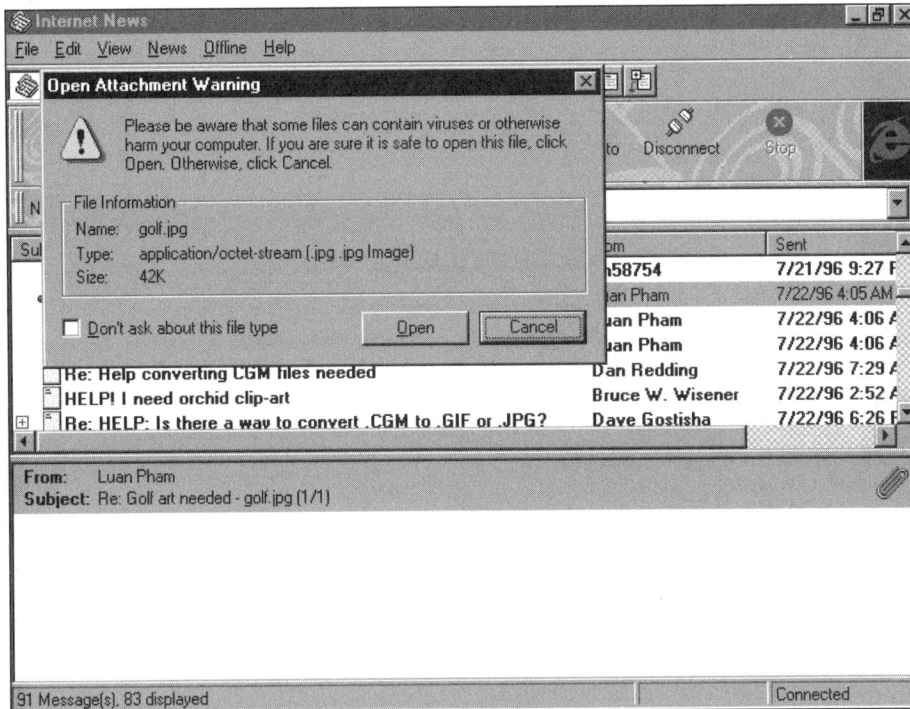

Figure 10.12: Viewing a downloaded file.

Then select the file, which will be represented as a Windows 95 short-cut until the file is uploaded to the server.

Subscribing to Newsgroups

If you find that you visit certain newsgroups more frequently than others, you may wish to subscribe to them. This does not involve money or automatic e-mails to your address. It does set up the news-groups to be easily accessible without having to sort through the entire list of groups. There are several ways to subscribe to a newsgroup. The first is automatic. When you leave a group after visiting, Internet News will automatically ask you if you want to subscribe (shown in Figure 10.13). If you click Yes, that newsgroup is placed in your Newsgroups folder list (directly below the icon bar). When you launch Internet News, you can go to your subscribed newsgroups by clicking

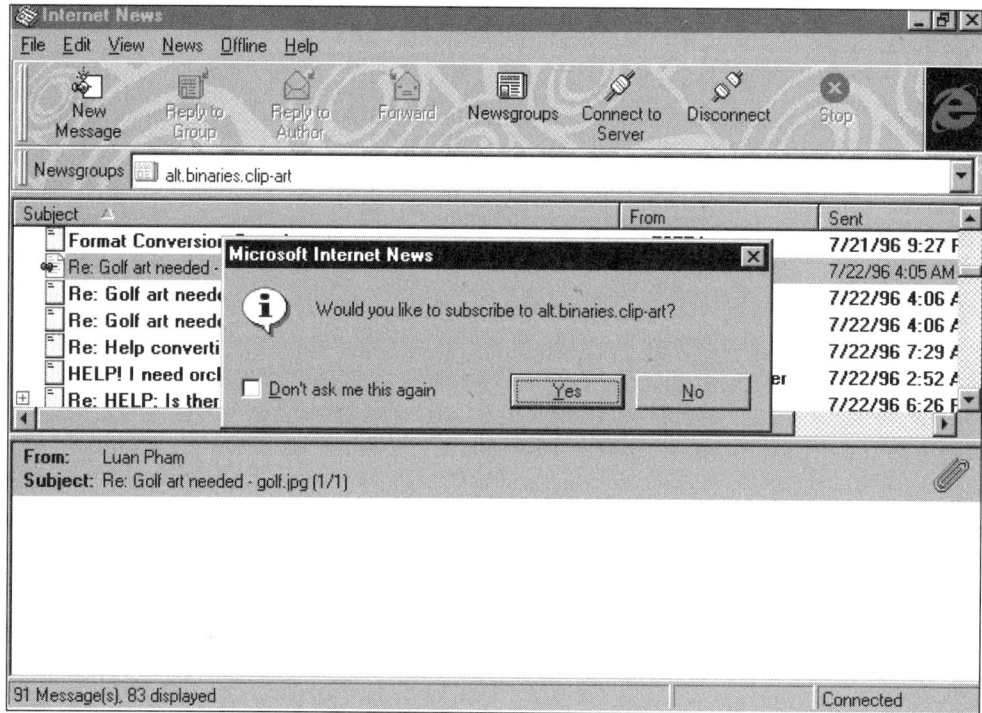

Figure 10.13: Leaving a newsgroup.

the down arrow on the Newsgroups section and selecting the desired group from the list.

You can also manually subscribe. From the Newsgroups window, highlight the group to which you want to subscribe. You now have two options. Either click the Subscribe button or double-click the newsgroup title. Either way, a picture of a newspaper will appear next to that newsgroup on the list. In Figure 10.14, I have subscribed to two newsgroups. These will be visible as I scroll through the list of all newsgroups available. The Subscribed tab at the bottom of the window will display a list of all subscribed newsgroups to make selecting easier. Highlight the desired group and select Go to to view the contents of that group.

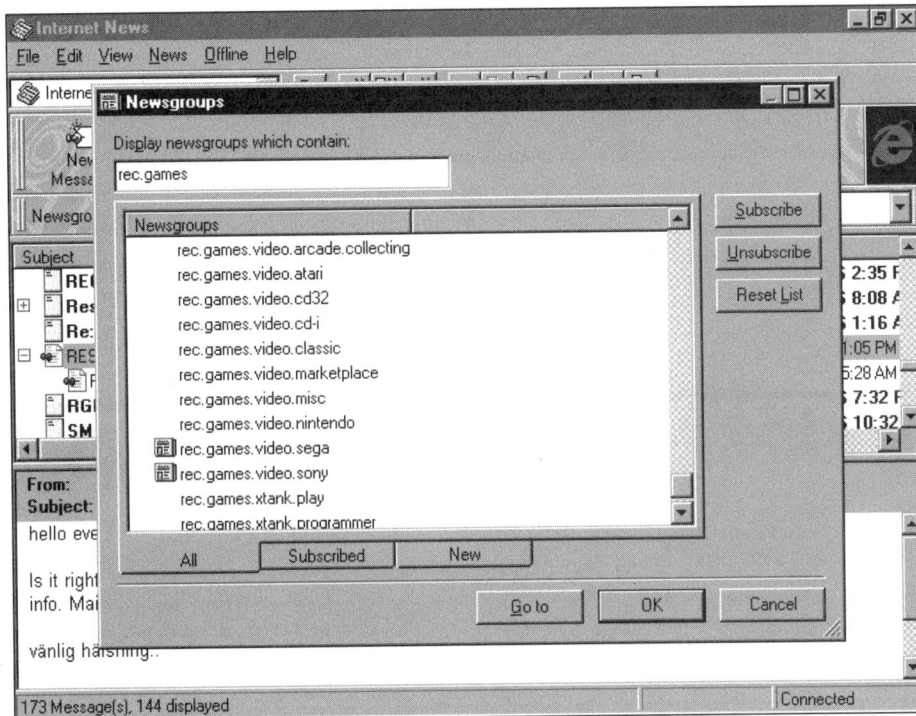

Figure 10.14: Subscribed newsgroups on the main list.

Working Off-line

For those of you who don't want to spend your on-line time connected to the news server, Internet News offers the capability to view messages while off-line. You must first connect to the desired subscribed newsgroups so that the message headers are cached. You can then disconnect and browse the threads at your leisure. If you see any topics that look interesting, you can mark them for download using the Mark for Download and Mark Thread for Download buttons on the toolbar. The Offline menu also offers the capability to select from specific subscribed newsgroups to download messages for off-line viewing with the Mark Newsgroups option. If hard drive space is not a concern, the Mark Newsgroups option also allows you to download entire messages instead of just the headers. After all messages are marked for download, connect with your ISP and select Offline Post and Download from the menu bar. Internet News will do the rest of the work.

ROT13

Occasionally, you will see a message that is scrambled but doesn't seem to be an encoded file. The message may be all "random" letters, but the strange ASCII symbols associated with encoded files are missing. What's going on? You have found a message scrambled using ROT13. This actually isn't a very complicated way to scramble a message. ROT13 stands for rotated 13. This means that the letters have been replaced with letters that are 13 spaces further along in the alphabet. Instead of A, the message displays N. Instead of B, you see O. C is replaced with P.

To read these messages, you don't need a secret decoder ring. MSN and Internet Mail can convert ROT13 messages back into standard format. With MSN, choose Tools ROT13 Encode/Decode. With Internet News, select Unscramble (ROT13) from the Edit menu. The real message is then displayed for you.

Why use ROT13? It's obviously not a code that people can't crack (most newsreaders have ROT13 unscramblers). It is mainly used to warn people that the message may be considered offensive. People who are easily offended can then stay away. ROT13 isn't very common, especially in the alt newsgroups. I guess people figure that if you are in the alt groups, you should be able to handle some strange stuff!

NETIQUETTE

Netiquette is a term for computer etiquette. Usenet newsgroups are places for interaction, and without a little courtesy, they can turn into mud-slinging arenas. Before you post anything to a newsgroup that will be publicly viewed, read through my list of suggestions. This could make Usenet a more friendly place to be as well as save yourself from ridicule, flaming, and spamming!

Do

- Read the newsgroup for a few days before posting. This will help you learn the "style" of the group and keep you from asking questions that might be considered out of place or that were asked only a short time ago.

- Look for a FAQ and read it. A FAQ is a list of Frequently Asked Questions. Not all newsgroups have them, but if they do they can save you some time. If a group has a FAQ and you post a question that is included on that FAQ, you will be subject to the scorn of all the group participants.
- Stick to the subject of the group. People on the Sony Playstation group don't want to hear about the Sega Saturn or the Nintendo 64. If they did, they would go to that group.
- Make a real contribution. Posting a reply that says "me too" doesn't add anything to the discussion. If you disagree with something, go ahead and say it. But if you agree, keep it to yourself to minimize clutter on the thread.
- Read as many of the threads as you can to avoid posting a subject that is already covered.

Don't

- Post to a list that you are unfamiliar with.
- Spam. Spamming is posting the same message to many newsgroups or posting the same message several times on the same group. There are cases where this is appropriate (such as posting a message about a new video game to several groups if that game is available on more than one video game system), but too often people post messages to totally unrelated newsgroups.
- Criticize spelling or grammar. I know that many people have poor English skills, but the Internet is a place to exchange ideas, not give grammar lessons. Many people who post messages use English as a second language, so cut them some slack.
- Post a message when you are mad. Calm down before you post. Remember, the whole world could see how silly your message is.
- Post a message if a private e-mail would be more appropriate. Newsgroups are for public discussion, not one-on-one conversations.

You will find after visiting just a few newsgroups that many people ignore suggestions like these. In fact, many threads are nothing more than collections of sophomoric insults strung together rather than meaningful debate. Rather than take the "everyone else is doing it" position, try to place yourself above the masses. If even a few of us can reduce the nonsense on Usenet, it will make it a much better place to visit.

WHAT'S AHEAD?

- Look into the future of Web browsing in Chapter 11
- Learn how to create your own Web page in Chapter 12

Chapter 11

THE FUTURE OF CYBERSPACE

Voice-operated wireless personal supercomputers that link to a centralized information network over a subspace carrier wave and offer a 3-D user interface are sure to be the standard in ten years. Okay, maybe I've been watching too many science fiction TV shows. Everybody knows that dedicated machines that work with a virtual reality interface and plug in to your TV set will be all the rage in two years. Did I say virtual reality? I meant portable cellular terminals that link to the Internet and have pen interfaces.

This group of examples may seem possible (except for the first one, maybe), but in truth, nobody really knows what the future will bring to the Internet. If you ask ten so-called experts, you will probably get seven or eight different opinions as to what the future (even the near future) will bring. One thing is rather certain, however: The Internet of the future will be more interactive and more involved in the lives of most people.

A few glimpses into the future are available today. Virtual Reality Modeling Language (VRML) is an established 3-D interface on the Web that offers a way to "move" through Web pages. Microsoft's ActiveX offers new levels of control for both developers and users. And Java, by Sun Microsystems, has been a huge success and something of an Internet sensation. So those of us who aren't professional developers aren't left out of the fun, VBScript and JavaScript are there to fill the void. We will cover all of these developments, shedding some light on the possibilities the Internet has to offer.

KEY POINTS IN THIS CHAPTER

- What does VRML do?
- How do I move around in a 3-D world?
- What is ActiveX?
- What is Java?
- Where do VBScript and JavaScript fit in?

VIRTUAL REALITY MODELING LANGUAGE

Internet Explorer 3.0 has built-in support for VRML, a three-dimensional interface for maneuvering through Web sites. Unlike standard Web pages, which are flat and two-dimensional, VRML allows the user to rotate an object 360 degrees and move completely around it. While many of the current VRML pages seem rather primitive (some are merely objects that you can spin around), the potential for this technology is immense. Imagine being able to "walk" through a shopping mall while doing your on-line shopping! How about an architect sharing a three-dimensional plan of a building with prospective clients thousands of miles away? Car designers could create a VRML representation of an auto body in their California design studios and engineers in Detroit could examine it as closely as a clay model.

VRML sites can be identified by the .wrl file extension used. Even if you don't notice the file extension of the Web address, Explorer will still be able to automatically load a VRML page. When the site is accessed, you may see the window shown in Figure 11.1 (depending on your security settings). This is the same warning that appears when opening program files. As usual, if you are not familiar with the site, you should be cautious of viruses. If you are confident that the site is safe, choose Open it and OK to continue. You will then enter the VRML world.

Note: If Explorer is not configured to automatically play animations, VRML sites will not load. To configure Explorer for animations, go to the tab in the View Options menu. Make sure that Play videos is checked.

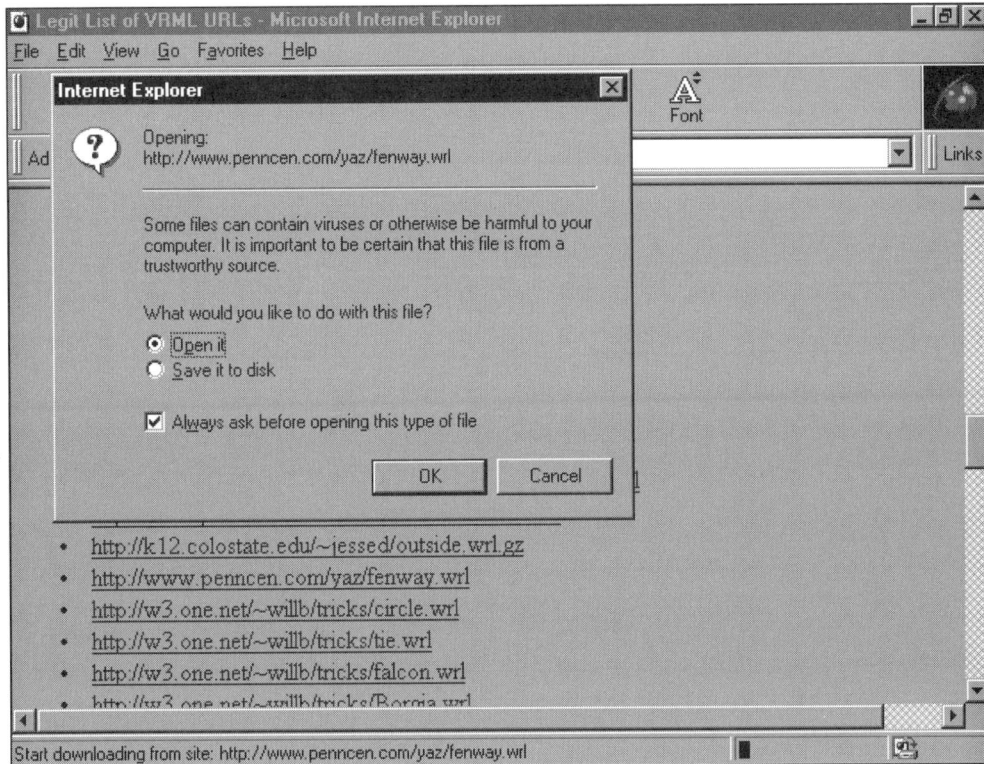

Figure 11.1: Warning before opening a VRML file.

Moving in a 3-D World

Figure 11.2 shows the outside of a theater on a VRML site. Notice the toolbar at the bottom of the screen. These are the movement controls in VRML sites. You have the option of moving by using the mouse, keyboard, or joystick.

Using the Mouse To move using the mouse, click one of the buttons on the toolbar (described below). Point to the page with your cursor. Holding the left mouse button down, move the cursor in the direction you want to go.

Tip: If you want to go directly to an object, double-click that object.

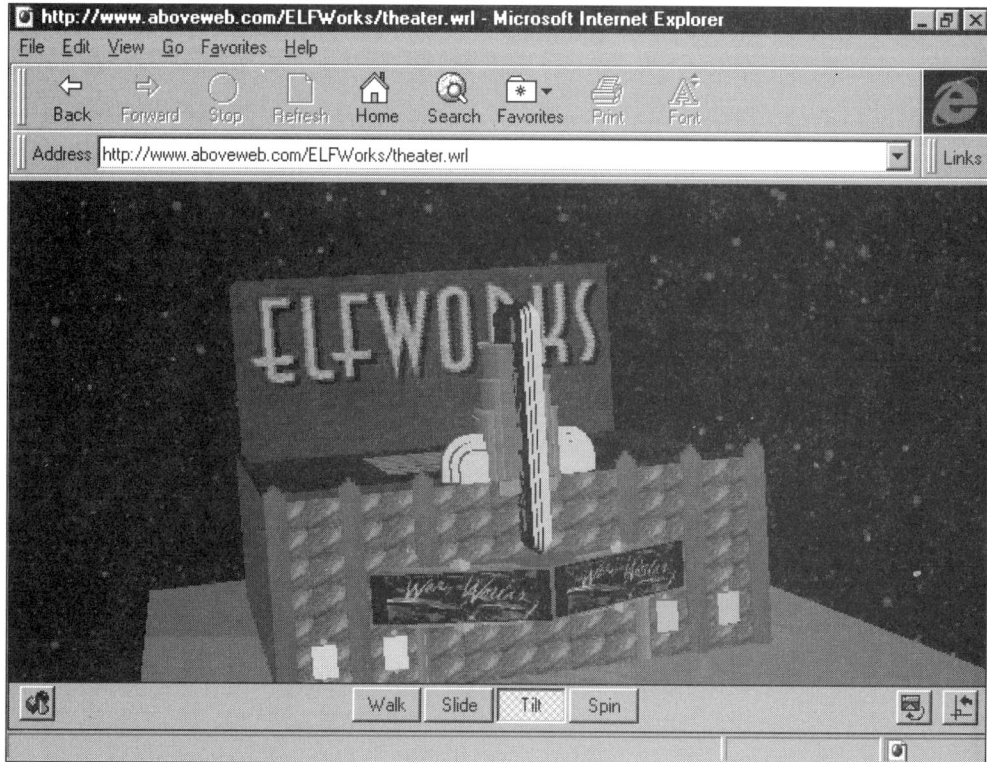

Figure 11.2: A VRML theater.

This Menu button displays the VRML support menu. This menu duplicates the functions on the toolbar. It also sets collision detection and textures (described later in this section). This menu can also be displayed by right-clicking a point on the VRML page.

The Walk button allows you to move forward, backward, and turn.

The Slide button allows you to move horizontally or vertically.

The Tilt button changes viewing angle by tilting up, down, right, or left.

The Spin button rotates the VRML world around its center.

The Reset button returns to the starting location and orientation.

The Straighten button returns to the original orientation.

Using the Keyboard The arrow keys move forward, backward, left, and right. Holding down the Shift key while pressing the arrow keys will tilt the image. Holding down the Ctrl key while pressing the arrow keys will slide.

Using the Joystick Move the joystick in the direction you want to go. The Shift and Ctrl keys on the keyboard work to tilt and slide, respectively. If your joystick has a view hat, you can use it to slide instead of the Ctrl key.

Note: Be sure your joystick has been properly calibrated within Windows 95. This is done through the Joystick Configurations icon in the Windows 95 Control Panel.

Linking to Other Sites

VRML pages can contain hyperlinks to other sites just like regular Web pages. When you see these links, your mouse cursor will change from a pointer to a hand. To go to the link, click it.

VRML Quirks

With some VRML sites, you can literally walk through walls. Many times this can be disorienting, but not always. For example, in Figure 11.2, you can walk inside the theater to see links to other pages in the "lobby." If the site you are viewing is too confusing, disable the Walk Through Walls option on the VRML menu. This may slow some pages down or completely prevent you from moving in some pages, so be prepared to change it back if necessary.

If the page you are viewing is too slow and difficult to control, you can turn off the detail of the images. Open the VRML menu (from the toolbar or by right-clicking) and select Options. Disable the Load Textures and Load Inlines options. This may significantly improve your performance. Of course, upgrading your hardware (CPU, modem, and video card) will also increase the speed of VRML.

VRML Examples

The following figures are a few more examples of VRML sites. They are perhaps not as flashy as the virtual reality presented in some recent Hollywood movies, but they do show examples of the potential of the technology as it becomes more widely supported.

Figure 11.3 is a map of the Earth's ocean topography. Using the Spin control, you can rotate the globe to see the surface of the entire planet. For this and other representations of VRML sites, visit **http://www .geom.umn.edu/~daeron/bin/legitlist.cgi**.

Figures 11.4 and 11.5 are from the Intel Web site. They allow you to navigate inside a Pentium processor. This VRML site contains many

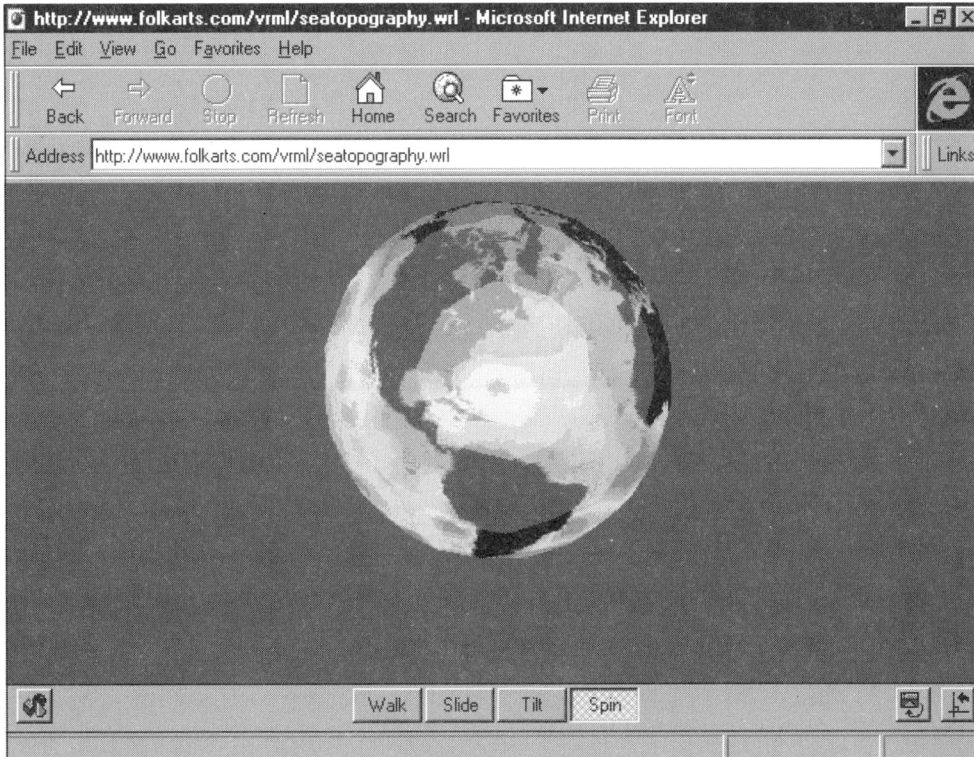

Figure 11.3: Ocean topography in VRML.

links that will take you to other VRML pages describing the capabilities of the Intel Pentium line of CPUs. This site is located at **http://www.intel.com/procs/ppro/intro/vrml/nav.wrl**. Other than its main purpose of selling computer chips, this is one of the better examples of the uses of VRML technology.

ACTIVEX

One of the most significant improvements added to Internet Explorer 3.0 is ActiveX. But what is it? To an end user, ActiveX doesn't offer any tangible benefits. It doesn't let you view 3-D worlds, animations, and sounds, and it doesn't let you interact with Web

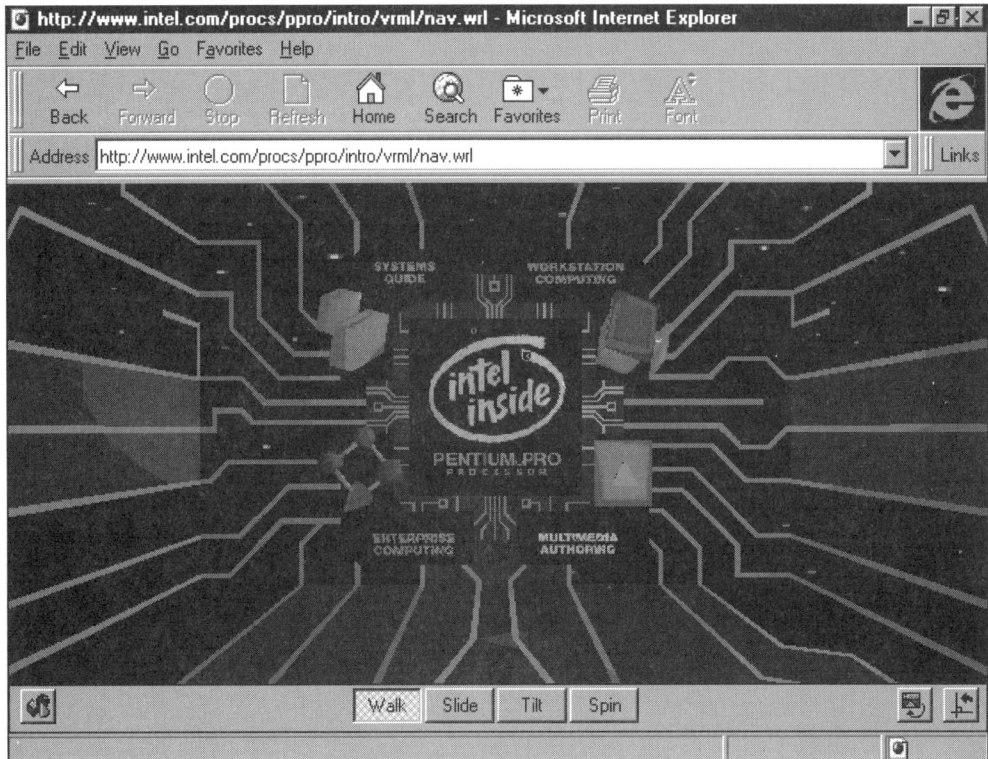

Figure 11.4: Intel VRML site.

pages. Or does it? ActiveX actually does all of these things; it just does them in the background.

ActiveX doesn't let you move within a VRML world, but it does control the VRML interaction with Explorer. ActiveX doesn't give you an interface to play video clips and sounds, but it does allow these sounds to be played. And ActiveX doesn't let you fill out electronic forms on a Web page, but it does allow that Web page to respond to you depending on what you wrote. You will never launch an application that says ActiveX at the top, but ActiveX is always working to integrate different features within Explorer. Perhaps the easiest way to describe what ActiveX does is to compare it with plug-ins. Both add capabilities to Explorer, but ActiveX is much more advanced than normal plug-ins. Explorer comes with many ActiveX controls built in, and

Figure 11.5: Moving within the Intel VRML site.

new controls are being developed all the time that are available for downloading.

Think of ActiveX as a programming language used by developers that is powerful and flexible enough to do the following:

- Control plug-ins (such as Active Movie)
- Control interactivity (pages that update automatically or respond to user input)
- Control security (PCT and SSL)
- Control Java (discussed in the next section)

You can understand why there are no figures showing examples of ActiveX in this section—there are really no easy ways to represent it with a few pictures. For a more technical explanation, see the Microsoft Internet Explorer home page at **http://www .microsoft.com/ie**. This is also a great site to download new ActiveX controls.

SHOCKWAVE

A popular example of an ActiveX control is Shockwave. Developed to run Macromedia Director animations (called movies), Shockwave is a terrific example of multimedia on the Web. Shockwave movies are professional presentations complete with sound, animation, text, and graphics. Unlike the Director files in their native format, Shockwave movies are very small and, with a 28.8 modem, usually take very little time to download.

   To download the Shockwave ActiveX controls for Explorer, visit the Macromedia site at **www.macromedia.com/shockwave** (or the Internet Explorer home page listed above). The download is self-installing, so you will be ready to view Shockwave sites immediately. The Shockwave site also contains lots of examples and links to sites that have been "shocked." I didn't include any examples in this section (black and white pictures just don't do justice to colorful animations), but I highly recommend visiting.

JAVA

Java was not originally developed to be used on the Web, but things sure worked out nicely. Java is a scripting language (similar to ActiveX, but not as extensive) that allows interactive content on the Web. Java was one of the first tools that made animations and sounds on the Web possible. It also allows for pages that respond to user input (such as games and forms), and pages that automatically update. For example, without Java if you log on to a standard Web page that is displaying stock quotes, those quotes will always stay the same. Even if you leave the page and return later, the numbers will not have changed unless you manually refresh the page or have Explorer set to automatically refresh (instead of reloading from the cache). With a Java page, the numbers will update without having to refresh the page. Some sites even have moving stock tickers in a frame at the bottom of the screen, just like financial reports on television news!

Java programs (called applets) are not run over the Web. They are instead downloaded to the host machine and run from there. Java is written to be platform independent, which means that it can be run on any computer. You can run the same Java applet on your PC that your friend runs on his Macintosh. It is also secure. Java code is checked to ensure that no viruses will sneak by when you download a Java applet. Once again, animations and interactive Web pages are difficult to show in a book, but the following figures give you some places to look for examples of Java on the Web.

Gamelan (Figure 11.6) is a terrific site to locate Java applets and other sites of all kinds. The Java Centre (Figure 11.7) is another good

Figure 11.6: www.gamelan.com/index.shtml.

Figure 11.7: www.java.co.uk/javacentre.html.

source for Java material. For something a little different, try the Weird Java Applets page (Figure 11.8). After seeing how strange Java can be, visit the Expedition: Fossil site (Figure 11.9) run by the American Museum of Natural History to see Java's educational possibilities. Finally, after all that thinking on the fossil site, try your hand at a game of golf at the Virtual Open 96 (Figure 11.10).

VBSCRIPT AND JAVASCRIPT

It's really fantastic how interactive and involving the Web is becoming. In just a few short years of existence, the Web has evolved from a text-only interface to a multimedia showcase. There is one small problem with this advancement, however. The fancier the Web

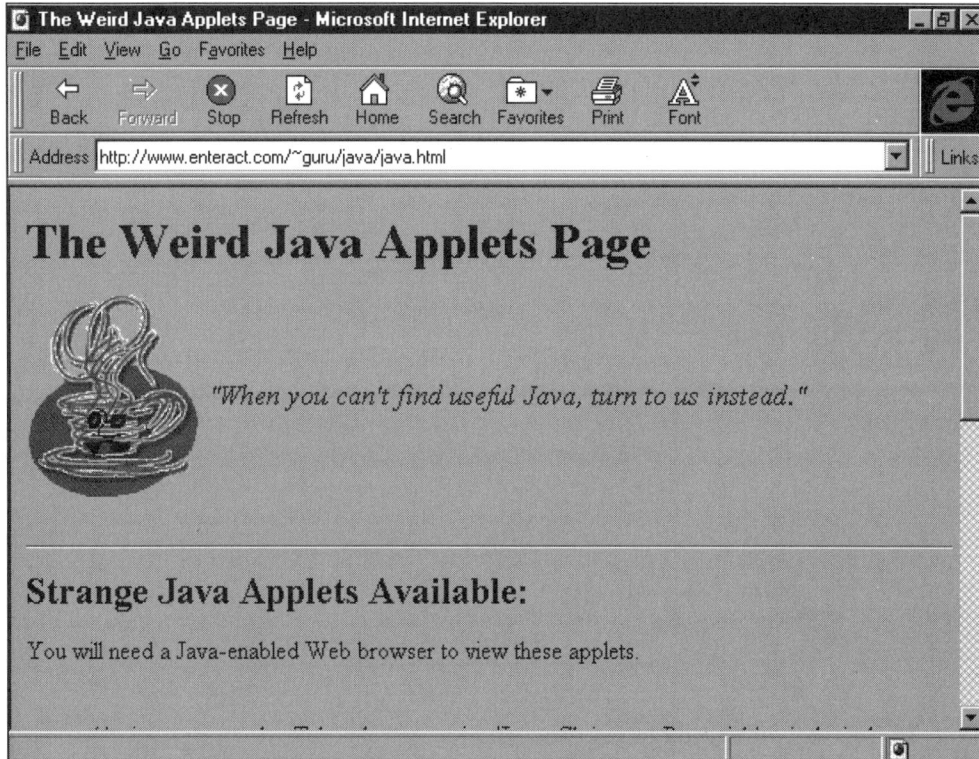

Figure 11.8: www.enteract.com/~guru/java/java.html.

becomes, the more professionals are needed to develop for it, leaving many amateurs behind. ActiveX, Java, and Shockwave are all amazing accomplishments, but they can be very difficult to master, especially if you have a full-time job that doesn't involve working with them!

Luckily, the rest of us have VBScript and JavaScript. These are two similar scripting languages that can be incorporated into HTML code. This way, when we are creating our own personal Web pages, we can add a little flash and interaction of our own! VBScript and JavaScript allow (among other things) Web authors to link ActiveX controls and Java applets, allow Web pages to respond to user inputs, and generally allow for a more interactive, richer experience on the Web.

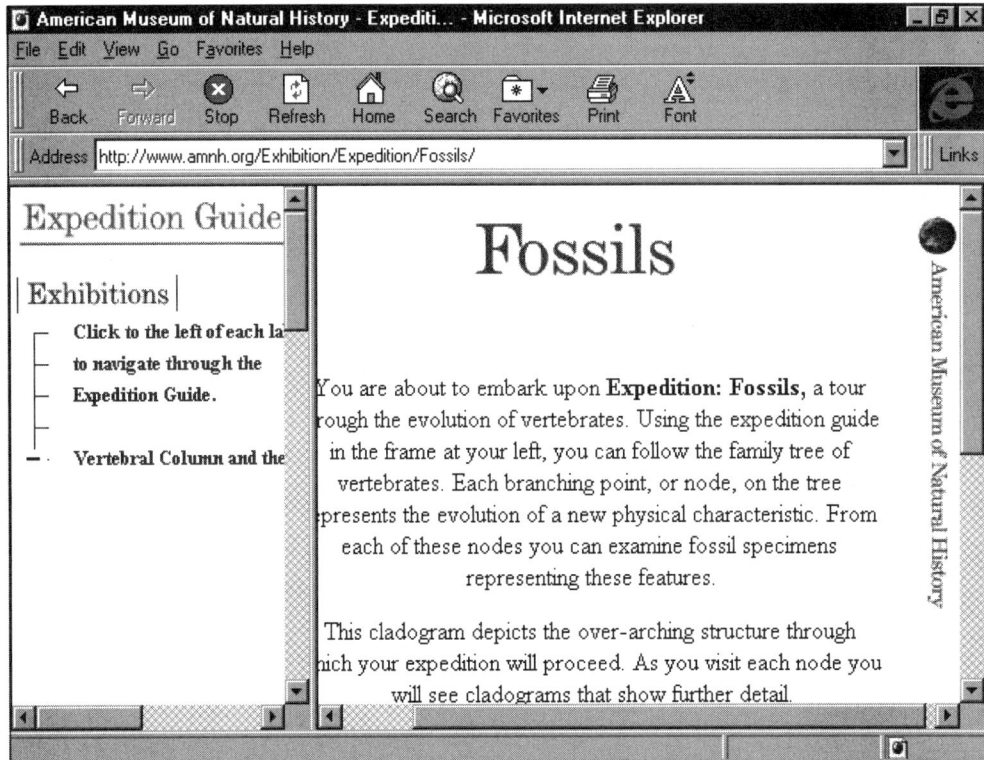

Figure 11.9: www.amnh.org/Exhibition/Expedition/Fossils/.

VBScript and JavaScript are, in my opinion, a bit more complicated than standard HTML (which we will learn in Chapter 12, by the way), but they are not out of reach for non-programmers like some of the higher-level languages. Now with some VBScript or JavaScript in our sites, we might not be as self-conscious when people click over from the Microsoft home page to our own personal Web pages!

WHAT'S AHEAD?

- Learn how to create your own Web page in Chapter 12

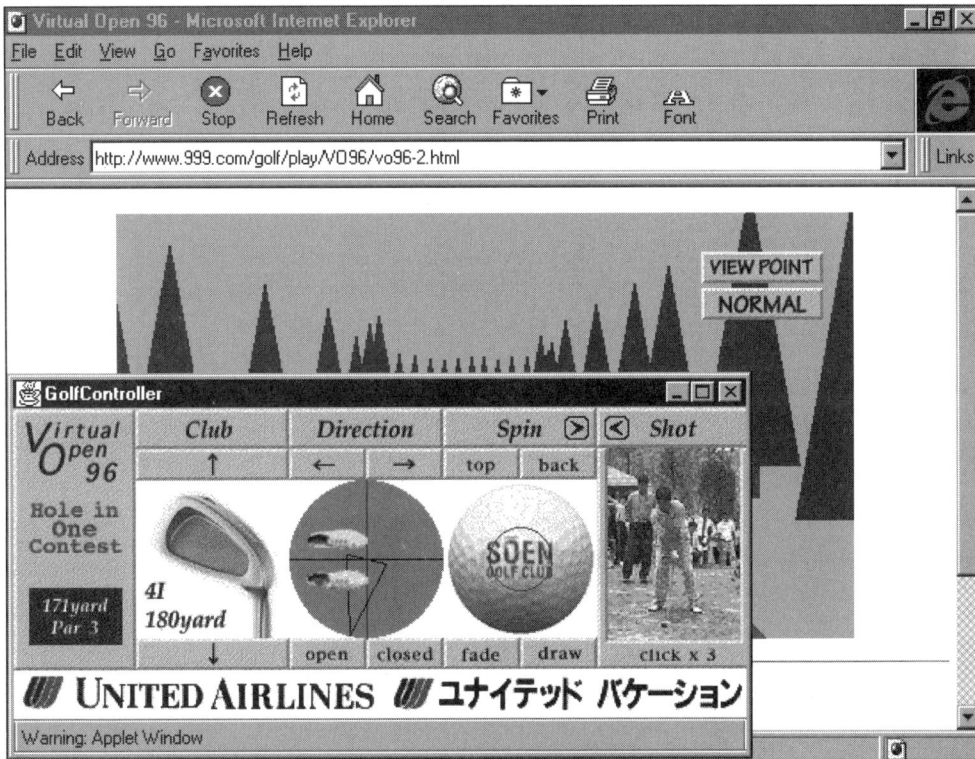

Figure 11.10: www.999.com/golf/indexe.html.

Chapter 12

CREATING YOUR OWN WEB PAGE

We have spent a good bit of time describing how to view Web pages (among other things) in this book. I bet you have thought at least once, "Gee. That sure would be cool if I had my own Web page to show my friends." You will actually be surprised how easy it is to design and create you own Web page. It may not look quite as polished as a professional designer's page, but you don't do this full time! In only one 30-minute session, you can have a page with a little flair to call your own.

You might remember some discussion about HTML throughout this book. HyperText Markup Language, or HTML, is the basic language with which Web pages are written. Web browsers such as Internet Explorer read this language and convert the HTML instructions into the Web pages we see when we are on-line. Don't think that just because it's a programming language that it's complicated, though. I struggled through my programming classes but was able to pick up HTML fairly quickly, and I think that most people can learn quickly, also.

Why create your own page? I can think of a few reasons. First, it's cool. You could go to parties and tell people to check out your site. You could put the address on your business card. You could make people think you are way smarter than you are. (Nothing personal; I'm sure you're plenty smart, but Web pages look more complicated than they actually are.)

Second, it can give people you know a centralized place to keep in touch. I use my page to keep a list of friends' and family members' e-mail addresses for everyone to access. I also add links to new sites that I think they would enjoy, and I put in a section on what's been happening lately.

Third, you can make it your Start Page in Explorer and customize it to display exactly what *you* want to see. If you learn to use frames, you can display other pages within separate frames. You can have news headlines in one frame, sports in another, and Letterman's Top Ten List in a third. Even if you don't master frames, you can still create links to commonly visited sites to act as a supplement for your Favorites list.

Don't be intimidated by HTML. It really isn't as complicated as it looks at first, and there are many great authoring programs available to help you on your way. At the very least, skim through this chapter to see what it's all about. I may cover only the basics, but the examples I provide will give you a solid foundation for HTML programming should you decide to move on to a dedicated HTML book.

KEY POINTS IN THIS CHAPTER

- Where can I find an HTML editor?
- What are the basics of HTML?
- How do I add hyperlinks and pictures?
- Can I have files available to download?
- What else do I need to know?

WHERE DO I GET AN HTML EDITOR?

The program in which you write the HTML code is called an HTML editor or HTML authoring software. To actually write a Web page, you have several options.

1. Use a word processor or text editor
2. Use an add-on to a word processor
3. Use a dedicated HTML editor

When using a word processor or text editor, you must write out all of the HTML code by hand, save it as an ASCII text file with an HTM or HTML extension, and upload it to your Web server manually. Not at all as difficult as it sounds, but this is the most time-consuming method. It is the least expensive option, though. Even Windows Notepad is enough to write HTML.

When you use an add-on to a word processor (like MS Word Internet Assistant for Microsoft Word), you can work in your word processor almost as if it were a dedicated HTML editor. You don't have to worry about converting any files, and you have the familiar interface of your favorite word processor to work with.

Dedicated HTML editors usually have time-saving enhancements that also make certain functions as easy as clicking on an icon. Extensive toolbars eliminate the need to memorize HTML commands, and some programs will even upload the completed files to your Web server for you. HTML editors often come with HTML help files and syntax checkers to find mistakes before you upload your files.

Note: If you use a method that requires you to upload your files to the Web server manually, check with your ISP for the correct way to do this for your service.

WHERE DO I GET A WEB SERVER?

When I say Web server, I mean the actual computer that is always connected to the Internet that contains the HTML files for your page. Where does this come from? Do you have to buy another computer or keep your PC turned on and connected to the Internet 24 hours a day? No. Usually your ISP will offer Web server services to its members. Some are free, but some do require fees. Check with your service to learn about setting up a space for your personal Web page.

Where do you get these types of programs? Many versions of all three types of HTML programs are available at retail outlets. Word processors like Microsoft Word are easy to find. Add-ins are readily available in stores. Dedicated HTML editors like Microsoft Front Page and Hot Dog Pro are also in stores.

Many HTML books come with shareware versions of add-ins and HTML editors. The best place, though, is on the Net itself. Probably two of the most popular HTML editors on the Net are Hot Dog and HoTMetaL, both available in shareware versions for downloading.

My best advice is to try some editors from each category to see which you prefer. For instance, a friend of mine won't do his pages in anything but his word processor, while I despise doing pages that way. I prefer to use a dedicated HTML editor. You may notice that the figures in this chapter show Hot Dog Pro in the Address Bar. This is the editor that I personally prefer, and it is available in stores or for downloading at **http://www.sausage.com**. No, I'm not paid by them, but I like their program. As I said before, try a few HTML editors to see which works best for your situation. Any HTML taught in this chapter will work the same for any of the program types that I have mentioned.

HTML BASICS

The first HTML file that you will create will probably be called "index.htm" or "index.html." You may immediately have two questions. One, why is it called "index," and two, why is it ".htm" or ".html"? The answer to number one is that it might not have to be named "index." Many Web servers and browsers require the main HTML file for a site be named "index," while any secondary files can be named whatever you choose. Check with your ISP. Number two also depends on your server and your authoring software. Because many HTML editors were designed to work for Windows 3.1, these programs can't save a file with a four-digit extension like ".html." However, many Web servers require the HTML files to have four digits. Editors like Hot Dog get around this problem by saving the files as ".htm" for use on your computer, and changing the files to ".html" when they are uploaded to the server. Check with your authoring software and your ISP to find out what you need.

Note: Notice that I said "most" and "many" a few times while describing filenames and extensions. Because these are computers, no rule is ever completely set in stone. Some Web servers don't care if the main file is called "index," and some do. Some Web servers prefer ".htm" and some prefer ".html." Editors also have different ways of dealing with these issues. As always, check with your ISP and editor's documentation to find out for certain.

Tags

The guts of an HTML file are its tags. Tags are the actual commands to the Web browser that define how the page looks and acts. These tags are always surrounded by < > brackets; they separate the HTML code from the text that you want to be displayed in the document. This basically means that if you actually want to use the symbols < > in your page, you have to use a special code to differentiate them from tag separators. Check Table 12.1 for a list of some of the special characters and the special codes that represent them.

If you start a function that pertains only to specific text rather than the entire document, you must "cancel" the function with a </>. For example, if I wanted to make a word bold, I would use the <B> command. After that word, I cancel the <B> with a </B>. Every word will be bold until the </B> appears in the code. That means that if you forget to cancel a bold tag, all of the text to the end of your document would be in bold type!

Tags on Every Page

There are a few tags that must be on every page. They identify the header, title, and body of your page. Don't leave these lines out, or something bad may happen!

```
<HTML>
<HEAD>
<TITLE> The title of your page goes here </TITLE>
</HEAD>
<BODY>
The main part of your page (the body) goes here.
</BODY>
</HTML>
```

Table 12.1: Special Characters

Symbol	Special Codes
<	&lt
>	&gt
&	&amp
"	&quote

Figure 12.1 is an example of the simplest form of a Web page. There are no formatting options of any kind. The HTML code for Figure 12.1 is below.

```
<HTML>
<HEAD>
<TITLE>This is the Title</TITLE>
</HEAD>
<BODY>
This is a simple page.  Notice that the text we typed after the
TITLE tag does not show up in the document.  Check the Title
bar at the top of the screen.
</BODY>
</HTML>
```

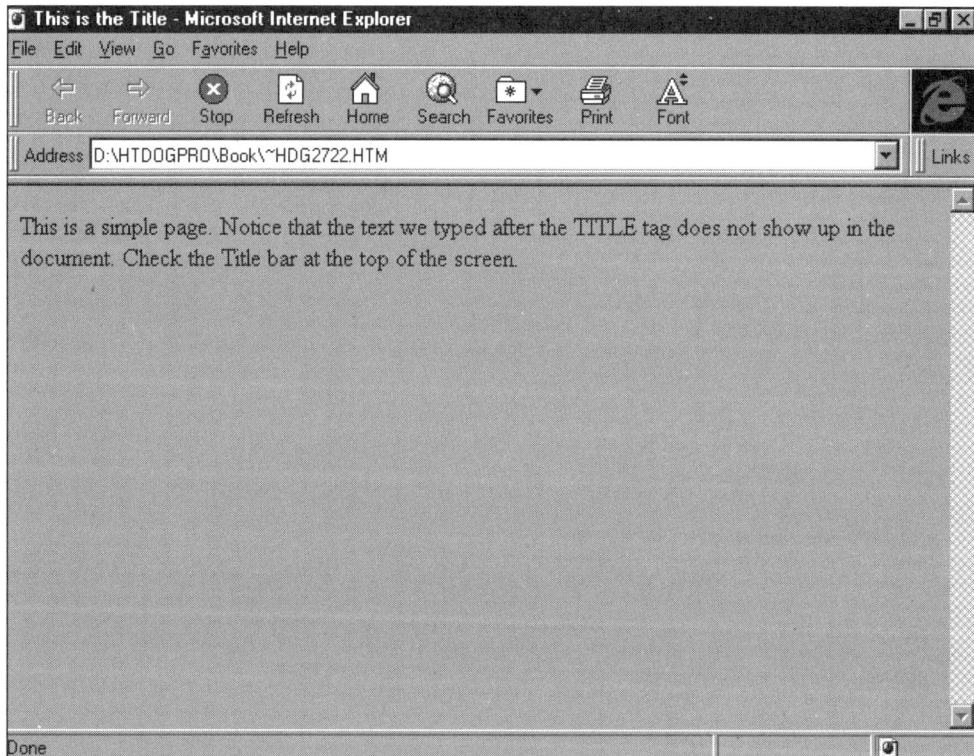

Figure 12.1: A simple Web page.

Commonly Used Tags

Several tags are used fairly regularly for tasks such as forcing line breaks, changing fonts, and dividing sections.

**<P> and
** When you type text in a Web page, HTML does not factor in any carriage returns at the end of a line like a standard word processor. Even if you hit Enter after each line, your page will be displayed as one continuous line of text. Notice how the text flows together in Figure 12.1 even though the text in the HTML code shows line breaks. <P> is used at the end of a line to force a paragraph. The text in the next line following will be left justified (or whatever justification you have chosen) and two lines down.
 forces a line break. The text on the next line will be left justified, but no line will be skipped in between.

<B>, <I>, and <U> These tags are used for bold, italic, and underlined text and are canceled with </B>, </I>, and </U>.

<H1> to <H6> The <H1> to <H6> tags identify text to be placed in headings. Basically, they change the font size and make the text bold. <H1> is the largest and <H6> is the smallest.

<HR> Horizontal rule places a line in the document, which can be used to divide sections of your page.

CREATING LINKS TO OTHER SITES

Now that we have the basic structure for a Web page, let's add some interesting items to it. One of the great features of the Web is the ability to jump to other sites using hyperlinks. Most Web browsers will support hyperlinks to HTTP, FTP, Gopher, Telnet, and Mailto (e-mail addresses). Web pages and e-mail addresses are the most common, so we will cover them. The other formats work the exact same way, though.

The tag to create a link is <A HREF="*URL*">*name*</A>. The URL must be the exact address of the site to which you are linking, and the name is anything you want to call it on your page. In Figure 12.2, I have created a link to the Microsoft Internet Explorer home page,

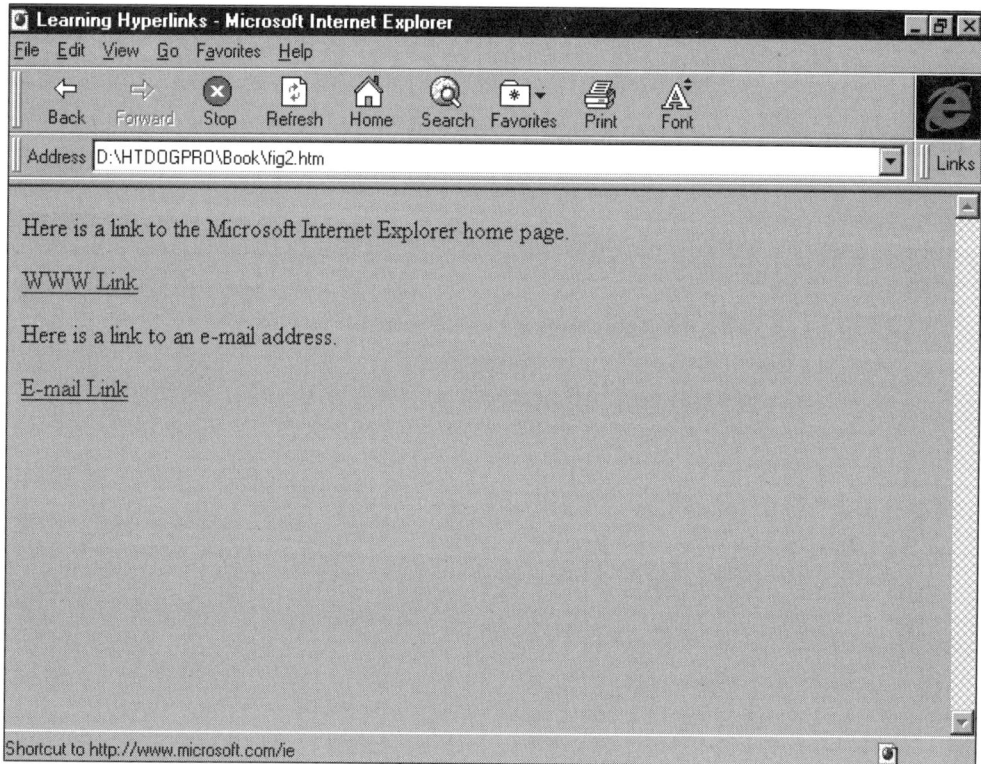

Figure 12.2: Adding hyperlinks to your page.

which is represented as <A HREF="http://www.microsoft.com/ ie">WWW Link</A>. Note that you must type the quotation marks to separate the actual URL from the rest of the tag. The e-mail link in Figure 12.2 is identical in form except for mailto:// being used instead of http://. Here is the HTML code for Figure 12.2.

```
<HTML>
<HEAD>
<TITLE>Learning Hyperlinks</TITLE>
</HEAD>
<BODY>
Here is a link to the Microsoft Internet Explorer home page.<P>
<A HREF="http://www.microsoft.com/ie">WWW Link</A><P>
Here is a link to an e-mail address.<P>
<A href="mailto:dsull@iquest.net">E-mail Link</A>
</BODY>
</HTML>
```

Remember that anything typed without a tag preceding it is treated as plain text. Note that I used the <P> at the end of the text. Without it, my links would have been on the same line as the text, making it more difficult to read. Also note that the link's address appears in the status bar when the cursor is placed over the link.

ADDING PICTURES

What kind of page would it be if there were no pictures? After all, the Web can handle multimedia, why not use some of it? This time the tag is <IMG SRC="*file name and location*">. Note that there is no need to cancel this command. Figure 12.3 shows a simple picture added to a Web page.

Note: Remember loading times when inserting pictures into your pages. Many people go overboard and add so many pictures that their pages take several minutes to load. Pictures are great, but most of us hate waiting to see them. Try to exercise some restraint!

Also in Figure 12.3, we have turned a picture into a link. This is done by placing the <IMG SRC> in the *name* spot in the <A HREF> tag. This looks a little confusing in the HTML code, but it makes the links more interesting. Note the link's address in the status bar. Here is the HTML code for Figure 12.3.

```
<HTML>
<HEAD>
<TITLE>Inserting Pictures</TITLE>
</HEAD>
<BODY>
Here is a simple picture<P>
<IMG SRC="smiley.gif"><P>
You can use a picture as a link to a Web page, e-mail address,
etc.<P>
<A HREF="http://www.microsoft.com/ie"><IMG SRC="msie30.gif"
ALT="This picture is a link to the Explorer home page."></A>
</BODY>
</HTML>
```

Two notes on this code. First, you may notice the ALT= inside the <IMG SRC> tag. This specifies what to display if the browser being used to view this page does not support graphics (or has images turned off). Internet Explorer will also display this text when the cursor is held over the image.

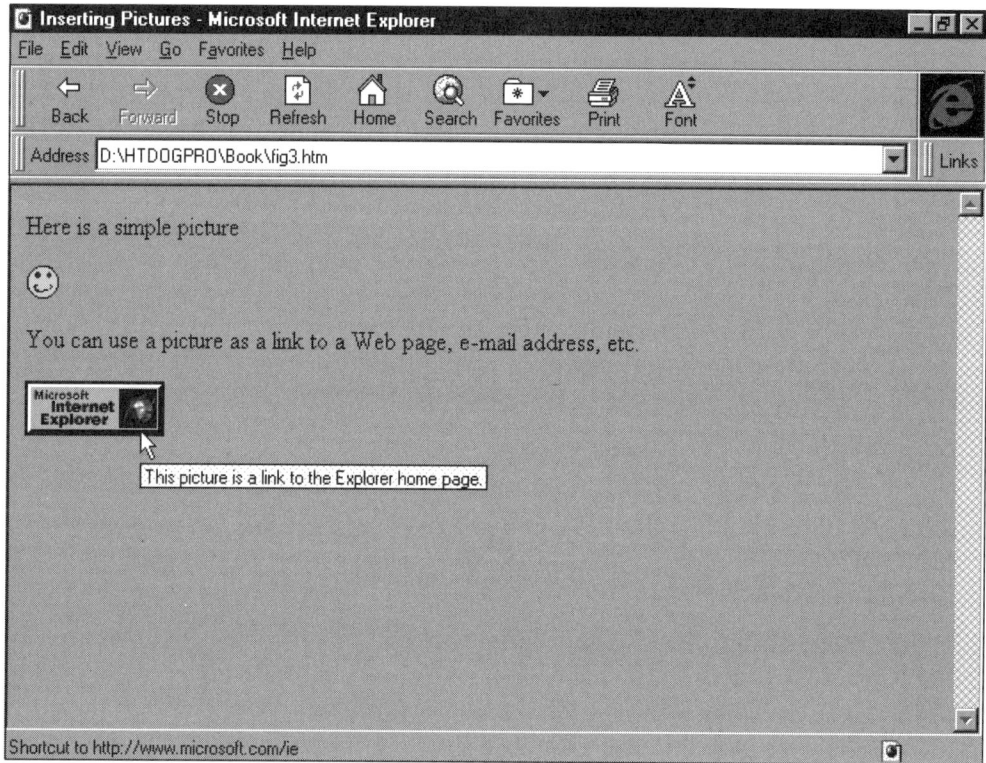

Figure 12.3: Adding images to your page.

Second, the title of the picture being used can be important. If you do not type a directory path (directory is a UNIX and DOS term similar to folders in Windows 95) for the image, the browser will assume that the image is in the same directory as the HTML file itself. If the image is in a different directory, you *must* tell the browser where to look for it. For example, <IMG SRC="file://D:/web/graphics/smiley.gif"> tells the browser to look for the file "smiley.gif" in the web/graphics directory on the server's D drive.

MAKING FILES AVAILABLE TO DOWNLOAD

If you want to have people visit your site to download files, you must first upload the files to your Web server (or know the address of another server that has them). Then you must create a link to

download them. Here again, we use our friend <A HREF=
"*file*">*name*</A>. *File* is the actual name of the file to be downloaded, and *name* is your description of it on the page.

Once again, you can jazz things up by using a picture to represent
the file to download. This is again a combination of <A HREF> and
<IMG SRC>. This time, note that the link in the status bar that is
shown when the cursor is pointed to the link is the location and name
of the file to be downloaded. Here is the HTML code for the page
shown in Figure 12.4.

```
<HTML>
<HEAD>
<TITLE>Downloadable Files</TITLE>
</HEAD>
<BODY>
You can place links to downloadable files into your page, even
if the files are on another server!<P>
```

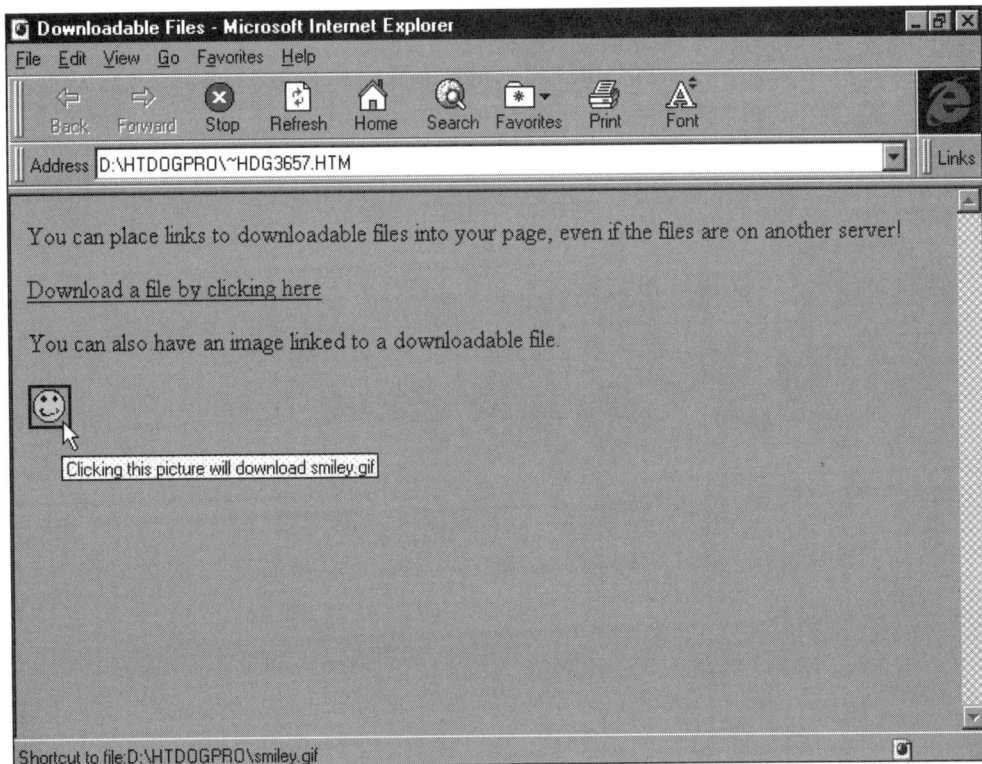

Figure 12.4: Downloadable files in your page.

```
<A HREF="smiley.gif">Download a file by clicking here</A><P>
You can also have an image linked to a downloadable file.<P>
<A HREF="smiley.gif"><IMG SRC="smiley.gif" ALT="Clicking
this picture will download smiley.gif"></A>
</BODY>
</HTML>
```

Just as with pictures, you must tell the browser where to locate the file to be downloaded. If you do not specify an address, the browser will look only in the same directory as the HTML file itself. If you do not have the space to keep files on your Web server, you can reference them at different sites by specifying their addresses in the *file* section. For example, to allow users to download a file from the Microsoft Explorer home page, you would enter <A HREF="http://www .microsoft.com/ie/smiley.gif">. This should be done only with the permission of the targeted site, however, because these links can adversely affect the performance of the targeted server.

MOVING WITHIN THE PAGE

There may be times that your page is so long that it takes too long to move from top to bottom and back to the top again. Or you may want to place a list at the top of your page and have more detailed descriptions toward the bottom. In either case, it may be best to create targets within your page that allow you to move instantly from one spot to another. These targets are essentially links, but they don't take you to other sites on the Internet.

The example in Figure 12.5 shows three links at the top of the page named 'a,' 'b,' and 'c' that are aimed at targets at the bottom. At the bottom is a link that aims back up top to a target named "top." In this example, the user would click on the appropriate *"here"* to go to 'A,' 'B,' or 'C' at the bottom of the page, or click the *"here"* at the bottom of the page to return to the very top. The links are made using the <A HREF> tag, while the targets use the <A NAME> tag.

First you must decide what your link is going to be. It is usually a word, but it is possible to use a picture. Then you must decide where your target will be located. The link uses the form <A HREF="#*target name*">*linked word*</A>. The target uses <A NAME="*target name*"></A>. Note that the pound sign (#) is necessary in the link tag, but not in the target tag. Also note in Figure 12.5 that the target name appears in Explorer's status bar when the cursor moves over the link.

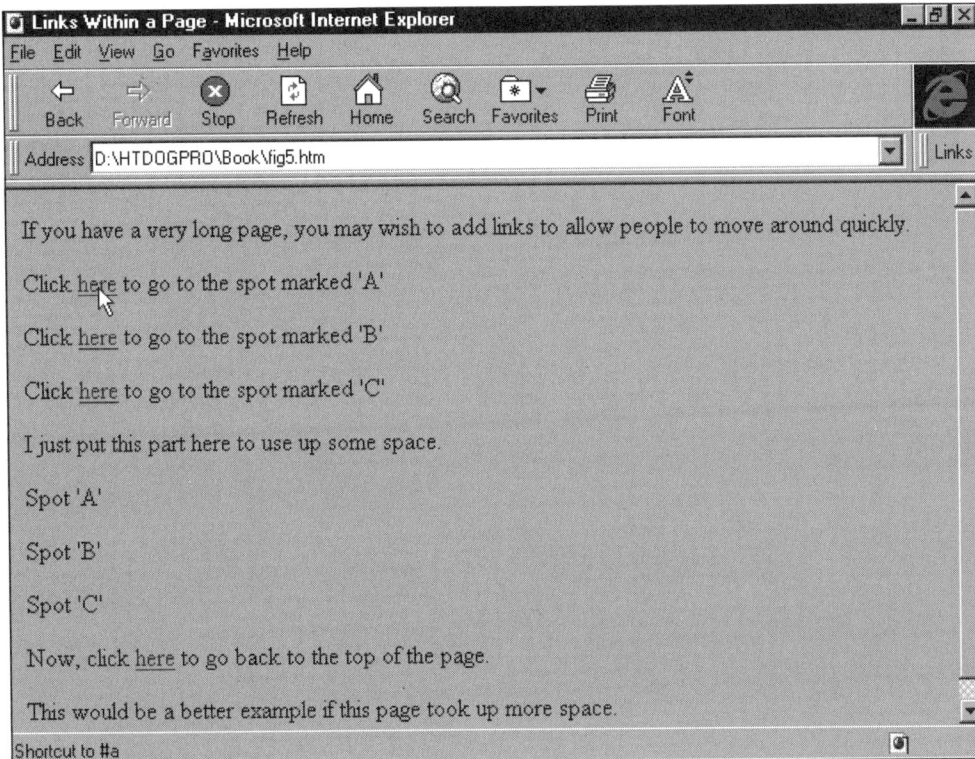

Figure 12.5: Creating links within a page.

```
<HTML>
<HEAD>
<TITLE>Links Within a Page</TITLE>
</HEAD>
<BODY>
<A NAME="top"></A>If you have a very long page, you may wish to
add links to allow people to move around quickly.<P>
Click <A HREF="#a">here</A> to go to the spot marked 'A'<P>
Click <A HREF="#b">here</A> to go to the spot marked 'B'<P>
Click <A HREF="#c">here</A> to go to the spot marked 'C'<P>
<P>
<P>
I just put this part here to use up some space.<P>
<P>
<P>
```

```
Spot '<A NAME="a">A</A>'<P>
Spot '<A NAME="b">B</A>'<P>
Spot '<A NAME="c">C</A>'<P>
Now, click <A HREF="#top">here</A> to go back to the top of the
page.<P>
This would be a better example if this page took up more space.
</BODY>
</HTML>
```

CREATING LISTS

If you have information that you need to display in a list, HTML can make one for you. You can choose from three kinds of lists: bulleted, ordered, or definition. The bulleted list starts with the <UL> tag and ends with the </UL> tag. In between, each item has its own <LI> tag. The ordered list uses <OL>, </OL>, and <LI>. The definition list uses a slightly different format. The main tags are <DL> and </DL>. The term being defined uses <DT>, while the definition itself uses <DD>. Figure 12.6 shows examples of the three types of lists.

```
<HTML>
<HEAD>
<TITLE>Creating Lists</TITLE>
</HEAD>
<BODY>
Here are examples of lists.<BR>
<UL>
<LI>Bullet one
<LI>Bullet two
<LI>Bullet three
</UL>
<P>
<OL>
<LI>Number one
<LI>Number two
<LI>Number three
</OL>
<P>
<DL>
<DT>The defined term goes here
<DD>The definition goes here
```

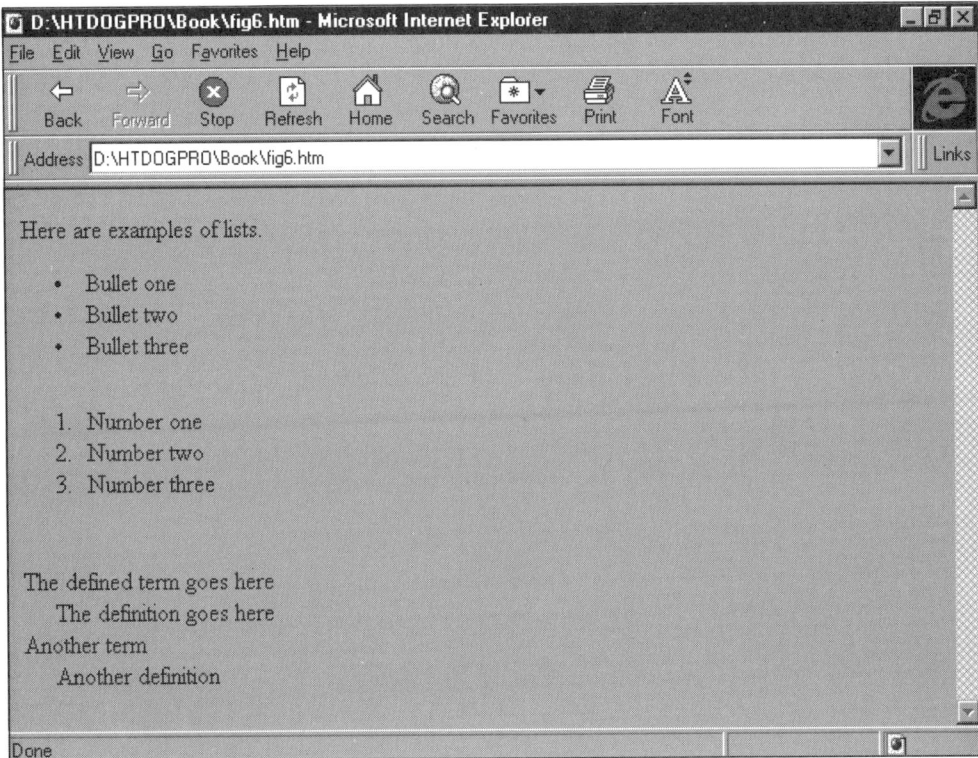

Figure 12.6: Creating lists.

```
<DT>Another term
<DD>Another definition
</DL>
</BODY>
</HTML>
```

Notice in this example that you do not have to use the <P> or <BR> after an item that is part of a list. The next item on the list will automatically be placed on the next line as long as it is preceded by <LI> or <DD>.

OTHER COOL STUFF

Believe it or not, you have now learned enough basic HTML to create your own page and do a pretty decent job of it! Just for inspiration, I have provided another example for you to use. Figure 12.7 shows

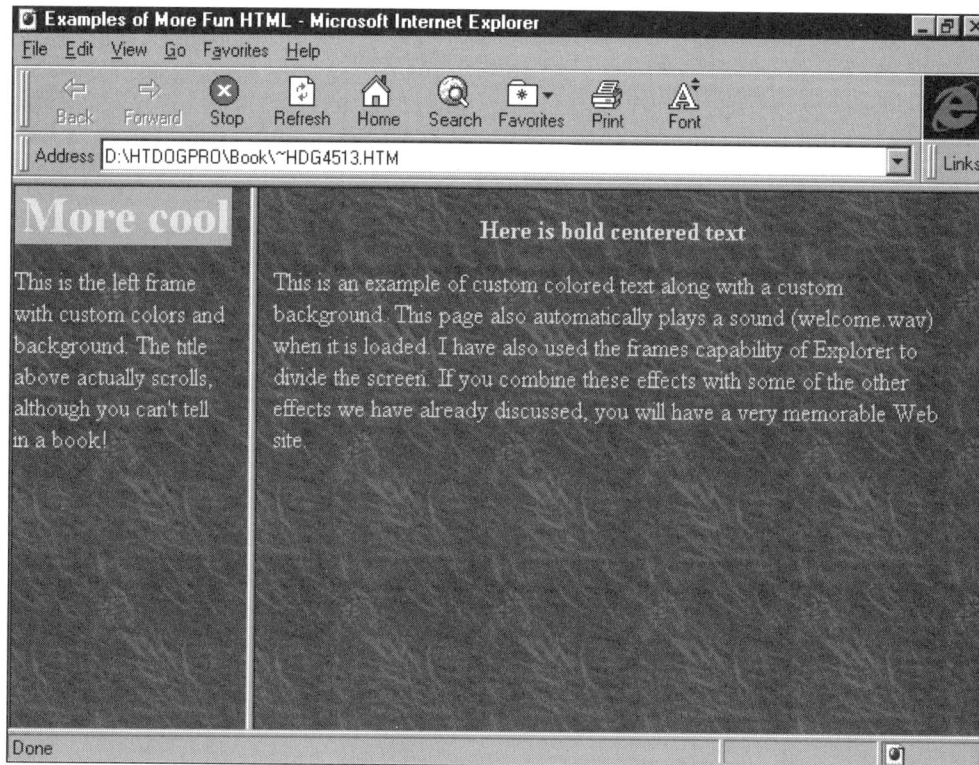

Figure 12.7: More HTML for you to learn!

some other cool tricks to add a little excitement to your Web page. This page has a custom background; text alignment (centered); bold, large fonts; scrolling text (difficult to see in a picture!); sound (*really* difficult to see!); and frames (two, if you didn't notice).

Rather than explain how to do all of this, you should have enough basic knowledge of HTML to pick parts out of this code and try them out in your own. In fact, a great way to learn HTML tricks is to look at the code from other pages that you like. You can view the source code from within Explorer by choosing View Source from the menu bar. Then you can cut and paste to grab any parts that look good.

Caution: As more pages are being designed by professionals, it is becoming more common for the source HTML code to be copyrighted. If you want to use some of the code that you see, it is always safest to ask for permission rather than just copying it and pasting it into your page.

The page shown in Figure 12.7 is a little different because it uses frames. It is actually made up of three separate HTML files—one file for each frame and a control file. When you view the source code, only the main file's code is displayed. Here is the code for all three files for your review. The first batch of code is for the main file, which controls the layout of the frames but is not displayed itself.

```
<HTML>
<HEAD>
<TITLE>Examples of More Fun HTML</TITLE>
</HEAD>
<FRAMESET COLS="25%,*">
<FRAME NAME="left" SRC="fig7b.htm" NORESIZE>
<FRAME NAME="right" SRC="fig7c.htm">
</FRAMESET>
</HTML>
```

This next file is in the left window of the frame.

```
<HTML>
<HEAD>
<TITLE>More Cool HTML</TITLE>
</HEAD>
<BODY BACKGROUND="marble.gif" TEXT="#FBFF43" LINK="#00FFFF"
VLINK="#00FF00" ALINK="#DD00FF">
<BODY TOPMARGIN=0 LEFTMARGIN=0>
<FONT SIZE=6><B><MARQUEE BEHAVIOR=SCROLL DIRECTION=LEFT>More
cool
HTML!</MARQUEE></B><FONT SIZE=3><P>
This is the left frame with custom colors and background.  The
title above actually scrolls, although you can't tell in a
book!<P>
</BODY>
</HTML>
```

Finally, this is the right window of the frame.

```
<HTML>
<BGSOUND SRC="welcome.wav">
<HEAD>
<TITLE>More Cool HTML</TITLE>
</HEAD>
<BODY>
```

```
<BODY BACKGROUND="marble.gif" TEXT="#FBFF43" LINK="#00FFFF"
VLINK="#00FF00" ALINK="#DD00FF">
<BODY>
<CENTER>
<B>Here is bold centered text</B><P>
</CENTER>
This is an example of custom colored text along with a custom
background.  This page also automatically plays a sound (wel-
come.wav) when it is loaded.  I have also used the frames capa-
bility of Explorer to divide the screen.  If you combine these
effects with some of the other effects we have already dis-
cussed, you will have a very memorable Web site.<P>
</BODY>
</HTML>
```

If you find yourself really interested in HTML now, then I've accomplished my goal. If you want to learn more, however, this is not the place to do it! Definitely go to your favorite bookstore and pick up a book dedicated to HTML. I have shown you only a few small pieces of what you can do with your own Web page. And remember, after you learn HTML, you can learn VBScript or JavaScript to really add some punch to your pages!

PLANNING FOR DIFFERENT BROWSERS

One of the hassles of designing a Web page is making sure that everyone can get something out of it. This means giving alternatives to people who don't have the latest version of Internet Explorer. An example of this was the alternate description we gave when loading a picture for people whose browser does not do graphics or whose images are turned off.

Explorer has some great HTML features that are not supported by other browsers at all (yet). An example is True Type font support. With most browsers, the <FONT SIZE=> is the only way to change the font. Explorer, however, lets you use specifc fonts on your page. So, for example, if you wanted Arial used in your headings and Times New Roman for your body, you can specify Arial and Times New Roman. Again, there are too many of these types of features for me to cover in this book, but the Microsoft web site is full of information about Explorer's extraordinary capabilities.

If you are sure that most of your friends use Netscape, then it is probably not wise to fill your page with tricks like scrolling marquees that only Explorer can view. Get your friends to switch, or keep those features out. Try to write your page with the lowest common denominator in mind, but don't make it text only! People have to upgrade sometime, after all!

WHAT'S AHEAD?

You have now finished this book! Congratulations! By now you are an accomplished user of both Microsoft Internet Explorer and the Internet itself. Happy surfing!

Appendix A

INSTALLATION AND CONFIGURATION

If you don't already know how to get Microsoft Internet Explorer, keep reading! If you haven't chosen an ISP, you will also get some information here on the most popular methods to choose. Finally, if you need to configure your ISP account, the required steps are listed.

SYSTEM REQUIREMENTS

I won't be kind. If you have a 386 with 4MB of RAM, Explorer 3.0 is not the program for you. Look into Explorer 2.0 or find a version of Mosaic. You'll never miss the ActiveX and Java applets; you'd grow old waiting for them to run! If you aren't quite that technically challenged, here are the minimums.

- A personal computer with a 486 or Pentium processor
- Windows 95
- 8MB RAM
- Approximately 15MB free hard drive space (more is needed for the cache to be effective)
- SVGA color monitor (256 colors or greater)
- Sound card and speakers (for multimedia)
- 14,400 bps modem or faster (ISDN is supported with an extra download from Microsoft)
- Mouse

WHERE CAN I GET EXPLORER?

The easiest way to get Explorer is to download it from Microsoft's Web site at **www.microsoft.com/ie**. To do this, you will need another Web browser (many ISPs will give Mosaic to new subscribers) or an FTP program (Windows 95 has an FTP program built in). You will also need to have an ISP chosen and configured. If you have yet to do this, see the "Choosing an ISP" section later in this appendix. Other places to find Explorer are the Microsoft Internet Starter Kit and the Microsoft Plus! pack, both of which are available at many software retailers.

Note: The Internet Starter Kit and the Plus! pack might contain earlier versions of Explorer. If you find this to be the case, click the button on the toolbar called Product Updates. This will take you to the Microsoft Internet Explorer home page where you can download version 3.0.

INSTALLATION

If you choose to download Explorer, you may need to open the file once the download is completed. If your browser allows it, have it open the file automatically after downloading. If the file does not open automatically, run Windows 95 Explorer, locate the file, and double-click it. The installation will begin. The installation Wizard will ask a few questions about the destination folder in which the program will install, and the rest will be automatic. A shortcut will be created on your desktop called The Internet. Double-clicking this shortcut will connect to your ISP and launch Explorer.

CHOOSING AN INTERNET SERVICE PROVIDER (ISP)

You basically have three options to connect to the Internet with Internet Explorer: The Microsoft Network, a local ISP, or a national ISP. The local and national ISPs are essentially the same as far as configuration, so they will be treated as the same entity. I will just call them local ISPs to keep things simple.

MSN

The Microsoft Network offers full PPP Internet access in most areas of the country and is constantly adding more lines. MSN is more than just an Internet provider, though. It is a full on-line community that offers dedicated news and information services as well as unique user groups and support services. It also is generally more expensive than dedicated ISPs. MSN does offer a 30-day free trial period with unlimited usage during this period. Once on-line, you can check the current subscription rates in MSN Central by selecting Tools Billing from the menu bar.

Local ISP

When choosing a local ISP, you should prepare a list of questions to ask the sales representatives. Be ready to shop around, as most large cities have several providers from which to choose. Some of the national long distance carriers have entered the arena, offering competitive rates, also. Here are some questions that you need to ask before subscribing.

- Is it a local call from your home?
- Is it PPP access or SLIP? You want PPP.
- Do they provide installation software and/or written instructions for setup?
- What are their technical support hours, and do they charge extra for tech support calls?
- What is their user-to-modem ratio? Around 10-to-1 is optimal.
- How often has their system been down recently? Are these chronic problems?
- Do they offer unlimited usage plans, or is there a time limit each month?
- Do they charge more for faster modems?

On average, expect to pay around $15 to $20 per month for 100 to unlimited hours of access.

CONNECTING WITH MSN

Microsoft has made it fairly easy to subscribe and configure MSN and Internet access. If you haven't deleted it, there is an MSN shortcut on your desktop. Double-click it to launch MSN. The first time you do this, instructions will appear to enroll you in the service and configure your computer. You may need your Windows 95 disks or CD-ROM to complete the installation. Figure A.1 shows one of the first screens of

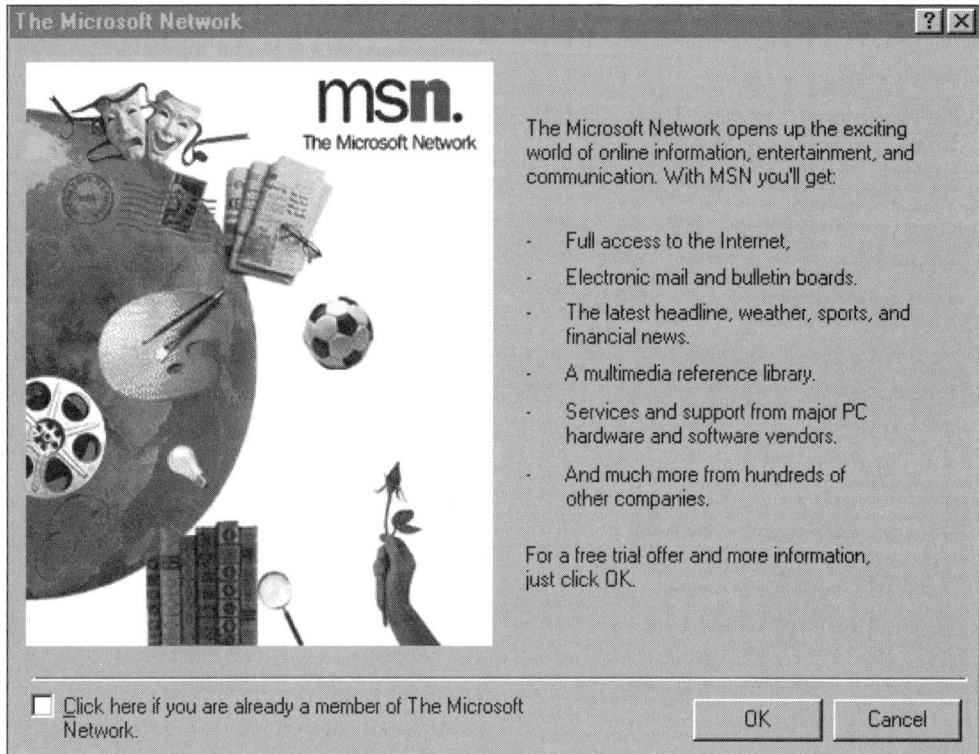

Figure A.1: Starting MSN for the first time.

the MSN installation. The installation will walk you through the entire process, from finding a local phone number to creating a username and password.

Note: If you do not have the MSN shortcut on your desktop, here is how to get it. Select Start Settings Control Panel. Double-click Add/Remove Programs and select the Windows Setup tab. In the Components box, check the box next to The Microsoft Network. Click OK to leave the Add/Remove Programs window. Windows will now install the needed files for MSN. You may need your Windows 95 disks or CD-ROM.

When the MSN software is installed, you will need to run the Internet Connection Wizard. This is run by selecting Start, Programs, Accessories, Internet Tools, Get on the Internet. Choose the Automatic option from the window shown in Figure A.2. Windows will take over from here. All you have to do is select the Microsoft Network as your Internet provider when prompted.

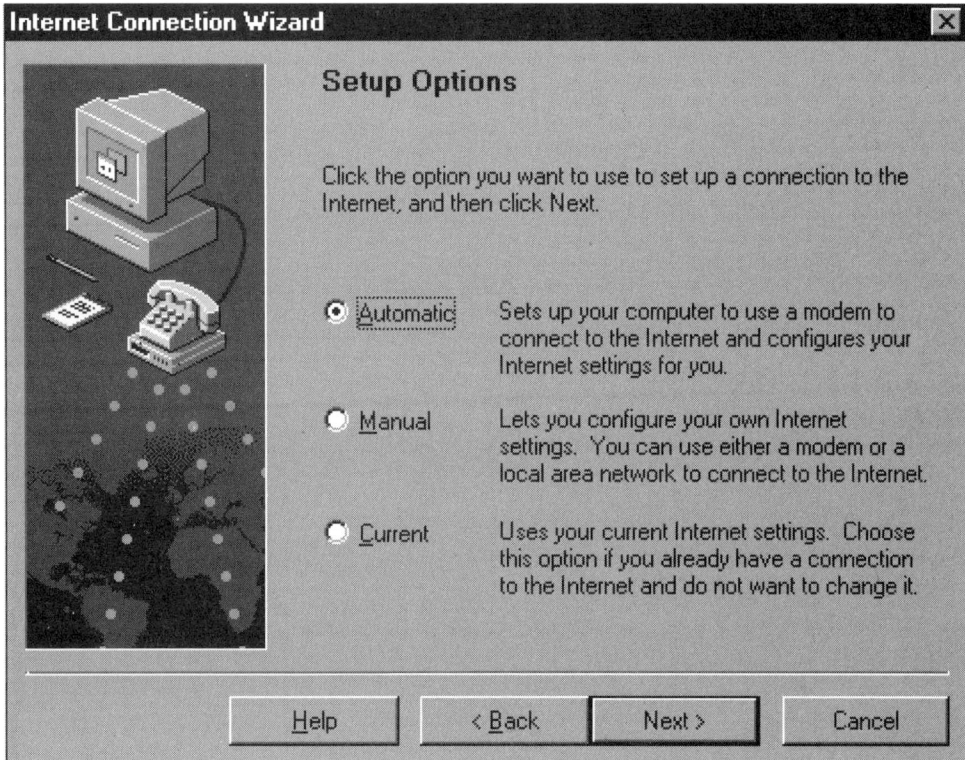

Figure A.2: Choosing the installation method for Internet Access.

Note: Your computer may have the Internet Setup Wizard instead of the Internet Connection Wizard. There are a few differences between the two, but the basic process is identical.

Once MSN is configured, you can connect to the Net in one of two ways: through the Internet Center of MSN or by double-clicking The Internet on your desktop. The first method is entirely through MSN; Explorer is launched from within MSN itself. The second method bypasses the Microsoft Network and just gives you Internet access.

CONNECTING WITH A LOCAL ISP

If you decide to take the dedicated Internet route, the first thing you need to do is subscribe to a service. If you haven't already, use my list of questions above and get to it! Once your ISP has sent you its welcome packet, it's time to configure.

The easiest way to go is if your ISP provides you with a setup disk. If it does, use the disk to connect to the Net, if necessary, and download Explorer. If you got Explorer from somewhere else, then you are all ready to go once the setup disk has been installed.

Some ISPs do not provide setup disks, however. The least they can do is provide you with a detailed list of instructions and a tech support phone number. Assuming the worst, let's say that you have none of this, that the tech support lines are always busy, or that you just hate calling people for help and you want to do this by yourself. If any or all of these are true, you must know some basic information about your connection before you continue.

- The name of your ISP
- The phone number of the ISP (for the computer, not tech support)
- Your username and password
- Your ISP's IP address—this may be provided automatically each time you connect
- The primary DNS number (and sometimes a secondary DNS number)
- Your e-mail address (yourusername@yourprovider.com or .net)
- Your mail server address
- Your news server address
- Your ISP's domain name

Once you are armed with this information, you are ready to start the configuration.

Using the Internet Connection Wizard

This is the second easiest method for configuring (next to using a disk provided by your ISP). Once you have collected the information listed above, the Wizard will walk you through the setup by asking for each piece of information one at a time. The Internet Connection Wizard is launched by selecting Start, Programs, Accessories, Internet Tools, Get on the Internet.

1. Choose Next at the Get Connected window.
2. Choose Manual at the Setup Options window (refer back to Figure A.2).
3. Choose Next at the Internet Setup Wizard.

4. Choose between using your phone (modem) or your network and select Next.
5. Enter the name of your service provider and select Next.
6. Enter your phone number and select Next—check with your ISP about the Bring Up Terminal Window.
7. Enter your username and password and select Next.
8. Select your IP address according to your ISP's instructions.
9. Enter your DNS server and alternate DNS server (if applicable) address and select Next.
10. Check Use Internet Mail.
11. Enter your e-mail address and your mail server address and select Next.
12. Select Exchange and then Next at the Windows Messaging Profile window.
13. Select Finish.

You will now connect to your ISP whenever you launch Internet Explorer.

Note: You may have the Internet Setup Wizard instead of the Internet Connection Wizard. There are essentially no differences between these versions, although the menus may appear a little different than described here.

Manually Configuring Windows Dial-up Networking

If you do not have the Internet Connection Wizard or the Internet Setup Wizard, these are the steps you need to take to configure Windows 95 manually to connect with your ISP. First, you need to determine if Dial-up Networking has been installed on your computer.

1. Double-click My Computer on the desktop. If you see a Dial-up Networking folder, skip to the next section. Otherwise, continue to step 2.
2. Double-click the Add/Remove Programs shortcut and select the Windows Setup tab.
3. Highlight Communication in the Components box and select Details.
4. If the Dial-up Networking box is checked, skip to the next section.

5. If the Dial-up networking box is not checked, check it now and select OK.
6. Select OK or Apply.
7. Insert Windows 95 disks or CD-ROM if prompted by Windows.
8. If asked to name your computer and workgroup, name them anything you like.
9. Reboot your computer and proceed to "Manually Configuring TCP/IP."

Manually Configuring TCP/IP

1. Select Start, Control Panel, Network.
2. Double-click the Network icon.
3. If there is no Dial-up Adapter listed, select Add.
4. Double-click Adapters.
5. Select Microsoft in the Manufacturer's box on the left.
6. Double-click Dial-up Adapter in the box on the right. The Dial-up Adapter should now be listed in the Network Configuration window.
7. In the same window, check for TCP/IP. If none, select Add.
8. Double-click Protocols.
9. Select Microsoft in the Manufacturer's box on the left.
10. Double-click TCP/IP. TCP/IP should now be listed in the Network Configuration window.
11. Double-click the TCP/IP item that was just created.
12. In the IP Address tab, make sure the IP address is properly entered or selected automatically depending on instructions from your ISP.
13. Select the DNS Configuration tab.
14. Select Enable DNS.
15. Enter your username in the Host box.
16. Enter the domain name in the Domain box.
17. Enter the domain name server address in the DNS Server Search Order box and select Add.
18. Enter the domain name in the Domain Suffix Search Order box and select Add.
19. Select OK at the bottom of the Network installation window.

20. Insert Windows 95 disks or CD-ROM if prompted by Windows.
21. Reboot if requested by Windows.

To create a shortcut to your Internet account on your desktop, follow these instructions.

1. Select Dial-up Networking folder from the Control Panel.
2. The first time you make a connection with Dial-up Networking, a new connection will automatically be created. If you have used Dial-up Networking before (or just snooped around in the folder), you must choose the Make New Connection icon.
3. Replace My Connection with the name of your ISP.
4. Enter the access phone number in the Telephone Number box.
5. Select OK.
6. Holding the right mouse button down, drag and drop your new shortcut on your desktop and select Create Shortcut Here from the pop-up menu.

To connect to the Internet, you can double-click the shortcut that was just created and then launch Explorer, or you can launch Explorer, which will automatically connect to your ISP.

Appendix B

WINDOWS 95 REFRESHER

Many people using Explorer will be new to computers and new to Windows 95. Several terms used throughout this book may not make any sense to you newbies. If this is you, don't be ashamed! Keep reading, as this appendix will brief you on the basics of Windows 95. It is by no means a substitute for a complete Windows 95 book, but it should help you with using this book and Explorer.

WINDOWS 95 DESKTOP

First, let's start with the desktop, which is the area that you see when Windows 95 is started. This is where your programs are placed while they are running. Imagine that it is a real desktop, and your programs are spread out over it like papers while you are using them. Figure B.1 shows a typical desktop, with a few extra shortcuts added.

What's a shortcut? It is a link to a program. Each program that is installed on your computer has a file that is used to launch that particular program. Normally to find that file, you would have to open the Start menu and search through all of the programs on your computer. Or you could open Windows 95 Explorer and search through all the files on your computer. If you use a certain program very often,

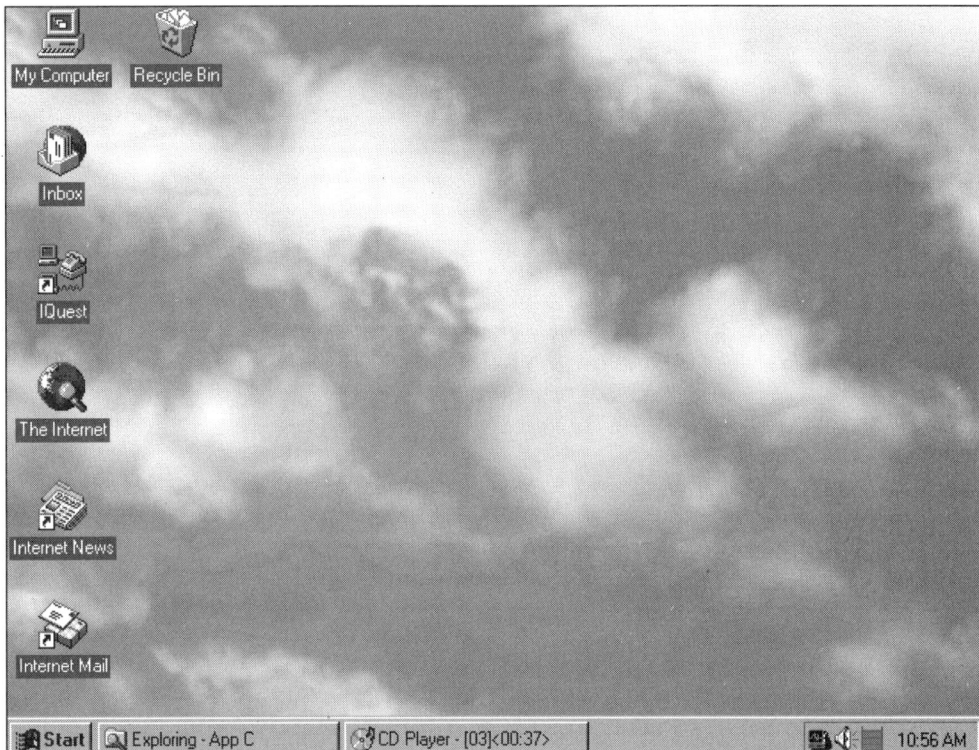

Figure B.1: A Windows 95 desktop.

you can see that it would be faster just to put it on your desktop to save you the time of searching through everything else to get to it. That's a shortcut. It is a mini program that jumps to and loads the desired program. Shortcuts save time, but be careful not to put too many shortcuts on your desktop or you risk cluttering up everything. Then you lose the advantage of having the shortcut at all!

THE MOUSE

The mouse is the main input device for navigating through Windows 95. It is used to open and close programs and windows, move items around, highlight areas, and perform countless other tasks. A few of the most common tasks are covered here. Always assume that a double- or single-click uses the left mouse button unless specifically told otherwise.

Double-Clicking

This is the staple of Windows operation. Double-clicking is used to open windows and launch programs. But what does double-click mean? Well, it means to click the left mouse button twice in rapid succession. I see many people struggle with the double-click, usually because they can't hold the mouse still while clicking. Their first click is fine, but their second click ends up across the screen! If this describes you, don't worry. You just need some practice. In the meantime, you can slow down the speed at which the button is clicked. When your skill improves, you can speed things up again. Follow these directions to change the double-click speed.

1. From the Start menu, select Settings and Control Panel.
2. In the Control Panel, double-click (you can do it!) the Mouse icon.
3. On the Buttons tab, move the marker in the Double-Click Speed box to the left. This is accomplished by clicking and holding the left mouse button while your cursor is over the marker and moving the mouse to the left.
4. You can test the speed in the Test area to the right. If you double-click successfully, the jack-in-the-box will pop out.
5. Play around until you find a comfortable double-click speed.
6. Select OK.

The Mouse Properties window is shown in Figure B.2.

Dragging and Dropping

This feature is used to copy and move files, create shortcuts, launch Web pages, and countless other tasks. Dragging and dropping involves clicking on an object and holding the mouse button down, moving the object, and releasing the mouse button. Generally, dragging and dropping an object using the left mouse button will move that object to the new location. Using the right mouse button will open a pop-up menu, giving you the option to move the object, copy the object, or create a shortcut for the object in the new location.

Minimizing and Maximizing

This isn't strictly a mouse feature, but it is done mainly using the mouse, so I decided to put it in this section. When you are running a

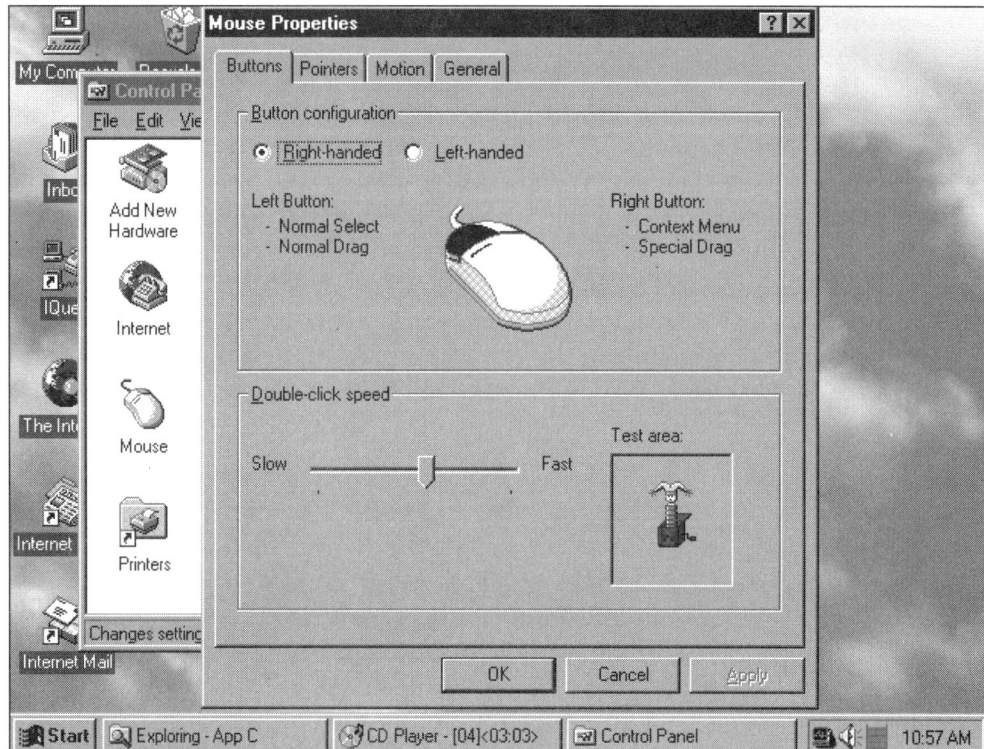

Figure B.2: Changing the double-click speed.

program, you can have that program fill the entire screen, which is considered maximized. If you need to access something on your desktop or another program, you can minimize the window partially or completely to reveal any items underneath. A partially minimized window can still be seen, but it does not fill the entire screen. A completely minimized window is visible only on the taskbar; the rest of the screen is clear.

Each window has several small buttons in the top right corner that control minimizing and maximizing. The first button, which looks like a minus sign, completely minimizes the window. When a program is completely minimized, it can be restored by clicking on its button on the taskbar. The window will restore to its previous state. The second small button changes to fit the circumstances. When a window is maximized, it looks like two overlapping boxes. This means that selecting it will partially minimize the window. When the window is partially

minimized, this button will look like a square. This means that selecting it will maximize the window. The X button to the far right completely closes the window, ending the program.

THE START MENU AND TASKBAR

Figure B.3 shows the Start menu and the taskbar. The Start menu is displayed by pressing the Start button, while the taskbar is always visible
at the bottom of the screen. The Start menu is where most of your programs will be launched (except for the programs that have shortcuts on
your desktop). The Start menu leads to any of several submenus, represented by the arrows next to the names in Figure B.3. When you position the cursor over these areas, the submenus are displayed. To launch
a program from one of the submenus, single-click its name.

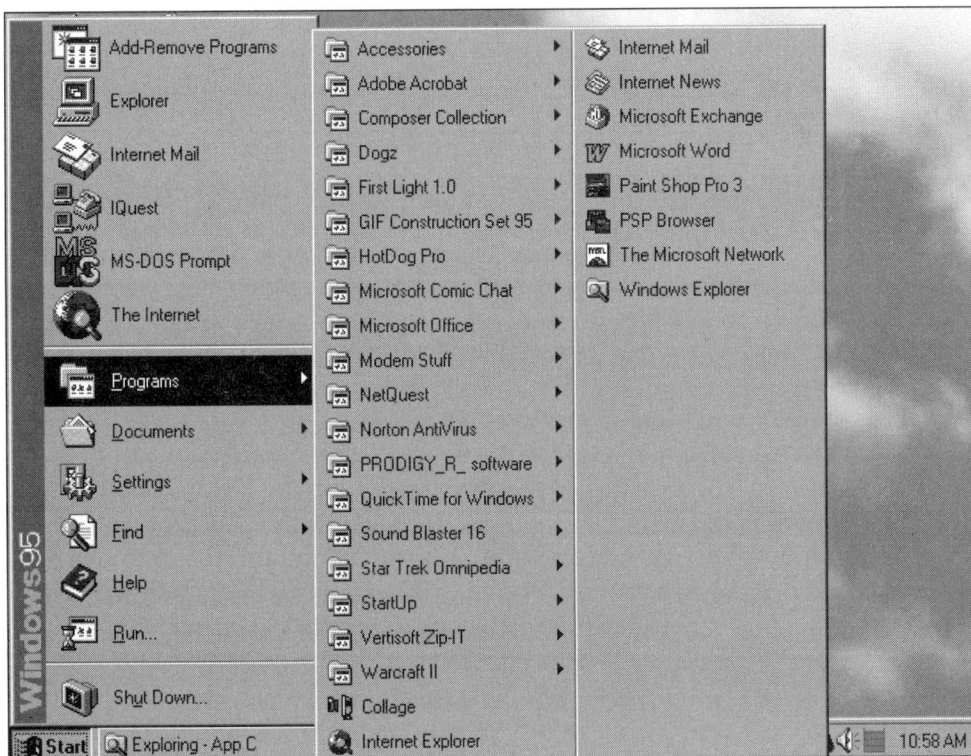

Figure B.3: The Start menu and taskbar.

Tip: The standard Start menu contains only about half of the features shown in Figure B.3. I have added everything above Programs myself. This is done by finding the executable files for the programs (either in Windows 95 Explorer or in My Computer) and dragging and dropping them on the Start button. This is a simple way to make commonly used programs available at all times.

The taskbar is used to keep track of all active programs. Switching back and forth between programs is accomplished by clicking on the corresponding button on the taskbar. This will make the selected program active. An active program is represented on the taskbar by a depressed button. In Figure B.3, there are two programs running, although neither is currently active. Right-clicking a button on the taskbar will bring up a pop-up menu with several options including restore, minimize, maximize, and close.

Tip: You can hide the taskbar to create more viewable space on your screen. To do this, select Start Settings Taskbar. Then check the box next to Auto Hide and click OK. The taskbar will now be visible only when your cursor moves to the bottom of the screen.

MENUS

You have heard me discuss pull-down menus and pop-up menus, but what is the difference? As far as basic operations are concerned, there are no differences. You make a selection from each the same way, and the task is carried out the same way. They do appear in different circumstances, however.

Figure B.4 shows a pull-down menu. Pull-down menus appear when you select an option from a menu bar. To select an item from a pull-down menu, move your cursor over that item and single-click.

Figure B.5 shows a pop-up menu. This type of menu usually appears when an object is right-clicked. To select an item from a pop-up menu, move your cursor over that item and single-click.

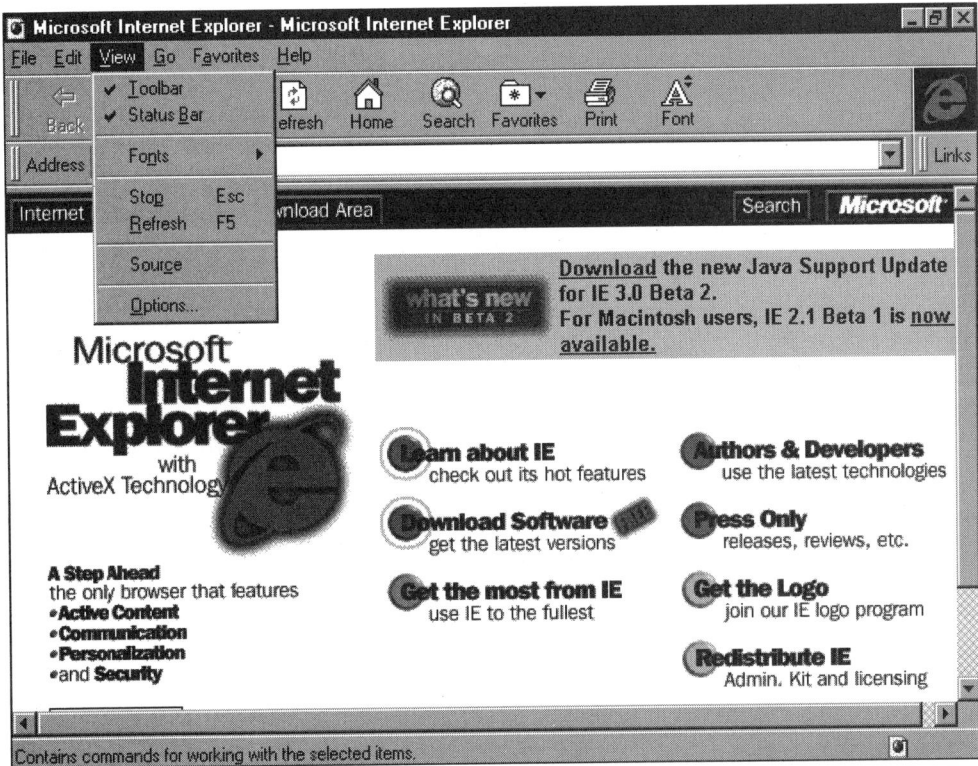

Figure B.4: A pull-down menu.

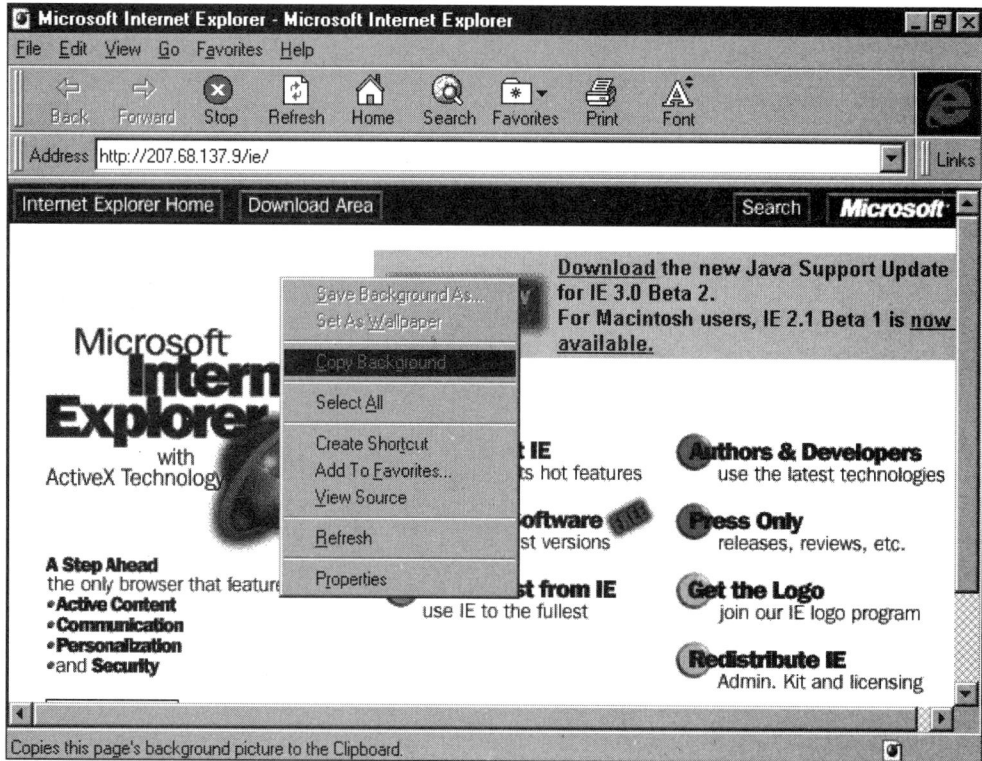

Figure B.5: A pop-up menu.

Appendix C

INTERNET EXPLORER 2.0 FOR WINDOWS 3.1

Not to leave out users of Windows 3.1 or Windows 3.11, Microsoft has developed a version of Explorer just for them. With this offering, Windows 3.x users have a fast and stable method to access the Internet. But how does it compare with Explorer 3.0 for Windows 95? Well, that's sort of like comparing a 1996 car with its all new 1997 version. Yes, you can see some common lineage here, but if you can afford it, you are better off with the 1997 model.

Explorer 2.0 includes many of the features that we have come to expect in Web browsers: support for multiple windows, multimedia playback, a hard disk cache system to improve performance, and stability. It does lack many of the power features that make up a top-of-the-line browser, however. Absent features include: ActiveX support, Java support, inline video support, background sound support, short-cut creation and use, opening pages by selecting their files from the hard disk, and stable newsgroup support.

The system requirements are much less demanding for Explorer 2.0, however, so it may be the only option for some users.

- A personal computer with a 386 processor or higher
- Microsoft Windows 3.1 or 3.11 or Microsoft Windows for Workgroups 3.1 or 3.11
- 4MB of RAM

- Approximately 5MB free hard drive space (more is needed for the cache to be effective)
- VGA monitor or better
- Mouse
- Sound card and speakers (for multimedia)
- 9600 bps modem or faster

Several versions are available for download. The first is the standard Internet Explorer 2.0. The second includes support for TCP/IP and a dialer. These are important if they are not already installed on your computer (Windows 3.x does not come with any versions of these). The third version includes e-mail and a newsreader. All versions have a setup Wizard to guide the installation process, although you will need to have your ISP information ready. See Appendix A, "Connecting with a Local ISP," for the information that you'll need. MSN requires Windows 95 and therefore does not support Explorer 2.0.

EXPLORER 2.0 BASICS

Figure C.1 shows the basic screen for Explorer 2.0. Note that while it is not a twin of Explorer 3.0, there are some similarities. Both versions have a title bar, a menu bar, a toolbar, an address bar, a logo (in this case the Windows logo), and a status bar.

Title bar

This space at the very top of the window shows the title of the current Web page.

Menu bar

This contains all the pull-down menus that control program operations and customization. While not identical to the menu bar in Explorer 3.0, it is similar enough to be familiar to 3.0 users.

Toolbar

The toolbar buttons are mostly familiar. There are a few different buttons that are not part of 3.0. At the far left is a folder button that is used

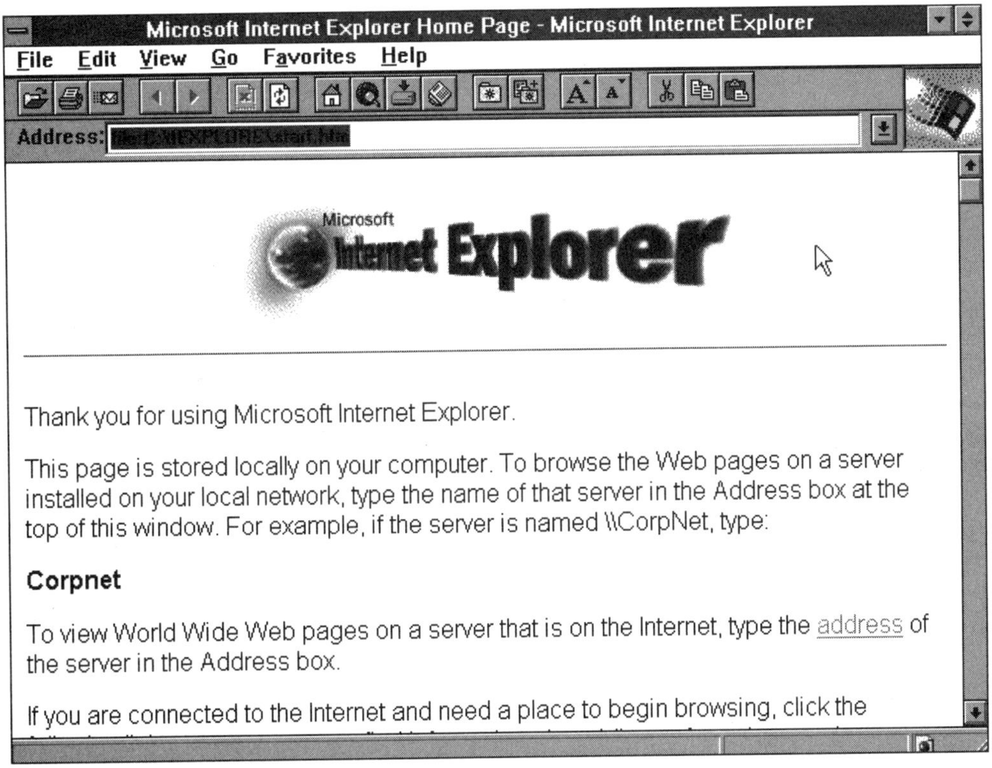

Figure C.1: Internet Explorer 2.0.

to open a new Web page. This button gives you the option of opening a new window or replacing the current window (a new window is shown in Figure C.2). Two buttons over is a button used to launch the built-in e-mail program. Underneath the Help menu are two new buttons. The button with a hard drive is used to load the Explorer home page to download new versions (this feature was moved to the Quick Links in version 3.0). The newspaper button launches the built-in newsreader. Next to the Favorites folder is an Add to Favorites button. Changing fonts is done with two buttons in this version. Finally, Cut, Paste, and Copy have been placed on the toolbar as well as in the Edit menu.

Address bar

The operation of the address bar is identical to that of Explorer 3.0.

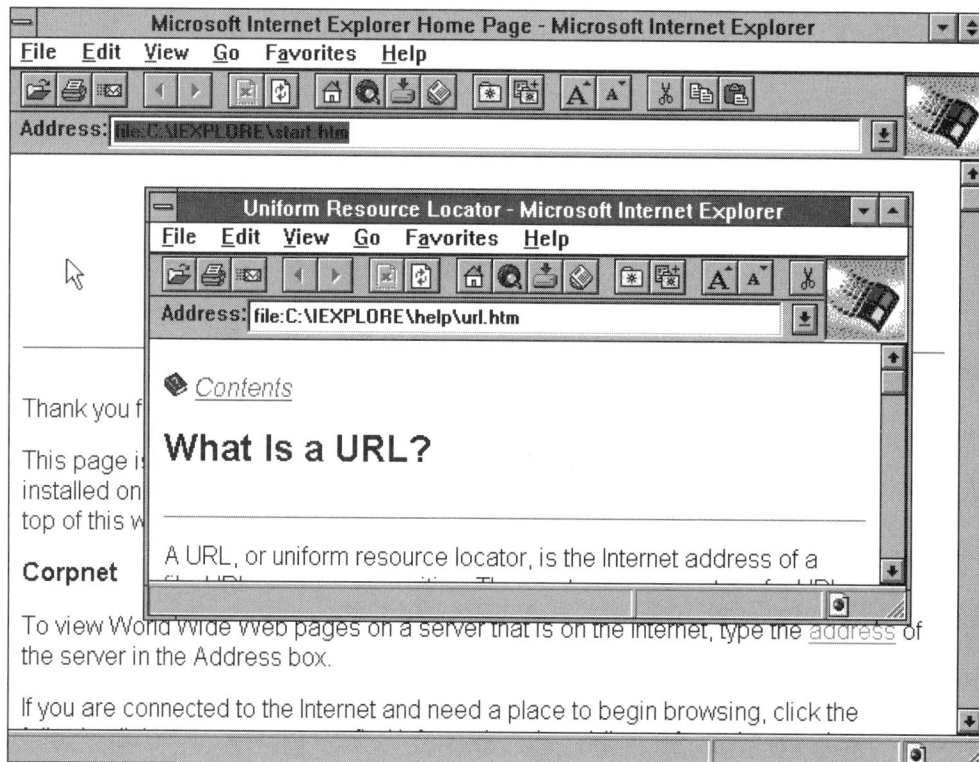

Figure C.2: Opening a second window in Explorer 2.0.

Logo

The logo performs the same function as in 3.0. In this version, the clouds are in motion when a page is being loaded or a file is being downloaded.

Status Bar

The status bar displays the address of a hyperlink or file being downloaded in the bottom left corner. The bottom right shows small icons that represent document status.

Operation

The basic operation of Explorer 2.0 is not very different from 3.0. You can still view Web, FTP, Gopher, and Telnet sites. Hyperlinks work the same way, as does the address bar. Explorer 2.0 supports off-line viewing, so you can copy pages for later viewing. Its cache and history list also work in much the same way as Explorer 3.0. Even customizing features is a very similar process. Figure C.3 shows the View Options menu. Anyone familiar with 3.0 can certainly find his or her way around in here. The Favorites list, while different in appearance, works the same way as 3.0 to save frequently visited sites. There is even a button on the toolbar to add a site to the Favorites list.

Downloading and playing multimedia files is essentially the same process as in version 3.0. Explorer 2.0 supports many of the popular audio and video formats, although you must download plug-ins for MPEG audio and video as well as for Quicktime movies. Inline video (video images that are displayed as a regular image on a Web page) are not supported in version 2.0. For HTML authors, frames and scrolling

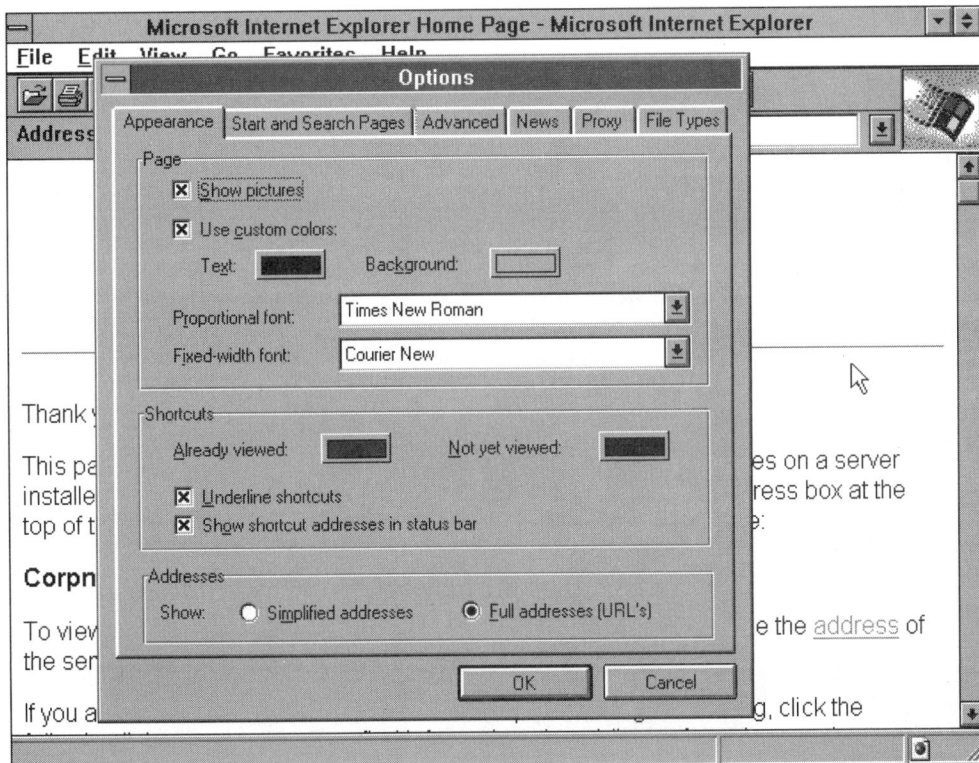

Figure C.3: Configuring Explorer 2.0.

marquees are supported, although 2.0 does not support the new style sheets and True Type fonts like version 3.0.

E-MAIL AND NEWSGROUPS

The built-in e-mail program and newsreader are not nearly as feature rich as Internet Mail and News, included with Explorer 3.0. Figure C.4 shows the main e-mail screen. Notice that it does have several folders to store messages (called the Local Message Store). The toolbar also covers most commonly used functions such as writing a new message, finding a message within a folder, reading the previous or next message, and forwarding, saving, replying to, and sending messages.

Writing and sending a new message are nearly identical to Internet Mail in Explorer 3.0. When you select New Message from the toolbar,

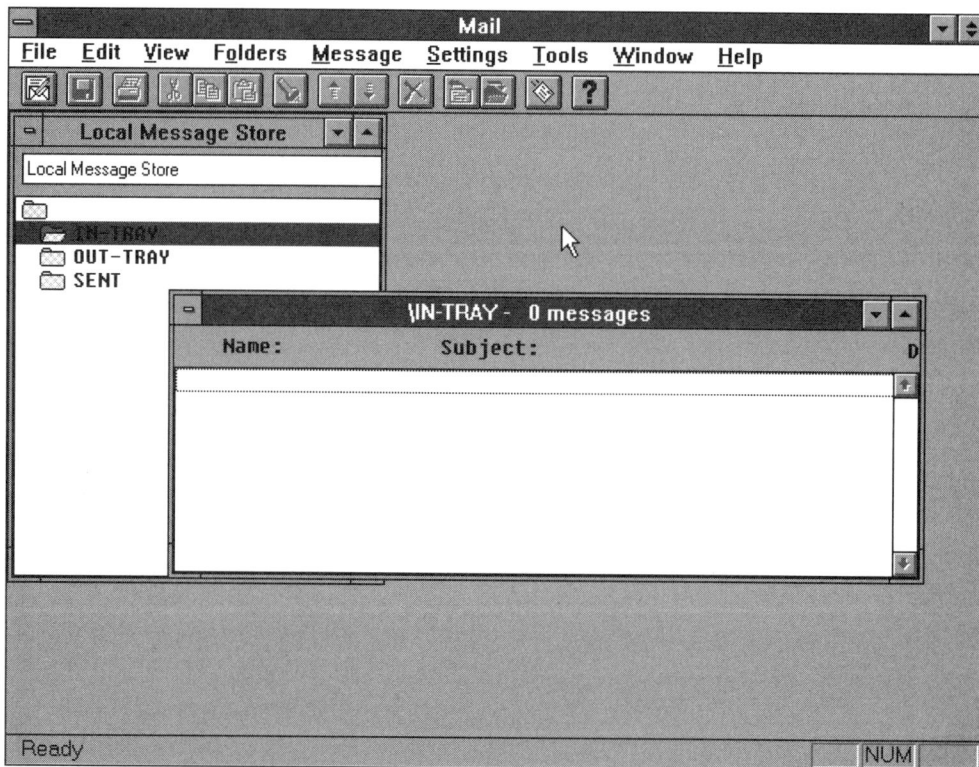

Figure C.4: E-mail from Explorer 2.0.

a new window appears in which you can address and type your message (shown in Figure C.5). You can send the message to multiple addresses, choose from an address book, and add a personal signature to the end of the message. File attachments are also permitted.

If you wish to use your own e-mail program, you can set it up as the default rather than using this built-in mail program (or you can download the version of Explorer that doesn't include the e-mail program and newsreader). Exchange is also compatible with Explorer 2.0.

The newsreader for 2.0 is perhaps its weakest feature. The menu system is awkward and confusing and is not easy to work with. The newsreader program itself has trouble working with news servers that have more than 16,000 newsgroups. Since many have over 20,000, I recommend downloading a separate newsreader and configuring it as the default instead of this one.

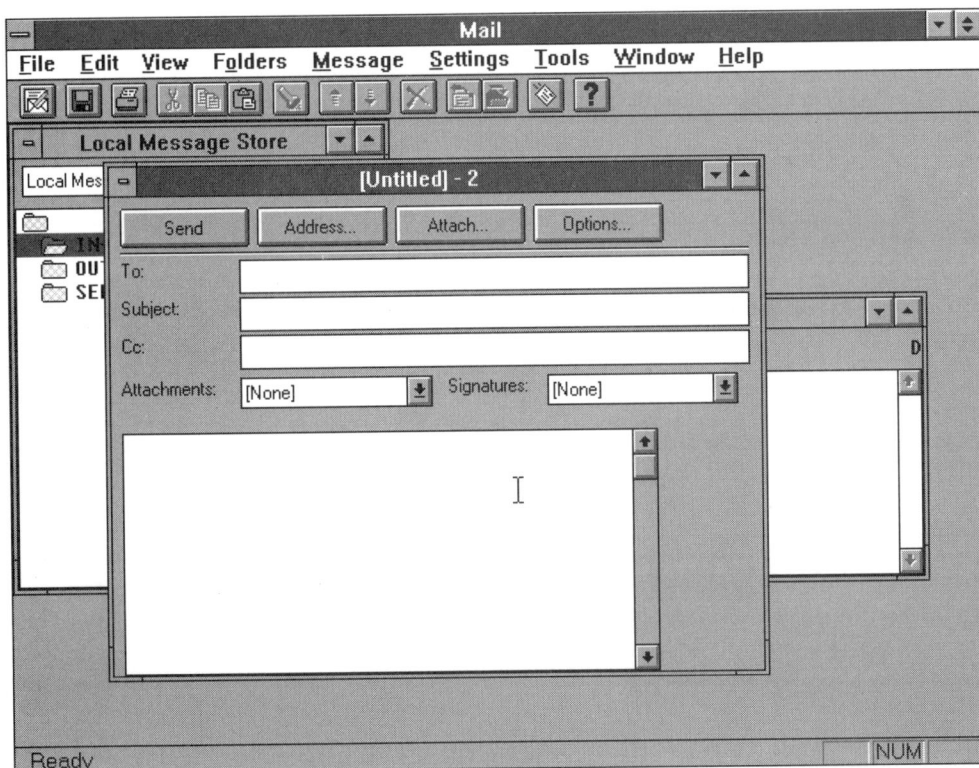

Figure C.5: Writing a new message.

Index

A

Acrobat, 187

Active Content, 167–169, 262

ActiveMovie, 179–181

ActiveX, 26, 27, 167, 179–259, 265, 307

Add to Favorites, 68, 69, 70, 80, 82, 83, 84, 309

add-ons, 41, 177, 186–192

Address Bar, 40, 41, 46, 48, 56, 60, 66, 75, 87, 111, 112, 122, 138, 141, 148–152, 160, 235, 308, 309, 311

addresses
e-mail, 22, 24, 33, 195, 202–203, 206–210, 216–218, 219
Internet, 22, 66

Address Book, 202, 203–218, 219–313

AIFF, 87, 179–182, 189

Alta Vista, 97–100

AND operator, 93, 94–98, 99, 101–102, 104

anonymous FTP, 108